JUVENILE DELINQUENCY

(Treatment and Rehabilitation of Juvenile Drug Addicts)

HEARINGS

BEFORE THE

SUBCOMMITTEE TO INVESTIGATE JUVENILE DELINQUENCY

OF THE

COMMITTEE ON THE JUDICIARY

UNITED STATES SENATE

EIGHTY-FOURTH CONGRESS

SECOND SESSION

PURSUANT TO

S. Res. 173 and S. Res. 303

EIGHTY-FOURTH CONGRESS

INVESTIGATION OF JUVENILE DELINQUENCY IN THE
UNITED STATES

DECEMBER 17 AND 18, 1956

231391

GREENWOOD PRESS, PUBLISHERS
NEW YORK

Originally published in 1954 by U.S. Government Printing Office

First Greenwood Reprinting, 1968

Library of Congress Catalogue Card Number: 68-55116

CONTENTS

EXHIBITS

NUMBER AND SUMMARY OF EXHIBIT

III

EXHIBITS—Continued

NUMBER AND SUMMARY OF EXHIBIT—continued

TREATMENT AND REHABILITATION OF JUVENILE DRUG ADDICTS

MONDAY, DECEMBER 17, 1956

UNITED STATES SENATE,
SUBCOMMITTEE OF THE COMMITTEE ON THE JUDICIARY,
TO INVESTIGATE JUVENILE DELINQUENCY,
Washington, D. C.

The subcommittee met, pursuant to notice, at 10:10 a. m., in the caucus room, Senate Office Building, Senator Estes Kefauver (chairman of the subcommittee) presiding.

Present: Senators Kefauver and Langer.

Also present: James H. Bobo, general counsel; Ernest Mitler, special counsel; and Peter N. Chumbris, associate counsel.

Chairman KEFAUVER. We are here today to learn what constructive steps can be taken to improve our treatment program for juvenile drug addiction.

I am glad that our very faithful member of this subcommittee, Senator Langer, is with us today.

This, of course, is the subcommittee of the United States Senate Committee on the Judiciary To Investigate Juvenile Delinquency. In addition to Senator Langer and myself as chairman, the subcommittee is composed of Senators Thomas C. Hennings, Jr., of Missouri, Alexander Wiley, of Wisconsin, and Price Daniel, of Texas.

We were given the responsibility by the Senate of studying the extent and character of juvenile delinquency in the United States and (1) its causes and contributing factors; (2) the adequacy of existing law in dealing with youthful offenders of Federal laws; and (3) the problem of juvenile drug addiction.

The subcommittee has been in existence more than 3 years. During the first year, the subcommittee focused its attention on the overall environmental factors leading to the increase of juvenile delinquency at that time.

Hearings were held in many of the major cities throughout the United States, and local officials were given an opportunity to testify as to the problems in their area and their preventative programs.

After these initial hearings, studies and further hearings were held on specific problems relating to the juvenile delinquency problem. An exhaustive and complete study of the comic book industry was conducted and hearings were held.

As a result of these hearings, many of the extremes in brutality and cruelty which had been commonplace in comic books have been reduced. In addition, a self-regulatory body was established within the comic-book industry to set standards.

1

Hearings were held concerning the traffic in pornography. Loopholes in the existing laws, which enabled this traffic to flourish, were closed by means of Federal legislation. Many of the major operators in this field have since been arrested or put out of business.

A series of hearings were held on the interstate baby-selling racket, the effect of television on juvenile delinquency. I am happy to report in that connection—and also in motion pictures—in these connections that the new motion picture code is certainly an improvement in lessening and tightening up the code on unnecessary brutality and in other respects, and also that there has been, I think, some improvement on a self-action basis by the television industry on the type of pictures they have been showing.

We have held hearings on youth employment, delinquency among the Indians, where Senator Langer has taken the load, held many hearings in many parts of the country, and there has been a great improvement in the treatment and facilities for Indian children and Indians generally in the various reservations, in the fields of health, education, recreational opportunities, as a result of Senator Langer's hearings and great interest in the problems of Indians.

In addition, staff studies were conducted on venereal disease among juveniles, care and treatment in juvenile institutions, juvenile courts and the handling of delinquents, and education.

The overall impact of these hearings, studies, and reports has resulted in not only constructive legislation on a State and Federal level, but in the dissemination of information on the local community level, enabling these communities to more effectively come to grips with many of the problems leading to juvenile delinquency.

The last hearings we held in Newark last week dealt with a new problem, as far as juveniles are concerned, and that is, there has been a substantial increase in the confidence game, in the victimizing of elderly people, taking their life's earnings, in which an increasing number of juveniles is being used at the present time, and we have one witness today who was supposed to have testified in Newark but could not get there, who will testify on this subject matter today.

The present hearing, dealing with narcotics, is the result of a staff study and survey made during the past 3 years. Upon the recommendations of the Attorney General and Mr. Bennett, we are not going to have some of the witnesses from some of the Federal institutions. It is their feeling that it is not in the best interest of their rehabilitation, and we have abided by their decision.

But we will have other witnesses who will present their cases.

Representatives of the subcommittee have visited many of the centers where drug addicts are being treated in the United States. Many addicts, both in and out of institutions, have been interviewed. Police officials, experts in the field of drug addiction, and social workers have been consulted.

This study has been directed at the treatment and rehabilitation aspect of the juvenile drug problem, and to assist the effort to further develop an effective program to combat juvenile drug addiction.

A Senate subcommittee headed by Senator Price Daniel, of Texas, has just completed a thorough and exhaustive study of many of the facets of the narcotics problem, and has succeeded in making more rigorous the laws relating to the sale and distribution of narcotics in the United States. The work of this subcommittee has been a continuation of the work done by Senator Daniel's subcommittee, with special emphasis on the treatment of drug addicts under the age of 21.

We will be especially concerned today with learning whether a juvenile addict, as well as all addicts, can be effectively treated and cured and turned into a useful citizen. Some persons subscribe to the view that once a person becomes addicted, it is imposible to cure him permanently of the habit.

Witnesses will tell us today about the results of some very hopeful and enlightening recent studies made concerning the possibility of curing drug addicts.

The subcommittee will also examine existing treatment facilities and the program within these facilities to determine their present adequacy and effectiveness in meeting the addiction problem. An effort will be made to learn whether there is an adequate after-care and follow-through program from the existing treatment centers.

It is axiomatic that a constructive treatment program requires an intelligent and diligent after-care program to assist and guide the individual after he has left the treatment center.

Witnesses who will be heard today will include leaders in psychiatry and medicine who have had vast experience in the drug addiction field, as well as addicts who have been exposed to institutional treatment for drug addiction.

It is the subcommittee's desire that today's hearing will stimulate the expansion and improvement of the treatment facilities throughout the United States for juvenile, as well as all, drug addicts.

Law enforcement standing alone cannot solve the narcotics problem. Only through the combination of a sound enforcement program with a sound treatment program will the vicious narcotics traffic be completely defeated.

Senator Langer, do you want to add any thing to the statement?

Senator LANGER. Nothing, Mr. Chairman.

Chairman KEFAUVER. Mr. Mitler, our special counsel, will conduct the hearings today. He is on my left.

Mr. Bobo, our chief counsel, is on Mr. Mitler's left.

Mr. Mitler, will you proceed.

Mr. MITLER. I first want to introduce into the record Senate Resolution 173, the resolution authorizing the existence of the committee, at this time.

Chairman KEFAUVER. Let it be made a part of the record; and also what else, Mr. Mitler?

Mr. MITLER. Also the resolution signed by the five members of the subcommittee, authorizing and permitting the holding of these hearings today.

Chairman KEFAUVER. Let these be made a part of the record.

(The Senate resolution, and subcommittee resolution were marked "Exhibits 1 and 2," and read as follows:)

[S. Res. 173, 84th Cong., 2d sess.]

RESOLUTION

Resolved, That the Committee on the Judiciary, or any duly authorized subcommittee thereof, is authorized under section 134 (a) and 136 of the Legislative Reorganization Act of 1946, as amended, and in accordance with its jurisdiction specified by rule XXV of the Standing Rules of the Senate insofar as they relate to the authority of the Committee on the Judiciary to conduct a full and complete study of juvenile delinquency in the United States, including (a) the extent and character of juvenile delinquency in the United States and its causes and contributing factors; (b) the adequacy of existing provisions of law, including chapter 402 and 403 of title 18 of the United States Code, in dealing with youthful offenders of Federal laws; (c) sentences imposed on, or other correctional action taken with respect to, youthful offenders by Federal courts, and (d) the extent to which juveniles are violating Federal laws relating to the sale or use of narcotics.

SEC. 2. For the purposes of this resolution, the committee, from March 1, 1956, to January 31, 1957, inclusive, is authorized to (1) make such expenditures as it deems advisable; (2) to employ upon a temporary basis, technical, clerical, and other assistants and consultants; and (3) with the prior consent of the heads of the departments or agencies concerned, and the Committee on Rules and Administration, to utilize the reimbursable services, information, facilities and personnel of any of the departments or agencies of the Government.

SEC. 3. The committee shall report its findings, together with its recommendations for legislation as it deems advisable, to the Senate at the earliest practicable date, but not later than January 31, 1957.

SEC. 4. Expenses of the committee, under this resolution, which shall not exceed $55,000, shall be paid from the contingent fund of the Senate upon vouchers approved by the chairman of the committee.

[S. Res. 303, 84th Cong., 2d sess.]

RESOLUTION

Resolved, That Senate Resolution Numbered 173, agreed to on March 20, 1956, be amended by striking out in section 4, lines 21 and 22, "Expenses of the committee, under this resolution, which shall not exceed $55,000" and inserting in lieu thereof the following: "Expenses of the committee, under this resolution which shall not exceed $80,000".

RESOLUTION

Resolved by the Subcommittee of the Committee on the Judiciary to Study Juvenile Delinquency in the United States, That pursuant to subsection (3) of rule XXV, as amended, of the Standing Rules of the Senate (S. Res. 180, 81st Cong., 2d sess., agreed to February 1, 1950) and committee resolutions of the Committee on the Judiciary, adopted January 20, 1955, that Senator Estes Kefauver and such other members as are present are authorized to hold hearings of this subcommittee in Washington, D .C., on December 14 and 17, 1956, and such other days as may be required to complete these hearings and to take sworn testimony from witnesses.

Agreed to this 30th day of November, 1956.

> THOMAS C. HENNINGS, Jr., Missouri.
> PRICE DANIEL, Texas.
> WILLIAM LANGER, North Dakota.
> ALEXANDER WILEY, Wisconsin.

Chairman KEFAUVER. Mr. Neeb, will you come around?

We are very glad to see you, Mr. Neeb.

Mr. NEEB. I am very glad to see you, Senator.

Chairman KEFAUVER. Mr. Neeb is appearing here as a friendly expert in this field, who has devoted a lot of time and interest to this problem, so that he will testify in that capacity, and I do not think we need to swear you in.

I am very happy to have a telegram from my good friend, Tom Carroll, of the San Fernando Valley, who said you were going to be here. I am glad to see you here again.

Mr. NEEB. It is a pleasure to see you.

Chairman KEFAUVER. I was glad to see you at Los Angeles.

Mr. NEEB. I happened to run into Tom Carroll at the airport, and he asked me where I was going, and I told him——

Senator LANGER. Senator Hayden just came in.

Won't you come up here and sit with us?

Chairman KEFAUVER. Come up here and sit right here by Senator Langer and Mr. Chumbris, who is also an associate counsel, on the right here.

We appreciate the presence of the dean of the United States Senate now, Senator Hayden of Arizona.

STATEMENT OF ROBERT A. NEEB, JR., ATTORNEY AT LAW, BEVERLY HILLS, CALIF.

Mr. MITLER. Your name is Robert Neeb?

Mr. NEEB. Yes; it is Robert A. Neeb, Jr.

Mr. MITLER. What is your occupation, Mr. Neeb?

Mr. NEEB. I am an attorney at law, practicing in Beverly Hills, Calif.

Mr. MITLER. And you have come here to testify before this committee, from California, to cooperate with us; is that correct?

Mr. NEEB. Yes, I have.

Mr. MITLER. Would you give us your background in connection with this particular problem?

Mr. NEEB. Well, my background, briefly, is this: I have practiced in the courts of California and the Federal courts for about 19 years, most of it in the criminal field, and I have handled many juvenile matters.

I became interested in the juvenile problem during the World War, and became special deputy attorney general of California for the express purpose of making a juvenile delinquency survey of that State; and I believe I made the first statewide survey of juvenile delinquency in California's history. We set up at that time a department on juvenile delinquency in the attorney general's office.

Since that time, I have been in private practice, and continued to be interested in the subject. I was a special adviser to the former district attorney of Los Angeles County, Mr. Dockweiler, on the subject of juvenile delinquency. I have served on a number of boards in Los Angeles, child guidance clinics; and in 1953 the present attorney general of California appointed a statewide citizens' committee to advise with him on crime prevention and juvenile delinquency, and I had the honor to be chairman of that committee for 3 years in southern California. There are two branches; because the State is so large, it was handled in that manner.

The first subject we took up was the subject of narcotics, and we have thousands of words and hundreds of pages of testimony taken over nearly 2 years, from all of the experts on this subject in the United States, and we had the privilege of hearing from one inspector from Scotland Yard who had handled narcotics in the British Isles.

But, not being satisfied with that, we went into the prisons and there took the testimony of addicts, most of whom were serving long sentences for serious crimes, all of which had been while they were on the outside, addicts.

This committee of yours, gentlemen, is a committee primarily concerning itself with juvenile delinquency, and to begin with I want to say this so you will understand our feeling:

We in California feel that the narcotics problem is almost a hundred percent a juvenile delinquency problem because of this fact: We don't find any addicts, to speak of, in California who do not give a direct history of learning about narcotics in their early teens, some as early as 13 and 14 years of age.

Mr. MITLER. Mr. Neeb, I know that you have a statement. Would you submit that for the record, please?

Mr. NEEB. Yes, I will.

Chairman KEFAUVER. Well, Mr. Neeb, you can either read your statement, or it will be printed in the record and you may summarize it and tell us about it.

Mr. NEEB. I would rather not read it. I think it is rather dull to do so, and if Mr. Mitler would ask me some questions on anything the Senators are interested in, I would be glad to try to answer them.

Mr. MITLER. I will ask that your statement be incorporated in the record.

Chairman KEFAUVER. It will be printed in full in the record.

Has it been released to the press?

Mr. MITLER. It has been, Senator.

(Mr. Neeb's prepared statement is as follows:)

STATEMENT BY ROBERT A. NEEB, JR., ATTORNEY AT LAW, BEVERLY HILLS, CALIF.

I greatly appreciate the opportunity to appear before this committee and to present some views and recommendations based upon an intensive 2-year study in California of crime-prevention problems. This study was made by two citizens' committees appointed by California's attorney general, Edmund G. Brown, one for southern and one for northern California. I was chairman of the southern California citizens' committee, and Dr. Milton Chernin, dean of the School of Social Welfare at the University of California in Berkeley, was chairman of the northern committee.

While my specific subject is treatment for narcotic addiction, it is impossible to speak of treatment without some deference to the growing drug evil itself. Any attack on this evil must involve both control of the source and the handling of those who have fallen prey to the living death drug addiction represents.

Our California studies involved many meetings and investigations, and the taking of hundreds of pages of testimony by experts concerned with narcotics, crime prevention and law enforcement; by sociologists, psychiatrists, and medical practitioners; and by addicts themselves.

Several facts stand out in a review of these investigations and testimony. Some are contrary to public belief.

For example, it may be the common view that the addict loves the drug which masters him. The contrary is true. He hates the drug, hates his addiction, hates the peddler. He hates them as the tortured slave hates his master. But society offers him no help in breaking the chains that bind him. The bond of his addiction may lead him to theft, burglary, robbery, forgery, even to murder. These things he will do rather than face the tortures of withdrawal in jail. He cannot go to a physician, because under the law a physicias may not use drugs in treating him. Addicts have told us that, much as they might yearn to be free of heroin addiction, they cannot face the agony of sudden withdrawal.

Another fact not commonly known is that addiction is more mental than physical. Addicts who have spent months or years in jail or prisons are physically free of the drug. Their bodies no longer require it. Yet, immediately upon their release they return to the habit.

We were told by law-enforcement agents that there is no case of a heroin addict being cured. Some agents conclude that there is no use wasting time or money in treatment. Our California committees could not accept this view. Our reasons were not alone humane consideration for the individual. One out of four California crimes may be traced directly or indirectly to narcotics. I would estimate that crimes of the addicts in support of their drug habit cost the people of California at least $100 million a year. I am counting the cost of the crime to the vicitms and the cost of law enforcement, apprehension, trial, and incarceration.

The cost to the Nation of heroin-inspired crime must be staggering, many times the cost of treatment facilities.

Another reason we cannot afford as a Nation to leave the untreated heroin addict loose in our society is that these people form the principal source of revenue of organized crime. The average heroin addict pays $50 a day for the drug. Multiply this by 150,000 addicts in the United States—certainly not a high estimate—and you have $7,500,000 a day or $2,737,500,000 a year being paid to support the world crime syndicate. It is interesting that evidence of the Mafia, with its general headquarters either in Sicily or in the United States, appears frequently in investigations of the drug traffic. There is other evidence, which I shall discuss later, that narcotic export is part of the Kremlin pattern of aggression.

Organized crime in America was supported during the 1920's by bootlegging. With the end of prohibition, the underworld turned to other sources, including various rackets and especially gambling. Today its chief revenue appears to come from narcotics.

Our California study led to the introduction of bills before the last session of the California Legislature which would have dealt with the treatment problem along these lines:

1. Instead of being confined in jails, untreated, to face the prolonged torture of withdrawal, the addict would be confined to a special narcotic ward in a hospital. There both the physical and mental addiction would be treated. When there was sufficient evidence that he might return to society free of addiction, he would be released, but only on the condition that he regularly visit an outpatient clinic.

2. The outpatient clinic would provide no drugs, but would give psychiatric, social work, and employment aid where needed. Any evidence of new addiction, or failure to report, would bring about a return to the narcotic ward.

These outpatient clinics would be staffed with doctors of medicine, psychotherapists, social workers, and employment counselors.

Testimony before our committees indicated that an addict may not be considered cured until he has gone without the drug for 4 years. Pharmacology has supplied a new drug called nalline which apparently can detect an addict within minutes.

I would recommend that in all cases involving an addict probation should be for a period of not less than 5 years after release from the narcotic ward. During this period regular visits would be required to the outpatient clinic.

Both the California Assembly and Senate agreed to this legislation, which was introduced by Assemblyman H. Allen Smith, recently elected to the United States House of Representatives. But the program was vetoed by the Governor on the ground insufficient funds had been appropriated to implement the program adequately. We expect the same legislation to be introduced at the 1957 session of the California Legislature, and fervently hope that this time it will be accompanied by adequate financial support and will be adopted by the legislature and approved by the Governor. The savings to California taxpayers will be many times its cost, and law enforcement will gain great strength in its war against crime.

Again let me stress that it is not sympathy with the addict that provides the strongest argument for this proposal. We know from our studies that the addict will go to any length to avoid the torture of sudden withdrawal in jail. He will not willingly commit himself to this truly terrible ordeal. He has no other way, no matter how strong his desire, to break his heinous, consuming bond with the drug. So he perpetuates his own slavery by committing any crime necessary to buy the narcotic. And thus he continues to rob, steal, and otherwise plunder society to support his masters, the Fagans who control the drug trade. He hates them, but he will do anything for his daily "fix."

Those already "hooked" by heroin become a great recruiting army for new addicts. They are willing peddlers, since in this manner they can support their own addiction. So, in a measure, the confinement and treatment of addicts would serve to slow new addictions.

This California approach to the drug problem appears to be unique. We believe that it could best be done on a national scale, with all States and the Federal Government participating.

As I suggested earlier, any effective attack on the drug evil must include both treatment and hard blows at the drug traffic itself. Our California studies led us to this conclusion. The Mexican border and our west coast ports and airfields are highways for the narcotic traffic into this country. Most of our marihuana, and a good deal of our heroin, is smuggled into California from Mexico. As it was pointed out to our committees, our sister republic to the south has not taken effective action to stop the raising of poppies far in excess of the need for legitimate medicinal export. Nor has the Mexican Government effectively acted to help stop the flood of marihuana into California. It is sold to American visitors in Mexican border cities. If the flood of marihuana and other illegal drugs over the 1,800 miles of the Mexican border continues, I would suggest we consider closing the border entirely to free access, and permit exchange of visitors with Mexico only on the basis of passports and visas, as we do with other foreign nations.

Large supplies of illicit narcotics also find their way to the United States from Yugoslavia, Turkey, Iran, Iraq, and India. Some of it is processed in final form in France and Italy. I suggest we consider stopping all aid to nations which will not enter into effective agreements with us to reduce the manufacture and illegal export of narcotics.

It is to be noted that cocaine has been stamped out as a major problem because the Central and South American countries where it was manufactured destroyed the factories.

The most deadly of all narcotics, almost pure heroin, enters the west coast from Red China via ship and plane. This leads to another observation.

While every American is affected directly by the narcotics evil, it has more than a casual bearing on the future of the free world. As you no doubt know, narcotics addiction had fallen to such a low ebb in 1948 that the Government was considering the closing of the two Federal hospitals for narcotic addicts. With the end of World War II and the full control of China by the Communists, the United States and other nations suddenly found an alarming rise of heroin addiction. It is well known that heroin of almost pure strength became a principal export of the Communists from Red China; that the manufacture and export of enslaving drugs has been vigorously encouraged by the Communists where they gained control of satellites. Drug addiction in the free nations is a subtle and diabolical form of conquest in which the victims pay for their own enslavement. This is even more cruel and mind destroying that the techniques devised by the masters of the Kremlin to force the innocent to confess crimes punishable by death. The export of narcotics brings about mass self-destruction among peoples marked for slavery by the Red imperialists. We have seen this pattern in Thailand and we are seeing it in Japan, where addiction is higher than in this country, and never was known before. That this conspiracy also has had its effect upon America cannot be doubted, and the growth of narcotics addiction has alarmed all of us.

Coupled with this evident pattern of Communist narcotic aggression is the fact that the narcotics trade offers huge rewards, and comparatively small risks, to the world criminal element. A pound of heroin purchased in Red China for $1,000 is easily worth $200,000 here. Many law-enforcement agencies believe that the drug traffic is the principal revenue of the underworld. Cut it off and the criminal army would be isolated from its main source of supply and could be decimated by our law-enforcement officers, now fighting what seems a losing battle at times against the rising tide of crime.

Most of the Chinese heroin undoubtedly arrives at west coast ports and airfields. There are, it appears, other foreign sources of this diabolical drug, but that from China is of such strength that it obviously could be exported only with government approval. We were told that addicts accustomed to weaker heroin from Mexico and other countries have died under the shock of a shot of the Chinese variety.

No contract seems possible with Red China to stop its export of heroin. Even had we trade and diplomatic relations with Red China, we have learned from sad experience that the Communists honor obligations only when this is expedient to them.

Since we have no way to stop the flow of heroin at its source in Red China, we must look to the ports of entry. Once it leaves the harbor or airfield in the

United States it is very difficult to trace the drug. It has been cut and dispersed into a thousand channels. Yet we deny our Federal and State narcotics agents the power to search vessels and planes and incoming baggage and cargo for drugs in their uncut form. This power is reserved to an undermanned customs staff. No wonder the odds are almost 99 to 1 against detection for the heroin smuggler.

It is my belief that the Congress should give Federal and State narcotics agents concurrent jurisdiction with the Customs Service over incoming ships, aircraft, and other means of transportation which can be used to bring narcotics into our country.

Another problem is that we have too few narcotics officers, they are paid too little, and they lack the weapons to fight the drug traffic effectively. This war demands men of high courage and intelligence and such a dangerous and difficult career should offer commensurate pay.

Only rarely is a higher up in the narcotics racket arrested. Why? Partly because we are too niggardly in our appropriations for the work of the agents. Until recently, the State of California allowed its narcotics officers only $7,500 a year to spend in making purchases of narcotics. This now has been doubled to the unrealistic sum of $15,000. No wonder they cannot get far beyond the little peddler. It is like trying to land a big fish on a spool of string.

It is evident that some of the rulers of the racket are outside the jurisdiction of the United States. Most of the overlords, foreign and domestic, never come close to the actual drugs. They are not users. They do not handle the narcotics directly. They bankroll the purchases. Some of the peddling is done in the following manner, in California: The addict runs low in supply, he obtains financing and goes to Mexico for a couple of days; there he buys the narcotics— more than he needs for a period; he returns and peddles to his fellow addicts until he runs low again; and then repeats the process.

A high proportion of the sales do not occur in bars or back alleys but in apartments rented for a brief period by the addicts. It is very difficult for agents to detect this type of operation.

One further point deserves mention, and this involves the greatest tragedy and crime of all.

Most, if not all, heroin addicts in California start in their teens through marihuana parties. They are told marihuana is harmless and not habit-forming; that the feeling is wonderful. This is the bait. Once they become accustomed to marihuana and its spurious thrills, the teenagers are introduced to "hard" narcotics. The hook is set. At first, they do not feel it, fool themselves that they can quit. Suddenly they realize they are "hooked," helplessly enslaved to a drug they will come to hate but cannot live without. They are on their way to physical and moral dissolution, a living death.

A gay adventure has turned into tragedy for the victim and his family, a new menace to society.

We rarely find a heroin addict without a history of narcotics in his teens, beginning with marihuana. Many begin at 14 and 15 years of age.

In California, unlike other areas, addiction is not limited to racial groups and certain neighborhoods. It cuts across racial, neighborhood, and economic lines. It invades the wealthy district as well as the poor neighborhood. Many addicts are of average or superior intelligence. Some made excellent witnesses before our committees.

No matter what cultural or economic status they may hold, no family is safe from this contagion. Their beloved teen-age child may easily be lured into an experiment with marihuana, then into heroin addiction.

I recall one case of a 13-year-old girl, arrested for forgery to support her heroin habit.

Society must stamp out this evil, make it such a serious crime to provide juveniles with narcotics in any form that the traffic will be discouraged, the price of drugs beyond reach of the thrill seeker. California has increased its penalties for the sale of narcotics to juveniles. The Federal Government has imposed drastic penalties, even to capital punishment.

This is one field in which severe punishment does act as a deterrent.

To summarize, we believe these steps are essential:

1. Create hospital narcotic wards for confinement and treatment of addicts. Supplement this treatment by drugless outpatient clinics providing psychiatric, social work, and employment aid. Require those discharged from the hospitals to report regularly to these clinics—or, in a small city, to an authorized local

physician. Upon evidence of renewed addiction, return the individual to custody. This is the California plan.

2. Provide Federal and State narcotic agencies authority for search of incoming ships, aircraft, and other conveyances, concurrent with that now granted the Customs Service.

3. Arm our agencies fighting the war on narcotics with adequate, properly paid personnel and the appropriations and other weapons necessary to win this war.

Mr. MITLER. As the result of a study made by your committee, would you tell us the scope and extent of juvenile drug addiction in California?

Mr. NEEB. Well, as to the numbers who are addicts, that is a pretty difficult question to answer. But I can tell you this: That the commitments of juveniles—and in California that means any age down to 9, 10, 11, or 12 years of age up to the youth authority, which takes them to 23, but there are very few over 21—has been steadily increasing on the narcotics side. The increase, or the last figures, which would be 1955 and 1956, show about 6 percent of the total commitments are known addicts, even though they are still in their teens.

Last year the increase in boys was 1 percent over the previous term and 2 percent for girls. We don't have any idea why there are more girls getting into trouble than boys.

Mr. MITLER. What has been the overall trend since 1950?

Mr. NEEB. Well, it is a general trend; yes. I don't have each year, but there is one interesting figure, and that is, we have over 5,000 young people on parole in California, that is the parole load of our parole officers, and they have a very heavy load; and, of those, somewhere between 450 and 500 of them are known narcotics cases. And we know a lot of them are narcotics cases we don't know but because, very strangely, those that are listed as narcotic problems, 25 percent of them became narcotic problems either after they got out on parole or were never arrested for it and were discovered later to be users.

Mr. MITLER. Mr. Neeb, what are the overall figures with respect to juvenile delinquency; is there an upward or downward trend?

Mr. NEEB. The general trend is up.

Mr. MITLER. In the State of California?

Mr. NEEB. Yes.

Mr. MITLER. Have you got some general figures on that?

Mr. NEEB. No; only on the narcotic figures. I limit it to that.

Mr. MITLER. By the way, the figure you gave us you received through the courtesy of the California Youth Authority, Mr. Heman Stark?

Mr. NEEB. Yes. Those were released as of December of this year, so they are pretty accurate and pretty recent.

Mr. MITLER. To fill in the picture, do you have any figures with respect to the overall narcotics picture in California?

Mr. NEEB. Yes, I do have.

We expect 1956 will show about 9,000 felony arrests for narcotics in California, and we figure that if you arrest 1 out of 5 users in a year, you are doing pretty good; and if those figures hold, you would have about 45,000 narcotic addicts in the State of California, juvenile and adult.

Mr. MITLER. As a result of your examination of these people and the institutions in your overall study, could you tell us about what age do most of these people have their first contact with narcotics in California?

Mr. NEER. Well, I personally have never interviewed addicts—and I have interviewed a lot of them—who didn't say they started in their early teens, and every one of them says the start was with marihuana.

Mr. MITLER. Can you tell us something about the population make-up of those people who are addicts, and especially those under 21?

Mr. NEEB. Yes. Nationally, you have a trend in every State, it is racial, and depends on locality or neighborhood problems. California has no connection whatever with race or locality. The narcotic problem there cut across all phases of society, and we cannot find out why we are different than the national trend, but we are.

Mr. MITLER. Tell me——

Chairman KEFAUVER. By "all phases," you mean well-to-do children——

Mr. NEEB. Yes.

Chairman KEFAUVER (continuing). Poor, regardless of their ethnic background?

Mr. NEEB. Yes. It doesn't seem to run like it does in other cities.

For instance, I haven't been there, but the investigation indicates that in New York you can draw a line around the area where you have narcotic addiction; but in California, you can't draw a line around anything, and you can't limit it to just the big cities.

Chairman KEFAUVER. Well, you undoubtedly have more in slum areas than you do in nonslum areas.

Mr. NEEB. Yes, you do. I think if you interviewed a hundred addicts, you would find the two reasons they give for addiction is availability and environment.

Mr. MITLER. Mr. Neeb, did you discover what the source of the drugs was that were used by these young people in California, where did they mostly come from?

Mr. NEEB. Well, we made an extensive study of sources of supply. There are three sources of drugs in California, and by that I mean the heroin drug. One is the Mediterranean heroin that comes out of Iran, Iraq, Turkey, Yugoslavia, and India. It is manufactured in France and in Italy, and some of the other countries, and exported through the Mediterranean.

We have positive indication that it is run by the Mafia, because if you wanted to check the arrests for smuggling on the eastern seaboard for 10 years back, I think you would find you would be surprised how many Sicilians are involved, and there those same names turn up again in Central and South America, still in the smuggling business, after they are released from some incarceration in this country.

The second source is Mexico. Mexico supplies us with what is known in the trade in California as brown heroin. It is called brown heroin because it is not refined very well, and it is not as strong. And Mexico is almost the exclusive source of marihuana.

Stopping there a moment, I want to say this to you gentlemen: The marihuana problem in California is far more serious than anyone in this country realizes, because it is the cause of addiction. The young people can get it for a dollar, and it is child's play to obtain it.

The third source is becoming perhaps an international incident, almost, and that is the tremendous quality of the heroin that comes from China. It is getting——

Chairman KEFAUVER. You mean "quantity"?

Mr. NEEB. Quantity and quality. The examination of this heroin indicates that it is about as pure as you can produce it, about 87 percent pure. Actually, we have had cases in California where some addict has gotten some Chinese heroin, and one shot will kill them because it is so strong. It is not diluted enough.

The heroin that comes from other sources is always diluted and cut down.

Our committee came to this conclusion, Mr. Chairman: The heroin from Mexico is pure ground; the heroin from the Mediterranean is cut to about 5 percent of strength when it gets to California, because it travels through hands. The heroin from Communist China comes in pure, and we don't think you could have it so pure unless it was sponsored by the Government of Communist China.

As a matter of fact, they have said they were in the business, they used it in the conquest of Thailand. Today they are pushing it into Japan. There is more addiction in Japan today than there is in the United States.

Mr. MITLER. Mr. Neeb, do young people go into Tijuana, across the border, and get narcotics?

Mr. NEEB. That is one of the sad tales of California. We have a tremendously long border with Mexico. It is simple and easy for young persons—here is the modus operandi in California: Four or five people want some heroin or they want some marihuana. So they each put up a few dollars apiece, and somebody borrows a car or they take the family car, and 1 or 2 of them go to Tijuana. They simply go over the border and say, "We are Americans"; they simply come back and say "We are Americans." Very seldom is there any search, and they can buy all the heroin and all the marihuana they want in Mexico.

And the thing that disturbs us out there is this: The Mexican Government apparently does very little, if anything, about these peddlers, and we are sure they know them because our border guards give them money when they inform as to who they sold to.

Mr. MITLER. Could you explain that, Mr. Neeb?

Mr. NEEB. Yes. Our border guards apparently, in an effort to do a good job—and I don't criticize them; I criticize the Mexicans for not clamping down on the peddlers—they have a standing offer of $500 of our money to any peddler in Tijuana who will inform and give the license number of a purchaser in Mexico.

Now, that applies to juveniles. I know juvenile cases where it is happening . They get paid for the heroin or the marihuana with American money, and then they get $500 from the border guard for giving the license number.

Mr. MITLER. Mr. Neeb, will you turn now to what the treatment program is, to the State——

Chairman KEFAUVER. Let us turn a little more to this problem with Mexico.

We have had some hearings, Senator Langer in El Paso, under Senator Hendrickson in San Diego, about this border problem. At that time there was some recommendation of stopping the boys going back and forth across the border without some written authorization of their parents, and there is a bill filed, Mr. Chumbris reminds me, S. 959. We thought that might be a way of getting at it.

But then we found that brought a great deal of criticism and complaint from our friendly neighbor to the north, the Canadians, where there was no traffic; also a great many other places where there was no traffic, where good, normal relations in going back and forth existed, and we did get—so we were never able to work out a bill which would fit the situation to stop this traffic.

I think we did get something which was helpful. Congress authorized a little more money for control, and got some agreements and cooperation from some of the Mexican officials.

But what is the solution to that problem?

Mr. NEEB. We feel there is a solution. It may sound drastic, but actually I think it would be workable, and that would be for us to close the border except as we have borders open and intercourse with other countries. That means by passport and visa. If a person has business in Mexico, they could go just as easily as they could go to Sweden or England or anywhere else. But it is the people without business who are bringing in the narcotics.

Chairman KEFAUVER. Well, that, of course, is a policy of our Government, to encourage vacation exchange in going from country to country, just visiting. Do you think that such a closing of the border, requiring passports, would interfere with vacation visitation?

Mr. NEEB. I think this, Senator: that if we did it for a limited period of time, I think we would find that the use of marihuana in this country would fall off so greatly that the closing would be found to be justified.

Chairman KEFAUVER. In Tijuana, you can buy marihuana anywhere, in the stores, almost.

Mr. NEEB. Well, I don't know about stores, but they have enough peddlers there that the young persons who don't have any contacts, they can just go down there and find it. You don't have to be a big man in the peddling business to be able to buy it over the border.

Chairman KEFAUVER. And heroin, too?

Mr. NEEB. Heroin, yes; usually brown heroin. That is the Mexican variety.

Chairman KEFAUVER. And searching kids coming back is not a very adequate way of stopping it?

Mr. NEEB. Well, Senator, the answer is this: The records of that one part show 1,200,000 purchases, and 5 million people, each 12 months. You just can't—the border patrol is too thin, you couldn't possibly do it.

Of course, you would have opposition by the racetrack people and the gambling interests, because they are running races and bookmaking in Tijuana, and thousands of people go, and they say, "We have a right to go to the races."

But I think that helping these young people is more important than letting people go to the races. We honestly feel, Senator, if we could lick the marihuana problem in California, we would lick the narcotic problem, because that is the road that leads to heroin.

Chairman KEFAUVER. I think we all understand that when the thrill of marihuana wears off, they look to heroin or something stronger.

Mr. NEEB. That is right.

Chairman KEFAUVER. Well, is this the recommendation of the juvenile commission of which you have been chairman?

Mr. NEEB. No. We didn't come to a unanimity of opinion on that, because, as you pointed out, there are two schools of thought about closing the border. But we certainly did recommend—there is one other recommendation that we made, Senator, that we did agree upon, and that is that the narcotic officers of the State and Federal Government have a right that they do not have now, and that is the right of search and seizure.

On the incoming boats and planes into California, no narcotics officer, however well trained, has a right to search any person or any baggage on those boats or planes. They have to have with them customs officers.

Now, I don't mean to imply they do not cooperate. They do. But without costing the Government 1 more cent, think of the personnel that you could add to the power of the customs officers if you gave this right to State and Federal narcotics officers. It wouldn't cost anything.

Chairman KEFAUVER. I have here, Mr. Neeb, the narcotic addiction report to Attorney General Edmund G. Brown by the Citizens Advisory Committee to the Attorney General, on Crime Prevention, and you as chairman of the southern committee.

This is the book you are speaking about?

Mr. NEEB. Yes, that is the book; correct.

Chairman KEFAUVER. And Dr. Milton Chernin.

Mr. NEEB. Yes.

Chairman KEFAUVER. Yes.

Mr. NEEB. He is the professor of sociology at the University of California at Berkeley.

Chairman KEFAUVER. He is the northern chairman?

Mr. NEEB. Those chairmanships are changed. We are rotating them.

Chairman KEFAUVER. These matters of closing of the border or giving authority to make searches to narcotics agents, have you taken that up with any Federal officials?

Mr. NEEB. No, we have not. We made recommendations, and that is about as far as we could go.

Chairman KEFAUVER. Senator Langer, do you have any questions you wish to ask at this time?

Senator LANGER. No.

Chairman KEFAUVER. All right, proceed, Mr. Mitler.

Mr. MITLER. Mr. Neeb, would you tell us now about the treatment program in the State of California, with special reference to those in the under-21-years-of-age group? What is being done to get at the root of the problem in terms of treatment?

Mr. NEEB. Well, Mr. Mitler, I think California has gone out in front in this regard. We actually have legislation that passed the senate and the assembly in California, which we think will lick the problem of treating the addict.

We felt, after this long investigation into our own State, that you cannot lick the narcotic problem unless you do it in two ways: First, you have to be vigorous in your enforcement, you have to cut off the peddler and the source of supply. But you also have to cure the addict who is on the street, because as long as he is a customer, an addict, a supplier will spring up.

You ask the man in prison, and he will say as long as you have customers you will have peddlers.

So we have this proposal——

Chairman KEFAUVER. Wait just a minute, Mr. Neeb.

Mr. Cunningham, would you come up?

Mr. Cunningham is the Deputy Director of the Bureau of Narcotics, a Tennesseean.

Mr. CUNNINGHAM. We have a representative down here to wait for you. If you want me this afternoon, I will be glad to come back.

Chairman KEFAUVER. We certainly do appreciate your coming up, Mr. Cunningham.

Mr. CUNNINGHAM. Mr. Diordano is here.

Chairman KEFAUVER. Thank you very much for your cooperation, Mr. Cunningham.

Senator LANGER. Mr. Cunningham——

Chairman KEFAUVER. Senator Langer wanted to ask you something.

STATEMENT OF GEORGE W. CUNNINGHAM, DEPUTY COMMISSIONER OF NARCOTICS, FEDERAL BUREAU OF NARCOTICS, TREASURY DEPARTMENT

Mr. CUNNINGHAM. Yes, Senator.

Senator LANGER. I was interested in what Mr. Neeb said about having additional people having authority to search.

Have you ever considered that question?

Mr. CUNNINGHAM. Well, no, Senator; we haven't. I don't think that would be very difficult, as a matter of law, just to give these Federal narcotics agents the same rights as customs agents to search.

Whether they would agree to it or not, I have no way of knowing. It wouldn't be a very difficult law to pass.

Senator LANGER. It would be a simple matter to introduce a bill——

Mr. CUNNINGHAM. That is right.

Senator LANGER (continuing). Giving you this authority.

Mr. CUNNINGHAM. That is right.

Senator LANGER. Well, in your reports have you ever asked for that authority?

Mr. CUNNINGHAM. No, sir; we have not.

Chairman KEFAUVER. I think it would be a different problem giving State narcotic agents authority.

Mr. CUNNINGHAM. I would think so.

Chairman KEFAUVER. But your agents would be a simple matter, would it not?

Mr. CUNNINGHAM. Back in the early days, I had a commission in the customs, and I still have it. I can search boats, planes, or anything else, but I don't know of many narcotics agents that have that. I think I had one in the early twenties, and I still have it.

But it might not necessitate a law. It might be done through the Treasury Department, that is, the Commissioner of Customs.

Chairman KEFAUVER. Mr. Cunningham, would you be so good as to research or have it researched, if possible we would like to have it today, whether you do have law or authority, what you need to have authority, so we could include in our report.

Mr. CUNNINGHAM. Right. I am sure there is no statutory authority to first engage in searches, which is similar to what the customs do.

But I think it could be done administratively.   I may be wrong about it, but I think those powers could be extended administratively, to Federal narcotics agents.   I am not saying about the State narcotics agents, Mr. Chairman.

Chairman KEFAUVER. Anything else on that, Senator Langer?

Senator LANGER. Yes.

Take, for example, in wheat inspection, the Federal Government can authorize a State official——

Chairman KEFAUVER. Why don't you sit down, Mr. Cunningham. Sit down with Mr. Neeb.

Senator LANGER. They can authorize a gentleman working for the State, for example. to do the inspecting.   Why couldn't the Federal Government deputize the State agents here?

Mr. CUNNINGHAM. Well, that would be very beneficial on the Texas and Mexican border.

Senator LANGER. I do not see why it couldn't be done.

Do you have any reason you see why it could not be done?

Mr. CUNNINGHAM. I know of no reason why it could not be done.

Senator LANGER. Mr. Neeb?

Mr. NEEB. You are speaking to me, Senator?

Senator LANGER. Yes.

Mr. NEEB. We have given it a lot of consideration, and we gave it consideration in 1955, and we have talked with a lot of narcotics agents on the coast.   I don't know what Mr. Anslinger thinks about it. We talked to him about it, and——

Senator LANGER. How many State agents are there?

Mr. NEEB. You mean in California?

Senator LANGER. In California.

Mr. NEEB. I can't give you the exact number, but we have in the department in California about 30 agents.

Chairman KEFAUVER. You mean the California department?

Mr. NEEB. Yes.   We have our own narcotic agency on the State level, and we have on the county level and police departments, also.

Chairman KEFAUVER. And there is very close cooperation, I know, between the California narcotics agents and the Federal agents.

Mr. NEEB. Yes, there is no problem of cooperation.   But there are times we found when there were boats coming in through the Golden Gate when, for one reason or another, you could not find more than 3, 3 customs agents, to take care of the matter.

It is not their fault.   They just don't have enough.

Chairman KEFAUVER. Mr. Cunningham, can you also give us some information as to the research and what the status is, authorizing this to be done: that is, to give the State agents authority to be deputized by the Federal Government to assist in searches?

Mr. CUNNINGHAM. Consistent with the authority that the customs agent has, do I understand you to mean that?

Chairman KEFAUVER. Yes, sir.

Senator LANGER. Your agents are all men, are they, or have you some women agents?

Mr. CUNNINGHAM. We have all men.

Chairman KEFAUVER. How about yourself, Mr. Neeb?

Mr. NEEB. I don't think we have any women agents.   I think they are all men.   I don't know of any personally.

Chairman KEFAUVER. You have not heard about the equal-rights amendment out there.

Mr. NEEB. We have heard about it, but not in that department.

Chairman KEFAUVER. The local squads, like Los Angeles, San Diego——

Mr. NEEB. They employ women police officers and sheriff's officers.

Chairman KEFAUVER. In talking of the 30, you are not talking about the narcotics squad of the cities?

Mr. NEEB. Oh, no. The Los Angeles Police Department has a large squad, the sheriff's office has a large squad. As a matter of fact, there is no lack of manpower, but there is a lack of power, if I make myself clear.

Chairman KEFAUVER. Lack of authority.

Mr. NEEB. Yes, lack of authority. We are informed by the customs agents in Los Angeles that so far as airplanes are concerned, they just don't have the manpower to search more than about one plane once a month, and that is not, of course, doing the job.

Chairman KEFAUVER. You are talking about the local——

Mr. NEEB. No; I am talking about customs. They can't search planes, either. They don't have the manpower. And we have two of the biggest airfields in the country at San Francisco and Los Angeles, and many planes from overseas.

Chairman KEFAUVER. Of course, heroin and marihuana come in that way as well as being smuggled across the border directly.

Mr. NEEB. Well, it can come in—a pound of it that you would pay about a thousand dollars for in Shanghai, we know 1 place where they make 300 pounds a day, you can buy it for a thousand dollars, and when you get it to Los Angeles it would be worth about $200,000, and the customs officers have told us that as far as Chinese heroin is concerned, they get about 1 percent of it at the point of entry. The rest of it is confiscated later by local officers and by Mr. Cunningham's men, when it is already in the State.

Again, I am not criticizing the customs officers, but they just don't have enough personnel to do the job in California.

We have a thousand miles of coastline, and a hundred or several hundred miles of border with Mexico, and it is a tremendous problem.

Chairman KEFAUVER. Do you agree generally with that situation, Mr. Cunningham?

Mr. CUNNINGHAM. Yes, Mr. Chairman; I do.

Chairman KEFAUVER. Well, may I ask you also while you are here, Mr. Cunningham—for the record, this is George W. Cunningham, Deputy Commissioner of the Bureau of Narcotics—by closing the border, I am sure Mr. Neeb means requiring visas.

Mr. NEEB. That is right.

Chairman KEFAUVER. You do not mean just to close the border.

Mr. NEEB. Oh, no.

Chairman KEFAUVER. But requiring a person to have some kind of a permit or visa.

Mr. NEEB. Yes. If they have legitimate business, they certainly could go back and forth.

Chairman KEFAUVER. We certainly don't want to close the border with our Mexican friends, but they as well as we should not object to reasonable measures to stop this traffic.

Mr. NEEB. That is correct.

Chairman KEFAUVER. And visas are what you have in mind?

Mr. NEEB. Visa and passport, and if they have legitimate business, they could obtain it.

Chairman KEFAUVER. What is your feeling about that, Mr. Cunningham?

Mr. CUNNINGHAM. Mr. Chairman, I wouldn't be qualified to speak on that, because it involves a lot of international relations, and I have long since learned that it might be well to let the State Department take care of that.

Now, at the last session of Congress, in Senator Daniel's bill, with which you are very familiar, they closed the border under certain instances to addicts, making those addicts register in going to Mexico under penalty.

As to what success they have had with that, I don't know. But I can say with that border as long as it is, and the many places you can cross it, not only by Mr. Neeb's description of the amount of people and the amount of cars that go from southern California to Tijuana, it would be a rather hopeless task.

Chairman KEFAUVER. You have the same thing at Juarez and other places?

Mr. CUNNINGHAM. Well, you don't have the traffic at Juarez that you have in southern California.

Chairman KEFAUVER. You recommended favorable action on our bill, S. 959, requiring permits of some kind for minors to go back and forth, authority from their parents. But that got into international complications, also.

Mr. CUNNINGHAM. That is right.

Chairman KEFAUVER. We would appreciate it if you will send up what you can this afternoon so we can put it in our record.

Mr. CUNNINGHAM. I will get in touch with the enforcement people over at customs, and see what their idea is about it. I am sure they would welcome any help that they can get.

Chairman KEFAUVER. And if we can have it so we can put it in our record and release it to the press this afternoon.

Mr. CUNNINGHAM. Would you like me to ask one of the enforcement people in customs if he might come down this afternoon?

Chairman KEFAUVER. Yes; and bring whatever he can—whatever information or research on what can be done in these matters we are talking about.

Mr. CUNNINGHAM. I will be glad to ask them.

Senator LANGER. What are your total appropriations?

Mr. CUNNINGHAM. The Bureau of Narcotics?

Senator LANGER. Yes; each year.

Mr. CUNNINGHAM. This year it is about $3,400,000.

Senator LANGER. That is not as much as we have appropriated for the wetback enforcement law, is it?

Mr. CUNNINGHAM. I don't know how much you appropriated to those, Senator Langer.

Chairman KEFAUVER. How many agents do you have?

Mr. CUNNINGHAM. On the rolls Friday, we had 271.

Chairman KEFAUVER. Two hundred seventy-one for the whole United States, all of our territories?

Mr. CUNNINGHAM. And Europe.

Chairman KEFAUVER. And Europe.

Mr. CUNNINGHAM. We are recruiting now to the extent of our ability. I might say that we have the money to put on more men, but we are having trouble locating the right type of people. We are attempting to recruit for about 300 as quickly as we can.

Chairman KEFAUVER. I remember when we started these hearings, you had only about 181.

Mr. CUNNINGHAM. 175.

Chairman KEFAUVER. 175?

Mr. CUNNINGHAM. Something like that.

Chairman KEFAUVER. Mr. Mitler, do you want to ask Mr. Cunningham anything before he leaves?

Mr. MITLER. I have no questions.

Mr. CUNNINGHAM. Thank you very much.

Chairman KEFAUVER. Thank you, sir.

Mr. MITLER. Mr. Neeb, you were telling us about the present and existing treatment program in California.

Mr. NEEB. Well, I was about to, and was going to say that we actually prepared a bill. It is rather interesting, because I think there were about 59 narcotic bills introduced at the last meeting of the legislature. Our committee met at the Fairmont Hotel at San Francisco, and we stayed in session about 2 solid days, and we put together what we thought was a bill that was workable, based upon our 2 years of effort and study.

I have copies of it here, if anybody wants to look at it.

Chairman KEFAUVER. It is similar to Bill No. 2334.

Mr. NEEB. Yes, Senator.

Chairman KEFAUVER. Let's make this an exhibit here to your testimony, and have it printed in our record.

Mr. NEEB. All right. I have other copies, if anybody wants them.

Chairman KEFAUVER. All right.

(The bill referred to was marked "Exhibit No. 3," and is as follows:)

ASSEMBLY BILL No. 2334

CHAPTER_____

An act to add Article 2.1 to Chapter 4, Division 10 of, and to amend Section 11721 of the Health and Safety Code, relating to the treatment and punishment of narcotic addicts.

The people of the State of California do enact as follows:

SECTION 1. Article 2.1 is added to Chapter 4, Division 10, of the Health and Safety Code, to read:

"Article 2.1. The California Commission on Drug Addiction

"11397. The purpose of this article is to protect the health and safety of the people of the State of California from the menace of drug addiction, to prevent the further spread of such addiction, especially among minors, to provide for the treatment and cure of addicts, to bring about a better and wider understanding of the evils of drug addiction, and to develop through scientific knowledge more effective methods of treatment for those who are chronically addicted to the use of drugs.

"11398. There is in the State Government the California Commission on Drug Addiction.

The commission shall be composed of 11 members and shall include a representative of the Department of Justice, the Department of Public Health, the

Department of Mental Hygiene, the Department of Corrections, and the Youth Authority, designated by the representative heads thereof, and six other members appointed by the Governor of whom three shall be physicians and three shall be laymen. Of the three physician members, at least one shall be a psychiatrist, and of the laymen, at least one shall be a woman. The chairman of the commission shall be elected by the commission each year from the members of the commission other than the ex officio members herein mentioned.

"The appointive members of the commission shall be appointed for a term of four years. The terms of office of the appointive members expire as follows: one on September 19, 1956, two on September 19, 1957, two on September 19, 1958, and two on September 19, 1959, and thereafter in the same relative order. Vacancies shall be filled for the unexpired portions of the terms in which they occur.

"11399. The commission shall appoint an executive secretary whose duties shall be specified by the commission and who shall be paid such compensation for his services as the commission may determine. The commission may employ and appoint such other personnel as may be required in accordance with law.

"The commission shall meet at least every two months and at such other times as called by the chairman or by request of any four members.

"Members of the commission shall serve without compensation, but shall be reimbursed for the necessary expenses incurred in the performance of their duties as members of the commission.

"11400. The commission is empowered to establish general and specific policies relating to the treatment of drug addicts and the other provisions of this article. Preventive and treatment programs shall be carried out by the commission as hereinafter provided.

"The commission shall, in addition to its other duties herein set forth, investigate, study and evaluate all phases of the treatment and rehabilitation of drug addicts and other facts in the reduction and prevention of drug addiction and shall periodically report its findings thereon to the Governor and to the Legislature with its recommendations. The commission shall have the power to have placed at its disposal any and all records pertaining to narcotics or drug addiction from any state or local agency.

"11401. As soon as practicable the commission, in cooperation with appropriate local authorities, shall promote and develop counseling and other services for juveniles to prevent drug addiction.

"The commission shall coordinate existing medical facilities and may contract with existing state or local licensed facilities and services for the purpose of treatment of narcotic addicts as provided by this code.

"11402. There shall be established at places designated by the commission outpatient treatment facilities subject to the control of the commission for narcotic addicts for the purpose of giving cure and treatment to narcotic addicts released under the provisions of Section 11721 of this code as amended. In such communities where it is not feasible to establish such outpatient treatment facilities, the superior court therein shall be empowered to designate any competent physician, who is also a psychiatrist, to give treatment and care to any person still subject to the jurisdiction of said court as provided in Section 11721 as amended. Such outpatient treatment facilities as shall be established by the commission shall be staffed by competent professional personnel, including licensed physicians and surgeons and psychiatrists.

"Nothing contained in this article shall give the right to any physician to administer narcotics to any person in any outpatient treatment facility established hereunder and should it come to the attention of any physician in such outpatient treatment facility that any person subject to its care has returned to the use of narcotics, said physician shall report the same in writing to the superior court. Upon the ascertainment of such facts, said court may then revoke the probation and return said person to the facility to which such person was sent by the court for treatment for a period of not less than one year."

Sec. 2. Section 11721 of the Health and Safety Code is amended to read:

"11721. No person shall unlawfully use or be addicted to the unlawful use of narcotics. No person shall be under the influence of narcotics except when such narcotics have been administered by or under the direction of a person licensed by the State to prescribe and administer narcotics. Any person convicted of violating any provision of this section is guilty of a misdemeanor and shall be sentenced to serve a term of not less than 90 days nor more than one year in the county jail. The court may place a person convicted hereunder on probation for a period not to exceed five years and shall in all cases in which probation is granted require as a condition thereof that such person be confined in the county jail for at least 90 days, or the court may, in its discretion, place the person upon probation for not more than five years and as a condition of said probation, commit said person to a state hospital or other treatment facility authorized by Section 11391 and such person shall be committed to such treatment facility for not less than 90 days and shall remain in said treatment facility or state hospital until such time within the limits of said probationary period when the authorities of such institution may recommend to the court that the said person is ready for release. No person shall be committed to a state hospital pursuant to this section unless the superintendent thereof certifies that facilities are available for the treatment of the person in such hospital. In the event that the superintendent of the state hospital does so certify and the person is committed to the hospital, the county from which the person is committed shall be responsible for the cost of his care in such hospital in the same manner as provided in Sections 5356.1 and 5356.2 of the Welfare and Institutions Code. If the court approves the release of said person from such commitment prior to the completion of the period of probation the court may, as a further condition of probation, order said person to undergo outpatient treatment at an outpatient treatment facility designated by the commission pursuant to Section 11402 of this code. In no event does the court have the power to absolve a person who violates this section from the obligation of spending at least 90 days in confinement in the county jail, treatment facility, or state hospital."

——— ———, *Speaker of the Assembly.*

——— ———, *President of the Senate.*

Approved_____, 1955.

——— ———, *Governor.*

Passed the Assembly June 6, 1955.

——— ———, *Chief Clerk of the Assembly.*

Passed the Senate June 3, 1955.

——— ———, *Secretary of the Senate.*

This bill was received by the Governor this_____day of_____, 1955, at_____o'clock_____M.

——— ———, *Private Secretary of the Governor.*

Mr. NEEB. This bill actually passed unanimously.

Chairman KEFAUVER. Go ahead, Mr. Neeb.

Mr. NEEB. This bill passed. I might say that all the other bills were abandoned when the senators and the assembly read this one, and this was the only narcotic bill, and the legislature united on it and it was passed by both houses.

And then for one reason or another, which I haven't been able to figure out, our Governor vetoed it. At any rate, it didn't become law.

It provides what I think will be the ultimate workable method of treating addicts. It sets up at the State level a State commission on narcotics. That commission would have as a duty, to oversee the handling of narcotic hospital facilities in already existing hospitals, no necessity for spending additional money.

These hospitals, under the supervision of the commission, would be the place where a judge would have to send an addict. The person would be convicted of a misdemeanor only, and they could surrender voluntarily. They would receive a minimum of 90 days at the State hospital, whichever one the judge sent them to.

After 90 days, the superintendent and doctors of that hospital, it being staffed by proper doctors, medical doctors, psychiatrists and social workers, would then report back to the judge that Mr. So-and-So or Miss So-and-So is ready for society.

The judge then would have the prisoner returned to the courtroom, where he would then be placed on probation for, I suggest, not less than 5 years, because you can't say an addict is cured unless they are off of the drug for 4 years.

This person would be ordered, as a condition of probation, to report regularly to out-patient clinics to be established in the major communities. In the small areas where it would not be feasible to have a clinic, the bill provides that the judge can designate a local medical doctor, preferably a psychiatrist, to administer to the person.

The bill provides that no drugs, under any circumstances, are to be given at the clinic; only psychiatric help, care, and guidance.

After the person has remained on probation for the period of time set, under our law—and many other States have the same law, section 1203.4 of our probation law provides that a man who has completed his probation has a right then to come into court and make a motion to have the probation terminated or set aside, and have his guilty plea changed and a not-guilty plea entered, the record expunged, and be relieved of all penalties and disabilities for the conviction; and then he can honestly testify in court that he has never been convicted of a crime.

Now that, in essence, is the provisions of the bill.

We believe that it will work because of these factors: The superintendent of your big hospital in Lexington came out to California and spent some time with us. He says that 95 percent of those who go through your hospital, at great expense, return almost immediately to the use of narcotics.

We have talked to many, many addicts and taken their testimony, and they all give the same answer, even though they don't even know each other or haven't talked about this matter.

The answer is always this: "We can be cured of the physical properties of addiction in about 90 days or 6 months. We are all right. But when we get out and we become subject to the same pressures, the same neighborhood, the same associations, the same phobias and worries, we turn again to the crutch we learned to use before. We can't make it alone."

You can hear them, every one of them will tell you that, "We need some psychiatric help, we need guidance, we need work help, we need a place we can go to talk to someone instead of going back and associating with those who got us in this in the first place, who are addicts."

If you had that program, gentlemen, and you enforced it, I am sure you would make great inroads in curing the addict.

There is one other thing the bill provides, and that is, if the doctor in the clinic finds the person has returned to the use of narcotics, he must immediately, in writing, report this to the judge, probation is revoked, and the proceeding starts all over again.

Mr. MITLER. However, that bill, unfortunately, was not passed.

Mr. NEEB. It was passed by both houses, but the governor vetoed it. He said there wasn't sufficient appropriation with it.

Mr. MITLER. Mr. Neeb, turning back to the existing situation at this moment, what are the treatment facilities in California?

Mr. NEEB. There aren't any. The procedure now is that when you arrest a young person who is an addict, you just throw them in jail and let them sweat it out for a month or more, and I think that is one of the worst phases of this, because it leaves a mental scar, particularly on young people. They never get over that, and they will commit any crime in the book to avoid going through that again, once they go back on the drug.

That is what causes these serious crimes. An addict who has had the experience of going through 30 or 60 days in jail, no medical help, the terrible sickness of a real withdrawal, he is not going to get put back in jail again. He will kill before he will do it, before he will let you take him in.

Mr. MITLER. In other words, there is no active treatment program.

Of course, there is withdrawal and physical buildup. There is no psychotherapy.

Mr. NEEB. There is nothing, no. Our law provides in California that a doctor is guilty of a felony if he treats an addict by giving him any withdrawal help by way of drug injection or otherwise.

Mr. MITLER. Now, Mr. Neeb, what is your philosophy about the approach to this problem? Do you think it is medical or punitive? What do you feel about that?

Mr. NEEB. I think the peddler—and we do in California—is the worst criminal America has. I think that it is absolutely without question the basis of organized crime in the United States today is the drug traffic. It makes billions of dollars. All you have to do is figure we have got about 160,000 addicts, and the cost, at least in California, is about $50 a day to supply the habit. Add it up, and look at the cost.

Chairman KEFAUVER. Well, let's see, let's add it up. One hundred sixty thousand addicts.

Mr. NEEB. Over $2 billion a year in actual money that goes through the drug traffic. And a lot of it is paid by juveniles who commit crimes to get the drug.

Now, in answer to Mr. Mitler's question directly, it is our feeling that almost all prisoners in our State institutions who are incarcerated for serious crimes and who are addicts, are not criminals except by reason of their being addicts and being forced to commit crimes to get money to buy the drug. About 13 percent or 16 percent of our burglaries in California are committed by addicts to get money to feed the habit.

So your answer is this Mr. Mitler: Half of the problem is enforcement, but you cannot lick the problem simply by being tough with sentences in the courts. You have to cure the addict and remove the profit to the peddler, because as long as the addict is around, the peddler will take a chance and sell.

Mr. MITLER. I have no further questions, Senator.

Chairman KEFAUVER. Mr. Neeb, we have the narcotics-treatment hospital at Lexington. To what extent is that used by juvenile or adult addicts in California?

Mr. NEEB. It is used almost never by any State court. I don't know of it ever being used.

Our Federal courts do use it. They send them from our Federal district courts, San Diego, Los Angeles, San Francisco, Fresno; but as far as I do know, with all due respect to the money spent at Lexington, it is not a success.

Chairman KEFAUVER. The State courts are not authorized to send addicts?

Mr. NEEB. No, I don't think you could get into Lexington if you tried to. You would have to try to get him to go down there and voluntarily commit himself.

Chairman KEFAUVER. As a matter of fact, because of the distance, there is no Federal treatment center in the Pacific area—let's see, there is one at Fort Worth.

Mr. NEEB. Fort Worth, Tex., but that is just not very much closer.

Chairman KEFAUVER. Then what percentage of—or do you have any figures—juvenile addiction do get to either Lexington or Fort Worth?

Mr. NEEB. I don't think we have any out of California, so I don't know how many juveniles there are at Lexington. You have 1,200 beds out there, and I understand they are full. But what their ages are, I guess the records of the hospital would have to tell us. I don't know.

Of course, Senator, again we have to realize that by the time the person reaches the addiction stage, he may be an adult, but it still is a juvenile problem because he learned it when he was in his teens.

Mr. MITLER. You are talking about 16, 17, and 18, not necessarily 15; is that correct?

Mr. NEEB. Yes. We had, not too long ago, a girl who was arrested for forgery, to supply her habit, and she was 13 years old.

Chairman KEFAUVER. Are you going to make an effort to get this bill passed at the next session of the legislature?

Mr. NEEB. Yes, it will be introduced again, and I am sure it will pass both houses, and we hope there will be enough appropriation for it for the Governor not to veto it.

Chairman KEFAUVER. With this bill, would you have facilities to give treatment and supervision to all of your addicts?

Mr. NEEB. Oh, yes.

Chairman KEFAUVER. And juveniles?

Mr. NEEB. Oh, yes, because California has between 7 and 9, I forget how many, large mental hospitals. I don't mean to infer that California needs a lot of mental institutions, but we have them, anyway.

Chairman KEFAUVER. Are you in position to tell us how many of the States have farseeing, modern legislation of this type on their books?

Mr. NEEB. I don't think any State legislature has ever seen a bill like this one. There is one hospital, I believe, operating in New York, which is trying to work this out, but I do not think it is on the scope of this.

I might say this, too, gentlemen: It is our hope that the Federal courts will use this, and you see, you have a right now to commit to our county jail from your Federal courts, and it would seem to me a rather simple matter for your Federal courts in California, for instance, instead of sending a man to Lexington, they could send him to one of the State hospitals in California, and pay the appropriate costs. Instead of sending them to Lexington, let them stay in their own State.

Chairman KEFAUVER. We, of course, know how the States sometimes don't like advice from Senators, but Senator Langer and I, I am sure, would be glad to urge the Governor to get enough money so he would be justified in signing the bill and putting this into operation.

Mr. NEEB. We hope he will, anyway.

Chairman KEFAUVER. So you tell him what we thought about it.

Mr. NEEB. All right.

I might say this, Senator, that according to our figures of commitments in the State, and arrests, as far as the scope of narcotic problems in California is concerned, it appears that about 1 crime of 4 that we now suffer with is a direct or indirect result of this problem, and that is a pretty high percentage.

Chairman KEFAUVER. I was looking at the members of your committee, both north and south, that you have had on your committee which made this outstanding study, and, of course, you have some very excellent physicians, lawyers, people representing a fine cross-section of the life and interest of the community of California.

Mr. NEEB. Yes.

I might say a lot of those people are very busy professional men and heads of large corporations, and they devoted many, many months to these, and we are regular attendants at these meetings.

And, also, I might add, we did it all at our own expense. It didn't cost the State of California one cent. We paid our own way.

Chairman KEFAUVER. You mean it was a nonpaid commission?

Mr. NEEB. Oh, yes; not only nonpaid, but we paid our own expenses in the matter. This book was printed at the expense of one of the members of this committee.

Chairman KEFAUVER. And looking at the list of witnesses you had, you seem to have had about every professional expert in the whole country testify.

Mr. NEEB. We did, Senator, and we came to this conclusion: For some reason, I don't know why it is, but narcotic enforcement officers are very unsympathetic to anybody who talks about treatment. They take the position that you are wasting the people's money and wasting time, because once an addict, always an addict. And with this, we do not agree.

Senator LANGER. Have you an extra copy of this report?

Mr. NEEB. Yes; here is another one right here.

Chairman KEFAUVER. He is talking about this report here.

Mr. NEEB. Yes, I have one here—the blue book.

Chairman KEFAUVER. Yes.

Mr. NEEB. We can send some more on, if you wish it.

Senator LANGER. I would like to have about a dozen of them, if I could.

Mr. NEEB. All right, I will make a note of that, because I will have them sent from the attorney general's office in California.

Senator LANGER. Thank you, Mr. Neeb.

Mr. NEEB. I have another suggestion, if I might, gentlemen, about this matter of what to do.

Chairman KEFAUVER. Mr. Neeb, I had ordered this report just to be made an exhibit, but it is obvious from your testimony and from what Mr. Mitler tells us that this is probably the best citizens' report which has been prepared, so we are going to have it copied as a part of the hearings.

Mr. NEEB. All right. I will send on some others, too, then.

Chairman KEFAUVER. It will be exhibit No. 4.

Mr. NEEB. All right.

(The report referred to was marked "Exhibit No. 4," and portions are printed below.)

NARCOTIC ADDICTION

(Report to Attorney General Edmund G. Brown by the Citizens' Advisory Committee to the Attorney General on Crime Prevention, March 26, 1954)

*   *   *   *   *   *   *

CHAPTER VI. TREATMENT

The committee heard considerable evidence reflecting the fact that under our present treatment facilities, very little rehabilitation of drug addicts is accomplished. Statements of addicts interviewed by the committee (see appendix), and opinions expressed by medical and law enforcement experts in the field, showed that less than 5 percent of reported heroin addicts who undergo treatment at the Federal and State hospitals manage to remain cured for any appreciable period of time upon release from those institutions. Most addicts receive no medical treatment and are left to "kick the habit" on their own—usually unsuccessfully. The committee is greatly concerned over the apparent lack and failure of present treatment facilities and in its studies on this phase of the problem submits the following—

1. General principles

Narcotic addiction is fundamentally a problem in mental hygiene. It is primarily a psychobiological illness, and only secondarily is it a legal or criminal problem. The legal, criminal problem arises as a result of existing laws and as a consequence of the fact that it is necessary for addicts to resort to crime in order to secure money for the drugs. The general philosophy, therefore, should be that the management of narcotic addicts ought to be oriented in the direction of social rehabilitation and not that of punishment. It is, of course, at all times important to realize that the goal of rehabilitation may in some areas come into conflict with the necessary element of protection of society. This problem arises particularly in association with the quandry of the small peddler because most of the addicts will to a greater or lesser extent engage in some degree of peddling in order to sustain themselves. The chapter on penalties attempts to clarify some of the issues involved in this particular problem.

2. Management program

The management of the narcotic addict is envisioned in two stages: The initial phase would consist of a period of at least 90 days of institutionalization during which time the patient would be withdrawn from narcotics and exposed to an overall educational, psychiatric program. The second phase would consist of outpatient supervision. This would be done in an outpatient type of clinic where supervision and control would be exercised and the patient exposed to every modality of therapy conceivable. In association with the program in the outpatient clinic it would be well to emphasize one thing, in view of the fact that too often psychiatry is looked upon as the golden answer to all human problems: namely, the problem of narcotic addiction is something which is wider than just its psychiatric aspects. The why of addiction—why is one person more prone than another—must be at all times considered in the broadest spectrum possible. Not only psychological, but also sociological, economic, cultural, and other elements play a role in determining the narcotic proneness of an individual. In keeping with this orientation the management program in the outpatient clinic would be therefore viewed broadly as an attempt at a specific kind of educational experience which would involve every type of individual who could potentially have social meaning for the patient addict. This would include, therefore, not only psychiatrists and psychologists, but also social service workers, religious counselors, and similar individuals.

The particular character of the institution which would be used in the initial phase of treatment and the character of the outpatient clinic, with all the problems of organization and personnel involved in that, was an issue which was laid aside until the fundamentals of the approach could be agreed upon.

A very important part of this management procedure would be the element of compulsion to the continuation of outpatient treatment supervision. Either on the basis of direct arrest or on the basis of a special, new, legal provision for voluntary self-commitment, individuals would be placed in the situation of being compelled to continue the treatment supervision. From a psychological viewpoint it was felt wise to refer to the followup outpatient treatment not as probation but as treatment supervision.

In both the initial as well as the outpatient phase of addict management, the time element purposely is left indeterminate. The suggestion is made for the consideration of a new kind of approach, namely, the formation of a disposition tribunal—a group of individuals experienced broadly in the field of human relations who would act as the ones to evaluate the disposition of cases, would determine how long a person should remain in an institution for the initial phase, would regulate the time the patient should be kept in outpatient treatment and control.

In association with the element of outpatient treatment there is one recent development in the field of pharmacology which can be of enormous help in getting around a great problem in the procedure of diagnosis of narcotic addiction. Thus far physical examination of the patient for evidence of needle injection or the restraint of the individual for 24 to 48 hours for the production of withdrawal symptoms have been the only techniques available for diagnosis. At the present time, however, there is in existence a drug called Nalline which within a matter of minutes can produce withdrawal reactions within an individual who is addicted. This could be a very potent instrument in the outpatient clinic because it is an objective technique for determining whether an individual who is in outpatient treatment has returned to the use of narcotics. If the Nalline showed that the individual had withdrawal reactions and that he once more was addicted, the disposition tribunal would have the privilege of determining what might be done with him and he might then be returned to the primary institution. There probably would be individuals who would go through this procedure 2, 3, or 4 times. When direct evidence of that would be gathered, the issue that would arise at that time then would be, "Is this a person who can be helped?" or "Is he an individual who might be characterized as incurable?" This issue of what to do with the incurable individual provoked some degree of dispute in the subcommittee since one group felt that individuals of this sort should in some sense be certified or registered and then through some governmental agency be given narcotic drugs in a regulated manner so as to remove the addicts as a potential market for criminally or illegally secured narcotics. Because of the subcommittee's disagreement on this particular point it was finally resolved that instead of committing itself to a definite recommendation we would be able within a year or two after the institution of the overall management program to have gained direct experience as to whether the residue of incurables would be around 5 percent or 95 percent. At that time, when the problem could be a more direct and concrete one, the issue of certification or registration could be considered more realistically.

In association with the problem of marihuana and barbiturate addiction, the former could be integrated into the outpatient treatment program since there are no withdrawal reactions associated with marihuana, while barbiturate addicts who showed withdrawal reactions to barbitals could go through the same procedure as the regular narcotic addicts.

Several members expressed the particular opinion that any kind of a program of this sort will inevitably cost a certain amount of money, but that if research were instituted to show how much could be saved by not having the individuals brought up for trial, imprisoned, and their families in a variety of ways affected, the cost actually would be no more than at the present time.

CHAPTER VII. REPORT ON PREVENTION

The most serious aspect of the increase in the use of narcotic drugs is the reported number of young persons involved. Consequently this chapter is concerned principally with our youth. The data presented to the committee failed to substantiate the somewhat sensationalized statements reported in certain areas to the effect that there has been a marked increase in the number of juveniles who are using narcotics (see appendix for arrest data). The effects of narcotics is so ravaging, however, that even if we had only a few youthful addicts, steps must be taken to stamp out the menace. Law enforcement alone cannot accomplish this. Drug addiction has two main factors, availability of the drugs and predisposition to addiction. Law enforcement can control the first but not the second.

Prevention must include education and understanding of the causation of addiction.

Education

The education code of California states:

"SECTION 8253. Instruction shall be given in all grades of schools and in all classes during the entire school course, in manners and morals, and upon the nature of alcohol and narcotics and their effect upon the human system as determined by science."

"SECTION 20456., In all teachers' training classes in the State colleges, adequate time and attention shall be given to instruction in the best methods in teaching the nature of alcohol and narcotics and their effect upon the human system."

The reported increase in the number of youthful addicts in the last few years has realerted many school systems in the State to the importance of these sections, with the result that they have reevaluated and revised their curriculum material. Most schools incorporate this teaching in health, physical education, science, senior problems, social science and/or family life classes. Narcotics should not be dramatized nor "glamorized" by special assemblies. The committee feels that the revised curriculum material is good but we recommend that the State board of education urge all school systems in the State to see that sections 8253 and 20456 of the education code are constantly carried out.

It is not only youth, however, who must be taught about the effects of narcotics. There is need for education of parents, teachers, law-enforcement officers, and other community youth leaders. In considering the problem of narcotics the importance of marihuana should not be minimized. The consensus of doctors is that marihuana causes a mental habituation without the physical dependency brought about by the overuse of opiates; it leads to a breakdown in the fundamental social and moral principles and the transfer to heroin is easy. This is its chief danger, particularly to our youth.

Only those persons become addicts who have addictive personalities, the addiction having developed from some basic emotional maladjustment or insecurity. Narcotic addiction, representing one form of antisocial behavior, centers primarily in urban communities which previously have had a high delinquency record, but addicts are found in all economic brackets of society. Drug addiction is a result of human weakness, and may result from cultural conflicts, family tensions, insecurity, lack of parental training, or personality maladjustment.

While it is true that the narcotic habit is adopted by some adolescents who are looking for a thrill, the majority of juvenile users of narcotics are those who have somehow missed the satisfactions of normal social life and work, youngsters from slum areas, or from inadequate homes, or from communities which provide no wholesome youth activities or interests.

The committee believes that consideration should be given to a new type of counseling agency for young people intended to serve individuals who have already violated the criminal law by experimentation with narcotics. There are unfortunately very few places where such a person may now go to, should he become concerned about the drugs he has been offered or has already taken or has seen his friends use, the exceptions being that the department of mental hygiene maintains mental outpatient clinics in Berkeley, Fresno, Long Beach, Los Angeles, Marysville, Riverside, San Francisco, and San Diego, and in connection with some of the State hospitals they are developing some degree of outpatient clinic work. Unfortunately these are so overcrowded that they cannot meet the demands for service with the present complement of personnel.

You must also have a community environment which satisfies their needs for normal, wholesale social and work experiences. It will take large sums of money to equip a community with adequate recreational, welfare, and cultural services, but the providing of these resources will not in the long run be so costly as the present staggering sums spent on law enforcement and judicial agencies, prisons, and mental hospitals. Our concept in law enforcement has rightfully changed from punishment of the offender to treatment of the offender, for we believe that treatment is less wasteful than punishment, but even treatment is inferior to prevention.

CHAPTER VIII. PENALTIES

The consensus of experts heard was almost unanimous that the punitive approach to the narcotic problem has been a failure. Case histories studied, together with the recidivist records of convicted addicts who have served sentences for addiction, show that very few remain free of addiction for any appreciable period of time following release from incarceration. Commissioner Anslinger and other Federal narcotic officers point out with some degree of force that whenever and wherever the penalties become more severe and more strictly enforced the incidence of addiction in that area decreases proportionally. There is no evidence, however, that these addicts were cured or diminished their intake of narcotics. On the contrary it would appear that the addict merely moved to another climate.

Insofar as the basic problem of addiction is concerned it would appear that stiffer penalties merely result in brushing the problem under the carpet; the problem remains in spite of our complacency in wearing blinders. On the State level, the philosophy toward penalties may be summed up in the statement that—"It is not the severity of punishment that acts as a deterrent to crime but rather, the certainty of punishment." This statement was voiced by such experts as Austin MacCormick, Walter Creighton, George Maloney, A. V. Beckner, Orville Hawkins, John Misterly and others.

While the experts and the committee abhor the purely commercial peddler of narcotics, on the other hand they recognize that the great majority of addicts and a large percentage of addict-peddlers should be regarded as mental-health problems and that penalties meted out to these two groups should be on a mental-health approach. The records are replete with case histories of addicts who might have been helped medically had they received treatment during the early stages of their addiction. Almost every addict interviewed revealed that his first commitments to city or county jails had no beneficial effect on him but instead merely served to introduce him to other addicts and peddlers who were likewise serving sentences. Through mutual exchange of experiences among these addicts and peddlers they became further indoctrinated in the use, source of supply, names of users and peddlers throughout the State. This information was used by them in the furtherance of their addiction upon release.

The studies of the committee brought into focus the realization that its studies on penalties should be considered in three separate phases:

1. The addict.
2. The addict who peddles to support himself.
3. The professional nonaddict peddler.

It was agreed that the addict who has found that he is addicted should be able to surrender himself to a proper institution and admit his addiction without the necessity of being charged with a felony for which he may be incarcerated. Such person should be able to voluntarily surrender to any superior court by petition and may, without arrest, appear in court and upon determination that he is an addict, the court shall place such person on probation and as a condition thereof shall send such person to a State medical institution for care and treatment.

Through the courtesy and cooperation of Mr. Ronald H. Beattie, chief of the Bureau of Criminal Statistics, Department of Justice, State of California, the following data is submitted:

Comparative figures of the United States district courts in California and the superior courts of this State, showing the disposition of narcotic cases together with the sentences imposed on those convicted for the fiscal years 1952 and 1953.

	California—United States district courts		California superior courts	
	Fiscal year 1952	Fiscal year 1953	Calendar year 1952	Calendar year 1953
Convicted and sentenced	146	180	1,824	2,075
Prison	128	154	547	584
Youth authority			102	111
Probation	18	26	83	347
Jail			1,092	1,033

It is interesting to note that over 92 percent of all the prosecutions in the State of California for narcotic felonies occurred in the State courts. The fact that most of the prosecutions occurred as a result of enforcement activities by State and local agencies, and that many cases involving Federal enforcement activities are turned over to State courts illustrates the need for wider sentencing discretion on the part of the State courts as compared with the Federal courts to take care of a relatively large number of minor violations.

The legislature gave further recognition to this need in its action last year by returning to the State courts the judicial discretion to use probation in cases of first narcotic offenders. This change became effective in September 1953, and accounts for the greater use of probation shown in 1953 in the above figures relating to California superior court sentences.

The following table shows sentences set for narcotic cases by the Federal courts throughout the United States, and sentences set by the Federal district courts in California, as compared with the sentences set by the California State Adult Authority in narcotic cases committed to prison. In studying these comparative figures it should be remembered that the adult authority in these cases does not generally hear and set sentences until after the prisoner has been incarcerated and has been in prison for approximately 1 year. Consequently those of the sentences referred to in the following table, as set by the adult authority in 1953, involve defendants who had been committed under legislation passed in 1953 which extended the penalties for narcotic addiction.

	United States district court sentences		State prison sentences set by the adult authority	
	Fiscal year 1952	Fiscal year 1953	Calendar year 1952	Calendar year 1953
Total Federal prison commitments	1,551	1,556		
Average sentence in months	35.2	38.4		
Prison sentences in California cases	128	154	198	460
Less than 2 years	31	8	5	5
2 to 3 years	30	79	19	19
3 to 5 years	46	47	89	196
5 years	17	17	56	181
Over 5 years	4	3	29	59
Average sentence in months	37.1	34.4	51.1	53.8

It is interesting to note that the California Federal sentences in 1953 were less in narcotics cases than they were in 1952, and that despite the fact that the State sentences set in 1953 involve persons committed before the 1953 changes in the California law, the State average sentence in 1953 of 53.8 months is 56 percent greater than the average Federal sentence of 34.4 months set in 1953.

It would seem to be apparent from these facts that State and local operations account for over nine-tenths of the enforcement activities in the narcotics field, and that the State penalties invoked for those sentenced to prison are at present more than one and one-half times as great as the Federal imprisonment penalties.

CHAPTER IX. RECOMMENDATIONS

Supply

1. That in view of the critical lack of adequate enforcement personnel in all Federal agencies that deal with traffic in narcotics for the proper investigation and inspection of persons, vehicles, ships, and aircraft coming into the United States from other countries, and the lack of funds to support proper investigation and undercover work in foreign countries, Congress be strongly urged to increase appropriations for these purposes to a level more nearly consistent with the enormity of the problem and the menace to the public welfare which it represents.

2. That a new Federal agency or bureau, with adequate enforcement personnel, be created to deal specifically with the problem of preventing the smuggling of narcotics across our border, and that the Customs Bureau be relieved from primary responsibility for this function; consideration should obviously be given to the feasibility of authorizing the Federal Bureau of Narcotcs to exercise the function suggested for the new agency or bureau.

3. That a central clearinghouse, through which all information of value to narcotic-law enforcement officials on the local, State, and Federal level can be channeled, be created jointly by the Federal Government and by the several States.

4. That the armed services be urged to set up special narcotics control units to protect our overseas military personnel against the danger of becoming addicted in countries where narcotics are readily available, and to prevent the smuggling of narcotics into this country by returning military personnel.

5. That the attorney general of the State of California address to the Secretary of the Treasury of the United States a resolution expressing the deep concern which the members of the attorney general's committee feel, and which is shared by all informed and public-spirited citizens, that the personnel of the Customs Bureau are so inadequate in numbers that it is impossible for them to prevent the entrance into this country of more than a small percentage of the huge quantities of narcotics smuggled over our borders by land, sea, and air. The resolutin should make it clear that the committee recognizes the enormity of the problem, but believes that a wealthy and powerful Nation such as ours must staff its protective forces more adequately than we are now doing, and that the reductions recently made in the appropriations for the Customs Bureau are indefensible. The Secretary of the Treasury should be urged to bring this resolution to the attention of the Director of the Budget and appropriate congressional committees. It is recommended that a similar resolution with reference to the Federal Bureau of Narcotics be addressed to the Secretary of the Treasury, and that it refer to internal law enforcement as well as to the international traffic.

Enforcement

6. That the Federal Government increase the appropriation for the pay, training, and staffing of its narcotic enforcement agency.

7. That the appropriations available to the attorney general of the State of California for the operation of this bureau of narcotic enforcement be increased to the same end.

8. That provision be made for the regular conduct of in-service training schools conducted under the supervision of appropriately trained Federal and State narcotic officers for the more thorough indoctrination of local police and deputy sheriffs.

Treatment

9. Upon a medical determination that a person is an addict, he shall be institutionalized for a period of at least 90 days, during which time the patient will be withdrawn from narcotics and exposed to an overall educational and psychiatric program.

10. On release from this institutional treatment, the patient will be assisted by outpatient supervision. Here the patient will receive benefit of all reasonable conceivable therapy. It will include phychological, sociological, economic, cultural, and other elements in an effort to determine the narcotic-proneness of the individual.

11. Treatment should be on either a voluntary self-commitment basis or involuntary. The patient must be required legally to continue the treatment supervision in the outpatient clinic. This phase shall be known as treatment supervision.

12. It is recommended that a disposition board be established consisting of individuals experienced in the field of human relations who shall evaluate the disposition of cases and the duration of treatment and control.

13. If during outpatient treatment it is ascertained by administration of Nalline or other means that the patient is again using narcotics as indicated by his withdrawal symptoms, then the disposition board would have the responsibility of determining the further disposition of the case.

14. Should the disposition board conclude, after repeated failures, that the patient is incurable, he might then be certified or registered so that thereafter he shall receive indicated dosages of narcotic drugs from a determined governmental agency and thereby remove said addict as a potential market for criminally or illegally secured narcotics. The establishment of this phase of the program should be deferred until 2 years after the institution of the overall management program.

15. Barbiturate and marihuana addicts should be integrated into the outpatient-treatment program. Barbiturate addicts evidencing withdrawal reactions could be subjected to the same procedure as the regular narcotic addicts.

Prevention

16. It is recommended that greater emphasis be placed in all schools on the importance of moral and spiritual influences.

17. It is not only youth who must be intelligently indoctrinated about the effects of narcotics—there is likewise need for the education of parents, teachers, law-enforcement officers, and other community youth leaders. It is, therefore, recommended that the State department of justice establish a broader program of assistance to counties and/or cities in setting up training courses and institutes for such adults, so that they may intelligently and accurately recognize the signs of potential addiction.

18. It is recommended that the State department of justice receive adequate appropriations for the production and dissemination of educational and informational mediums.

19. Recognizing that the home must share the responsibility of prevention, it is, therefore, recommended that the schools and parent-teachers organizations expand their programs of parent education and family life education classes and intensify their efforts to enroll more parents in such classes.

20. Teachers often recognize signs of personality maladjustment sooner than parents; it is, therefore, recommended that more and better guidance and counseling services, both psychiatric and psychological, be provided by schools.

21. It is recommended that communities organize community councils in which the citizens, together with the community agencies—governmental, fraternal, church, and educational representatives—may join together to study the needs of their communities and to plan how to provide the necessary services.

22. Recognizing that needed services are now being given in nine California cities by the department of mental hygiene through its mental outpatient clinics, it is recommended that this service be increased and the clinics extended.

23. The committee received ample medical and other testimony attesting to the fact that alcohol is a narcotic drug. It was stated by Committee Member Karl M. Bowman, M. D., that: "Alcohol cannot be left out as a cause of juvenile delinquency, that it is far more important in this respect than marihuana, and produces far more crimes of violence and is just as much a precursor of heroin as is marihuana."

The committee felt that the problems identified with the ingestion and abuse of alcohol are so numerous and perplexing that a separate study of this drug should be undertaken by the committee at some date in the near future.

Penalties

It is recommended that the following three distinct phases be kept in mind in considering the question of penalties:

    I. The addict.
    II. The addict who peddles to supply and support himself.
    III. The professional nonaddict peddler.

Any change or purported legislation on penalties takes on meaning only in relation to this differentiation in offenders.

I

24. It was, therefore, recommended that a new section of the penal laws be enacted providing that a person who is an addict may voluntarily surrender himself to any superior court and, upon being found to be an addict, the court shall place said person on probation and, as a condition thereof, shall send such person to a suitable State security hospital for cure and treatment. Such conviction shall constitute a misdemeanor for all purposes. It is further recommended that the judge, in his discretion, shall be able to impose as a further condition of the probation, a direction that upon the addict's discharge from such security hospital he should submit himself to outpatient psychotherapy treatment at an outpatient clinic.

Such hospitals and clinics should be first-class institutions, staffed by the best available doctors and psychiatrists, and maintained at public expense.

25. It is further recommended that this security hospitalization be established as part of the new medical center of the department of corrections and shall be for the treatment of men.

26. It is likewise recommended that a proper treatment facility for women be established at the present institution at Corona.

27. It is recommended that the records of said addicts' voluntary commitment be sealed and, should the addict successfully complete his treatment of probation, he may then return to court, and by motion under section 1203.4 of the Penal Code be relieved of all penalties and disabilities resulting from the conviction.

II

28. With regard to the addict who peddles to support himself, it was recommended by the subcommittee on penalties that the court be given discretion under this same section to determine whether such person should be given consideration as outlined in No. I above, or prosecuted as a peddler. If such discretion is given, the court should then have the power to recommend to the prosecutor that the charge be changed to being a "user of narcotics" and dismiss the charge of peddling in the interest of justice. The courts could then proceed to order a penalty, the same as provided under No. I hereof.

29. If, however, the court, in its discretion, believes that said addict-peddler is a danger as a peddler, then there should be enacted into law one penalty of State prison for not less than 5 calendar years of incarceration, and not to exceed 15 years. This sentence should apply whether the person suffered a previous conviction of a felony or not. Such person should be incarcerated in the place of incarceration, as provided in Part I above, until the treatment phase of his sentence is completed, and then should be subject to transfer to another institution as directed by the department of corrections.

30. The duration of treatment before release shall be determined by a board of three members appointed by the director of corrections.

Editor's note: These recommendations listed under No. II carried by a vote of—Yes, 12; No, 6; not voting, 4.

III

31. The subcommittee on penalties recommended that the law be changed with regard to the professional nonaddict peddler, that will charge one penalty for selling, transporting, furnishing, or giving away of narcotics, or offering to do any of these things—that said penalty be a minimum of 10 calendar years to life, said minimum to apply whether such person has a prior felony conviction or not.

32. The subcommittee further recommended that there be created a statutory presumption that the illegal possession of a narcotic in excess of an amount specified in section 11392 of the Health and Safety Code is with intent to sell or otherwise illegally dispose of such narcotic.

33. It is generally recognized that addicts obtain the money for the support of their addiction from some illegal enterprise. In order to relieve society of this condition it is recommended that: After an addict who has received treatment for his addiction to the extent that competent medical authorities believe any further attempt at rehabilitation to be futile, such addict shall, by certification of such authorities, be permanently confined to a State institution.

IV

34. The committee further recommended that, as to Nos. II and III above, the court would not be, by law, prevented from giving probation if under the particular circumstances the court felt such to be proper, instead of the heavy penalties fixed by law.

V

35. None of the foregoing recommendations relate to marihuana.

36. It is further recommended that all other penalties relating to narcotics, and especially those relating to vehicles, doctors, pharmacists, and in relation to prescriptions as now contained in sections 11000–11576, except 11391, which relates to places of treatment, remain unchanged.

37. It is likewise recommended that the dangerous drugs section of the Health and Safety Code, sections 29000–29043, remain unchanged.

TREATMENT FOR NARCOTICS ADDICTION IN CALIFORNIA

That part of California's narcotics problem which is borne by the State mental hospitals is a small one, and the number of nonpsychotic narcotics addicts committed to State hospitals gives little evidence to indicate whether narcotics addiction or just the awareness of it is increasing in this State.

Last year there were 327 persons committed as narcotics addicts (214 male, 113 female). On the whole, treatment is similar to that offered for those ad-

dicted to alcohol; vitamins, subcoma insulin, tolserol, and hyocine for quick
alleviation of withdrawal symptoms, and then whatever psychotherapy and
rehabilitation therapies are indicated. However, since those hospitals who have
any such patients at all usually have perhaps 1, or at the most 3 or 4 at any
1 time, it is difficult to stabilize a specific program for them. Length of stay is
little more than the minimum 3 months (maximum to 2 years), and there are
many recidivists in this group. Norwalk, as soon as adequate carbon dioxide
therapy equipment is received, plans to institute a program to treat some of
their alcoholic as well as narcotic drug addicts in this manner; particularly
those where it is quite apparent that addiction is a result of anxiety and chonic
tension.

Since most narcotics addicts are involved in crimes of one sort or another in
order to get the money for the drugs, few of those arrested ever find their way
to the State mental hospitals.

There is also provision for commitment of addicts to habit-forming drugs such
as barbiturates. There were 51 such admissions last year.

There is some evidence that addiction to some of these habit-forming drugs
may present a greater medical (and perhaps social) problem than even the
narcotic drugs, since physiological dependence is so great.

NARCOTIC COMMITMENTS—STATE HOSPITALS

Recent concern over an apparent increase in the use of narcotic drugs has led
to a survey of Department of Mental Hygiene records with the discovery that
commitments for narcotics addiction have almost tripled in the past 5 years.
During 1946–47, 86 persons were so committed to State hospitals and during
1950–51 the figure was 227. Commitments of all types only increased about
one-fifth as much during the same period. The actual number of drug-addict
admissions during 1950–51 was 246, counting those actually committed as drug
addicts under section 5355 of the Welfare and Institutions Code; those committed under other sections subsequently diagnosed as nonpsychotic narcotics
addicts; and those whose primary diagnosis was mental illness but who were
also addicted to the use of narcotics.

At present, new admissions for narcotic addiction are averaging 25 a month.
Average length of stay in the hospital for this type of patient was 8 months.
Ninety-five percent of the patients were discharged as having benefitted from
hospitalization. Of the remaining 5 percent, about half were discharged as
unimproved and half as cured.

Since by far the greater majority of narcotics users come under the jurisdiction of Federal authorities, these figures are by no possible means a reliable
indication as to whether or not more and more people in California are becoming
narcotics addicts. Most narcotics addicts come to the attention of authorities
charged with some form of crime; therefore, the vast majority are either given
the "iron cure" of imprisonment or are sent to a Federal hospital. The California
law provides that "if evidence is submitted showing that a person is of bad
repute or character apart from his habit * * * and that there is a reasonable
ground for believing that the person, if committed, will not benefit from treatment, the judge shall not commit the person to a state hospital."

The value of the statistics quoted above is in the indication that there might
be more and more acceptance of the belief that narcotic addiction is basically
a medical problem and requires medical treatment. The laws as now constituted
provide the opportunity for anyone who wants to be helped to have himself
committed to a State hospital without stigma, much the same way an alcoholic
is committed.[1]

Once the narcotics user becomes a responsibility of the department of mental
hygiene, there is no discrimination between his sickness and the sicknesses
suffered by thousands of California citizens now in the State hospitals. Perhaps
considering the narcotics user as a medical problem is the first step towards
solution of the social problem.

---

[1] Welfare and Institutions Code, sec. 5350 et seq.

Admissions to State mental hospitals diagnosed as drug addicts without psychosis, by age at admission

Fiscal year	Total	15 to 19	20 to 24	25 to 29	30 to 34	35 to 39
1948–49:						
Total	98		8	13	15	12
Male	56		4	7	10	5
Female	42		4	6	5	7
1949–50:						
Total	168	6	34	22	10	23
Male	106	6	21	15	5	14
Female	62		13	7	5	9
1950–51:						
Total	242	14	64	34	19	30
Male	153	5	41	17	11	21
Female	89	9	23	17	8	9

Fiscal year	40 to 44	45 to 49	50 to 54	55 to 59	60 to 64	65 to 69	70 and over
1948–49:							
Total	17	18	8	2	4		1
Male	11	11	5	1	2		
Female	6	7	3	1	2		1
1949–50:							
Total	25	18	12	8	7	3	
Male	15	9	8	6	5	2	
Female	10	9	4	2	2	1	
1950–51:							
Total	28	20	17	9	6	1	
Male	15	15	15	8	4	1	
Female	13	5	2	1	2		

Commitments under welfare and institution, sec. 5355 (narcotic)

	Total	Male	Female
1948–49	97	55	42
1949–50	153	101	52
1950–51	227	143	84

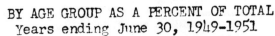

BY AGE GROUP AS A PERCENT OF TOTAL
Years ending June 30, 1949-1951

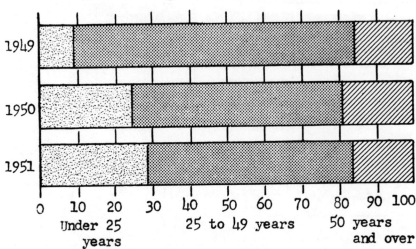

Chairman KEFAUVER. Senator Langer.

Senator LANGER. You said you had some other suggestions. What were they?

Mr. NEEB. I have one other suggestion in relation to this, and I might explain it this way: The stopping of the importation of drugs with the customs officers and the narcotics officers is a tremendously difficult problem. The only way you can do it is the way we stopped the cocaine problem.

You don't have a cocaine addiction problem in America today, and the reason is very simple: They smashed up all the factories down in Central America and Peru where they were making it, and they did it with the fine cooperation of those governments.

Now, our suggestion is this: We are sending, spending millions and billions of dollars in aid every year to other countries, and I would suggest that the Congress of this country seriously consider refusing to grant any aid whatsoever to any nation which will not enter into a workable agreement to stop the export of opium and its derivatives from that country.

We recently sent a great deal of money to Yugoslavia. They export four times as much opium out of Yugoslavia, according to our information, as they need to grow for any medicinal purposes. Of course, it is proper to grow opium to make morphine and things of that sort, but they are growing a lot more of it than is necessary.

One of our friendly countries is Turkey. But you can buy narcotics, I understand, in Turkey about as easy as you can buy tobacco.

Those countries are not carrying their weight when it comes to stopping the export from their own country of the basis of heroin, within which is the black substance that comes out of the opium poppy.

And I think the Congress could very well give serious consideration to at least saying or proposing that we stop aid to countries that do not aid us in this terrible problem.

That is the other suggestion that I would like to offer.

Chairman KEFAUVER. Anything else, Senator Langer?

Senator LANGER. No.

I still want those copies, if I could have them.

Mr. MITLER. No further questions.

Mr. NEEB. Senator Langer, do you want the bill?

Senator LANGER. I mean those 12.

Mr. NEEB. I have those. Do you want any more of those bills?

Chairman KEFAUVER. We wish you would leave them here.

Mr. Neeb, we are very grateful to you for giving us your thoughts and the summary of your study and your experience in California. I think you have rendered a very fine public service.

Mr. NEEB. I want to say that I appreciate the honor of being here before you gentlemen, and I might say in behalf of all the very distinguished members of that committee, we appreciate your interest in this problem.

And if in the future there is anything that we can do to aid you in your splendid efforts, we would like to have a part in it.

Thank you very much.

Chairman KEFAUVER. Thank you very much, Mr. Neeb.

Senator LANGER. Don't forget to send me those 12 copies.

Mr. NEEB. I have already written it down, 12 copies to you.

Chairman KEFAUVER. We would be glad for you to sit with us up here during our hearing today.

Mr. NEEB. Thank you.

Chairman KEFAUVER. Mr. Mitler, who is our next witness?

Mr. Mitler, who is the associate counsel of our subcommittee, has, at the direction of the committee, made a detailed study of this problem, the matter of addiction and treatment of juveniles, and I am going to ask him to come around to testify and give us any information he has secured.

Mr. Mitler, do you talk about any people so that you need to be sworn?

Mr. MITLER. No, I am not mentioning the name of any person.

Chairman KEFAUVER. All right. Will you first tell the extent of your study, and proceed in your own way?

TESTIMONY OF ERNEST MITLER, SPECIAL COUNSEL, UNITED STATES SENATE SUBCOMMITTEE TO INVESTIGATE JUVENILE DELINQUENCY

Mr. MITLER. On behalf of the subcommittee, I interviewed drug addicts and institutions in the Midwest, the west coast, State of Texas, and in New York State, and I interviewed altogether about 200 addicts who were, most of them, in institutions, and some of them were out of institutions.

I interviewed police officials in most of the major cities throughout the United States, and I also interviewed psychiatrists and psychologists who worked in these institutions and were interested in the problem, and I made a visit to the border at the point where Tijuana comes in contact with California, and I want to here simply report on the composite picture.

Chairman KEFAUVER. Mr. Mitler, before making your report in addition to your experience with this subcommittee, you for a number of years were assistant district attorney with Mr. Frank Hogan of New York and you had a great deal of experience in narcotics cases, matters?

Mr. MITLER. Yes. I tried a great many narcotics cases and presented narcotics cases to the grand jury, court of special sessions, while I was in Mr. Hogan's office.

I want to report simply on the composite result of these interviews. I am not an expert in this field; I am simply bringing back to you the observations and what I was told. There are here today the outstanding people in this field who can tell us exactly what is being done in the different treatment centers. Now, of those people interviewed the great majority had had their first contact with narcotics at the age of 17 or 18. Occasionally they had had their contact at 15 or 16. It was usually 6 months to a year later where they had their first conflict or first arrest so that you have to subtract a year or 6 months from the date of the first arrest to give you any indication of the age when these young people came into contact with drugs.

Chairman KEFAUVER. How many did you say you interviewed?

Mr. MITLER. About 200.

Chairman KEFAUVER. What was the age of the people you interviewed?

Mr. MITLER. I interviewed people from the age of 15 up to the age of 45. The majority were between 23 and 27. There was a cross section, but I did focus on those under 21, and I interviewed a great many 17 and 18.

Chairman KEFAUVER. About half males and half females?

Mr. MITLER. Yes. I think I interviewed more men than women.

Chairman KEFAUVER. All right.

Mr. MITLER. I should add that some of the interviews were conducted under the jurisdiction of the narcotic squads in different parts of the country. I did not interview any addicts at the United States Public Health Service at Lexington or at Fort Worth. That is not in conformity with their policy to have their patients interviewed there.

Now, of those interviewed the majority and especially those of the young group had their first contact with drugs through the use of marihuana. That is universally true. Some started in immediately with heroin and of course it is commonly known heroin is the preponderant drug right now.

Of those interviewed, and this is not mapped out statistically but about half had had some conflict with the law before they started to use drugs and about half had had no conflict with the law before they started to use drugs. But they all had committed crimes or had arrest records after they used drugs as the result of their need to get money to sustain the habit.

Of those interviewed I should state they were usually cooperative and they did not indicate any of the belligerency or aggressiveness that is a common denominator of those identified with armed robbery or with different types of crime, but they were cooperative during the course of the interviews.

Those interviewed—and they were not interviewed as I said at Lexington or Fort Worth—of those that had been in Lexington the great majority had been removed from the use of drugs at the United States Public Health Hospital at Lexington or Fort Worth.

There are 2 types of persons that go on to these 2 installations, hospitals—there are those who go on their own initiative and those who go there as Federal prisoners. Those who had gone there as volunteers and were permitted to leave when they wanted to, the majority did not stay the recommended period of time which is 4 months and 15 days. They had stayed at those two hospitals simply long enough to be drawn from the drug and then they had left the hospital and had relapsed very shortly thereafter into the use of drugs.

With respect to the prisoners who had been to the Public Health hospitals at Lexington and Fort Worth and this is with special reference to those who were in the younger group, they too had relapsed into the use of drugs after having been at these hospitals.

However, of those interviewed, they all did know of other persons who had permanently remained off the use of drugs after having been at both of those hospitals.

In the United States there are three institutions that are exclusively devoted to the treatment of drug addiction. One is the United States Public Health Service Hospital at Lexington. The second is the hospital under the same service at Fort Worth, Tex., and a third is the Riverside Hospital in New York, which is the only hospital, I believe, in the world which is exclusively devoted to the treatment of drug addicts and those in the under-21-year-old age group.

Those who went to Lexington reported to me that the attitude of the staff was helpful and cooperative, but they had been built up very well physically, that Lexington had done a full and good job for them, but as the result of the fact that there was no follow-through or after-care program especially with reference to the volunteers, in other words after they left Lexington they were sort of dumped back into the community, that they felt they had relapsed into the use of drugs, the biggest point made by all of these addicts who had been to Lexington and Fort Worth was that they felt there was a need to have representatives of those hospitals in the major cities to give them guidance, cooperation, and help when they return back into the community.

Now, I just want to briefly report on some of the other things that they said, which have been confirmed by other officials. Many of the addicts who had been to Lexington and Fort Worth stated they felt Fort Worth Hospital had more of an atmosphere of a mental hospital and a treatment center. Some of them felt Lexington had somewhat of a prison atmosphere. They did not object to it. They simply stated that it had something of a prison atmosphere. Some who were in the 17- and 18-year-old group stated to me that they had discussed with the older addicts who were Federal prisoners at Fort Worth and Lexington drug addiction. I asked them about the mixing of volunteers who came as patients and Federal prisoners. The majority said they felt they had a common denominator and that was drug addiction and they did not feel it was wrong to mix the two.

However, some volunteers were reluctant to be mixed with Federal prisoners.

The Riverside Hospital—and there will be testimony about that, I don't need to touch on that, there is the only program for those in the under-21-years-old group and it is the only hospital where there is existing a followup clinic which exists in the Metropolitan Hospital in New York.

When the patients leave the Riverside Hospital there is available a clinic they can report to to give them help and guidance after they have left the Riverside Hospital.

I spent about 6 weeks in the State of California and I visited some of the mental hospitals which is where drug addicts are committed under civil commitments. In other words if they have not committed a crime they can volunteer and go to a mental hospital. I was told there my be a program there. I think I should report to the subcommittee an interview I had in one of the hospitals near Los Angeles. I interviewed a 17-year-old boy from a nearby community who said that he had been told in his community that he would get guidance, therapy, and help at the hospital. He said to me all that has happened since I have arrived here is that I have been confined in this ward. The mental patients have the availability and the privilege of the grounds and I am staying here for 90 days. I asked the other patients where the treatment program was and they said there simply wasn't any. All the other people who were in that ward who were drug addicts confirmed the fact that there was no program. They were just sitting out the 90 days. The officials at the institution, and I think this is something they want to overcome, stated that with one psychiatrist with so many hundreds of patients and these drug addicts coming for such a short period of time they are not able to provide a full treatment program.

Chairman KEFAUVER. That is a State institution in California?

Mr. MITLER. That's right.

Chairman KEFAUVER. So that confirms testimony that we have had from Mr. Neeb that there is just no program there?

Mr. MITLER. There is no program and the officials are the most anxious to be able to develop one.

With respect to the border, I went to the border——

Senator LANGER. Just a minute. How many inmates are there at Lexington and Fort Worth and Riverside? Do you have them at each institution?

Mr. MITLER. Can you help me?

Dr. LOWRY. Population yesterday was 1,173.

Mr. MITLER. How many at Fort Worth?

Dr. LOWRY. I don't know.

Mr. MITLER. Fort Worth is smaller; I believe more of the patients are mental patients there than drug patients. I think the drug patients there are about 250 and the mental patients are 800. Am I correct?

Dr. LOWRY. I can't answer that.

Chairman KEFAUVER. About 1,423 altogether?

Mr. MITLER. At the Riverside Hospital there are about 200 to 250 young people so those are the number of people receiving treatment at the moment.

On the border—I just wanted to supplement what Mr. Neeb said—there is one additional factor. The sheriff's department of San Diego County has appropriated money and is trying to do a job at the border. The sheriff is Bert Strend. He has there, stationed at the border in the entrance to Mexico, late in the day, three of his deputies. Of course, they don't have full authority to physically stop people but they do have a curfew law and whenever they see young people trying to come over the border they speak to them and ask them the reason for wanting to go into Mexico. They use every power they can to persuade them if it appears that they are going there on a lark and probably to secure drugs and I myself observed them turn back by persuasion some young people.

So that is a voluntary step that has been taken by the sheriff's department in San Diego County.

I want to just report two other things. A lot of addicts said they had been also helped by narcotics squads in cases when they had become addicted. They had been urged to go to Fort Worth and Lexington and had been given guidance and help. However, there were some instances—this was reported to me by a former officer who got into difficulties and is in an institution right now and later confirmed by responsible officials—that there is in some places and in isolated cases but there occasionally has developed a practice whereby addicts who are arrested are given narcotics by the officials while they act as informants and I know that it is not done in New York or Philadelphia but it seems inconsistent with the overall policy of the narcotics law and I have spoken to some of the officers who are here today and they feel that very strongly. But there have been situations that have been confirmed by prosecution whereby addicts have been given narcotics and sustained on the habit while they go and act as informants and it seems that if doctors are not to be given that discretion, that discretion should not be given to anybody else.

Chairman KEFAUVER. That is not done with official sanction by the Bureau of Narcotics?

Mr. MITLER. No; not by the Bureau of Narcotics. It is done in a few areas with official sanction directly and indirectly with the intent of getting behind the scene.

Chairman KEFAUVER. Are you referring to State officers?

Mr. MITLER. State.

Chairman KEFAUVER. State narcotic people? Do you know of any instances where Federal narcotic agents engaged in such practice?

Mr. MITLER. It wasn't reported to me in a reliable enough way to—I wouldn't want to comment on that because unless it is confirmed by an official——

Chairman KEFAUVER. It is not confirmed to you that any Federal officers were engaged in such a practice?

Mr. MITLER. It was stated to me by someone who I do not feel was completely reliable. But it was confirmed on the State level. I have been told of isolated instances where it did happen on the Federal level but was not confirmed and I do know it has happened on the State level.

In the interviews in the institutions I think it is only correct to report that the great majority I interviewed—and they are a cross-section—were not addict pushers. It was very rare that I encountered anyone who had been selling drugs who himself was not addicted. There are some. But the great majority of those who are in institutions that were interviewed were addicts who claimed that whatever they did in the way of dispensing of drugs had been done in order to sustain their habit. Addicts are notoriously unreliable in what they say. I am merely reporting what most all of them told me.

Now, one other point—and this is a suggestion that I think should be passed on and that is not only is there a need for treatment facilities throughout the United States, but when they are developed there certainly is a need for followup treatment. It is just like starting an operation and not finishing it, not to have any followthrough or aftercare treatment.

This has been recommended by a lot of reliable people who have thought on this subject that not only should there be followthrough treatment but there should be a sort of a halfway house.

In other words when the addict leaves the treatment center instead of being returned back to the old environment it would be the same old faces, that there be developed some kind of a program perhaps kindred to the forestry camps or an intermediate place where they could live with nonaddicts and a cross-section of the population but still not be put directly back in the community, but this intermediate step might be very helpful in having them assimilated in their environment. Every addict who knew of others who were removed from drugs very often told me that the addict who had been removed from drugs personally had gone to live in another community, had a complete break of the old environment. That apparently from the point of view of all addicts as well as public officials is a very important factor. Those are the things I have to say.

I'm not an expert on the field, I want to report what I was told.

Chairman KEFAUVER. We thank you very much for your report. Senator Langer, do you have any questions?

Senator LANGER. No questions.

Chairman KEFAUVER. Mr. Bobo, any questions?

Mr. BOBO. No questions.

Chairman KEFAUVER. Mr. Chumbris, any questions?

Mr. CHUMBRIS. No questions.

Chairman KEFAUVER. Mr. Neeb, do you want to ask any questions?

Mr. NEEB. No questions.

Senator LANGER. No questions.

Mr. MITLER. Mr. Winick, Charles Winick.

Chairman KEFAUVER. You are not going to talk about any people by name, are you?

Mr. WINICK. No.

TESTIMONY OF DR. CHARLES WINICK, RESEARCH DIRECTOR, NARCOTIC ADDICTION RESEARCH PROJECT, NEW YORK, N. Y.

Mr. MITLER. You name is Charles Winick?

Dr. WINICK. That's right.

Mr. MITLER. In a word would you tell us—you are a psychologist?

Dr. WINICK. That's right.

Mr. MITLER. You are the head of a voluntary group in New York who has made a study of the treatment of drug addicts and drug addiction under the age of 21.

Dr. WINICK. I am the director of research of the narcotics addiction research project which is a group of 27 psychiatrists, psychologists, and social workers who organized in the summer of 1955 for the specific purpose of determining how accessible drug addicts are to psychotherapy. The reason that it is a voluntary group is that attempts were made at that time to obtain institutional financing but we were told that there was very little hope for the psychoherapy of drug addicts.

Mr. MITLER. Mr. Winick, if you don't mind, I will get to the part I think is the most significant.

Senator KEFAUVER. Mr. Winick, you have several degrees in medicine, psychiatry.

Dr. WINICK. No; in psychology.

Senator KEFAUVER. All right.

Mr. MITLER. How many were in this group, how many addicts were in this group of patients that you did this study on?

Dr. WINICK. There were 70 addicts, 51 men and 19 women ranging from teenagers to 56 with a median age in the early twenties.

Mr. MITLER. Now, would you give us or summarize the results of that study and tell us—over how long a period have you been working on this?

Dr. WINICK. We began in the summer of 1955, that would be almost a year and a half ago and the procedure was to alert community agencies, hospitals, the United States Public Health Service follow up in New York City and any other agency or individual in New York who might have access to drug addicts. We let it be known that we would accept for psychotherapy any addict who would come forward and solicit psychotherapy. The addict was screened by an intake psychiatrist who then referred him to a psychotherapist, one of the 27 participating therapists. After he reached the participating psychotherapist he then made his own arrangements for frequency of appointments, any payments that were involved, although it were generally known and so forth. Of these 70 patients, 35 entered the project under the erroneous assumption that they would get drugs. I should emphasize that none of these patients at any time during the course of their psychotherapeutic treatment did receive drugs. Most of these 35 patients had the vague impression that they would get drugs or they did not have an accurate impression of what psychotherapy is.

Therefore within the time from the first phone call to the time they got to the original therapist 50 percent dropped out. That leaves exactly 35 patients. Of the 35 who have been seen from the fall of 1955 to the present time, a number dropped out for various factors, such as their being arrested, having to leave town or various other reasons of that type.

Of the 35 who originally dropped out, we also had some who were arrested or had to leave the project for reasons outside their own jurisdiction.

Eighty percent more or less of the addicts who began therapy are still in therapy. Of the addicts who got to the therapy situation at all, the great majority have been off drugs. The decision to get off drugs was accomplished between them and the therapist relatively early in the treatment process and we found that this was actually perhaps the less important part of the therapy process.

Mr. MITLER. I think you ought to emphasize that you have been successful with 80 percent of those persons who remained in therapy.

Dr. WINICK. Yes. Are off drugs. Now, our major focus was not only to determine what percent of the addicts we could cure because obviously with a relatively small number of patients like this to take percentages may be somewhat misleading. Our purpose was to establish the fact that addicts can be reached and treated psychotherapeutically. In the entire history of psychiatric literature dealing with the treatment of addiction I found exactly three cases in which addicts were treated by psychoanalysis or by psychotherapy and were considered cured by the psychoanalyst or psychiatrist. This has led to a general pessimism on the part of psychiatrists and psychoanalysts about their ability to do anything with or for addicts.

One of the things we did in our study was to conduct a simple poll of the participating psychotherapists as well as of a number of other psychoanalysts. We wanted to find out from them what stereotypes they had about the treatment of drug addicts, what their preconceptions were about how difficult or easy a drug addict was to cure.

We found a general stereotype among the great majority of psychoanalysts who answered all this although we were dealing with relatively sophisticated people.

A number of these referred to addicts as not being human and this phrase has been used by a number of medical authorities who say that the addict enters into a mysterious world of his own which makes him not accessible to verbal communication.

We feel that we have established that it is possible to reach at least certain kinds of addicts via psychoanalytic therapy, other forms of psychotherapy with no special hazards to the psychotherapists. One of the traditional stereotypes about the treatment of addicts is that they cause special problems by showing up with robberies, stealing things from the therapist's offices and so forth.

In our 70 cases we did not find one such hazardous incident and this project has been going on for almost a year and a half.

I should mention also that since most of the patients were seen under the regular situations of private practice; that is, they saw the therapist for a couple of hours a week, 1 hour at a time, they had the very difficult hurdle of summer vacation for the therapist. During the summer the therapist usually takes a substantial vacation, usually at least a month. This means that the patients were deprived of the contact with the therapist from anywhere from 1 to 2 months and yet the bulk of these patients survived that hurdle and most of them are still in.

Mr. MITLER. I want to ask you about the thing that I think is the most striking, the high degree of people you have been successful with. Would you just highlight why you think that your group has been able to have this high degree of potential success, because it is only a year and a half and perhaps the treatment centers of the United States have not been able to have that same high percentage. Could you just hit the highlights of that?

Dr. WINICK. The treatment centers are doing a remarkably fine job of withdrawing the patients from drugs. Unfortunately the severe personnel limitations they have make it extremely difficult for them to do much else in a way of support of psychotherapy. Our group consisted entirely of persons who were psychoanalytic therapists. They had no direct concern about the withdrawal of the patient from the drug. Of course that was a necessary and crucial part of the treatment process, but they are trained in the treatment of emotional disorders. They treated the patients, the human being, the person rather than the symptoms by addressing themselves to the underlying personality problem which we presume that practically every addict has. They were therefore able to address themselves to those situations which arose after the patient had been withdrawn from the drug.

Under usual conditions of treatment the addict is withdrawn from the drug which has been meeting all of his needs. The drug releases, job, personal and family satisfactions. He's then left to go out and hassle, as the addicts say, in the world outside with nothing to replace the satisfactions which the drug had afforded him.

Mr. MITLER. In a nutshell, is it true that in the larger institutions they are not able to have individual therapy because there are not enough psychiatrists and psychologists?

Dr. WINICK. That's right.

Mr. MITLER. You were able to give individual therapy?

Dr. WINICK. That's right. We had a group consisting exclusively of persons who were trained to treat emotional disorders.

Mr. MITLER. Without going into the many interesting parts of the study, could you submit for the record—I believe you have written an article on this.

Dr. WINICK. Yes.

Mr. MITLER. And that will be incorporated in the record, or we will have it submitted a little later.

Chairman KEFAUVER. Is it something which we should have printed in the report?

Mr. MITLER. Yes.

Chairman KEFAUVER. Exhibit 5 to the subcommittee's hearings.

(The document referred to was marked "Exhibit No. 5," and is on file with the subcommittee.)

Mr. MITLER. You have often heard it said that it is an impossible task to cure or treat addicts, Dr. Winick.

Dr. WINICK. Yes, I have. That is one of the things that we wanted to address ourselves to.

The hopelessness of the medical profession in general is one of the major reasons for the fact that we have to have these hearings now and the fact that there have been so many meetings and groups discussing this problem. The status of drug addiction today is roughly like that of the whole problem of juvenile delinquency of 20 years ago or the treatment of schizophrenia was 10 or 15 years ago, or the treatment of syphilis was 30 or 40 years ago. The persons who require perhaps the most immediate education in terms of whatever success our particular project or any other success is reported, the group which perhaps most needs the reinforcements of the need for hope, the need for experimentation of a close examination of what success there is, is the various branches of the healing profession itself, medicine, social work and psychology. If we had adopted 20 years ago the same hopeless attitude toward juvenile delinquency that we have toward addiction today, juvenile delinquency would not be in the situation which it is now of having various tests, measures, clues to its predetermination and so forth.

Mr. MITLER. You yourself made this study of a group of 1,500 high school pupils who had gone to see a motion picture about drug addiction?

Dr. WINICK. Yes.

Mr. MITLER. Did you make such a study?

Dr. WINICK. Yes, I did.

Mr. MITLER. Without going into all the details of it, what was the net outcome of this study, did it tend to stimulate the students or to warn them about drugs? What was the outcome?

Dr. WINICK. Well, there is as we all know a great deal of discussion, a lot of novels, films, and so forth dealing with drug addiction and related subjects. The whole American attitude toward taking chemicals is changing. Ten or fifteen years ago if a person took a chemical to make himself feel better that would be regarded as immoral or something oriental or something to be frowned on by Americans. Nowadays we find the tranquilizing drugs, which represent chemicals that you take to make you feel better, are the largest selling pharmaceutical item in the country. There is a subtle evolution in attitude taking place toward the taking of chemicals to make you feel better.

Mr. MITLER. What is the outcome of the study?

Chairman KEFAUVER. Let him go ahead.

Dr. WINICK. We can speculate that the change in the general public's attitude toward process of ingesting a chemical to make one feel better is suddenly changing. It is well known that many of these chemicals do not have the desired effect or, if it does, it wears off after a while. We may speculate that one unfortunate boomerang effect of these tranquilizers is that a person may become aroused to other chemical sources of emotional reassurance or satisfaction. The study of the film The Man With the Golden Arm was conducted among a group of 1,500 high school students in the New York City area. The purpose of the study is to find out whether there is a boomerang effect from even extremely worthwhile solid production dealing with narcotics. This film had a very laudable goal, was very well produced, and was a fine film. It had a well-known actor in its leading role, it was hypothesized that by giving a group of students a before and after test—that is, taking a group of students some months before the film could be shown to them and giving them a test of their attitudes on matters related to addiction and then come back months later giving them the same test—it would be possible to find out, first, who had paid the money to see the film, which would represent a self-selected group, and then it would be possible to see whether there had been a change in their attitudes.

This change of their attitudes can be compared with a group of persons who had not seen the film, which would provide a baseline for a change of attitude resulting from current events, committee hearings, and other media of news.

It was found that in general there was a boomerang effect in many cases, that many young people particularly the more disturbed ones—I should mention that we had data on the degree of this disturbing, their disturbance whether they were more or less disturbed. This was obtained before our study.

The particularly more disturbed ones carried away from the film not only the comment message of the film that taking drugs is dangerous, can be frightening and lead to criminal activities, but many carried away a message which wasn't in the film but which they saw there because of the association of glamorous personalities who were taking drugs. So if I can conclude very hastily about this, the effect of this film with its excellent message on many young people particularly the more disturbed ones and the more impressionable ones and susceptible to the influence of mass medium, the effect of this film was to heighten their interest in drugs as a source of emotional support and to give them the vague feeling that perhaps there might be something good to be derived from taking them.

Of course they got the bad part of the film too, the negative part but there was a statistically significant number of young people who picked up feelings about drugs which perhaps that in an appropriate setting might lead them to begin experimenting with them. Since the age for onset of addiction at least in the New York City area is steadily declining, it seems to me that this may be a very serious effect of some of our otherwise excellent mass media material.

Mr. MITLER. You think a person can cure the habit or get off drugs simply by will or does it require some more assistance or help?

Chairman KEFAUVER. Before you answer that, let me see if I can get straight with that what the result of your experimentation with this film was. You find that a larger number were reinforced in their determination not to fool with drugs and treat them dangerously or a larger number were—their will power to be influenced by these chemicals that make you feel good was reinforced?

Dr. WINICK. I don't know of any——

Chairman KEFAUVER. Was it good or bad? I didn't exactly get your testimony.

Dr. WINICK. I don't know any test for willpower and I was not measuring that. I was measuring the degree of interest in drugs and the degree of tolerance toward the use of drugs. This was measured by various questions. In a statistically significant number of cases especially in the cases of the more disturbed youngsters the degree of tolerance toward drugs was increased and the degree of interest in the use of drugs was increased as determined by comparing the pre and post answers. The majority of all the youngsters did not increase their tolerance of drugs but a large enough minority did.

Chairman KEFAUVER. In other words the minority of the 1,500 did have a tolerance toward drugs and related chemicals increase?

Dr. WINICK. Yes, Senator.

Chairman KEFAUVER. As a result of seeing the picture?

Dr. WINICK. Yes. They developed a more emancipated attitude toward using these drugs.

Chairman KEFAUVER. By emancipated you mean they would be more likely——

Dr. WINICK. To experiment——

Chairman KEFAUVER. Than those who did not see the picture?

Dr. WINICK. Yes, sir.

Chairman KEFAUVER. Did seeing the picture do anybody any good?

Dr. WINICK. There were a number of persons who had their negative attitudes toward taking drugs reinforced by seeing the film.

Yes; many of these young people came away with the feeling of horror and grimness.

Chairman KEFAUVER. But overall on balance, the attitude and the position of these 1,500 young people was not helped by seeing the picture?

Dr. WINICK. The attitude of a goodly number of them was not helped. We want to emphasize it is very difficult to isolate the effect of one communication like a film or speech or talk. Therefore we are guessing here but I believe we can guess with a certain amount of statistical precision because we have a group and we have a baseline before and after the exposure to the film.

Chairman KEFAUVER. I suppose the best way to get at it, would you recommend your children or your neighbor's normal children go to see the film or not?

Dr. WINICK. I wouldn't know how to answer that. I would say that the more disturbed a youngster is, the more likely he is to pick up a more emancipated attitude about taking drugs from the film. The healthier the youngster is the more revolted and horrified will he be about the effect of the film. In other words it is impossible to generalize because we have all kinds of children and on the basis of more disturbed and less disturbed the effect varies greatly.

Chairman KEFAUVER. Senator Langer, you have a question?

Senator LANGER. I wish he would define what he means by "disturbed youngsters."

Dr. WINICK. By a "disturbed youngster" I mean a young person who has an emotional problem which involves his relationship with other people, his relationship with himself, his expression of anxiety, his being exceptionally aggressive, having difficulty in behaving in a schoolroom.

Not being able to determine as well as he can perform as determined by tests, teachers' ratings, parents' comments, and trouble with other children and so forth.

Chairman KEFAUVER. Dr. Winick, by the way, all these are experimentations in treatment and have all been conducted by you on a voluntary basis by you and your group; is that right?

Dr. WINICK. Yes. Every participating therapist has volunteered and has received no payment from any source.

Chairman KEFAUVER. How many are there?

Dr. WINICK. We have 27 equally divided among psychiatrists, social workers, and psychologists. What they have in common is knowledge and experience in the application of psychotherapeutic methods.

Chairman KEFAUVER. These treatments were started in 1955.

Dr. WINICK. In the summer of 1955; yes, sir.

Chairman KEFAUVER. So that it has been conducted for a year and a half?

Dr. WINICK. A year and a half; yes.

Chairman KEFAUVER. Do you feel that addiction can be permanently cured by therapy, by psychoanalysis or treatments of psychology? That is given normal assistance and cooperation?

Dr. WINICK. Our experience has shown that first addicts are accessible to psychotherapy and it is generally believed that the most lasting cures, the most ultimate type of change in a person which can be affected by any kind of psychiatric treatment is that affected by psychoanalytic psychotherapy. This is generally regarded to be the case in the field. I would say if any group has any chance of remaining permanently cured if we can use an ambiguous term like "cure," it is a group that has had psychoanalytic psychotherapy. Their chances of never going back to drugs are far greater than any other group.

There is a group of persons we know that cures itself. The typical addict in the New York area undergoes four cures. These are people who taper off with an increasing amount of time between each time they kick the habit and then go back to it. But we have no statistics on these people. We can't organize any treatment in which people treat themselves and so far as I know this is the best kind of treatment where ultimate modification of personality is needed.

Since the addict is an emotionally sick man and this treatment tries to cope with his basic emotional illness, it would seem to me this offers certainly the best possibility for ultimate cure.

Chairman KEFAUVER. You said that people who cure themselves according to statistics taken in New York City were 4, you mean 4 percent?

Dr. WINICK. No; various studies have shown that the typical addict has undergone four cures. He may have undergone a cure himself. He may have gone to Lexington for four times. He may have gone to private hospitals four times. But I believe that the typical one has undergone 4 cures and we know that a series of relapses is part of the disease. We don't regard it as alarming that a patient who has an organic disease like diabetes if he has to go back to the hospital for a checkup now and then and get more shots. But we have our moral attitudes toward human behavior so closely interwoven with our attitudes toward drug addiction that we regard it as more or less morally wrong for an addict to have these many cures and relapses.

People assume that an addict is an addict because he does not exercise his will.

Chairman KEFAUVER. What you are testifying to is of great importance to us and to the public and to the committee of Congress with appropriations for treatment of these unfortunate people at Lexington and Fort Worth. I would like to get it as specific as I can. Do you feel that with therapy, psychiatry or psychology, that you can in good number of cases give reasonable cooperation and help the patients to be in a position to lead a normal life without going back to drugs?

Dr. WINICK. Yes; I would certainly say so and I would say the younger the patient and the fewer the number of years he has been on drugs, the better the chances for psychoanalytic therapy.

Chairman KEFAUVER. You have had there thirty-odd patients under treatment for a year and a half. How long do you contemplate taking the normal ones, with reasonable cooperation, the length of your therapeutic treatment would have to last?

Dr. WINICK. That is a matter to be decided entirely by the therapist depending on each individual case and you would make your decision in conjunction with a patient.

Chairman KEFAUVER. I know one might take much longer than the other.

Dr. WINICK. Yes, of course.

Chairman KEFAUVER. What is your general concensus?

You are working on this project. The average one would be 2 years, 2½ years, 3 years?

Dr. WINICK. It is impossible to generalize. I would say that we might look at the general range of time that is needed to cure severe neuroses where figures like the ones you cite are often typical, in other words 2½ years, 3 years, and so forth. Since the addict is usually likely to be suffering from very severe emotional disorder, that would probably be almost a minimum period. I am not talking about merely getting the addict——

Chairman KEFAUVER. Then does the frequency of therapeutic treatments taper off with the passing of time if the patient has been making reasonable progress?

Dr. WINICK. Not necessarily, no. Usually a set number of visits per week is established and that is maintained until the end of the treatment unless there are factors why it should be shortened.

Chairman KEFAUVER. All right, Mr. Mitler, do you want to ask any further questions?

Mr. MITLER. I don't have any other questions. If you will submit for the record the two articles——

Dr. WINICK. I will.

Chairman KEFAUVER. Senator Langer?

Senator LANGER. No questions.

Chairman KEFAUVER. As I get it from you, Dr. Winick, you feel that with addiction that there is a sufficient hope that psychiatry and other treatments can help cure people with their cooperation and that they should not be considered as once an addict, always an addict, a hopeless drag on society?

Dr. WINICK. I would certainly agree that there is a goodly number that can be reached this way and that can be cured and what we need is more study of successful experience, more research and less hopelessness within the healing profession itself.

Chairman KEFAUVER. All right. Thank you very much.

Dr. WINICK. I appreciate the opportunity of appearing before you.

Chairman KEFAUVER. Well, we appreciate it very much. We are interested in this.

Senator LANGER. When you speak of therapy, does that mean chiropractic?

Dr. WINICK. No; when we speak of psychotherapy we mean one person, a therapist listening to what another person, the patient, says and then a mutual discussion about these communications, involving interpretation of what the patient says and so forth. In other words, there is a verbal communication back and forth. There is no necessity or provision or requirement for any manipulation of the body.

Senator LANGER. Of course, in some of these chiropractic clinics, as a matter of fact, they have accomplished just what you have accomplished; isnt' that true?

Dr. WINICK. I don't know enough about it to say. I have heard of many successes.

Senator LANGER. Our subcommittee made a study of chiropractic about 2 years ago. We had doctors in from the Sears Clinic in Denver, Colo., and they made the claim that their treatments had cured some of these addicts. I thought you might interested in that.

Dr. WINICK. Yes; I am.

Senator LANGER. All right.

Chairman KEFAUVER. But the therapy you refer to is not physio-therapy, it is mental.

Dr. WINICK. No; it is psychotherapy where the patient talks and the therapist listens and the therapist interprets what he learns from the patient.

Chairman KEFAUVER. Thank you very much, Dr. Winick.

The subcommittee will stand in recess until 2 o'clock this afternoon.

(Whereupon, at 12:40 p. m., a recess was taken, to reconvene at 2 p. m. of the same day.)

AFTERNOON SESSION

Chairman KEFAUVER. We will get started now.

Senator Langer will be here shortly, and he asked us to proceed.

Mr. Mitler, who is your next witness?

Mr. MITLER. The next witness, Senator, is testifying. His name is not to be used.

Chairman KEFAUVER. Let's use some other name.

Mr. MITLER. We will use the name of "Paul Taylor."

"Mr. Taylor," you come from the——

Chairman KEFAUVER. Do you want Mr. Taylor sworn?

Mr. MITLER. I think it would be wise to have him sworn.

Chairman KEFAUVER. Stand up, sir.

Do you swear the testimony you will give will be the truth, so help you God?

"Mr. TAYLOR." Yes, sir.

Mr. MITLER. Of course, his picture is not to be taken.

TESTIMONY OF "PAUL TAYLOR" (A FICTITIOUS NAME SUPPLIED BY THE SUBCOMMITTEE)

Mr. MITLER. "Mr. Taylor," you come from the District of Columbia?

"Mr. TAYLOR." Yes, sir.

Mr. MITLER. Could you talk a little closer to the mike.

When you were 17 years old, did you become a drug addict?

"Mr. TAYLOR." Yes, sir.

Mr. MITLER. And you became addicted to what drug?

"Mr. TAYLOR." To heroin.

Mr. MITLER. I see.

Did there come a time when you——

Chairman KEFAUVER. How did you get addicted? Did you have marihuana first?

"Mr. TAYLOR." Yes, sir.

Chairman KEFAUVER. Won't you tell us about it?

"Mr. TAYLOR." Well, the first shot I ever took, I was on a Navy ship, and out of curiosity I took a shot of morphine tartrate. I drank a lot, and I liked to get "high." And I later found access to mari-huana. I smoked for a few months, and then began using heroin.

Mr. MITLER. Did there come a time when you decided you wanted to get assistance, and you went somewhere for help?

"Mr. TAYLOR." Yes, sir. After being addicted about 5 years, I went to Lexington for voluntary treatment.

Mr. MITLER. At Lexington there were really three kinds of patients at the time you went there?

"Mr. TAYLOR." Yes, sir.

Mr. MITLER. The volunteers——

"Mr. TAYLOR." Yes, sir.

Mr. MITLER. You go ahead and tell us the other kinds there were.

"Mr. TAYLOR." Voluntary patients, prisoners or ones sent there by court, and probationers.

Mr. MITLER. How long did you remain at Lexington?

"Mr. TAYLOR." One hundred and thirty-five days.

Mr. MITLER. Now, while you were at Lexington, what did you do, what was the program?

"Mr. TAYLOR." I was withdrawn and put to work on a farm.

Mr. MITLER. Did you have any group therapy at that time?

"Mr. TAYLOR." Yes, sir. Group therapy, as such, conducted by doctors; and group therapy in AA.

Mr. MITLER. I know you are extremely interested in AA, and we will come to that.

Could you tell us what the group therapy consisted of at Lexington?

"Mr. TAYLOR." It was headed by a psychologist. There were different groups in the hospital. The one I attended was headed by a psychologist, and we discussed freely personal problems.

Mr. MITLER. Did you feel that was some help, was of some value to you?

"Mr. TAYLOR." No, sir.

Mr. MITLER. Why not?

"Mr. TAYLOR." Well, I felt that group therapy, and I feel it is helpful, but I think the nature of my disease requires the help of a higher power, not found in group therapy.

Mr. MITLER. I see. In any event, you checked out of the hospital with or against medical advice?

"Mr. TAYLOR." I checked out with medical advice at that time.

Mr. MITLER. I see.

Now, when you were at Lexington, did you observe how long the volunteers stayed? Did they stay long enough for them to really do an effective job, or did they leave too soon?

"Mr. TAYLOR." Generally leave too soon.

Mr. MITLER. When you left, what happened? Did you relapse and use drugs again?

"Mr. TAYLOR." Yes, sir.

Mr. MITLER. Then what finally happened?

"Mr. TAYLOR." I went back again as a volunteer, and was withdrawn; I checked out against medical advice after 49 days, went back to AA, and I have been well since then.

Mr. MITLER. Now we will get to the AA. How long was it, how long a period elapsed, after you came out the first time, before you started to use drugs again?

"Mr. TAYLOR." Maybe 2 or 3 months.

Mr. MITLER. I see.

Now, at Lexington, are there some young people there as well as adults?

"Mr. TAYLOR." A few; yes, sir.

Mr. MITLER. Are there also Federal prisoners and volunteers?

"Mr. TAYLOR." Yes, sir.

Mr. MITLER. What is your feeling about the volunteers and the prisoners being together?

"Mr. TAYLOR." I don't feel that it is harmful.

Mr. MITLER. After you came out, you say you found a great deal of help in AA. I know that that is—you have done a good deal of work in the District of Columbia helping others.

Would you tell us what their program was and how it helped you?

"Mr. TAYLOR." Their program was to teach me that I had a disease.

Mr. MITLER. What is the AA, to begin with?

"Mr. TAYLOR." AA is Alcoholics Anonymous.

Mr. MITLER. Yes.

"Mr. TAYLOR." They taught me that I had a disease that was incurable, that I could find that it would be arrested if I refrained from the use of drugs, and I generally bettered my life and took an inventory of myself, finally trying to help others.

Mr. MITLER. And you found that you have been able to be permanently removed from the use of drugs as a result of the help you got at Lexington plus the AA?

"Mr. TAYLOR." Yes, sir.

Mr. MITLER. And you have gone down to the Lorton Reformatory and tried to develop a program there, too?

"Mr. TAYLOR." Yes, sir.

Mr. MITLER. What is the status now of the work that you are doing on a volunteer basis?

"Mr. TAYLOR." The status is that the group we started, similar to AA, called Narcotics Anonymous, was not successful in the way that we wished. Numerically speaking, we have few recoveries. But that it was gratifying and is worth my time, and the others that are with me, to continue on our own.

It is a long way down there, and it is a long trip.

Mr. MITLER. You have asked—you wanted to say something about the history of AA. Could you do it very briefly?

"Mr. TAYLOR." Yes, sir.

We are concerned about the treatment of other individuals like myself. I, with others, have found a release from the compulsion to use drugs from the life I was in, through the Alcoholics Anonymous program.

I suggest to anyone who is sincerely interested, to study the history of Alcoholics Anonymous as described in the Alcoholics Anonymous book, because the pattern is similar, is parallel.

As the gentleman mentioned earlier, alcoholism was once considered a hopeless disease, a person was a social outcast; and today more than 200,000 alcoholics who have recovered through AA are respected, and I think we can find our answer there.

Mr. MITLER. Now, of the people that you dealt with at Lorton, were most of those sellers, or what is the average status of the drug case?

"Mr. TAYLOR." The status of the average drug case are ones that were users, convicted through entrapment, generally, of transfer of narcotics, and classified and sentenced as peddlers.

Mr. MITLER. Turning back to just one or two other questions about Lexington, what is the ordinary topic of discussion at Lexington?

"Mr. TAYLOR." Dope.

Mr. MITLER. Well, of course, people with that kind of problem are bound to discuss it; is that correct?

"Mr. TAYLOR." Yes, sir.

Mr. MITLER. And when you were there, was there an effort being made to separate the young from the old people?

"Mr. TAYLOR." Yes, sir; there was an effort began at that time.

Mr. MITLER. What do you think the impact was of the 18- and 19-year-olds being in contact with the veteran Federal drug prisoners?

"Mr. TAYLOR." I think that the younger fellows who are there for treatment for drug addiction, most of the young fellows were just as ornery as the old ones; and in view of the fact that there are so few down there, I don't think that segregation is practical.

Mr. MITLER. I see.

At the present time, you are no longer involved in the use of drugs, but you are trying to help other people.

"Mr. TAYLOR." Yes, sir.

Mr. MITLER. In other words, you have your own kind of follow-through or aftercare program; you have done it on a voluntary basis.

"Mr. TAYLOR." Yes, sir.

Mr. MITLER. Have you gone down to meet people who are about to leave, to help them?

"Mr. TAYLOR." Yes, sir.

Mr. MITLER. Just tell us about that.

"Mr. TAYLOR." Well, generally, anyone being released from a hospital or penitentiary is skeptical, for all of the reasons we know. I found it hard for some fellows to get interested in AA, because it is supposed to be for alcoholics. I found that the biggest problem is misunderstanding and lack of acceptance, lack of understanding from lawmakers and doctors and ones that could help.

Mr. MITLER. I have no further questions.

Chairman KEFAUVER. "Mr. Taylor," when you first got out of Lexington after a period of time, you went back to narcotics. How did you happen to do it? Did you go to your old environments, or did you——

"Mr. TAYLOR." I imagine it had something to do with it, sir. I had not fully resigned yet to leave it alone when I came out the first time.

Chairman KEFAUVER. Well, if you had some followup counsel and help, and someone to talk with and give you therapy, do you think that would have helped you?

"Mr. TAYLOR." I had access to that, Senator, in AA, but I just failed to accept it. It was there, but I didn't want it at the time.

Chairman KEFAUVER. And would you mind telling us how long you have been in Alcoholics Anonymous?

"Mr. TAYLOR." It has been about 5 years, sir, since my last release from Lexington.

Chairman KEFAUVER. And for 5 years you have been able to control it yourself?

"Mr. TAYLOR." I haven't used any drugs in 5 years; yes, sir.

Chairman KEFAUVER. This help that you give by going down to Lorton on your own, and talking with patients who are released, you pay your own expenses, you do it on your own?

"Mr. TAYLOR." Well, there is not a lot of expense involved, sir, but it is on my own.

Chairman KEFAUVER. That is a very commendable work, to me.

I am glad that you found relief in treatment, and that you have been able to restore your life. You certainly have given a good account of the work of AA.

"Mr. TAYLOR." Thank you.

Chairman KEFAUVER. Anything else?

Mr. MITLER. No, Senator.

Thank you very much for coming.

Chairman KEFAUVER. Who is our next witness?

Mr. MITLER. This gentleman, I am using the name of "Joe Dixon," and——

Chairman KEFAUVER. "Mr. Dixon," you swear the testimony you give will be the whole truth, so help you God?

"Mr. DIXON." I do.

Mr. MITLER. Thank you.

Chairman KEFAUVER. All right, Mr. Mitler.

TESTIMONY OF "JOE DIXON" (A FICITIOUS NAME SUPPLIED BY THE SUBCOMMITTEE)

Mr. MITLER. Would you testify right into the mike.

You come from Philadelphia.

"Mr. DIXON." Yes, sir.

Mr. MITLER. And you have come down here to cooperate and explain exactly how you were able to be helped with the drug habit; is that correct?

Chairman KEFAUVER. How old are you, "Mr. Dixon"?

"Mr. DIXON." Twenty-five.

Chairman KEFAUVER. "Mr. Taylor," how old are you?

"Mr. TAYLOR." Twenty-nine.

Mr. MITLER. How old were you when you first came in contact with heroin or any kind of narcotics?

"Mr. DIXON." Seventeen.

Mr. MITLER. Could you tell us briefly how that came about?

"Mr. DIXON." Well, a group of fellows I was hanging around with at the time, all the same——

Chairman KEFAUVER. Pull the microphone closer.

"Mr. DIXON." We were interested in music at the time.

Mr. MITLER. And you were in Philadelphia?

"Mr. DIXON." In Philadelphia. We started smoking marihuana.

Mr. MITLER. And that was in the group that you were with?

"Mr. DIXON." Yes.

Mr. MITLER. Did there come a time when you went to Atlantic City during the summer?

"Mr. DIXON." Well, we went to Atlantic City during the summer, and I took my first shot of heroin.

Mr. MITLER. What was it that brought that about?

Chairman KEFAUVER. How old were you then?

"Mr. DIXON." I was just turning 18.

Mr. MITLER. How did that come about in Atlantic City?

"Mr. DIXON." A friend of mine came up and said something better than marihuana, get a better kick out of it, and I went and tried it.

Mr. MITLER. And that was heroin?

"Mr. DIXON." Yes, sir.

Mr. MITLER. Did there come a time during the summer when some pusher came down there and released——

"Mr. DIXON." This occurred later.

Mr. MITLER. Would you tell us about that?

"Mr. DIXON." It was in the fall of the year when we went back to Philadelphia. A big marihuana pusher at the time came to us and said—we were getting it from—the syndicate had said that he couldn't get any more marihuana until he got rid of a certain amount of heroin, and he said he would sell it to us for a dollar a capsule at the time. And we raised a hundred dollars, and we bought a hundred capsules.

Mr. MITLER. And, of course, you continued to develop the habit then.

"Mr. DIXON." Yes, sir.

Mr. MITLER. And you were 18 at the time?

"Mr. DIXON." Yes.

Mr. MITLER. How soon was it or how long was it before you came into conflict with the authorities and were arrested?

"Mr. DIXON." It was around a year later, I was arrested for the first time.

Mr. MITLER. Were you using narcotics during that period of time?

"Mr. DIXON." Yes, sir.

Mr. MITLER. What was your occupation then?

"Mr. DIXON." I worked at music, and I also was a salesman.

Chairman KEFAUVER. What did you get arrested for, would you mind telling us?

"Mr. DIXON." Use of narcotics. At the time, they had an internal possession law in Philadelphia.

Mr. MITLER. What sentence did you receive?

"Mr. DIXON." I received a year's probation.

Mr. MITLER. Did you resume the use of narcotics while you were on probation?

"Mr. DIXON." Yes, sir.

Mr. MITLER. And you came to New York to live?

"Mr. DIXON." I moved to New York, and I started almost immediately.

Mr. MITLER. In other words, you hadn't received any kind of guidance or treatment at that time?

"Mr. DIXON." No.

Mr. MITLER. You just went right back to the habit. Then what happened in New York?

"Mr. DIXON." In New York, I was arrested again.

Mr. MITLER. And what was the disposition of that case?

"Mr. DIXON." It was discharged; lack of evidence.

Chairman KEFAUVER. Was that a charge of possessing narcotics?

"Mr. DIXON." Possession, yes. It was a legal technicality. That was the cause of the discharge.

Mr. MITLER. At this point, were you heavily addicted by now?

"Mr. DIXON." Yes.

Mr. MITLER. Did you go back to Philadelphia?

"Mr. DIXON." Yes, I did.

Mr. MITLER. Did there come a time when, on your own initiative, you decided you wanted to try to help yourself, and you went to some private treatment center in Philadelphia?

"Mr. Dixon." Yes. I went to a private hospital for cure, a few months after going back to Philadelphia.

Mr. Mitler. Now, was that a reasonable place, or did they charge you an awful lot of money?

"Mr. Dixon." Very expensive.

Mr. Mitler. You don't remember offhand how much it was?

"Mr. Dixon." Not the exact figure.

Chairman Kefauver. About; what is your estimate?

"Mr. Dixon." I am really not sure. I didn't——

Mr. Mitler. Did your parents pay for it?

"Mr. Dixon." My parents paid for it.

Mr. Mitler. And you remained there how long?

"Mr. Dixon." About a month.

Mr. Mitler. What did they do for you there, in the way of helping you cure the habit?

"Mr. Dixon." Well, they took me off the physical habit, but that is all they did.

Mr. Mitler. Did you have any problem getting out of that habit?

"Mr. Dixon." Yes, I did.

Mr. Mitler. Tell us about that, briefly.

"Mr. Dixon." They more or less tried to force me, not physically, but to frighten me into staying. They claimed I would be picked up by the Federal authorities if I was to leave.

Mr. Mitler. And did you finally get the help of somebody in the hospital?

"Mr. Dixon." Yes, I did.

Mr. Mitler. How did that come about?

"Mr. Dixon." One of the male nurses at the hospital had quit the place there one day, and he went to my family and told them the situation.

Mr. Mitler. Finally you did leave the private treatment place; is that correct?

"Mr. Dixon." Yes.

Mr. Mitler. How soon after you left there did you resume the use of narcotics?

"Mr. Dixon." Almost immediately.

Mr. Mitler. In other words, they had given you physical withdrawal, but they hadn't gone any deeper.

"Mr. Dixon." No.

Mr. Mitler. And how long did that continue, the use of drugs, this time before any other steps were taken?

"Mr. Dixon." For, I would say, a few years.

Mr. Mitler. Did there come a time when you decided to go to Lexington as a voluntary patient?

"Mr. Dixon." Yes, sir, I did.

Mr. Mitler. How old were you at that time?

"Mr. Dixon." I believe I was 20.

Mr. Mitler. At that time did you have any cases pending against you?

"Mr. Dixon." Yes, I did. I was arrested—no, I was placed on probation; I was on probation.

Mr. Mitler. When you went there as a volunteer, that meant that you could leave whenever you wanted to?

"Mr. DIXON." Whenever I wanted to.

Mr. MITLER. How long did you stay at Lexington?

"Mr. DIXON." About 3 weeks to a month.

Mr. MITLER. What was the program, what did you do during the 3 weeks while you were there?

"Mr. DIXON." I was mostly in the withdrawal ward, and with the population for no more than a few days.

Mr. MITLER. As soon as you were withdrawn, what did you do?

"Mr. DIXON." I went to the doctor and checked out, against medical advice.

Mr. MITLER. Do you think that was a wise thing to do, in view of all the circumstances?

"Mr. DIXON." No; I don't at this time.

Mr. MITLER. How soon were you using drugs again?

"Mr. DIXON." A few days later, when I got back to Philadelphia.

Mr. MITLER. By the way, is there any followup or aftercare treatment program, to your knowledge, at Lexington?

"Mr. DIXON." None that I know of.

Mr. MITLER. That is, the prisoners have probation, but you were a volunteer.

"Mr. DIXON." Yes.

Mr. MITLER. You went back there again as a volunteer?

"Mr. DIXON." Yes, in 1954.

Mr. MITLER. And you stayed how long this time?

"Mr. DIXON." Four months and fifteen days.

Mr. MITLER. Did you participate in any group therapy, or what role did you take?

"Mr. DIXON." It was offered, but I didn't participate, I didn't take advantage of it.

Mr. MITLER. Were you built up physically while you were there?

"Mr. DIXON." Yes, I was.

Mr. MITLER. What activity did you engage in while you were there?

"Mr. DIXON." Well, I played in the band. I went to the religious services that they had.

Mr. MITLER. Was it a good band?

"Mr. DIXON." At the time, it was excellent.

Mr. MITLER. And did the religious services help you, do you think?

"Mr. DIXON." Well, just a rabbi with whom I was friendly, it was just his—knowing that someone was there that was interested.

Mr. MITLER. How often did you see any psychiatrist while you were there?

"Mr. DIXON." Twice.

Mr. MITLER. In any event, you left Lexington, and how soon was it that you relapsed again into the use of narcotics?

"Mr. DIXON." About a month. And I was arrested last January, and I haven't used anything since then.

Mr. MITLER. I see. At this stage——

"Mr. DIXON." I have been going to a private psychiatrist.

Mr. MITLER. I see.

When you left Lexington and went back to your home, did you have any trouble locating drugs?

"Mr. DIXON." No. You could always seek out your old friends if they were still around.

Mr. MITLER. What was the topic of conversation at Lexington, principally?

"Mr. DIXON." Principally drugs.

Mr. MITLER. However, there were some groups—were you with a group that was interested in other subjects?

"Mr. DIXON." Some groups were interested in music, and we tried to talk about other things to keep our minds off drugs. There were different things.

Mr. MITLER. Well, do you think the program was useful and helpful to you at Lexington, except there wasn't any aftercare?

"Mr. DIXON." Yes, I do.

Chairman KEFAUVER. If there had been aftercare treatment, would you have availed yourself of it?

"Mr. DIXON." One of the good points down at Lexington, in my opinion, I thought was the occupational therapy, and there is a problem of finding the right type of work when you come out of any institution.

Chairman KEFAUVER. If there had been someone who was in an official position to give you followup advice or counsel or therapy, or whatever may have been useful, would you have availed yourself of it?

"Mr. DIXON." A lot of assistance had been offered, and I just wasn't ready to accept it at the time. I myself decided within myself that I had to stop, and I wanted to.

Mr. MITLER. The Philadelphia authorities and police have been helpful to you in working with you in helping you rid yourself of the habit?

"Mr. DIXON." Yes, they have.

Chairman KEFAUVER. I guess one trouble is that you get back to your old environment; is that it?

"Mr. DIXON." Yes, that is one of the main problems.

Chairman KEFAUVER. Have you changed your environment?

"Mr. DIXON." Yes, I have.

Chairman KEFAUVER. Getting away from the old cronies that you had?

"Mr. DIXON." Yes, sir.

Mr. CHUMBRIS. Mr. Dixon, how much money did you spend a day for narcotics while you were on it?

"Mr. DIXON." Average of $20 a day.

Mr. CHUMBRIS. $20 a day?

"Mr. DIXON." Yes, sir.

Mr. CHUMBRIS. And you stated about getting with your cronies. Did they spend a similar amount of money on narcotics as you did; would you say?

"Mr. DIXON." Some did, some spent less, some more.

Mr. CHUMBRIS. Do you know from your own knowledge whether yourself or others, the other persons with you, committed any crimes to raise money for narcotics?

"Mr. DIXON." I know of instances.

Mr. CHUMBRIS. You say you do know of instances?

"Mr. DIXON." Myself, I haven't.

Mr. CHUMBRIS. And would you say they were serious instances of crime?

Chairman KEFAUVER. I suppose you got money from your family, and others did not have a family to get money from.

"Mr. DIXON." That is right. It depends on the individual situation.

Chairman KEFAUVER. So they stole from somebody else.

"Mr. DIXON." I worked, and I made a good salary working, and I worked in music, also, and made extra money.

Mr. CHUMBRIS. That is all.

Chairman KEFAUVER. Well, we wish you good luck, and we hope you keep up your strong determination.

"Mr. DIXON." Thank you.

Chairman KEFAUVER. Thank you for your cooperation.

Who is our next witness?

Mr. MITLER. Dr. Lindesmith.

Chairman KEFAUVER. We are glad to have you here.

STATEMENT OF DR. ALFRED LINDESMITH, PROFESSOR OF SOCIOLOGY, INDIANA UNIVERSITY

Mr. MITLER. Your name is L-i-n-d——

Dr. LINDESMITH. L-i-n-d-e-s-m-i-t-h.

Mr. MITLER. And your first name is?

Dr. LINDESMITH. Alfred.

Mr. MITLER. What is your background, what is your position?

Dr. LINDESMITH. I am at present professor of sociology at Indiana University. I am on leave at present and attached to the School of Law of the University of Chicago.

I have been interested in the narcotics problem since 1935, and at that time, beginning at that time, I have had close contact with considerable numbers of addicts, who were also usually criminals in one way or another, and often peddlers of drugs, also.

And I have written a book on the subject, which was published in 1947, and a number of articles.

Chairman KEFAUVER. What is the title of your book, Doctor?

Dr. LINDESMITH. The title of my book is "Opiate Addiction."

Mr. MITLER. Dr. Lindesmith, you have just returned from Great Britain, and you have been studying the British approach to this problem; is that correct?

Dr. LINDESMITH. Yes, sir. I was—I spent this last summer in England, and I spent the previous summer in England, and I was particularly interested in the manner in which the British handle this problem because I had read about it before, and there has been some controversy about whether they in fact did what I and other have said they do.

Mr. MITLER. Before you go into it, I want to clarify one thing.

Dr. LINDESMITH. Yes, sir.

Mr. MITLER. Do the British or is there any suggestion that they dispense drugs indiscriminately, or is there a different kind of a program?

Dr. LINDESMITH. Well, that is sometimes misunderstood. That is a mistaken impression that is known. It is not dispensed indiscriminately. That is very far from it.

Mr. MITLER. Would you tell us about the program there?

Dr. LINDESMITH. The basic principle of the program is that the matter of drug addiction is separated from peddling drugs, that the matter of drug addiction is regarded as a medical problem, and that the medical practitioner is permitted to prescribe drugs to addicts provided that he first makes a prolonged and persistent attempt to cure the addict, and also provided that he keep appropriate records, and keep the dosage minimized.

In the case of addicts which are deemed to be incurable by the physician, he is advised to call in another medical opinion before continuing the drugs. His records, his books, are subject to inspection by the Ministry of Health inspectors, and the drugstores also keep the prescriptions which he issues.

Chairman KEFAUVER. Does he not have to report every so often who he is treating, or the status of his patients?

Dr. LINDESMITH. When he has a case, the case, of course becomes immediately a matter of record through the prescriptions, and through the records in the doctor's office; and this becomes a matter of record with the police and with the Home Office, and there are periodic check-outs made.

Chairman KEFAUVER. When you say "Home Office," you mean the Ministry of Health?

Dr. LINDESMITH. No. The Home Office is a kind of nonpolice agency which exercises a supervisory sort of function and a coordinative function over the activities of the police, and coordinates these activities with the activities of the medical profession and the Ministry of Health on this matter.

So the doctor, however, is not required to report a case of addiction when he begins to treat it. He very often does.

The doctor ordinarily, as I understand it, requires from the addict who submits himself, that he agree to a course, a program, of treatment designed to cure him, and the doctor may include as a condition that the addict agree to have his name sent in to the Home Office.

Mr. MITLER. What is the cost of the drug to the addict? Any special circumstances?

Dr. LINDESMITH. The doctors are ordinarily—well, they are encouraged to see addicts at least once a week, and preferably more, and the cost is 14 cents or 1 shilling per prescription, so it would be 14 cents a week, or 28 cents a week if they saw them twice, and this would be the cost of the drug habit, that is the direct cost, under the National Health Service Act, I should say.

Prior to the National Health Service Act, the matter was handled as a matter of private practice, and no charge was specified. It could be whatever the doctor charged for such a service.

Mr. MITLER. How many dope addicts are there in Great Britain?

Dr. LINDESMITH. Well, the Home Office, the British Home Office keeps a file which it divided into two categories, medical addicts and nonmedical addicts, and their latest report for 1955 was 335 addicts.

Mr. MITLER. How many juvenile drug addicts are there in Britain?

Dr. LINDESMITH. All that they report concerning these known addicts is that almost all of them are over 30 years of age.

I judge—they don't report on whether any are under 20 or not, but I gather that juvenile addiction—that is, to heroin and morphine—is rather extremely rare.

Mr. Mitler. Would you tell us about the law enforcement? Are drug pushers arrested in England just the same as they are here?

Dr. Lindesmith. Yes. The English laws with respect to peddling drugs are much the same as here, except the penalties are not as severe and they are not mandatory.

If anyone is detected violating the law—for example, the addicts sometimes, even though they are receiving drugs legally at low cost, may object to the doctor's not giving them what they regard as enough, and supplementing this by forging prescriptions usually, or going to two doctors simultaneously.

In that case, the addict is arrested and punished, usually with fines. If there is a question of illicit trafficking in this drug or in marijuana, then usually there are jail sentences.

I would like to state, Mr. Mitler, that the use of opium is not—what I have said applies solely to heroin and morphine, and does not apply to marijuana or smoking opium.

Opium smoking is forbidden, as it is here, and so is the use of marijuana. This, incidentally, is a problem that has been growing, to some extent, in England.

Mr. Mitler. Is there drug racketeering in England, in drugs?

Dr. Lindesmith. There is said to be a small black market in drugs. I can't say that I know too much about it, but apparently it is believed to be very small and to be, consisting largely of sales, sales of drugs diverted from legal sources by a few unethical doctors.

This is what I am told.

Also, perhaps a certain amount of smuggling, but the British Government reports very little evidence of any organized traffic. Cocaine and marijuana are found.

Mr. Mitler. The British did not have a traditional background of drug using, such as our country did. Am I fair about that, Dr. Lindesmith?

Dr. Lindesmith. No. When the British—the history of the present British laws begins from 1920. Prior to that they had relatively little control, but they have never arrested, never treated, addicts as criminals.

As a matter of fact, I would like to add that I believe there are quite a few other European countries, all of them with very small drug problems, all of them, also, with almost no juvenile addicts, who handle the drug problem in the same way.

I have evidence here from the reports of these nations to the United Nations, from a number of countries like Norway, and the Netherlands, and so on, which indicate this.

So this practice is actually not unusual, the British scheme is not unusual. In fact, I think it is the most common scheme in the Western Hemisphere.

Mr. Mitler. Also, Great Britain has a different cultural setup than we do.

Dr. Lindesmith. Yes.

Of course, our cultural—culturally, we are very closely allied with Britain. The culture is not different. But I would like to say that addicts are much the same, in essential respects, the world over, and what differences there are I think are largely the way in which they are handled.

Mr. MITLER. What do you think we can learn of value, contrasting the two systems? What things can we derive from that?

Dr. LINDESMITH. Well, sir, I believe we would have to be cautious, I am willing to concede this, in applying wholesale, and without critical examination, the experiences of foreign countries which have much smaller problems than we have.

But I believe that we could benefit by a close study of what these nations do.

The principal advantage, as I see it, in the English program and in some of the other programs of this kind abroad, is that the addict is placed in the hands of what a gentleman here has called the "healing professions," and he is not sent to jail for what is called a "cure."

Mr. MITLER. Are there any other things that you think we can learn from the British experience?

Dr. LINDESMITH. Well, I don't know if you are going to bring this up later, but there has been some talk of what is called a clinic system, and I might mention, if it is appropriate now, that this system is not a clinic system.

It involves the medical profession taking care of what I think most medical men regard as a medical problem, and I believe that most of the people who know about this problem regard it as a medical problem in a broad sense.

Mr. MITLER. Apart from this study that you made in England, you also have been making studies of the situation in the United States?

Dr. LINDESMITH. Yes. I more or less continuously have been concerned with it since 1935.

Mr. MITLER. And you have also made a statistical study based on the FBI figures?

Dr. LINDESMITH. I wouldn't say I have made a statistical study.

Mr. MITLER. Well, you observed things.

Dr. LINDESMITH. I am acquainted with the figures.

Mr. MITLER. What would you say with respect to the trends and developments with respect to the drug, based on those figures?

Dr. LINDESMITH. I would say, in the first place, we have no realiable estimates, either of the number of addicts in the United States 30 years ago, or now. All we have is varying estimates, which I would call "guesses," varying so widely that they are totally unreliable.

We have figures on the number of arrests; and basing one's conclusion on the number of arrests, the arrest figures, I believe, have been setting new records every year.

I recall some figures which compared 1951—I picked 1951 because it was the year the Boggs bill went into effect—with 1955. These are from the Uniform Crime Reports issued by the Federal Bureau of Investigation, concerning the activities of local police squads, not Federal cases.

The arrest rate, that is, for narcotics offenses, per 100,000 population, approximately doubled during those 4 years.

And over all of the years since 1930, when the Federal Bureau of Investigation began to make those reports, the percentage of young persons involved in these figures has been steadily going up.

Also, I might add that the percentage of Negroes involved has also been going up steadily, and is now over half, usually.

Mr. MITLER. Is there a leveling off at present, of the use of drugs as evaluated from these standards, by young people? Or what is the situation?

Dr. LINDESMITH. There has been in the last year or so, I believe, in these figures which I refer to, there has been a slight decline, percentagewise.

But this decline percentagewise has been brought about by an increase in the number in the higher age groups, not by a decline in the numbers in the lower-age groups. I think you understand that.

Mr. MITLER. Are there any other observations that you would like to make which you think would be useful?

Dr. LINDESMITH. Well, sir, I believe that the operation of our present laws is, in my opinion, unjust and ineffective. I believe it is unjust primarily because, if I might make a distinction between the addict and the trafficker, and include among the addicts the petty pushers who support their habits by peddling, I would say that the penalties are primarily on the addict; that the traffickers, who are the ones who make substantial sums of money from the traffic, are not caught often enough to be punished by any law.

I think at a previous hearing it was proposed to get at least traffickers through the tapping of telephone conversations, but in the meantime, I don't believe that you can deter a criminal from his criminal activity by punishing his victim.

Mr. MITLER. Now, are there any other points that you wish to make?

Dr. LINDESMITH. I can't think of any offhand.

Mr. MITLER. I have no further questions, Mr. Chairman.

Chairman KEFAUVER. Dr. Lindesmith, of course in Britain they have a different medical system from the one we have here. Doctors are—all come under the socialized medical system; don't they?

Dr. LINDESMITH. That is true. But this system which I spoke of was used before and has no necessary connection with socialized medicine. You understand prior to socialized medicine or what we call socialized medicine in Britain, the addicts were simply taken care of by the doctors and were regarded as patients.

Chairman KEFAUVER. So the point you make is that you think that regarding the addicts as patients and more or less bringing out into the open and with some kind of supervision and treatment it is preferable to just classifying them as criminals and throwing them in a penal institution?

Dr. LINDESMITH. The English addict or an addict in this system has an out. He doesn't have to be a criminal if he is an addict. The American addict generally unless he is favored in someway or another has to be a criminal. That is, he has to peddle drugs or engage in prostitution or steal or something like this to raise the money to buy the drug, but an addict in a system of this kind does not.

Chairman KEFAUVER. And also if a person is taking narcotics under the—until he can get some kind of permanent treatment under a physician, he is not at the mercy of—I mean at least there is some limit on the amount that he gets; is that another point?

Dr. LINDESMITH. Yes. There are standards set up for the medical practitioner which are not enforced by the criminal law, by the police, but they are more or less enforced through these medical inspections carried out by the Ministry of Health in visits from these persons.

Chairman KEFAUVER. I take it from that you think rather than making a criminal in this country of a person unfortunately addicted, that if they could be placed in an institution or given some medical treatment without putting a criminal record down against them that would be a step in the right direction?

Dr. LINDESMITH. I believe that is a step in the right direction, and I believe that is eventually where we have to go.

Chairman KEFAUVER. All right. Anything else?

Mr. MITLER. I have nothing further.

Dr. LINDESMITH. Sir, I have a statement on the English system and another article.

Chairman KEFAUVER. We will have those printed in the record as exhibits 6 and 7 to your testimony. Thank you very much, Dr. Lindesmith.

Dr. LINDESMITH. Thank you. It was a privilege to appear.

(The statement and article referred to were marked "Exhibits 6 and 7," and read as follows:)

THE BRITISH SYSTEM OF NARCOTICS CONTROL

(By Alfred R. Lindesmith)

Assuming that there is a relationship between the means adopted by a country to control drug addiction and the extent and seriousness of the problem, a consideration of the British system of control should be of special interest in the United States, because it is an example of a relatively successful way of dealing with narcotic drugs. The lowest estimate of the number of addicts in the United States known to the authorities is 60,000. In the United Kingdom, 335 such addicts were reported in 1955. In Washington, D. C., alone, police estimate the number of addicts at about three times the all-Britain total. Even if one accepts the minimum estimate cited above, there appear to be more drug users in the United States than in all of the rest of the Western World combined.[1] The British system of control, as an example of a system commonly used in Western European countries, allows the addict to have legal, but regulated access to legitimate low-cost drugs.

There is, of course, more than one type of drug problem. However, when reference is made to the narcotics problem in the United States, it is generally understood that what is meant is the use of opiate drugs (morphine, heroin, etc.), and their equivalents. It is this type of drug abuse with which we shall be primarily concerned in this paper.

BRITISH DRUG LAWS

British practices with respect to controlling addiction have not changed materially since the act of 1920, which was the first legislation on this subject. This law, known as the Dangerous Drug Act of 1920, with subsequent additions, interpretations, and consolidations over the years, puts the treatment of addicts squarely into the hands of the medical profession. It defines the addict as a patient, treats addiction essentially as a disease, and makes the doctor the final judge as to the circumstances under which drugs are to be prescribed and in what quantity. Thus, in the British Government's annual report to the United Nations for 1955,[2] it is stated, "In the United Kingdom, the treatment of a patient is considered to be a matter for the doctor concerned. The nature of the treatment given varies with the circumstances of each case." In line with this conception, there is no compulsory treatment or registration of addicts; and doctors are not required to notify the authorities when they begin to treat an addict, although they are encouraged to do so.[3] Similarly, the National Health Act

---

[1] See the 1956 report of the U. S. Senate Subcommittee on Improvements in the Federal Criminal Code (of the Committee on the Judiciary); chairman, Senator Price Daniel.

[2] The Traffic in Opium and Other Dangerous Drugs. Report to the United Nations by Her Majesty's Government in the United Kingdom of Great Britain and Northern Ireland, 1955, p. 4.

[3] Memorandum as to Duties of Doctors and Dentists, Dangerous Drugs Act, 1920–32. D. D. 101 (5th edition), Home Office, October 1948, p. 9.

applies to addicts as well as to all other types of medical patients, so that the doctor who has addicts in his care receives compensation from the Government for treating them, and the drug user gets his supplies at a nominal cost of one shilling (14 cents), per prescription. However, an addict securing a regular supply of drugs from one doctor violates the law if, at the same time, he secures drugs from a second doctor without informing him that he is already under treatment. The punishment in such a case, it is important to notice, is not for securing a dual source of supply, but for withholding information from the second doctor. Practitioners who provide such dual supplies are therefore not in violation of the law.

The act of 1920 and all subsequent laws require that all persons and firms handling dangerous drugs from manufacturers and importers to pharmacists, doctors, and dentists, be licensed or authorized to do so. They are required by law to keep full and accurate records of all drug transactions, and to preserve these records for at least 2 years. Records of retail pharmacies are routinely inspected by the police, while the records of doctors are examined by specially appointed medical inspectors of the Ministry of Health, these inspectors also being available for advice on cases of addiction.

Pharmacists are required to keep their drug supplies in locked receptacles, and doctors are urged, though not required, to do the same as far as possible. A doctor is not, however, required to keep a written record of the drugs which he personally administers to a patient, but only of those which he gives by prescription. If he fails to keep the proper records because, for example, he is trying to cover up his own addiction, he is soon detected by the medical inspectors because the records will show that he is receiving unusually large quantities of drugs not accounted for by the needs of his patients. Such a practictioner, if convicted of an offence under the dangerous drug laws, can be deprived of his authority to possess, supply, or prescribe drugs, but he cannot be deprived of his right to practice medicine. Among the 335 addicts reported in 1955 there were 70 doctors, 2 dentists, and 14 nurses.[4]

In the early years of enforcing the act of 1920 a question of interpretation arose with regard to a regulation specifying that the doctor was authorized to possess drugs "so far as necessary for the practice of his profession." The home office, which has general control over drug law enforcement, interpreted this to mean that doctors were not to be permitted to prescribe drugs regularly for addicts. In a 1948 memorandum of instructions to doctors and dentists which is still in effect, the home office called attention to the above qualification and added:[5] "* * * a doctor or dentist may not have or use the drugs for any other purpose than that of ministering to the strictly medical, or dental needs of his patients. The continued supply of drugs to a patient, either direct or by prescription, soley for the gratification of addiction, is not regarded as a 'medical need'; and in a number of cases doctors who had purchased drugs for the gratification of their own addiction have been convicted of unlawfully procuring and possessing these drugs."

On the other hand, doctors who had previously prescribed regular supplies of drugs for addicted patients continued to do so after the 1920 legislation in apparent contravention of the law. The home office noted this fact, but was reluctant to prosecute because it was felt that this was a matter for the medical profession to consider.[6] As a consequence, in 1924 the Government appointed a committee of prominent medical men, with Sir Humphrey Rolleston as chairman, to investigate and make recommendations to the home office. The report of this committee affirmed the right of doctors to provide drug users with regular supplies of drugs, and, in effect, defined this as "treatment" rather than as the "gratification of addiction."

The 1948 Home Office memorandum includes an appendix which reproduces those sections of the Rolleston report pertaining to the medical treatment of addicts. These sections have guided the interpretation and enforcement of the law ever since. On the central problem of whether the doctor could legitimately prescribe regular supplies of drugs for an addict, the Rolleston committee stated:[7]

---

[4] Op. cit., p. 5.
[5] Op. cit., p. 4, par. 6.
[6] Report of Departmental Committee on Morphine and Heroin Addiction to the Ministry of Health, H. M. Stationery Office, London, 1926, p. 1.
[7] Quoted in appendix A of the 1948 Home Office Memorandum, op. cit., p. 10.

"* * * morphine or heroin may be properly administered to addicts in the following circumstances, namely, (*a*) where patients are under treatment by the gradual withdrawal method with a view to cure, (*b*) where it has been demonstrated, after a prolonged attempt at cure, that the use of the drug cannot be safely discontinued entirely, on account of the severity of the withdrawal symptoms produced, (*c*) where it has been similarly demonstrated that the patient, while capable of leading a useful and relatively normal life when a certain minimum dose is regularly administered, becomes incapable of this when the drug is entirely discontinued."

The committee made other recommendations for the guidance of doctors who handle drug users; these do not have the force of law, but exert considerable moral pressure upon medical men.[8] They include warnings that the gradual withdrawal method of cure should be undertaken in an institution or nursing home, that the patient should be in the hands of a reliable and capable nurse, that a second medical opinion should be secured before the decision to administer drugs indefinitely is made, that the quantity of drugs prescribed should be carefully controlled, and that drugs should not be administered to a new patient who requests them without prior medical examination and relevant information from the doctor who previously handled the case.

Concerning incurable cases of addiction the committee observed:[9]

"They may be either cases of persons whom the practitioner has himself already treated with a view to cure, or cases of persons as to whom he is satisfied, by information received from those by whom they have previously been treated, that they must be regarded as incurable. In all such cases the main object must be to keep the supply of the drug within the limits of what is strictly necessary. The practitioner must, therefore, see the patient sufficiently often to maintain such observation of his condition as is necessary for justifying the treatment. The opinion expressed by witnesses was to the effect that such patients should ordinarily be seen not less frequently than once a week. The amount of the drug supplied or ordered on one occasion should not be more than is sufficient to last until the next time the patient is to be seen. A larger supply would only be justified in exceptional cases, for example, on a sea voyage, when the patient was going away in circumstances in which he could not be able to obtain medical advice. In all other cases he should be advised to place himself under the care of another practitioner."

The Home Office annually reports on the number of persons known to be using drugs regularly. It maintains a file in which the cases are classified into two sections, medical and nonmedical. The former contains data concerning persons regularly receiving drugs because of disease, such as cancer patients. The nonmedical file lists the cases of those persons who are simply addicts, that is, persons who are receiving drugs primarily because they are addicted to them, and not because of disease or any other medical condition. The figure of 335 known addicts in 1955,[10] mentioned previously, was evidently secured by counting the number of cards in the nonmedical section, and represents an increase of 18 over the previous year. At latest reports the number of cases in the medical section also numbered a little over 300. The information recorded in these files is obtained from data voluntarily supplied by pharmacists and doctors as well as from regular inspections of their records.

Skeptics are likely to inquire whether the Government's figure of 335 addicts for a country with a population of more than 50 million people can be taken as any real indication of the actual number of drug users. Might there not be a considerable number of concealed addicts who secure their drugs entirely from illicit sources? Officials interviewed by the writer admitted the existence of such addicts, but refused to estimate their number. It was said that there were drug peddlers and traffickers in the Soho district of London; but, it was argued, the extent of the traffic was quite small, even in such large cities as London and Liverpool, and that it was practically nonexistent in other cities. It was also contended that this market is mainly concerned with drugs such as marihuana and cocaine, which are not regularly prescribed by doctors and

---

[8] If the doctor does not know of these recommendations the Home Office may call them to his attention. If he does know about them, and disregards them, pressure can be exerted upon him by the medical inspectors of the Ministry of Health and by medical bodies such as those which supervise the National Health Act. Continued recalcitrance could theoretically lead to disciplinary measures by a medical tribunal authorized under the regulations for this purpose. Actually no such tribunal has ever been convened.

[9] Quoted in appendix A of the 1948 Home Office Memorandum, op. cit., p. 10.

[10] The Traffic in Opium and Other Dangerous Drugs, etc., op. cit., p. 5.

are prohibited in the United Kingdom as they are here in the United States. Two medical men who were interviewed estimated that there were 10 unkown addicts for every 1 that is known to the authorities. Other doctors and almost all Government officials who expressed an opinion regarded this estimate as extravagantly high and totally unreliable.

Among the reasons for believing that the number of concealed addicts is not large is the fact that very few addicts are sent to prison each year. During the last 5 years the number of addicts sent to prison for any offense whatever has run as follows:[11] In 1952, there were 6; 1953, 16; 1954, 11; 1955, 11, and up to July 1956, 11. These figures do not suggest the existence of any large number of addicts among the criminal elements. When the writer observed to a Scotland Yard officer that pickpockets and shoplifters in the United States were frequently addicted, the officer ventured the opinion that there was not a single addicted pickpocket in London. Probation, parole, and prison officials and doctors are largely unacquainted with the addiction problem from personal experience. A police officer with 20 years' experience outside of London stated that he had encountered only 1 narcotics case, and it involved an American soldier who used marihuana.

The black market in drugs, such as it is, appears to be very different from that in the United States. Thus, the 1955 Government report states:[12] "The 'addict' who is also a 'pusher' is unknown in the United Kingdom, though on occasions an addict may procure more than his own requirements in order to supply his friends." It is also stated that the black market in Britain is not organized; that it subsists to a considerable extent on addicts who wish to supplement their legally obtained dosage, and that it is supplied, primarily, by drugs unlawfully secured from legitimate sources, for example, from unethical or unscrupulous doctors. A London physician estimated that there were, perhaps, 5 or 6 such doctors in London. In the Government's 1955 annual report to the United Nations, the following statements about the illicit traffic occur:[13]

"The gradual decline in the traffic in opium, noted in the report for 1954, continued, and both the number of seizures of this drug, and the quantity confiscated, were the lowest for several years * * *. Illicit production of manufactured drugs and traffic in such drugs obtained from illicit sources is unknown. Isolated cases of the theft of legitimately manufactured drugs occur very occasionally, but in 1955 no such cases were reported. There were, however, some instances of addicts obtaining supplies from lawful sources by illicit means, for example, by forged prescriptions."

The Dangerous Drug Act of 1951 prescribes penalties as follows:[14]

"Every person guilty of an offence against this Act shall, in respect of each offence, be liable—(a) on conviction on indictment, to a fine not exceeding one thousand pounds ($2,800), or to imprisonment for a period not exceeding ten years, or to both such fine and imprisonment; or (b) on summary conviction, to a fine not exceeding two hundred and fifty pounds ($700), or to imprisonment for a term not exceeding twelve months, or to both such fine and imprisonment * * *."

A qualification of the above is that anyone convicted for inadvertently violating the regulations for the dispensing of prescriptions and keeping of books cannot be sentenced to prison without the option of paying a fine not larger than £50. No mandatory penalties are prescribed. It is left to the court to fix the precise penalties in accordance with the circumstances of the case and the nature of the offense. In practice, the maximum penalties are scarcely ever applied. The court is also free to place the defendant on probation, and often does. A judge may place an addict on probation on the condition that he agree to accept treatment from a doctor.

In 1955 [15] the actual sentences of imprisonment imposed for offenses involving manufactured drugs ranged from 6 weeks to 12 months; for those involving opium, from 28 days to 6 months; and for those connected with marihuana, the range was from 1 day to 3 years. Maximum fines for these categories of offenses were equivalent respectively to $140, $280, and $140. By comparison to American practice these penalties are extremely light; and one might suppose that they would have little or no deterrent effect. However, it must be remembered that laws carrying mild and flexible punishments are more likely to be enforced than those that impose harsh, inflexible penalties.

---

[11] Unpublished figures given the author by a Home Office official.
[12] Op. cit., p. 5.
[13] Op. cit., p. 6.
[14] Dangerous Drug Act, 1951, 14 and 15, Geo. 6, ch. 48, sec. 15.
[15] The Traffic in Opium and Other Dangerous Drugs, etc., op. cit., pp. 6–7.

During 1955, 184 persons in the United Kingdom were prosecuted for violations of the dangerous drugs laws.[16] Of these 169 were convicted, 17 for offenses involving opium, 115 for offenses involving marihuana, 30 for offenses connected with manufactured drugs, and 7 because they failed to keep drugs in locked receptacles or did not keep proper records. Sixteen of the seventeen offenses involving opium were committed by Chinese persons, usually opium smokers, who had prepared or raw opium in their possession, ostensibly for smoking, a practice expressly forbidden by British law. Persons convicted in the marihuana cases were largely of Asiatic, West Indian, and west African origin; and about 85 percent of the cases occurred in Liverpool and London.

The 30 convictions involving manufactured drugs were cases where the defendants were all British subjects of European origin, and most of them were addicts. Their offenses consisted mainly in forging prescriptions or obtaining prescriptions simultaneously from more than one doctor.

The nature and number of the offenses noted above gives no support to the idea that a considerable number of unknown addicts exists in the United Kingdom; rather, it supports the view of officials that the black market is of such a nature that an addict cannot rely on it indefinitely for his supplies. Even if he escapes arrest, it is felt that he will soon be forced to go to a physician. When he does, and the doctor prescribes for him, his name appears on the prescription and on the doctor's register; in short, he becomes a known addict. British officials are confident that if there were a substantial number of addicts depending upon the black market for their supplies, the situation would be bound to come to the attention of the law enforcement authorities.

The facts as explained are bound to raise two questions in the mind of any American familiar with the problem of narcotics control. Why is there a black market at all in a country where users can obtain low cost, legitimate drugs? And why do not all addicts go to physicians for their drugs? To answer them, the writer made extensive inquiries during the summers of 1955 and 1956 while he was in England. A doctor in London, who had considerable firsthand knowledge of addicts, said that one answer to these questions was that some addicts patronizing illicit sources were unaware that they could secure drugs from doctors. He urged a publicity campaign to inform them of this. Other addicts fear becoming known to the authorities, and avoid medical men for that reason. The responsible physician is apt to require, as a condition for accepting the addict as a patient, that he agree to cooperate in a treatment program designed to achieve a cure. The doctor may also ask the addict for his permission to inform the Home Office of his case at once, since the case will come to the attention of the authorities anyway as soon as the doctor's register is next examined. Addicts who are unwilling to accept these conditions may prefer to depend upon illicit sources in spite of the much higher costs to them.

In order to fully understand the manner in which the drug problem is handled in Britain, it is necessary for an American to appreciate that the entire problem is given very little publicity. The Home Office officials and the police officers who deal with it are largely unknown to the general public, and their pictures do not appear in newspapers and magazines. Nor are their accomplishments glorified in the movies and the press. The effect has been to make the public generally regard the details of medical treatment for addicts as technical matters to be settled by discussions among experts, rather than by public debate. It has also prevented the public, and sometimes also journalists, doctors, and addicts, from knowing much about how the drug problem is actually dealt with.

LAW ENFORCEMENT

Enforcement of the British drug laws is centered in the Dangerous Drug Branch of the Home Office, which is a nonpolice branch of the Government exercising general control over police policy, and cooperating closely with the police, the medical profession, pharmacists, and the Ministry of Health. A small narcotic squad in the London police force is assigned on a full-time basis to the narcotic problem; and the regular police are also empowered to arrest violators. As noted before, inspections of pharmacists' records are carried out as a matter of routine by the regular police, who report their findings to the Home Office. Inquiries to doctors and inspection of their records are made by the Home Office and by specially appointed regional medical inspectors. If violations of the

[16] Ibid.

law are suspected or discovered, the police may be brought into the case to make investigations. If no violation of the law exists, but it is felt that a doctor's handling of the case is not up to standard, pressure is apt to be exerted upon him through medical channels; for example, a medical inspector may call upon him to give advice, since that is one of the functions of these inspectors. Doctors are sometimes convicted of offenses involving improper prescriptions or records, for instance, when they are trying to cover up their own addiction.

During the summer of 1955 the writer attended a hearing in a London magistrate's court on the case of a London doctor charged with violating the law by aiding and abetting an addict in the deception of another doctor. It was established that the addict had received about 6 grains of heroin daily from each of two doctors. He had died early in 1955, and the cause of death at the inquest was stated to be an overdose of heroin. The magistrate who heard the case dismissed the charges with the following comment: [17]

"It may well be that the patient committeed an offense here. It is not for me to decide one way or the other, but to my mind it would make nonsense of these regulations, which are designed to give duly qualified medical practitioners absolute discretion as to how they treat their patients and the quantities of drugs they shall prescribe, if I were to hold that these facts amounted to an infringement of these regulations by this defendant.

"There is nothing in these regulations to which my attention has been directed which limits the quantities of drugs which may be lawfully prescribed by a doctor. It may well be that this conduct of the defendant was gravely improper. It is not for me to decide any such issue.

"It may be that it is a matter which may be referred to the disciplinary body of the medical practitioners, but I have no doubt that the prosecution have failed to establish a prima facie case against this defendant of aiding and abetting another person to be in possession of this dangerous drug and I therefore dismiss the information."

During the course of the hearings on this case a woman who was said to have been an addict in the past appeared as a witness. She stated that she was now respectably employed and was no longer an addict, and asked that her name be withheld. When she appeared on the witness stand her name was accordingly written on a slip of paper and handed to the magistrate, but was not mentioned publicly. This incident is representative of the attitude generaly taken toward drug users. The public attitude may best be described as pity. When addicts appear in court charged with criminal offenses if they are treated differently from other offenders, they are apt to be dealt with more lightly. An addict who secures additional supplies of his drug by forging prescriptions or secretly consulting a second doctor will usually only be fined if he is not a chronic offender. If he is old and ill besides, he may merely be placed on probation. However, if an offender against the drug laws is thought to be operating from mercenary motives, for his own financial gain, he is apt to be dealt with more severely by being sentenced to prison.

In 1954, an incident occurred which is an illustration of the manner in which the British drug laws operate. An American entertainer performing at the London Palladium, a vaudeville theater, was known by the police to be a heroin user and was therefore watched. This person consulted a doctor from whom he received a prescription for heroin under a false name and identity. He was arrested, charged, and convicted for having given false information to the physician, and then deported. The writer asked what would have happened had the defendant not given false information to the doctor. The answer was that in that case nothing would have happened, because there would have been no violation.

THE BAN ON HEROIN

The recent attempt of the British Government to impose a ban on the manufacture and importation of heroin provides an excellent illustration of the sensitivity of the British medical profession to what it regards as encroachments on its prerogatives. Heroin was banned in the United States in 1924 when it was discovered that addicts were using this drug very widely. Since the heroin that was being used by American addicts at this time was already being used illegally, the ban had no particular effect; in fact, heroin has become even more popular with American users since, but not because, it was banned. The congressional hearings held before the ban was put into effect revealed that the

[17] Quoted in the London Times, September 9, 1955.

medical profession in this country was divided on the question of the medical usefulness of heroin, a majority declaring that heroin was not indispensable. A minority opinion contended that heroin did have some therapeutic values not possessed by possible substitutes, and argued against the ban. This minority opinion was brushed aside, of course, by congressional action. Shortly after 1925, similar hearings were held in Britain which revealed a similar split in British medical opinion; but Parliament interpreted this as a reason for not imposing a ban because the medical profession was not in agreement.

In recent years American representatives to the World Health Organization of the United Nations spearheaded an international drive to ban heroin everywhere; and it is now an illegal drug in more than 50 countries of the world. It was the pressure of this drive that probably caused the British Government, to announce, rather suddenly in 1955, that the manufacture of heroin would be discontinued in 1956. Protests from medical sources were voiced immediately, and the issue was vigorously discussed in newspaper columns and in letters to the editor. The matter became a minor political issue in Parliament; and the part played by American pressure in the campaign to outlaw heroin was understood and discussed. The vigorous reaction of the British medical profession to the Government's action was based more on the feeling that the Government was interfering with the rights of the profession than on any attachment to heroin as a therapeutic agent. The Government was eventually obliged to postpone the banning of heroin to an indefinite date, and heroin is therefore still not a contraband drug in the United Kingdom as it is in the United States.

EFFECTS OF THIS SYSTEM ON THE DRUG PROBLEM

It would, of course, be a mistake to attribute the trivial nature of the British drug problem entirely to the control measures which have been sketched. Back in 1920, when present control measures were set up, the number of addicts in Britain was small in contrast to the situation in this country. Nevertheless, the fact that the problem has diminished since that time, and that the number of drug users is probably close to what one might call "an irreducible minimum," are strong arguments in favor of th British system.

Prior to 1920 English addicts were free to buy their supplies of drugs from pharmacies without consulting a doctor. After that time they were compelled either to give up the habit or to consult a physician. They had a third alternative—to obtain supplies from illicit sources—but this was scarcely practical because no illicit traffic that was sufficiently organized to provide regular supplies ever developed. By having to turn to doctors, addicts got the benefits of medical and psychiatric care and advice. Although the drug user is a difficult patient to handle, he is obviously better off in the hands of the medical profession than if left to his own devices.

British officials are concerned over the potential development of a clandestine traffic as it exists in the United States; but feel, in the main, that giving addicts access to low cost, legitimate drugs takes most of the economic motive out of such a traffic. At the same time, it is realized that the addict's access to drugs cannot be too free and unrestricted; hence the pressure on doctors to minimize dosage and to make prolonged attempts to achieve a cure. Undoubtedly there is some objection in Britain on moral grounds to indefinite administration of drugs; but this is counterbalanced by considering the greater evil of a large illicit trade in the hands of criminals. That the present system seems to work, in the sense that the problem is small and not growing larger, causes an understandable reluctance to change it in any important way.

English officials and the public do not regard addicts as criminals since their addicts are not criminals, or only in a minor sense of the term. They therefore have difficulty in understanding the American tendency to equate addiction with criminality, and to punish addicts more and more severely. It is felt in Britain that the addict is a weakling or an unfortunate person to be pitied and treated with compassion.

Since the British addict does not need as much money to secure drugs as he does to buy cigarettes, he does not have to steal, become a prostitude, or peddle drugs in order to support his habit. Indeed, there is a positive, special hazard and unnecessary disadvantage for him in such criminal activities, since they may lead to entanglements with the law and to sudden interruptions of his habit. It is also disadvantageous for the criminal to become an addict, for he thereby adds greatly to the hazards of an already perilous occupation. A London police officer was asked what might happen if one approached a prostitute to inquire about illicit heroin. He suggested that she might well report to the police, since she knows that if she sticks to prostitution alone, the worst that will happen to her is that she will be fined 40 shillings about every 2 weeks, whereas if she becomes involved with drugs she might go to prison.

Because the British addict can maintain his habit without becoming a criminal, and the criminals not especially exposed to addiction by the existence of a large, illicit traffic or by great numbers of addicts in the underworld, these two groups remain relatively separate. This works not only to the public advantage, but also to their own; it should not be surprising, therefore, that London thieves show no special tendency to become drug addicts, or that London addicts are relatively noncriminal.

It is interesting that the use of marihuana, which in this country often leads to the later use of heroin, does not seem to have this consequence in Britain; there marihuana smokers obtain their supplies entirely from illicit sources, and the British police deal with this problem much as it is dealt with here. The fact that heroin, on the other hand, is not contraband, and that it may be prescribed for those addicted to it, may account for this difference in the use of the two kinds of drugs.

It has been said that British addicts do not show the same disposition as their American counterparts to spread their vice, but instead warn others who may become interested in it. On this point several aspects of the situation are relevant. One is that in England there is little or no economic incentive to spread the habit to others; and if the addict is under a doctor's care, he will certainly want to keep the supplies he receives rather than sell or give them away. If he sells them, he violates the law. Moreover, if the addict is under a doctor's care, he can keep his habit from becoming publicly known, since all records with respect to it are confidential. Thus he risks forfeiting his anonymity, as well as his status as a law-abiding citizen, if he violates the law.

A frequent criticism of the British program is that it does not place sufficient stress upon curing addicts because drugs are made available to them, and because they cannot be compelled to seek cures. In answer to this it is argued that compulsory cures are ineffective anyway, and that a drug addict, like a person addicted to alcohol, can only be cured if he wants to be and cooperates in the process. By putting the drug user in the hands of a doctor, and by not removing him from his community and family, the British program maximizes the resources which may be drawn upon for effective treatment by persuasion rather than by coercion. However, no really effective method of curing drug addiction has been found in any country of the world.

It is sometimes believed that controlled legal distribution of low-cost drugs to addicts would make drugs easily available and lead to the rapid spread of the habit. It has not done so, of course. This belief is based upon the mistaken premise that drugs made available by a doctor's prescription are generally easy to get. Such drugs are readily available to the addict diagnosed by medical men to be in need of them, but are relatively inaccessible to all others. It is difficult to imagine a teen-ager approaching a doctor to ask for a large quantity of heroin with which to entertain his friends. It is even more difficult to think that a doctor would accede to such a request. It is because addicts can obtain drugs by prescription that those drugs are unobtainable otherwise.

The system of drug control in Britain, which we have discussed, is obviously based upon the premise that the medical profession, with a certain amount of instruction, experience, and supervision, can be trusted to carry out its obligations in good faith under a scheme of this kind. It is quite true that much responsibility is placed upon the individual doctor, and that this responsibility has sometimes not been met. An English doctor made the point that any scheme is bound to be abused to some extent, and that there are some irresponsible persons in all occupations. He did not believe, however, that there was any sense in abandoning a good program because of this small minority, or in making a new program adapted to the low ethical standards of this small minority. Specifically, he felt that measures which would keep the few irresponsible doctors in Britain in check, and punish them for unethical practices in respect to addicts, would set dangerous precedents and be detrimental to the medical profession as a whole.

On humanitarian and legal grounds, the British system may be defended as a just and humane one. Because the addict does not also have to be a criminal, it is made reasonable and just to punish him when he does offend. Addiction itself is not a crime, either in theory or effect, and the addict is never formally punished for it. On the contrary, the idea of such punishment is rejected by public and official opinion as contrary to the principles of British law and common humanity. Because the addict, as elsewhere, is regarded as ill, weak, troubled, and an unfortunate person, fines and prison sentences are not thought of as appropriate ways of dealing with him. He has, moreover, the same legal protection and rights in court as anyone else, and is not deprived of them by legal technicalities or subterfuges. As a doctor's patient, he has the same standing as any other patient. As already mentioned, all official records are confidential; and, as a matter of practice, special care is taken to protect the addict from unnecessary exposure or publicity. Perhaps ultimately the greatest strength of the system lies in the fact that it is publicly recognized to be just and humane.

MISCONCEPTIONS OF THE BRITISH SYSTEM

During recent years there has been a growing interest in the United States in the methods of drug control used in West European countries, especially in Britain.[18] Perhaps because the practices of these countries are different from our own, and seem to be more successful, American officials have not invited invidious comparisons by publishing information about them. In some instances false information has been disseminated.

A prevalent misconception equates the so-called clinic system, as used in the United States in the early twenties, with a program such as the one described in this paper. The alleged failure of the clinic idea in the United States is then cited as proof that any legalized distribution of drugs to incurable addicts must fail. There is little resemblance between the clinic idea and the British program, and any attempt to treat them as similar leads only to confusion.

In a recently published book on the narcotics question,[19] Mr. Harry J. Anslinger, head of the Federal Bureau of Narcotics, contributes to this kind of confusion by discussing the "clinic plan" under the heading, "Fallacy of Legalizing Drug Addiction." He describes such a plan as follows: "Under this plan anyone who is now, or who later becomes, a drug addict would apply to the clinic and receive the amount of narcotic drug sufficient to maintain his customary use." He does not describe the British system or that of any other West European country. Concerning the British system he writes: [20] "No government in the world conducts such clinics, no matter what is said about England. What about all the seizures there? What about the trouble doctors are having keeping their bags from being stolen?"

The latest official report of the British Government,[21] for 1955, states concerning these questions raised by Mr. Anslinger: "The isolated cases of the theft of legitimately manufactured drugs occur very occasionally, but in 1955 no such cases were reported."

As far as nonmanufactured drugs are concerned, 48 seizures of opium and 48 of marihuana were reported for 1955.

Elsewhere in his book,[22] Mr. Anslinger refers to "The present wave of drug addiction in the United States, Canada, Turkey, Egypt, England, Germany, and Japan," and makes the following specific remarks about England: [23]

"In England, the British Government reports annually only 350 drug addicts known to the British authorities—mostly doctors and nurses. When we ask them about the statistics of seizures of opium and hashish (marihuana), they say: Negroes, Indians, and Chinese are involved. In this country we don't distinguish; we take the situation as a whole. England, during the last year, has had a surge of hashish addiction among young people. A year ago they were looking at the United States with an 'it can't happen here' attitude. Suddenly hashish addiction hit the young people. Ordinarily hashish is only something for the Egyptian, the Indian. Now the British press is filled with accounts of cases of addiction of young people."

Apart from the fact that marihuana, or hashish, is not a drug of addiction in the sense that the opiate derivatives are, it should be noted that the number of persons prosecuted for offenses involving marihuana reached a peak in Britain

---

[18] For a recent example see Laurence Kolb, Let's Stop This Narcotics Hysteria, Saturday Evening Post, July 28, 1956.
[19] Harry J. Anslinger and William F. Tompkins, The Traffic in Narcotics, Funk & Wagnalls Co., New York, 1953, p. 185.
[20] Ibid., p. 290.
[21] Op. cit., p. 6.
[22] Op. cit., p. 11.
[23] Op. cit., p. 279.

in 1954 with a total of 152.[24] In 1955, there were 115 such cases. The number of these offenders who were of European origin, was 29 in 1954. These figures scarcely seem to justify the use of the word "surge" in describing the British situation.

Some deliberate attempts to misrepresent the nature of the British system have been made. In an anonymous mimeographed statement entitled, "British Narcotic System," distributed free of charge at the meeting of the American Prison Association in Philadelphia in 1954, the following statements appear:

"The British system is the same as the United States system. The following is an excerpt of a letter dated July 18, 1953, from the British Home Office, concerning the prescribing of narcotic drugs by the medical profession:

" 'A doctor may not have or use the drugs for any other purpose than that of ministering to the strictly medical needs of his patients. The continued supply of drugs to a patient, either direct or by prescription, solely for the gratification of addiction, is not regarded as a medical need.' "

The above quotation is an extract from the 1948 Home Office memorandum, and was also quoted and explained earlier in this paper. The failure to explain that the Rolleston report interpreted regular administration of drugs to an addict by a medical practitioner as "treatment," rather than as "gratification of addiction," gives the statement the opposite of its actual meaning.

Other statements from his document on the British system follows:

"No doctor would give a prescription for marihuana in the United Kingdom as he would be charged with a narcotic violation."

Comment.—A doctor would not, of course, prescribe a marihuana cigarette, but he could, conceivably, prescribe marihuana in some other form without violating any law since prescriptions of drugs are subject to control by medical practice and not by law.

"There is also a black market for morphine and pethidine in the United Kingdom. Twelve percent of the illicit trafficking cases in the United Kingdom related to forged prescriptions or *concurrent supplies from more than one doctor* to obtain morphine or pethidine to gratify addiction. The British Government arrests these addicts who forge prescriptions for morphine and pethidine. They are handled the same way in the United States." [Italics not in original.]

Comment.—The italicized part of this statement shows that the unknown author was aware of the fact that British addicts can obtain supplies legally from one doctor. The number of persons represented by "12 percent" was 14;[25] and there was probably no connection with the illicit traffic. Addicts who forge prescriptions and obtain dual supplies do so as a rule to supplement the supplies they receive regularly.

"There are also robberies by addicts of drug stores or other establishments handling narcotics in the United Kingdom."

Comment.—There are few such cases, and in 1955 there were none reported.

There follows a brief discussion of the clinic plan in the United States, indicating that it failed, and that the American Medical Association opposed it. The final sentence in this anonymous statement reads:

"A pamphlet, Narcotic Clinics in the United States giving the history of the opening and closing of clinics, can be obtained free of charge by writing to the Bureau of Narcotics, Washington, D. C."

Comment.—It would appear that any discussion of the clinic plan in the United States under the heading "British Narcotic System," is highly irrelevant since there are no clinics in the British system.

The idea of allowing morphine or heroin addicts to have access to legal drugs is often represented in American magazines and the press as a daring and revolutionary conception. It is nothing of the kind. It is the principle on which most drug control schemes in the Western Hemisphere are based, and on which American practice was based until about 1920. The annual reports of European nations to the drug control bodies of the United Nations demonstrate this.[26] Methods for internal control of the drug problem are not dictated by the United Nations, and are rarely discussed in its publications, probably because of various national sensitivities, including particularly American sensitivity, on this question.

---

[24] See the previously cited reports to the United Nations, 1954, pp. 4–5; 1955, p. 7. In 1951, the year referred to by Mr. Anslinger, the number of marihuana cases was 127.

[25] As checked by a home office official who read the mimeographed statement.

[26] Summary of Annual Reports of Governments, published annually by the Commission on Narcotic Drugs, Economic and Social Council, the United Nations, New York.

Because of his position as Commissioner of Narcotics, head of the Federal Bureau of Narcotics, and American representative to the United Nations on drug control matters, the opinion of Mr. Harry J. Anslinger are of special importance. They are often echoed by congressional committees and by the press, and are influential in shaping public opinion. Mr. Anslinger has been consistently and strongly opposed to any form of legalized distribution of drugs to addicts. He has, however, never described the British program, but has leveled his blasts at the clinic plan instead.

Some of his objections to the clinic plan are as follows: [27]

"This plan would elevate a most despicable trade to the avowed status of an honorable business, nay, to the status of practice of a time-honored profession; and drug addicts would multiply unrestrained, to the irrevocable impairment of the moral fiber and physical welfare of the American people."

"(Such a plan) is * * * in direct contravention of the spirit and purpose of the international drug conventions, which the United States solemnly entered into along with 72 other nations of the world."

"(It would be a) reversion to conditions prior to the enactment of national control legislation and a surrender of the benefits of 22 years of progress in controlling this evil, in which control the United States has been a pioneer among nations."

"To establish clinics in countries which have a narcotic drug problem would be as sane as to establish infection centers during a smallpox epidemic."

"It is believed that easy or unrestricted access to drugs tends materially to increase addiction."

Not a single one of these objections is applicable to the program now in force in the United Kingdom and in most other countries of Europe. In the first place, none of them have clinics. All or most of them are also parties to the same international agreements that the United States has entered into, and all of them combined do not have as many addicts as the United States. The systems do not give "easy or unrestricted access to drugs," and have apparently controlled the spread of addiction, especially among young persons, far more effectively than has the American program.

CONCLUSIONS

The very success of the British and other similar European programs of narcotics controls has been a factor in preventing them from being widely known in the United States. The number of heroin and morphine addicts in Britain, for example, is so small that very few persons there have specialized knowledge of this subject. The literature is extremely scanty, consisting mainly of official reports and a few widely scattered articles in medical journals.[28] Many of these works are not illuminating to American readers because they take for granted a knowledge of British medical practices. However, the apparent success of medically controlled, legalized distribution of drugs to addicts there is of obvious special significance for the United States.

It would be rash to advocate any wholesale indiscriminate importation of British methods to this country in the expectation of an immediate solution to the drug problem. The relatively large number of addicts here, their concentration in big cities and in certain segments of the population, clearly present special problems of extraordinary difficulty, as does the existence of a large-scale illicit traffic of many years standing. Nevertheless, with due allowance for the differences in customs and social organization that exist between the two countries, it is reasonable to suppose that there is much in British experience from which we could profit. Drug addicts, after all, are pretty much the same throughout the world in many essential respects. Allowing for the smaller number of them in Britain, they still do not constitute the social evil there that they do here. The trend in the United States toward more and more severe punishment, for users and peddlers alike, has reached such an extreme that demand for a fundamental reevaluation of the present punitive program is very much in order. When it is undertaken, British experience could, and should, play an important role.

---

[27] Op. cit., pp. 186, 189, 190–191.
[28] The only recent book on narcotics known to the author which contains a fairly adequate description of the British system is by an English author, E. W. Adams, Drug Addiction, Oxford University Press, 1937.

[From the Nation, April 21, 1956]

TRAFFIC IN DOPE—MEDICAL PROBLEM

By Alfred R. Lindesmith [1]

For 40 years the United States has tried in vain to control the problem of drug addiction by prohibition and police suppression. The disastrous consequences of turning over to the police what is an essentially medical problem are steadily becoming more apparent as narcotic arrests rise each year to new records and the habit continues to spread, especially among young persons. Control by prohibition has failed; but the proposed remedies for this failure consist mainly of more of the same measures which have already proved futile.

The number of heroin and morphine addicts (the use of marihuana, cocaine, and other drugs is a separate problem not included in this discussion) is conservatively estimated by Mr. Harry J. Anslinger, head of the Federal Narcotics Bureau, at 60,000. This figure is a guess; its main virtue is that it is the lowest offered. Even so, the contrast with European countries is spectacular. For example, the English Government reports slightly more than 300 addicts known to the authorities in all of Britain, with a population of over 50 million. There are probably more addicts in the United States than in all of the other western nations combined, and more juvenile users in New York City than in the whole of Europe. Almost all English addicts are reported to be over 30 years old, while close to half of ours is under 25. What is even more significant, European users appear to add to the crime problem in only a minor way, and the illicit traffic there is feeble compared to ours. The American market is the hub of the drug traffic in the Western Hemisphere.

In recent years there has been a growing interest in the English system of control. General Sessions Judge J. J. Goldstein, of New York, mentioned it recently in connection with his advocacy of a system of controlled legal distribution of drugs to users. Dr. Hubert S. Howe, of New York, has also long urged such a plan, adopted by the New York Academy of Medicine, and has made references to the apparent success of the English system. Since about 1940, the writer himself has periodically suggested that an adaptation of the British idea be tried in this country.

The crucial difference between the American and British control systems is that the English physician is permitted to prescribe drugs regularly for the morphine addict while the American doctor is not. The decision as to whether or not regular prescriptions are to be given to the English user is left to the doctor, usually after consultation with another medical man. He does not have to report on the addicts under his care, but records must be kept both by him and by the druggists who fill the prescriptions. Through these sources the British Home Office and the police can secure information about addicts and keep close watch on them. Addicts are arrested for obtaining supplies from illicit sources or from two medical sources simultaneously. The addict cannot be coerced into taking a cure, but there is pressure on the doctor to do everything in his power to persuade the user to quit the habit.

The British addict under medical care is included in the doctor's panel of cases under the National Health Act. Apart from the taxes he pays under this act along with the rest of the population, the addict's expenses for maintaining his habit consist only in the shilling (14 cents) paid for each prescription. It is therefore unnecessary for him to engage in criminal activities to get his drug. The black market is small, limited primarily to London and a few other large cities, and caters to users who either don't know that they can place themselves under a doctor's care or don't wish to do so. Sometimes an addict will refuse medical care because he is afraid his addiction will become known, or because he does not want to try to cure himself of the habit. All black-market activities are, of course, prohibited by law, and the addict who patronizes peddlers risks arrest and punishment. In 1954 about 30 addicts were arrested, most of them for forging prescriptions or obtaining supplies from 2 doctors at once, and the majority were punished with fines up to a maximum of $280. The smoking of opium and the possession and use of marihuana are completely prohibited.

[1] Alfred R. Lindesmith, author of Opiate Addiction, is professor of sociology at Indiana University. In 1955 he went abroad to study the English system of narcotics control under a research grant.

The obvious advantages of this system are that it removes the major motives for peddling narcotics and for the creation of new users, puts pressure on the addict to seek medical care and removes his incentive to engage in crime. And even though the addict is not treated as a criminal, addiction has not spread. The plan, in fact, has the opposite effect by making the doctor rather than the peddler the prime source of drugs. Another of the great advantages of the system is that a mantle of decent privacy is thrown over the unhappy details.

In this country the history of opiate-drug control has been very different. Because American patent medicines in the 19th century often contained opiate derivatives which were not controlled, relatively large numbers of addicts were created who were not, however, generally regarded or treated as criminals. The problem then was in no way as serious as now. Criminal addicts were few, the illicit traffic minor in nature and addiction was largely confined to adults (about two-thirds of them women). Because drugs were legally available at low cost the user did not have to become a criminal to support his habit. Even so, an increasing concern with the dangers implicit in the unlimited availability of drugs led to the trial of measures of control late in the 19th century and in the first decade of the twentieth. Given time, this experimentation, guided by growing medical knowledge of the opiate drugs, might well have led to the establishment here of something like the English system. This did not happen because of the intervention of Federal authorities imbued with the prohibition mentality.

The present system of drug control began with the passage of the Harrison Act late in 1914. This act made no mention of addicts nor did it in any way indicate how they were to be treated. It was a revenue measure designed to bring the flow of dangerous habit-forming drugs into the open through the exercise of the Government's taxing powers. All persons and firms handling such drugs were required to obtain licenses and to keep records of supplies received and dispensed. Penalties were provided for violations. An exemption was made for the prescribing of drugs "to a patient by a physician * * * in the course of his professional practice only." The interpretation of this part of the law became crucial in the early years of enforcement because on it hinged the whole matter of whether the addict was to be placed under the care of the physician or turned over to the police.

Between 1919 and 1925 a number of test cases—the Webb, Jim Fuey Moy, Behrman, and Linder cases—were brought before the Supreme Court. The first three involved doctors who had flagrantly violated medical ethics by dispensing large quantities of drugs at high prices to addicts. Rufus King has pointed out in the April 1953 issue of the Yale Law Journal that these cases were in effect rigged by the Government. The prosecution wanted a court ruling which would prevent addicts from obtaining drugs from doctors. They evidently hoped that the unprofessional action of the doctors in these three cases would influence the court to decide against them, which it did. From the language of the indictments the Government was then in a position to argue that these rulings had established that any administration of drugs to addicts by medical men, even when done in good faith to achieve a cure, was illegal.

The Linder case was designed to clinch the Government's position. Unlike the three earlier ones, it involved a doctor who had prescribed small quantities of drugs to a single addict in good faith and in what was clearly a professional manner. The Government attorneys asked the court for a ruling against the doctor on the basis of the precedent allegedly established by the earlier decisions. In this case, however, the court reversed itself by ruling against the Government. Despite this reversal, Federal narcotics authorities have continued to operate under a Treasury Department regulation which states that "a prescription issued to an addict * * * to keep him comfortable by maintaining his customary use, is not a prescription within the meaning or intent of the act: and the person filling such an order, as well as the person issuing it, may be charged with violation of the law." Threatened with criminal prosecution, the majority of doctors naturally ceased to treat addicts; the minority found themselves in trouble with the narcotics agents, and in many instances were sent to prison.

In 1920 a radical change in the Government's attitude toward addicts became apparent after the enforcement of the drug laws was turned over to a newly formed unit in the Bureau of Internal Revenue which was also charged with liquor-law enforcement under the Volstead Act. From 1915 through 1919, the annual reports of the Collector of Internal Revenue included expressions of sympathy for the drug user and concern over the fact that previously respectable addicts were being turned into criminals by the operation of the law.   The 1919 report notes that various local health authorities had been encouraged to consider the possibility of setting up clinics in which drugs could be dispensed legally to such persons.   The 1920 report, however, reversed this stand.   It deplored the fact that some 44 local clinics had already been set up and announced that they were to be closed down.   Neither the 1920 report nor any subsequent one expressed concern with the fate of the once respectable user who was being forced to the underworld to maintain his supplies.

It is a current myth that the clinics which operated between 1919 and 1923 demonstrated once and for all the perniciousness of any legal system of drug distribution and that they were closed solely because they failed.   The facts are quite otherwise and more complex.   It is true that the New York City clinic was generally admitted to have failed, but its failure was guaranteed in advance by the manner in which it was set up and operated.   The stories of the other clinics vary.   There is considerable reliable information extant about the clinic in Shreveport, La., established under Dr. W. P. Butler, which is discussed in some detail by Drs. C. E. Terry and M. Pellens in their book, The Opium Problem, a monumental and authoritative study.   This clinic was originally set up by the Louisiana State Board of Health in 1919.   In 1921 the board, after consultation with Federal narcotics authorities, withdrew its support and the institution was continued under the authority of the Shreveport City Council.   In the same year it was unanimously endorsed by the Shreveport Medical Society; other medical groups and the local police also expressed their support.   However, in 1923 the clinic was finally closed by order of Federal authorities in Washington.   Dr. Butler reluctantly agreed to the closing after a conference with Federal narcotics agents who said they had been sent to shut down the clinic "because it was the only one left in the United States."   When a Los Angeles clinic had been similarly closed in 1921, Dr. L. M. Powers, then health commissioner of the city, had remarked, "I have not been able to realize the actual purpose of the closing of our clinic for there has been some unseen motive prompting much opposition to clinics which I have not been able to comprehend."

The disappearance of the clinics marked the final triumph of the prohibition idea and the complete removal of the control issue from the medical domain. The drug problem is what it is today as the result of these moves by the Government.   The huge illicit traffic, directed for profit by nonaddicted lords of the underworld, has become the focal point of new infection.   These men are rarely apprehended or punished; it is the user, exploited by the system, who suffers the major portion of the heavy penalties that are imposed.   Police suppression, by increasing the danger of distribution and reducing supplies, keeps up prices and profits.

It is a popular misconception that the increase of drug use among young people is entirely a postwar phenomenon.   As early as 1921, Dr. E. Bishop, a noted authority on drug addiction, commented on the trend toward juvenile addiction and ascribed it to the prohibition control technique.   Statistical evidence of the trend itself can be found in Uniform Crime Reports of the FBI over the last 24 years.   In 1932, for instance, only 15 percent of narcotic law violators were under 25 years of age; in 1940, the figure had reached 26 percent; today is a little under 50 percent.

In 1930, drug law enforcement was separated from liquor law enforcement with the establishment, within the Treasury Department, of the Federal Bureau of Narcotics.   Federal narcotics officials, both before 1930 and since, have combined their policing functions with an active and effective campaign in support of the punitive conception of drug control.   The expression of dissident opinion was discouraged.   How well their campaign has succeeded in mobilizing legislative and public sentiment is indicated by the fact that Congress, in 1951, passed laws that more than doubled the average prison sentence of Federal narcotics offenders.   In January of this year a preliminary report of a Senate subcommittee indicated that the present Congress will again be asked to increase penalties, enlarge the budget of the Federal Bureau of Narcotics, and generally add to the punitive nature of the existing program.   The report expressed sympathy for the addict but makes no distinction between him and the peddler.   It admitted that the real culprits, the big profiteers of the traffic, are rarely caught, and proposed to deal with them by legalizing wiretapping.   Although the report explicitly stated that the number of addicts in this country probably exceeds the sum total of those in all other western countries combined, no reference appeared in it to the control systems adopted abroad.

The treatment and cure of opiate drug addiction under the best of circumstances is very difficult. The main hope of control must be based on prevention. The punitive program now in operation neither prevents nor cures and it actually nullifies the rehabilitative measures that are being attempted. The addict belongs in the hospital, not in the prison. If we recognize that punishment cannot cure disease, if we want to take the profit out of the illicit traffic we need to return the drug user to the care of the medical profession—the only profession equipped to deal with him.

Chairman KEFAUVER. Next witness.

Mr. Terranova, we are very glad to have you here. Just sit down. I don't think we need to place you under oath. Let's get your name.

Peter E. Terranova, former head of the Narcotics Squad; is that correct?

STATEMENT OF PETER E. TERRANOVA, FORMER HEAD, NEW YORK NARCOTICS SQUAD

Mr. TERRANOVA. That is correct, sir.

Chairman KEFAUVER. When did you retire as head of the squad?

Mr. TERRANOVA. First of July of this year, sir.

Chairman KEFAUVER. Is that the New York State squad?

Mr. TERRANOVA. No, sir; New York City Police Department, Narcotics Squad.

Chairman KEFAUVER. How long were you connected with the squad?

Mr. TERRANOVA. Twenty-nine and a half years of police department, 5 years with the squad, was commanding officer. We built that squad from 32 men up to 200 men and women both.

Chairman KEFAUVER. What have you been doing?

Mr. TERRANOVA. I am now security director for the Bull Steamship Co. We use——

Chairman KEFAUVER. What company?

Mr. TERRANOVA. Bull.

Chairman KEFAUVER. Bull Steamship Co.?

Mr. TERRANOVA. Yes, sir.

Chairman KEFAUVER. All right, Mr. Mitler.

Mr. MITLER. Inspector, I know apart from your function as head of the narcotics squad, you are also a student of this problem.

I want to first ask you your comment about the using of the English system or some aspects of it here in the United States, and then I will get back to your work in New York City.

Mr. TERRANOVA. The question that came to my mind when Dr. Lindesmith—and incidentally I read his book and I think it is a very fine one—came to my mind is that London alone admits to about 6,000 prostitutes, street walkers, and we have found that prostitution and drug addiction are very closely allied, so how could there only be 300 or 450 addicts in the British Isles? This was the big question that came to my mind. I can't understand that.

Mr. MITLER. Do you think that program is feasible in the United States?

Mr. TERRANOVA. I beg your pardon?

Mr. MITLER. Do you think any elements of the British program would be feasible in the United States?

Mr. TERRANOVA. It is a big step. Of course, being a law enforcement officer, I guess we just hate to give up the fact of enforcing the law, in other words, in joining them if you can't lick them.

But we do know that the old-time addict is going to have to have his drug. There is no question about it.

But will we create a condition, will we encourage it in the youngster, new person coming along, by acquiescence to this addition by the old-timer?

Iran has been licensing opium smokers, and 60 percent of the population was smoking opium in Iran when the present Shah took over the Government. He is discouraging that since he started his regime. He is outlawing the illicit traffic as much as he possibly can at this time.

He has stopped licensing new smokers. He has stopped licensing Government stores for dispensing narcotics. So here we are a new nation coming in, and we want to turn around and do what some of these old nations are experienced in and now changing their laws.

This is a program that will have to be studied and very, very closely and not just a brushoff or just over the surface. Dr. Howe's program, I think most of us are all acquainted with.

I worked with Dr. Howe personally for 5 years. I know him personally. I don't agree with his program a hundred percent and he knows it. There are lots of bugs to be ironed out in the whole thing.

Mr. MITLER. Who is Dr. Howe?

Mr. TERRANOVA. Dr. Hugo Howe of the Academy of Medicine of New York has suggested this type of a program.

Mr. MITLER. There is a difference, isn't there? His program is the clinic program with drugs dispensed to addicts.

Mr. TERRANOVA. Mr. Mitler, we are always timid about the word "clinic" because of the failures in 1919, 1920, and 1921 in various parts of the United States.

In Dr. Howe's program the person would have to register, something I would approve of. All addicts should be registered. You can't fight something we don't know what you are fighting; we don't know how many addicts we have at any given point in the United States, nobody can point that out.

Mr. MITLER. Dr. Howe's program—under his suggestion there would be clinics where the drug addicts could go and get a supply; is that correct?

Mr. TERRANOVA. No, Mr. Mitler, it would be something—quickly, I know the time is limited—so very quickly, the person would register, be placed in a hospital, determine whether they could or could not withdraw them and keep them off the drug, then they would be placed in the custody of a medical man, a doctor who would be licensed by the particular agency who would handle this whole thing and naturally it would have to be on a Federal basis, it could not be on a local basis because the community that would invoke, that would have every junkie in the 47 States right there to get his dope for nothing.

Mr. MITLER. Turning to New York City, could you tell us briefly about the juvenile drug problem in the city of New York and bring it up to the 16-, 17-, and 18-year-old group, if you would.

Mr. TERRANOVA. Well, in 1951, we can go back that far, when we really started to get conscious, I think, of drug addiction, there were 3,661 arrests made, and of those 27 were under 16 years of age.

There were 775 between 16 and 20, including 20.

Chairman KEFAUVER. Wait a minute, 3,600 arrests made and how many were under 21?

Mr. TERRANOVA. 775 plus 27.

Chairman KEFAUVER. 802?

Mr. TERRANOVA. That is right, sir, and in 1952 there were 5,297, and under 21 there were 252 and 8, which makes 260; under 21, 260.

In 1953 there were 3,605, 556 plus 17 under 21.

These are arrests made by the New York City Police Department and not by any other agencies which, of course, the Federal Narcotic Bureau is very active in New York City.

And in 1954 there were 4,316, 729 plus 20 under 21.

In 1955 there were 5,232, and 681 plus 16 under 21. And the laws in 1951, the State legislature passed a law whereby all addicts who come to the attention of attending or consulting physicians must be reported by that physician to our State board of health.

From 1952, when the returns started to come in, up until October of 1955, there were 81 under the age of 16 had been reported. There were 2,507 between 16 and 20, and there are 11,608 or a total of 14,196.

Now, there were 10,615 of male, and 3,581 female. You will see there was 11 percent under the age of 21 of known addicts in the city of New York; 57.9 percent Negro, 24.1 percent white, 14.9 percent Puerto Rican—we classify it that way, just to distinguish the race—and yellow, 3.1; 87.8 percent of the drug used was heroin in the city of New York.

Crimes to be committed by these people were approximately about eight categories starting with petty larceny as the first, burglary, prostitution, grand larceny, assaults, jostling, forgery, and armed robbery.

As you will notice the most serious one of them all, the armed robbery, there is the least of them as any. These people are very docile, and they don't go in for vicious crimes.

Mr. MITLER. Now, the narcotics squad was expanded about 1950 or 1951 in New York City.

Mr. TERRANOVA. 1951, in June of 1951 there were about 30, 32 members. The beginning of 1955 there were 200. That includes male and female detectives.

Mr. MITLER. You are familiar with the program of the Riverside Hospital?

Mr. TERRANOVA. Somewhat, yes.

Mr. MITLER. Could you tell us what that is briefly?

Mr. TERRANOVA. Well, Riverside, who is in conjunction with a court of the magistrates system in New York City, narcotic term court, the boy or girl is presented before the magistrate, and this is not a criminal proceeding, to determine whether or not the child is or is not using narcotics, an addict, not just a user.

The child is sent to the hospital for 5 days' observation and at that time they would have time to decide, and if the child is an addict, they are sent back to the hospital for a period of, under the jurisdiction, for a period of 3 years, regardless of what age prior to 21. They could be 1 day before their 21st birthday and still could be put under the jurisdiction of this hospital for 3 years.

They don't stay at the hospital for 3 years.   They stay just as long as the medical staff feels it was necessary to withdraw them and rehabilitate them and make them a safe risk to put back outside.

But as we have heard this morning and this afternoon, the biggest and the weakest point of all our programs is our aftercare and followup. We don't have any. We have a small amount as far as the hospital is concerned, but we in the police department have picked the kids going up there with the "works" right on their person, going to check in the rehabilitation stations, so it isn't—I mean ambulatory patients are a very poor risk.

Mr. MITLER. Could you just tell us, there is a project you are working on right now in New York City?

Mr. TERRANOVA. New York State.

Mr. MITLER. New York State, rather.

Mr. TERRANOVA. The government, there is a New York State Joint Legislative Committee of 15 members of the State that have been appointed, of which I am on the committee, to investigate the condition of narcotics in the State of New York, sir.

Mr. MITLER. Just one other point. When I was testifying I said something about occasional, in some place——

Chairman KEFAUVER. Let's see. What is the committee doing? When are you going to make the report?

Mr. TERRANOVA. We have only just started, sir. We will make an interim report in March and continue from there.

Chairman KEFAUVER. Then you are going to investigate the conditions and make legislative recommendations; is that the idea?

Mr. TERRANOVA. Yes, sir; anything that we feel can come out of it, to change our legislature a bit, make some recommendations probably for some hospitals.

Chairman KEFAUVER. You said there was no followup provision in New York. Of course, you have this——

Mr. TERRANOVA. This hospital was one, Metropolitan Hospital, where they go to but, from my point of view, it isn't successful as far as the followup is concerned.

As expressed we picked up at least in one particular case, another too, this one boy going in there had an eye dropper with a needle and a spoon on his person; he was going in to report and talk to the person in charge of the particular clinic, and we questioned him, asking him why he at least didn't frisk him.

He said, if they did, that none of them would ever come back in again, which would be true, I suppose.

Of course, we had no hesitancy as police officers to give the boy a quick frisk and we found the "works," as it is known, on his person.

We had one case where a JFA children's court called us in to talk to a youngster who had been smoking marihuana, and the boy had explained the sensations, and there was no question in our mind that he was smoking marihuana.

He said he had been smoking marihuana for a year, and that at this time he was 8 years old. And he said he belonged to a group in the neighborhood where he came from where there were the "seniors," the "juniors," and the "midgets," the three gangs.

The Midgets bought from the Juniors, the Juniors bought from the Seniors.

"Where do you get your money to pay for the narcotics or the marijuana?"

And he said, "Well, I ain't going to tell you." He was very willing to tell us who he bought it— purchased the marijuana from. He said there was a 16-year-old boy in the neighborhood and we had been able to pick the boy up in a couple of hours and we found he had been taking narcotics by injections and he was one of a group that met in a hallway, in a house, in the neighborhood and used it as a shooting gallery.

They range from the age of 12 to 18, the oldest one being the first year of college and the youngest one grammar schools. Two boys from parochial school—and I would like to say right now that all of the group there were no Negroes or Puerto Ricans among them. They were Irish and Italian and Jewish, this particular neighborhood.

Mr. MITLER. That is all.

Chairman KEFAUVER. Inspector, what kind of followup do you think would be useful?

Mr. TERRANOVA. I think if when they come out of these hospitals if we have regional hospitals, if we can't afford to have our own hospital in each State, or the Government can't afford to have them around them, perhaps the Government and the State could get around and have a regional hospital.

I don't think this is originally too much. Part is and part is not.

I think then we should carry the load pro rata as to the amount of addicts that we probably are putting into these particular hospitals. We should not turn them loose after four and a half months, because the individual himself, if he is willing, is going back to the same environment.

We have gone all through that, but if they could be put into some intermediate hospital such as that where he could be—or the boys perhaps to some camp. We had camps here some years back, if you will remember, for these youngsters out of work; perhaps we could invoke some of them again, get them out in the open.

But we must always remember that the individual himself must be willing to do this. We can't force him to do it, because 95 percent of any so-called cure is the individual wanting to stay away from it.

If we sit here and try to legislate, we tell what doctors should do but if they don't want to do it themselves there is nothing, Mr. Senator, you or I or anyone else or all committees in the world can do anything about it.

Senator KEFAUVER. You have given one or two instances of where you didn't think the treatment at the Riverside Hospital or the followup there was doing much good. You wouldn't mean to intimate that that is true of all cases?

Mr. TERRANOVA. Well, I remember Dr. Gamso over at the hospital admitting that 50 percent of his patients came back to him and when he was asked what about the other, he said he didn't know.

Fifty percent were recidivists coming back to the hospital. We have had cases where the drug was smuggled in on a weekend pass; trying to build the children back up again the drug was smuggled in through their person in the apertures of their body.

Chairman KEFAUVER. But haven't they changed and improved this system recently?

Mr. TERRANOVA. They are, of course, going along and increasing it at all times. That is true.

Chairman KEFAUVER. But they can't give followup for all of the addicts in New York City, can they?

Mr. TERRANOVA. No; I am afraid not.

Chairman KEFAUVER. Not just one hospital?

Mr. TERRANOVA. This one hospital, no.

Chairman KEFAUVER. Mr. Mitler says they can only handle 121— only under 21?

Mr. TERRANOVA. Only under 21, and I think they have about 130 in the hospital right now, something like that.

Chairman KEFAUVER. How many reported addictions are there of crimes committed?

I mean, how many addicts did you say there were in New York City at the present time?

Mr. TERRANOVA. 14,196 as of April of this year, sir. There is more than that right now. This is the known addicts that come to the attention of the medical profession.

Chairman KEFAUVER. You agree with these other witnesses there is really no way of knowing how many addictions there are?

Mr. TERRANOVA. That is correct, sir, no way of knowing. We should have registration so that at least we will have a fairly good idea as to the amount of addiction we do have so we know how to cope with it.

Right now we don't know what we have got.

Chairman KEFAUVER. Well, we thank you very much, Chief.

Mr. TERRANOVA. Thank you, sir.

Chairman KEFAUVER. And appreciate your contribution.

Mr. MITLER. Lieutenant Driscoll, this is more to thank you and Inspector Driscoll who both came in to cooperate with us in this hearing. Perhaps you want to come with the lieutenant.

Chairman KEFAUVER. Come around, Inspector Driscoll.

First, are you fellows brothers or what?

Inspector DRISCOLL. No, sir; we are no relation at all.

Chairman KEFAUVER. If we are not able to get the full story——

Inspector DRISCOLL. I am Inspector Driscoll.

Chairman KEFAUVER. And you are Lieutenant Driscoll?

Lieutenant DRISCOLL. Yes, sir.

STATEMENTS OF INSPECTOR JOHN F. DRISCOLL, DETECTIVE DIVISION, AND LT. GLASGOW DRISCOLL, PHILADELPHIA POLICE DEPARTMENT

Inspector DRISCOLL. Senator, Lieutenant Driscoll is most familiar with the situation. I came down here as a representative, I am second in command of the detective division.

Lieutenant Driscoll is charged with the responsibility and enforcement of the narcotics laws and he has had wide experience. And I think he can answer every question regarding the Philadelphia situation.

Chairman KEFAUVER. That is showing good confidence in your lieutenant, Inspector Driscoll.

Inspector DRISCOLL. Yes, sir.

Mr. MITLER. Lieutenant, you are the head of the narcotics squad in Philadelphia?

Lieutenant DRISCOLL. Yes, sir.

Mr. MITLER. I am going to ask you 1 or 2 questions. Can you tell us about the technique of mass raids very briefly that you have instituted in Philadelphia?

Lieutenant DRISCOLL. Yes, sir. Starting in 1954 we had a major narcotic problem in Philadelphia and at that time the present commissioner of police obtained funds for us to purchase narcotic drugs from pushers and we went to the police academy and picked out both young men and women and trained them and placed them in the field where narcotic drugs would be sold. Since 1953 there have been five mass raids usually an average of 100 to 125 persons being arrested for the sale of narcotic drugs. On one occasion we had a young nurse who had just graduated from one of our local hospitals. We took her, gave her a shopping bag and put 2 or 3 dresses in it and named her shopping bag Peg and we put her down in one of the neighborhoods where drugs were being sold and she posed as a shoplifter who was stealing dresses and so forth by shoplifting and selling them for drugs.

Over a period of 5 months that 1 young lady made 70 purchases of narcotic drugs from drug pushers. Through that technique of using young policemen and women we have reduced a major problem to an absolute minimum in Philadelphia at the present time.

Mr. MITLER. About those under 21, what was the situation and what is the situation very briefly, Lieutenant, as to the scope of drug addiction in those age groups?

Lieutenant DRISCOLL. In the past 4 years there have been only 5 persons arrested under the age of 18 years and each of those cases the child was smoking marihuana.

Each of those five cases for some reason or other had stopped attending school. The age between 18 and 21 the average is about 5 percent of the number of arrests run between the ages of 18 and 21. The usual age area is from 21 to 27.

Mr. MITLER. What is your view of the practicality of Dr. Howe's clinical plan? Do you think it is practical or impractical?

Lieutenant DRISCOLL. I don't approve of a clinic plan because in most cases a drug addict never gets enough of narcotics. If it was made that easy for him to get his drugs it would only increase his habit instead of tending to decrease it. If he would be treated on the ambulatory plan where he would be given 20 doses of drugs to take each day himself there is a danger of his giving those drugs to a person that has never used drugs. I don't approve of the clinic plan of treatment.

Mr. MITLER. Thank you very much.

Chairman KEFAUVER. Lieutenant Driscoll, by ambulatory plan you seem to speak about that as if the patient carries the drugs around himself.

Lieutenant DRISCOLL. Yes, sir.

Chairman KEFAUVER. That is not what we are talking about. We are talking about them reporting to the clinic for treatment.

Lieutenant DRISCOLL. Some of the clinics that is the way they treat the patient. I would approve of an oldtime drug addict if he has passed the stage of all redemption and we find out he is going to be a drug addict as long as he lives, if he would go to a clinic and obtain the drugs he needs at the clinic and no drugs be given to him to be taken away from the clinic, I would approve of treatment for him. But for the young addict I would not approve of clinic treatment for him. In the next session of the Pennsylvania legislature a bill is going to be introduced suggesting a farm hospital where the drug addict instead of being sent to prison where he mingles with all types of criminals would be committed to this farm hospital for a period of 1 year. During that time he would receive psychiatric treatment from the doctors in the hospital.

He would be allowed to work at farming to rebuild himself physically and we hope at the same time that we could set up an employment agency by the State where they could encourage employers to take a chance on these young people that have made a mistake by becoming drug addicts. A lot of employers today seem to think that a person who uses drugs is contagious with leprosy or something. They are afraid to take a chance on them.

We in the police department have obtained jobs for several drug addicts and in no case have they let us down. They have stayed away from drugs and they are working and we found by applying the human touch to these people that many of them can be rehabilitated.

Chairman KEFAUVER. Do you think by having someone that will stay in touch with them, show interest, either a police officer, psychiatrist, or psychologist or someone to counsel them to help them find employment, after they have been released from the farm or the institution that that would be a good help?

Lieutenant DRISCOLL. Yes, sir. That would help. They want to be made to feel that they belong as a member in society, a useful member and if they are made to feel that way, I am sure that most of the young addicts can be rehabilitated and take their place in society as a successful useful citizen.

Chairman KEFAUVER. Have you substantially reduced the amount of addiction or the number of crimes by addicts in Philadelphia during your program?

Lieutenant DRISCOLL. Yes, sir. During 1955 Commissioner of Police Thomas J. Gibbons announced figures that crime was reduced 28 percent and he attributed it mostly to those mass narcotic raids of getting the drug pushers off the street. The number of total arrests for sale, possession, and use in 1956 will be about half the total of the arrests made in 1953, 1954, and 1955. So we feel our program of mass arrests is beginning to pay off.

Chairman KEFAUVER. How many people have you added to the narcotics squad to accomplish this?

Lieutenant DRISCOLL. In 1952 there were only six members in the narcotic squad. At the present time there are 35 members in the narcotic unit.

Chairman KEFAUVER. So that backing up the enforcement division is one of the good things to do in a city?

Lieutenant DRISCOLL. Yes, sir. I think that Mr. Neeb who testified this morning that 50 percent of our problem is to eliminate the pusher of drugs and I firmly believe in that.

Chairman KEFAUVER. Thank you very much, Lieutenant Driscoll, Inspector Driscoll, for your appearance.

Lieutenant DRISCOLL. Thank you.

Chairman KEFAUVER. We also want to express our appreciation to the prosecutor, Mr. Victor Blanc for his cooperation. He was in Newark with us.

Lieutenant DRISCOLL. I might say the success of the mass raids is also due to the fine cooperation of Mr. Blanc's office and the cooperation of the courts.

Mr. Blanc has saw fit that immediately after these mass raids that all the persons arrested have been held under high bail. That they are brought to trial quickly and in the cases of the drug pusher who is not a user, that long prison sentences are meted out and we have received splendid cooperation from his office and from the courts in enforcing the laws.

Chairman KEFAUVER. All right, thank you very much.

Mr. MITLER. Dr. Lowry?

Chairman KEFAUVER. We will have a 10-minute recess at this time.

(Short recess.)

Senator LANGER (presiding). Call your next witness.

Mr. MITLER. Dr. Lowry, please.

TESTIMONY OF DR. JAMES LOWRY, MEDICAL OFFICER IN CHARGE, UNITED STATES PUBLIC HEALTH SERVICE HOSPITAL, LEXINGTON, KY.

Senator LANGER. Doctor, we are very happy to have you here.

Dr. LOWRY. Thank you, Senator Langer.

Mr. MITLER. Your name is James Lowry?

Dr. LOWRY. That is correct.

Mr. MITLER. What is your present position, Doctor?

Dr. LOWRY. I am medical officer in charge of the United States Public Health Service Hospital at Lexington, Ky.

Mr. MITLER. Can you briefly tell us your background prior to that?

Dr. LOWRY. I am a physician and I began work with narcotic addicts in 1938 when United States Public Health Service Hospital was opened in Fort Worth, Tex. I was chief of the psychiatric service at that hospital in 1943, clinical director of the United States Public Health Service Hospital in Lexington from 1943 to 1947 and I have been medical officer in charge since July 1954. From 1947 to 1954 I was chief of the community services branch of the National Institute of Mental Health. As such I initiated one part of the activities under the Mental Health Act which stand as a continuing tribute to Mr. Percy Priest. My medical specialty is psychiatry and I have been a diplomate of the American Board of Psychiatry since 1946.

Mr. MITLER. Your responsibility is that you are in charge of the medical staff at the United States Public Health Hospital at Lexington?

Dr. LOWRY. That's right.

Mr. MITLER. Would you tell us something about the hospital, what the program is and what the approaches of the hospital are toward the drug addict?

Dr. Lowry. Yes, I will be glad to do that. I want to say that what I do say today will be based on my experience with addicts at the hospitals at Lexington and Fort Worth and I think it should be remembered that the addicts admitted to the hospital there are not necessarily representative of the addicts in the United States, even though we admit about 3,000 a year. When I use the term addict I mean a person who is physically and psychologically dependent on an opiate drug or a synthetic drug with opiatelike properties.

I might say that in my presentation I am going to use tables and read from a paper which I have written and will be published shortly.

I ran across a quotation recently that explains why I do this. The quotation says:

In the excitement of the moment I am sure to say something which I will be sorry for when I see it in print,

so I have it here in black and white and there are no mistakes made.

People attach too much importance to what I say anyhow.

This was said by Mr. Lincoln.

I will tell you a little bit about our hospital at Lexington. It was opened in 1935. And it is located about 5 miles from the city of Lexington and has a functional capacity of about 1,200 patients. There are about 350 beds in the infirmary wards, medical surgical and psychiatric withdrawal, TB, and the rest of the beds are in dormitories.

The buildings are located on a 1,050-acre reservation and I might say that they are less prisonlike in appearance than most prisons and more prisonlike in appearance than most hospitals.

It is a minimum custody institution and about four Federal prisoners leave without authorization each year. The valid judgments of the patients who are there vary widely. Some of them regard it as very distasteful place to be living and others regard it as above what they have been used to.

I have for you a paper that contains most of this information.

However, I think I will go through some of the highlights of it. It has already been mentioned that we have voluntary patients who are admitted at their own request and we have authority to admit them if there are beds available after the Federal prisoners and probationers are accommodated.

And that is the way that the law reads.

These voluntary patients come into the hospital at their own request and they are free to leave the hospital when they make the decision. Of course we make every effort to point out to them the consequences of leaving if it appears to us that it is an inopportune time and they have not completed treatment.

I think some of the things that affect a hospital are the characteristics of the addict patients, and the addicts that we see at our hospital have changed over the years and I think one of the important items that I might bring to your attention is a comparison between the addict as he was seen at the hospital 20 years ago and as we see him today.

Mr. Milter. Would you make a special focus of your attention on those who are under 21 years old?

Dr. LOWRY. I certainly will. In 1936 Dr. Pescor published an article in which he spoke about a statistical addict and I compared this with a study of addicts we made in 1955. In 1936 the average addict was a white male prisoner 38 years of age who had a 2-year sentence. Today we find an average addict is a Negro male, voluntary patient who is in his twenties.

Chairman KEFAUVER. What would be the average age today?

Dr. LOWRY. He would be a Negro male in his twenties. His average was 38 20 years ago. Dr. Pescor found that his addict patients had intact homes up to 18. The patients we see today don't come from intact homes. Most of them can't remember seeing their father and their mother was usually working as a domestic.

Mr. CHUMBRIS. You said the age of 38?

Dr. LOWRY. That's right.

Mr. CHUMBRIS. Then you say in the twenties. Can you be more specific as to where in the twenties?

Dr. LOWRY. I will cover that point more thoroughly in a minute. The addict today becomes addicted to heroin usually in his early twenties, 20 years ago he became addicted to morphine late in his twenties. They used to prefer morphine and now they prefer heroin. Twenty years ago the patients had a number of chronic illnesses. Now we find they are an essentially healthy adult, young male population.

I think one of the changes that I have remarked on and I touched on briefly a moment ago was the change that is reflected in the increase in the number of young Negro addicts. I think I should bring out here that at the hospital we receive male addicts from east of the Mississippi River and women addicts from anywhere in the United States. What we have seen in the recent past, and by that I mean the last 6 or 7 years, is an increase in the young Negro addict. Whereas in 1935 the Negroes constituted 9 percent of the population at the hospital, now they account for over 50 percent. Now the age distribution of the white males at the hospital is similar to what it was 20 years ago. If you divide the white patients by decades, you will find that there are as many in the 20, 30, 40, and 50 as there were 20 years ago and the distribution is about equal. However, if you look at the Negro males you will find that 70 percent of the Negroes that we had in the hospital last year were under the age of 30. This same thing holds true for both men and women addicts at the hospital.

In Pescor's study fortunately he inquired as to the age of onset of the use of drugs. And I might point out that in 1936 he found that 16½ percent of the addicts said they began to use narcotic drugs at age of 18 or younger. In a study of a similar group which was prisoner addict patients at Lexington, in 1955 and 1956 we found out that 45 percent said they began using narcotic drugs at age 19 and under.

So you see there has been a shift there in the 20-to-29-age group in 1936, about half of the patients started and in 1955–56, 45 percent. So that you see by the age of 29 then there are 89.6 percent of the patients have started using drugs these present days.

I brought some figures for you so I could tell you what our experience has been with young addicts in the last 5 years. We have information covering this period. If you look at the addicts who were

18 years or under who were admitted to the hospital in the past 5 years, you will find that the first admission run like this: 1952, 46; 1953, 49; 1954, 60; 1955, 25; and 1956, 25. In other words we have 199 young, age 18, 17, 16, addicts at the hospital in the past 5 years.

Of these 199, 15 were readmitted during that period.

When I looked at the race distribution of these 199, I found out that 112 were Negro and 87 were white. You will recall I said that the males come from east of the Mississippi and the women from the entire country. If you look at the State of origin of these addicts 18 years of age and younger, you find that they come from New York, Illinois, and the District of Columbia. There were 59 from New York, 59 from Illinois, and 18 from the District of Columbia, and then there is a scatter from a fairly good number of large States each contributing 2, 3, 4, or 5. I can pinpoint this a little further for you. They not only come from New York but they come from New York City. There are studies that show they come from specific neighborhoods in New York City and these studies further show that they come from broken homes in these particular cases. I am sure you have had that testimony in New York.

Chairman KEFAUVER. Very few come from farming districts, is that right?

Dr. LOWRY. I could run through this: Georgia 2 in 5 years, Indiana, 4 in 5 years; Iowa, 2; Kentucky, 2; I don't see any from the Dakotas at all.

Mr. MITLER. While I was in Lexington, you told me something about the difference in the makeup of addicts who come from large cities and those who come from less densely populated areas. I think that would be interesting.

Dr. LOWRY. I probably mentioned to you that we see our Negroes coming from the large northern cities and a great many of the whites coming from smaller towns and rural areas in the South.

Mr. MITLER. Are there some professional men that come from the smaller communities? I think you mentioned something of that nature.

Dr. LOWRY. We admit about 40 physicians a year and I do not have a study showing where they come from; I don't know whether they come from the city or the country.

You may be interested in knowing that of these 199, 18 years old and younger, that 116 of them were voluntary patients and 83 came as prisoners or probationers.

Mr. MITLER. Dr. Lowry, could I ask you a few questions about the volunteers? I think it is significant to know whether the volunteers stay as long as they should or whether they leave prematurely to get the full benefit of your program.

Dr. LOWRY. I can give you some figures on that and there will be a chart in this material that I will submit and I can tell you what our experience has been because we have studied it each year for the last several years.

Mr. MITLER. Surely.

Dr. LOWRY. Let us take the male addict voluntary patients. For instance, a study of 765 who left the hospital between January and June 1955 showed that 25 percent of these voluntary patients left the hospitals within 7 days of the time of their admission. This is almost the same as saying that they were still in the withdrawal period and receiving narcotic drugs when they left. In addition a number left, so by the end of 2 weeks 40 percent of the voluntary patients had left the hospital and by the end of 30 days 55 percent had left the hospital. By this time, by the end of 30 days the patient is no longer receiving institution treatment. That is completed ordinarily in 7, 10, 14 days. He is beginning to get his appetite back and sleep better, but you cannot say that he has no clinical signs of abstinence remaining.

Mr. MITLER. How long do you require the volunteer to stay at the hospital to get some benefit from the program?

Dr. LOWRY. I think if we are discussing only the physiological program from addiction, I would say a period of 3 to 4 months is a minimum time to obtain physical return to normal. In the same period, the vocational rehabilitation and psychological rehabilitation can occur, but this will have to be carried on after the patient has left the hospital. We have learned to not use the word "cure" when we refer to narcotic addict patients who are leaving the hospital. If they stay until such a time as we feel they are ready to return to their home community, we group them in a class called hospital treatment completed, so that no one will get the idea that this is the end of the treatment process, what happens to those that are there at the end of 30 days, if an addict, voluntary addict is in the hospital at the end of 30 days, the chances are very good he will stay until the physician says he is ready to go home.

Mr. MITLER. Now, the word "blue grass law" has been mentioned. Could you explain what that is, and how that used to affect the volunteers?

Dr. LOWRY. The blue grass law is a Kentucky statute which says it is a crime to be an addict in Kentucky and if an individual goes to a police officer and says he is an addict, he can be taken into court and given a sentence. I believe the sentence is limited to 1 year and the courts can probate this sentence on condition, well, they can put any conditions they want to but they frequently make it a condition that the patients be treated for an addiction and remain in treatment until he is discharged. In the past we have had a number of addict patients admitted to the hospital under this procedure. However, we were informed, I think it was about two and a half years ago, that it was improper to require a person to go through with that, what amounts to a criminal procedure to be admitted to the hospital as voluntary patient.

Actually the blue grass law, there is something akin to it in many States, where a State court can probate a sentence on certain conditions and the patients could come to the hospital.

We find a number of addict patients who have been in the hospital and who have found that they can't stay once they come in, who have of their own accord come into the city of Lexington and gone to the court, got a sentence and come to the hospital because then the decision is out of their hands as to whether they will stay or not.

Those persons are decreasing in number in the past several years.

Mr. MITLER. Dr. Lowry, what is the program with respect to psychotherapy in the hospital? What services are offered there?

Dr. LOWRY. Well, I will start with the newly admitted patient. When he comes into the hospital, he is on the withdrawal ward for a

couple of weeks and then he goes to an orientation ward. While he is
there if he stays in the hospital, he is interviewed by a psychiatric
social worker, vocational rehabilitation officer, and a psychiatrist, and
then a report is compiled on this patient and the psychiatrist, the administrative physician discusses this with the senior psychiatrist and
the treatment program for that patient is discussed and the patient is
brought in and his program outlined for him.

This program will vary from one patient to another. It depends
on a number of factors. The motivation of the ptiaent, the staff
available, the treatment facilities available, but the patient may be
offered individual psychotherapy, group psychotherapy. He is also
given vocational therapy and social casework is done. With some it
is more and with some it is less. I think it is only fair to point out
to you that what I said this morning, we had 1,178 patients in the hospital, but 125 of those are nonaddicts, psychotic patients, and that
leaves about 1,050 patients.

We have a limited staff. With physicians, we have a limited staff of
social workers and psychologists, and I think if every physician on the
staff worked 50 hours a week and spent all of his time working with
patients that he would be able to devote—each patient would get less
than 1 hour per week.

When I say physicians, I include all of them in the hospital, even
those that devote all their time to the medical and surgical services.

Mr. MITLER. Dr. Lowry, you do have some of the 18- and 19-year-
old group at the hospital.

Dr. LOWRY. Yes; we have 18 years old, 19 and 20.

Mr. MITLER. What is your opinion about the feasibility, the problem of having those youngsters who are volunteers in the same group
and commingling with some older Federal narcotic prisoners?

Do you think that is any kind of a problem?

Dr. LOWRY. I think there are advantages and disadvantages to this
situation. If you ask whether it would be practical to separate them
I would have to say no. If you only admit 25 such persons a year
at any one time there wouldn't be more than 10 in the hospital. As
I pointed out earlier today to someone we have more physicians in the
hospital than we have juvenile addicts in the hospital. From a practical standpoint this could not be done. I will say this, the 18-, 19-,
and 20-year-old addict is a much more difficult patient to handle than
an older person. We know what the normal adolescent is like. We
have lived through it ourselves, and we have had children. They
are in a difficult period, and added onto that they are disturbed people. I think while we often think of what happens to the younger
person, I think we should not forget the impact of these younger
people in their behavior on the older person in the hospital.

Mr. MITLER. Do you think that some of the volunteers who might
potentially or some people who might be addicts who might want to
come as volunteers would be reluctant to go because they might be
apprehensive of being commingled with Federal prisoners?

Dr. LOWRY. I think this might be a problem with some people.
However, I think it might be worth pointing out, each year we admit
2,500 voluntary patients and 500 prisoners, and it certainly has not
deterred the 2,500 from coming in.

Mr. MITLER. Could you tell us about the question of the followup or aftercare program what your opinion is of the existing facilities on that score?

Dr. LOWRY. I can tell you what we do.

Our vocational training and our social work services and our physicians attempt to help the patient develop a posthospital plan. We have no facilities and no authority to work with the patient after they leave the hospital. They are in a sense temporary residents with us. They come from a community, they stay with us and they go back to a community. We try and prepare them for going back to the community. We correspond with employment agencies, we try to get them a place to live, and we can do this with the Federal prisoners through the probation officers, but I think this is one of the areas where we are unable to do as much as should be done.

Frankly, there is a provision in the law that says that the record of voluntary patients is confidential, and shall not be divulged. We do divulge their presence in the hospital if they will sign a request that we correspond with persons in order to be of help to them. We do this and we try and work out a plan for every patient that we can.

Mr. MITLER. Dr. Lowry, do you have available, is there any study of fitness to indicate the degree of success at Lexington that they have had with respect to the patients.

Dr. LOWRY. I can tell you that there is a study that has been made on the followup patients that left Lexington. I heard someone say this morning that some percentage of patients did or did not relapse from the use of narcotics drugs. I would like to know what the basis is for those figures. I don't know of any such figures. Pescor made a study back in 1935 and his results have been published. Let me see here, he studies 4,766 patients who were discharged from 1936 to 1940. He did this in various ways. He felt this method which he used, he used the FBI records, probation officers, also anyway to make contact with them. He felt this method was crude and I am inclined to agree with him, since he could only obtain information on 60 percent of the group. He did determine that 39.9 percent had relapsed in periods varying from 6 months to 6 years. And he found that the parole prisoners made the best record.

The parole prisoners are a selected group. He has to have a plan, he has to have a job, he has to have a place to live and he has to have a parole adviser. It is not surprising that this was the group that did the best.

All we can really tell from our standpoint at the hospital is whether a patient returns to the hospital. I can tell you what our experience is with that.

The fact that he does not return to the hospital does not mean that he is not using narcotic drugs.

Mr. MITLER. Dr. Lowry, apart from Lexington, would you mind if I asked you about your reaction to what Dr. Brown had to say while I was there or do you feel that was not in accord with the testimony? You remember the man from Singapore.

Dr. LOWRY. Oh, the visitor from Singapore.

Mr. MITLER. I was going to ask your reaction to that if that would be beyond the purview of your testimony. He stated in Singapore he was a director of the medical center there and that the opium, the distribution of opium was made unlawful and narcotic squads were set up in Singapore and before that there had been no racketeering and gangsterism. Prior to that the drug addicts were able to get a card which permitted them to go to a center and get the opium. And after the opium was made unlawful there was gangsterism and heavy trafficking in drugs.

I thought you might have some reaction to that.

I thought it was rather interesting.

Dr. LOWRY. I feel perfectly free to say that the information that Dr. Brown gave was very interesting but I find that I don't have any need to comment on it, because I don't know the facts about the real situation. This is not a medical problem.

Mr. MITLER. I see.

Just one other question, I would like to ask, that was the question of it, you have been also to Fort Worth and to Lexington.

Dr. LOWRY. Yes, I have been at both places on two different details.

Mr. MITLER. Do you feel there is any difference in atmosphere between the fact that Fort Worth seems to be more oriented toward a mental hospital, that there is any greater value to that? In other words there are not the same number of bars?

Dr. LOWRY. I think you will have to remember this, that both of them are prison hospitals, because there are prisoners there. Both have Federal prisons. The tradition at Lexington is a little different. It was started in 1935 and it was opened by having a number of prisoner addicts transferred from Federal penitentiaries and there were a lot of custody features that were set up then that we no longer utilize.

I am sure a person who had not been there in 20 years would be very surprised. All through the years there have been prisoners.

When Fort Worth was opened in 1938, the same thing occurred but it was a little different. The patients came from Lexington, the first group to Fort Worth and in the few years that Lexington had been opened a good deal was learned about the discipline and treatment of addicts. Then the population of addicts didn't get very large at Fort Worth before World War II broke out and if you will recall during the war the hospital at Fort Worth treated patients who were psychiatric casualties from the Navy and Marine Corps in the Pacific so there were relatively few addicts at the end of the war and that the number of addicts in the hospital—and by the way the figure at present is about 300—has increased gradually over the past few years.

This does bring a somewhat different orientation. Here you have a large number of nonaddict patients and a small number of patients. At our hospital we have a large number of addicts and a small number of nonaddict patients.

People have attitudes about the mentally ill and they have attitudes about narcotic programs. There is a difference I am sure in appearance. Fort Worth is a fine white brick hospital sitting on top of a hill. Lexington is sort of a darker brick, red, and it looks a little bit formidable.

I will say this, I think our staff at Lexington is as well qualified—although I wouldn't want this repeated, I think just a little better than they have at Fort Worth.

Mr. MITLER. I interrupted you while you were going through the statement. Are there additional things you want to bring out about the program at Lexington?

Dr. Lowry. I think it might be important to repeat something I said before. There are a good many illusions about the number of times patients are treated at Lexington. We made a study last year of the patients who had been in the hospital from 1935 to 1952, that is about 17,000 different patients, and we found that 64 percent of these 17,000 were treated in the hospital once and have not returned, that is they had from 3 to 20 years to return and had never returned. Another 2 percent came back a second time and did not come back a third time and so you see that there are 86 percent that have come into the hospital once or twice and have not come back.

There is a small segment that constitutes 3½ percent of the 17,000 that accounts for over 23 percent of the admissions to the hospital. These are the people that create the illusion like the small army that is in the theater; it consists of 6 men coming out in front and going behind the scenery and coming out again and this is where the impression comes that everybody is a repeater, when actually the number that come more than twice is relatively small.

Mr. Chumbris. Let me get that figure correct. Three and a half percent constitutes approximately 25 percent or about 4,200 of 17,000; is that about right?

Dr. Lowry. Three and a half percent of the patients account for 25 percent of the admissions.

Mr. Chumbris. That's right. That would mean of the 17,000 admissions?

Dr. Lowry. No, I am talking about 17,000 different patients. The actual number of admissions I think runs up to close to 40,000. I can give you that figure. I don't have it at my fingertips.

Mr. Chumbris. How much does it cost the patient per year at Lexington, would you say?

Dr. Lowry. It costs about $6.70 per day.

Mr. Chumbris. How much?

Dr. Lowry. $6.70 per day.

Mr. Chumbris. And how do you fare as far as appropriations are concerned? Do you feel that your appropriations meet the particular problem that you have at Lexington?

Dr. Lowry. We have limitations that I think are important; however, I feel that it is, well, somewhat unfair to ask me to comment on this particular question. I think this is something that you should ask of the persons in the headquarters at the service.

Mr. Chumbris. If you don't feel like you want to answer the question. The reason is this: There was a suggestion made earlier that we have more regional clinics or hospitals to take care of these addicts where the Federal Government and the States can coordinate their activity and send the boys and men to these various institutions. I just wanted to get a line on the cost of such a program if we had more regional institutions for the care of the addicts.

Dr. Lowry. You will find the cost at Riverside is approximately $30 a day.

Mr. Chumbris. How about Fort Worth? Do you know what the cost is there?

Dr. Lowry. There it would be about the same as ours.

Senator Langer. How do you arrange about these volunteers? How do they pay?

Dr. Lowry. The voluntary patients fill out an application and he has to list his income and assets on the application and the determination is made as to whether they can pay for their care. We collect a few thousands of dollars a year and most of the money that is collected comes from the physicians who are pay patients and their wives, some of the women come in and their husbands pay for their care in the hospital.

Senator Langer. Any further questions?

Mr. Chumbris. Mr. Winick testified as to the advantages of psychotherapy in the treatment of an addict. Now, first what is your impression of his testimony as to the psychotherapeutic treatment in his rehabilitation?

Dr. Lowry. All I can say is that I listened with a great deal of interest to the results of the program that they have started and he gave some figures that a certain number came to the clinic, I believe it was 70, and of those 35 remained in treatment or initiated treatment and he then went on to say that 80 percent of those that continued in treatment appeared to be moving toward recovery.

I find this a very interesting experiment and I am glad to know that someone is dealing with this group on this basis and will come up with some results that can be examined.

Mr. Chumbris. If funds were made available to your institution, do you think such a plan could be inaugurated at Lexington?

Dr. Lowry. We already have a good deal of psychotherapy, both group and individual, going on, but the limiting factor there is the availability of trained staff to do this. At the present time we have vacancies for psychiatrists, we have vacancies for social workers and they are very difficult to find.

If somebody talks about setting up a regional hospital, they are going to have to remember they will need a staff to be in that hospital and they are very difficult to come by. Especially at this time.

Mr. Chumbris. Then you have the same problem we find in many of our Federal institutions, that it is not so much the limitation of funds as it is the limitation of qualified personnel.

Dr. Lowry. I didn't say we didn't have any limitation on funds. I said we had a limitation on personnel.

Mr. Chumbris. That is what I say. In many institutions we found throughout the country like the Federal prisons and correctional institutions that they can't find a sufficient number of psychologists and mental hygienists and psychiatrists and so forth to fill the necessary positions if the funds were made available to them.

Dr. Lowry. I understand that is a universal difficulty.

Senator Langer. Any further questions.

Mr. Mitler. I want to incorporate in the record the statement and material that Dr. Lowry has. It is subcommittee exhibit No. 8.

Senator Langer. That will be made part of the record.

(The document referred to was marked "Subcommittee Exhibit No. 8" and is as follows:)

U. S. Public Health Service Hospital, Lexington, Ky.

First admission and readmission of 18 years and under, June 30, 1951–June 30, 1956

Year	1st admission	Readmission	Total
1952	40	3	43
1953	49	0	49
1954	60	7	67
1955	25	3	28
1956	25	2	27
Total (5 years)	199	15	214

First admission, 18 years and under, by race and sex, June 30, 1951–June 30, 1956

Year	Negro		White		Total
	Male	Female	Male	Female	
1952	28	0	12	0	40
19"3	24	4	20	1	49
19"4	20	10	11	19	60
1955	11	3	11	0	25
1956	9	3	9	4	25
Total	92	20	63	24	199
	112		87		

First admission, 18 years and under, by State, June 30, 1951–June 30, 1956

State	Year					Total
	1952	1953	1954	1955	1956	
California	1	0	5	0	1	7
District of Columbia	2	7	3	5	1	18
Georgia	0	0	1	0	1	2
Illinois	5	23	15	7	9	59
Indiana	2	0	2	0	0	4
Iowa	2	0	0	0	0	2
Kentucky	0	1	1	0	0	2
Louisiana	2	0	3	0	0	5
Maryland	1	0	1	2	0	4
Michigan	3	0	1	1	2	7
Miss"uri	0	0	2	1	2	5
New Jersey	0	0	2	0	0	2
New York	19	12	17	7	4	59
Ohio	2	4	2	1	1	10
Pennsylvania	1	1	3	0	1	6
Puerto Rico	0	0	0	1	2	3
Total	40	49	60	25	25	199

First admission, 18 years and under, by status, June 30, 1951–June 30, 1956

Year	Voluntary	Involuntary	Total
1952	32	8	40
1953	36	13	49
1954	7	53	60
1955	21	4	25
1956	20	5	25
Total (5 years)	116	83	199

HOSPITAL TREATMENT OF THE NARCOTIC ADDICT

(By James V. Lowry, M. D., medical officer in charge, United States Public
Health Service Hospital, Lexington, Ky.)

The treatment of a hospitalized narcotic drug addict is a relatively simple
and a relatively complex procedure. Treatment of the physical addiction resulting from the pharmacological properties of the opiates is relatively simple.
Treatment of the psychological addiction and of the basic mental disorder is
relatively complex.

This paper will discuss the treatment of addicts at the United States Public
Health Service Hospital at Lexington, Ky., and the characteristics of the addicts
as they are seen at that hospital. It must be remembered that the addicts
admitted to the hospital are not necessarily representative of addicts in the
United States even though about 3,000 are admitted each year. No attempt
will be made to explain some of the observations because the explanation must
be arrived at by studies that cannot be done at the hospital. The word "addict"
when used in this paper means a person who is physically and psychologically
addicted to an opiate drug or a synthetic drug with opiate-like properties
and who is or has been a patient at the hospital.

Why hospitalize addicts? It is expensive and requires specialized facilities
and scarce personnel. The primary purpose is to provide an opportunity for
treatment of the addict patient. Recovery from physical addiction can be
attained in a few months in a drug-free environment with modern methods even
if only passive cooperation of the patient is obtained. This is important because
the continued use of narcotic drugs by an addict is in part due to physiological
drives resulting from physical dependence. Hospitalization provides the opportunity to initiate or complete treatment of the psychological addiction and to
begin social and vocational rehabilitation. This requires active participation
of the patient. And therein lies the difficulty.

Hospitalization removes the addict from the environment that nurtured his
addiction to an environment where the use of narcotic drugs is controlled. This
is important not only to the person who lives in deteriorated metropolitan areas
where drugs are available but also to the nurse or physician addicts who have
access to drugs as an ordinary part of their occupations.

Hospitalization is a public health measure that prevents the spread of addiction by isolating a principal agent of dissemination—the narcotic addict. A
common method of introduction to the use of narcotic drugs of addicts at the
hospital was by another addict. This was often done by nonpeddler addicts
giving drugs to a nonaddict for psychological reasons that are difficult to understand. Some addicts were introduced to drugs by other addicts who sold drugs
for profit used principally to support their own addiction. Isolation to prevent
the spread of disease could be accomplished by means other than hospitalization
but this has been the accepted medical procedure for isolating sick people.

Some of the patients admitted to the hospital began their addiction in the
course of treatment of an illness by a physician. Hospitalization provides an
opportunity to terminate the addiction in those whose initiating illness is no
longer present. If the initiating illness is still present, hospitalization and
treatment can result in a reduction in the dosage of narcotic drug or in most
instances an elimination of the use of narcotic drugs because of improvement
resulting from specific treatment of the disease.

The hospital, located about 5 miles from Lexington, Ky., was opened in 1935.
The functional capacity is about 1,200 patients. Three hundred and fifty of
the 1,300 beds are in the infirmary wards—medical, surgical, psychiatric, tuberculosis, and withdrawal. The rest of the beds are in dormitories. The buildings
are surrounded by 1,050 acres of land and are less prison-like in appearance than
most prisons and more prison-like than most hospitals. It is a minimum custody
hospital and about four prisoners depart without authorization each year.
One patient was overheard telling a newcomer who was complaining about the
accommodations, "Dis place is a boid's nest on da ground."

GENERAL INFORMATION ABOUT THE UNITED STATES PUBLIC HEALTH SERVICE HOSPITAL
AT LEXINGTON [1]

The hospital is authorized by law to treat Federal prisoners and probationers,
addicts committed from the District of Columbia, and voluntary patients who

---

[1] This information is available from the hospital in a pamphlet entitled "Information
for Prospective Voluntary Patients."

are addicted to narcotic drugs as defined in the Federal law. These include cocaine, codeine, dihydromorphinone (dilaudid), heroin, Indian hemp (marihuana), laudanum, meperidine (demerol), methadone (dolophine), metopon, morphine, opium, pantopon, paregoric, peyote (mescaline), and any other narcotic drug, the sale of which is under the Federal Narcotic Act. Persons addicted to barbiturates, alcohol, or other drugs are not eligible for admission unless they are also addicted to a narcotic drug.

The prisoner addicts are sent to the hospital by the Bureau of Prisons after conviction in a Federal court. Escape risks, persons with marked antisocial records prior to addiction and persons otherwise unsuitable are not sent to the hospital. Most of the prisoners have been convicted of violating the narcotic law but some are convicted of stealing and forging Government checks or other crimes.

The probationers from Federal courts and committed patients from courts of the District of Columbia are required to remain in the hospital until treatment is completed and are under supervision after return to their home community.

Voluntary patients are admitted at their own request if beds are available after eligible prisoners and probationers have been admitted. Federal law provides that the record of admission, treatment, and discharge of a voluntary patient shall be confidential and shall not be divulged and that such voluntary patient shall not forfeit nor abridge his rights as a citizen of the United States, nor shall such treatment be used against him in any proceedings in court. However, the hospital does not furnish refuge for known fugitives from justice. Voluntary patients able to pay are charged $7 per day for their hospitalization. Application forms are obtained from the hospital and when completed are mailed directly to the hospital. About 250 applications are received each month. The applicant is advised by letter that either he is to report to the hospital by a certain date, that his name is being placed on a waiting list and he will be notified when a bed is available, or that he is not eligible for treatment. Separate waiting lists are maintained for men and women. Letters of authorization are sent out in the order of receipt of the applications. The Lexington hospital accepts female from any State and males from east of the Mississippi River, Male patients from west of the river usually are treated at the United States Public Health Service Hospital in Fort Worth, Tex. Applicants should not go to either hospital until they receive a letter of authorization. Patients who present themselves without written notification may not be admitted.

Clothing is furnished to patients while they are in the hospital. They can bring their own house slippers, black or brown shoes, solid color sweater and plain socks. Prisoners are required to send other clothing home or donate it to the hospital. Suitable clothing and a $25 gratuity are provided at the time of discharge if the prisoner is indigent. The hospital provides transportation home for prisoners, probationers, and those indigent voluntary patients who stay until hospital treatment is completed.

Patients may correspond with relatives and other persons approved by the hospital staff; outgoing letters are limited to two per week. Mail is opened and read. Patients may receive telegrams but not telephone calls. Outgoing telegrams and telephone calls are restricted to emergencies. Money sent to the hospital for deposit in a patient's account must be in the form of certified check or postal money order. Commissary facilities at the hospital sell cigarettes, candy and small articles purchasable with coupons from commissary books.

Men and women have quarters in separate parts of the hospital. There is no separation of patients by race or age, of prisoners, probationery, voluntary or District of Columbia committed patients.

THE ADDICT PATIENT

The important characteristics of addiction to opiate drugs are physical and psychological addiction. Physical addiction to opiate drugs is characterized by two unique phenomena. One of these is well known—physical dependence. Repeated intake of opiate drugs results in physiological changes which produce characteristic abstinence signs and symptoms when the opiate is discontinued. The other phenomenon, tolerance, is equally important. Repeated intake of opiate drugs results in the development of tolerance to some of the drugs's effects—the analgesic, euphoric, and sedative effects which are all-important to the addict. Little tolerance is developed to the gastro-intestinal or pupillary effects. Because of the development of tolerance the physiology of the addict requires increasing amounts of narcotic drugs to obtain the desired effects. For this reason it is very difficult for addicts with physical dependence to stabilize on a maintenance dose. Physical dependence and tolerance appear to be related to changes in the sympathetic and central nervous systems[2] and in the endocrine glands.[3] Changes in function associated with physical dependence may include cessation of menstruation in women and disinterest in sexual activity with impotence in the male. Meperidine (demerol) in addition to the usual effects of opiates produces impaired vision, mental confusion, and sometimes convulsions.[4] About 50 percent of the meperidine addicts admitted in a 3-year period were physicians, nurses or other persons associated with the medical profession.[5]

Why did the patients continue to use narcotic drugs once the introduction had been made? The answer varied with the particular individual. For some persons narcotic drugs provided an escape from anxiety, loneliness, despair, frustration, anger or hostility into a placid world of unreality. For some narcotic usage was the ultimate in hedonistic experiences which combined the pleasures that other persons derive from work, love of wife, family, or friends, personal or group accomplishments, or service to others. For others the intravenous injection of narcotics provided the ecstasy of the adult at orgasm and the somnifacient satisfaction of the satiated infant at the breast. The addict with his narcotic drug had little interest in any person, belief or thing; an addict without drugs was principally interested in obtaining a supply. This motivation for drug usage has to be replaced by a desire to live without narcotic drugs if treatment is to be successful.

Addiction to opiates, as stated above, is characterized by physical and psychological addiction. The psychological addiction is related to the basic mental disorder of the patient. A few patients are admitted to the hospital who have physical addiction without psychological addiction. They usually developed their addiction in the course of treatment of some physical disease.

In addition to the diagnosis of drug addiction there is usually enough information derived from diagnostic studies to establish the presence of a mental disorder. Kolb[6] and later Felix[7] developed classification systems of these disorders that were operationally useful. These have been superseded by utilization of the nomenclature in the Diagnostic and Statistical Manual of Mental Disorders, of the American Psychiatric Association, published in 1952. The mental disorders most frequently present are personality trait disturbances, sociopathic personality disturbances, psychoneurotic disorders, and personality pattern disturbances. Occasionally patients are admitted with schizophrenic or affective reactions.

Personality trait and sociopathic personality disturbances are present in the patients hospitalized here with progressively increasing frequency. These individuals appear to be the products of a disorder of maturation in emotional development. The behavior shown by such persons indicates that development is fragmentary and may include behavior that would be normal for an infant, a young child, a preadolescent, and adolescent all in the same person. At different times or at the same time they may be dependent, demanding, narcissistic, stubborn, pouting, passively obstructive, have temper tantrums. Today is the reality in time. Some have acted out their feelings in a manner that brings them into conflict with their immediate family, group, or with society.

The personal history of many of these patients shows the absence of the father or a weak father and/or mother during the patient's childhood. The failure of emotional maturation may be related to this absence of any constant person with whom identification could occur. If there was no chance of identification then there could be no introjection and formation of internalized emotional control and growth. With some patients identification and introjection may have occurred, but it was an unhealthy person that served as the model.

Some of the most interesting and unexplained phenomena observed at this hospital are the remarkable changes in the characteristics of the "typical" addict,

[2] Wikler, A.: Recent Progress in Research on the Neurophysiological Basis of Morphine Addition. Am. J. Psych. 105 : 329, 1948.
[3] Eisenman, A. J., Isbell, H., Fraser, H. F., and Sloan, J.: 17—Ketosteroid Excretion in a Cycle of Morphine Addiction and Withdrawal. Fed. Prof. 12 : 200, 1953.
[4] Isbell, H., and Fraser, H. F.: Addiction to Analgesics and Barbiturates. J. Pharmacol. and Exper. Therap. 99 : 355–397, August 1950.
[5] Rasor, R., and Crecraft, H. J.: Addiction to Meperidine (Demerol) Hydrochloride, J. A. M. A. 157 : 654–657, February, 1955.
[6] Kolb, L.: Types and Characteristics of Drug Addicts. Mental Hygiene, 9: 300–313, (April) 1925.
[7] Felix, R. H.: An Appraisal of the Personality Types of the Addict. American Journal of Psychiatry, 1 : 462–467, 1944.

if one can use such a concept. The 1955 model addict differs from the 1936 "statistical addict" described in Pescor's study of a thousand admissions.[8] He isn't a "white male prisoner 38 years of age given a 2-year sentence for illegal sale of narcotics." He is a Negro male voluntary patient in his twenties. He didn't have a parental home "intact up to the age of 18." He probably can't remember seeing his father, and his mother was away trying to earn a living as a domestic. He wouldn't "become addicted to morphine at the age of 27." He would start on heroin at about age 20. He would not "prefer morphine." He would prefer heroin. His first arrest would not "occur at the age of 28 for violation of drug laws." He would be a young voluntary patient whose FBI record could not be requested by the hospital. He would not "as an adult be subject to some chronic disease, such as heart trouble, arthritis, tuberculosis, or asthma." He would be free of such afflictions.

These considerations of the characteristics of the addict and of addiction must be given consideration in the planning and organization of a treatment program.

CHARACTERISTIC OF THE HOSPITAL ADDICT POPULATION [9]

The average daily population of addicts in the hospital has varied relatively little over the years, but significant changes have occurred in its composition. The average daily population was near 900 from 1945 to 1949. From 1950 to 1955 it has been about 1,100 except for 1951 and 1953, when it was about 1,200. Prior to 1946 there were less than 100 voluntary patients in the hospital. This daily average increased each year until the high points of over 600 in 1951 and 1953. A rapid fall in 1954 to 400 was followed by a decline to 328 in 1955. There has been a gradual decline in probationers in the hospital from a high of 86 in 1947 to 18 in 1955. The number of prisoners has varied from a high of almost 900 in 1944 to a low of 492 in 1952 and a steady increase to 732 in 1955. (See graph, Average Daily Population.)

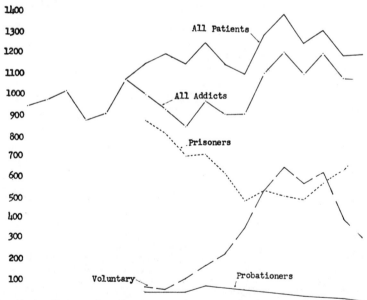

AVERAGE DAILY POPULATION
1938-1955
U.S. Public Health Service Hospital
Lexington, Kentucky

---

[8] Pescor, M. J.: A Statistical Analysis of the Clinical Records of Hospitalized Drug Addicts. Supplement No. 143 to the Public Health Reports, 1943.
[9] The basic data used in this part were provided by Mary L. Tonks, Medical Record Librarian, and Walter K. McCurry, Administrative Assistant.

The annual admission rate has varied considerably in the last 10 years. A rise from 1,753 in 1946 to 4,166 in 1953 was followed by a decline to 2,848 in 1955. The changes were due to the fluctuations in the annual rates of admission of voluntary patients—from less than 1,000 per year prior to 1946 to a high of 3,499 in 1953 and then down to 2,231 in 1955. The admission rate for prisoners has been fairly constant. The annual admission rate of probationers has declined steadily from a high of 222 in 1947 to a low of 53 in 1955. (Se graph, Annual Admissions.)

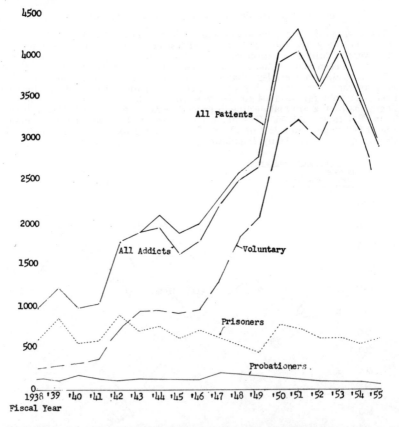

ANNUAL ADMISSIONS
1938-1955
U.S. Public Health Service Hospital
Lexington, Kentucky.

One of the changes in the addict population in the hospital is the increase in number of young Negro addicts. In Pescor's [8] 1936 series there was 8.9 percent Negroes. In 1955 the percentage was 52 percent. The age distribution of the white males in 1936 and 1955 was similar—a fairly equal distribution by decades from 20 to 60. In the 1955 study 70 percent of the Negro males were under age 30 as compared with 27 percent of the white males. A study of 347 females discharged in 1955 showed that 48 percent were Negro and 85 percent of these were under age 30 with no female Negro over 40. The white females, like the white males, were fairly evenly distributed by decades from 20 to 60. (See graph, Age and Race: Male Addicts.)

AGE AND RACE: Male Addicts
964 Discharged January — June 1955
U.S.Public Health Service Hospital
Lexington, Kentucky.

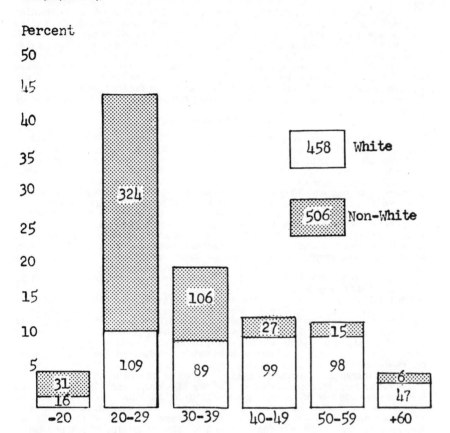

Age in years on admission

Since Pescor's 1936 group was mostly prisoners, a study was made of the medical records of prisoners to obtain information on the age of onset of addiction as given by the patient.   The data on the first 200 prisoners admitted in 1955 and the first 100 admitted in 1956 are compared with Pescor's findings:

Age of onset of addiction

[Percent]

	1936	1955-56
19 and under	16. 5	45. 0
20 to 29	53. 2	44. 6
30 to 39	21. 1	7. 6
40 and over	8. 9	2. 6
Not given	. 3	

These findings are in keeping with the age on first admission to the hospital of male addicts in 1955; 65 percent were 30 and under.

There has been a decrease in the number of Chinese addicts in the hospital from about 100, 10 years ago, to about 15 now. The number of Jewish addicts has decreased in the same period from about 100 to about 25.

Questions are frequently asked about the criminal records of addicts prior to addiction. A study was made of the Federal Bureau of Investigation records of the first 200 prisoners admitted to the hospital in 1955 and the first 100 admitted in 1956. This group is not representative of the patients admitted, since there were almost four times as many voluntary patients admitted in the same period. Voluntary patients were not included because Federal Bureau of Investigation records could not be requested. It is not necessarily representative of Federal prisoners who were addicts, because the prisoners who were sent to Lexington by the Bureau of Prisons are a selected group. It is obvious that it would not be representative of addicts generally. However, the findings were as follows: 30 percent of the prisoners had convictions prior to the stated age of onset of addiction.

The treatment program is based on more than 20 years of clinical experience and research. The planning takes into consideration the individual and group characteristics of the patients, the limitations in terms of the number and quality of staff, the limitations imposed by law, and the limitations in our knowledge. The goal of the treatment program is as simple to state as it is difficult of accomplishment—to prepare addict patients to return to their home communities where they can continue their rehabilitation and live without using narcotic drugs.

When the addict comes into the gatehouse at the entrance to the hospital grounds his treatment program begins. There he surrenders any narcotic drugs and enters an environment where he is protected from the misuse of drugs. As soon as the usual medical record information is obtained in the admitting unit, a physical examination is done and appropriate medication is ordered. The patient is admitted to the withdrawal ward if there is physical dependence on narcotic drugs and if there is no complicating disease requiring admission to some other infirmary ward.

Much has been written about the agonies of the opiate abstinence syndrome, and it is certainly a period of physiological upheaval. A system of measuring the intensity of the syndrome was developed by Himmelsbach[10] and Kolb.[11] If a patient has physical dependence on an opiate drug, the severity and time of onset of the abstinence signs will be related to the dosage and the particular drug used. The signs include sweating, lacrimation, rhinorrhea, yawning, dilation of pupils, gooseflesh, muscle jerking (not convulsions), and cramps, anorexia, vomiting, diarrhea, insomnia, increases in blood pressure and temperature. These signs may be precipitated by the use of nalorphine.[12] With competent medical care and use of the methadone substitution method the discomfort and dangers of the abstinence syndrome are minimal. This method is described in a number of publications by Isbell,[13] Wilker,[14] and Fraser[15] of the Addiction Research Center of the National Institute of Mental Health which is located at this hospital. The method, in brief, is to administer methadone orally in quantities just sufficient to keep signs of abstinence at a tolerable level and then to steadily reduce the dosage. The treatment of the acute phase of the abstinence syndrome which results from physical dependence on narcotic drugs usually requires less than 2 weeks. This is followed by a period of convalescence or subacute symptoms lasting about 2 weeks when the patient regains his strength, weight, and appetite, but is irritable, restless, and has difficulty in sleeping. Complete recovery from physical addiction takes about 4 months. The time and severity will vary somewhat according to the degree of tolerance and physical dependence of the patient and this in turn is determined by the drug used, duration of use, and daily dosage. When the patient is no longer receiving methadone and the acute abstinence signs and symptoms have abated,

[10] Himmelsbach, C. K., and Small. L. F.: Clinical Studies of Drug Addiction. Supplement to the Public Health Reports : 125, 1, 1937.
[11] Kolb. L., and Himmelsbach. C. K.: Clinical Studies of Drug Addiction. Supplement to the Public Health Reports. 128, 1938.
[12] Isbell, H.: Nalline, A Specific Narcotic Antagonist. Merck Report, 62, 2: 23–26, 1953.
[13] Isbell, H.: Medical Aspects of Narcotic Addiction. Bulletin of the New York Academy of Medicine, 31 : 886–901, December 1955.
[14] Wilker, A.: Rationale of the Diagnosis and Treatment of Addictions. Connecticut State Medical Journal. 19 : 560–568. July 1955.
[15] Fraser, H. F.: Treatment of Drug Addiction. American Journal of Medicine, 14: 571–577, 1953.

transfer from the withdrawal ward to an orientation ward is made. When necessary, patients are transferred to another infirmary ward—medicine, surgery, tuberculosis, or physchiatric.

Each patient has an administrative physician. He is the physician who is responsible for coordinating and supervising the patient's program from the time he leaves the withdrawal ward until he is discharged from the hospital. The administrative physicians are first-, second-, and third-year psychiatric residents. Their work is supervised by staff psychiatrists. The patient may be in individual or group psychotherapy with another psychiatric resident; he may have his most meaningful relationship with his vocational supervisor or dormitory aid; or he may be in casework therapy with a social worker, but the overall responsibility for the patient rests with the administrative physician. He formulates the program, follows the progress of the patient and, except for prisoners, decides when the patient is ready to return to his home community. This system has been in operation since July 1955, and is based in a large part on the research of Stanton and Schwartz.[16]

The patient remains on the orientation ward for about 2 weeks while convalescence is occurring. During this time group discussions for orientation purposes are held with the patients. The patients are interviewed individually by members of the vocational, correctional, social service, and psychiatric staffs for diagnostic purposes and written reports made. The patient's administrative physician prepares a diagnostic summary formulation from the reports. This is reviewed with him by a staff psychiatrist and a treatment program for the patient is formulated.

Every patient who is physically able to work has a job. Most of the young addicts have had erratic or no work records. One purpose of the work assignment is to enable these self-centered and many times hostile persons to work with other people and to accept authority. Immature adults, like normal children, resist and reject authority because it limits their freedom of action. To many of our patients authority is regarded in terms of their past experience with their parents and society—as hostile, punitive, and rejecting. Constructive, consistent relations with authority figures of a different type may permit a modification of previous reaction patterns.

The program varies from one patient to another according to the patient's needs and the limitations of staff time and facilities. One element is common to all programs—residence in a drug-free environment for a minimum period of 4 months to recover from the physical addiction. This period also initiates the disestablishment of the habit of using narcotic drugs as a pattern of living to relieve anxiety or for euphoria. Those patients who appear to be suitable are offered the opportunity for individual psychotherapy and/or group psychotherapy. It is not expected that all patients will remain in the hospital until psychotherapy is completed because this may need to be continued beyond the time when hospitalization is indicated.

Group psychotherapy and activity therapy appear to be more suitable than individual psychotherapy for patients with personality trait or sociopathic disturbances. Because of their emotional immaturity, dependency, and hostility the most useful program seems to be one similar to the activity programs used with disturbed children. The immediate "therapist" is the person with whom the patient spends the most time. In most instances this would be the vocational supervisor. Consideration is given not only to the vocational needs of the patient but when indicated to the needs of the patient for continued association with a particular kind of staff person. The vocational supervisors are apprised of the patient's problems when it appears to be indicated and the supervisor can phone or otherwise discuss the patient with the administrative physician at any time. Staff psychiatrists provide consultation in discussions with groups of vocational supervisors.

The hospital is not a vocational training school but it does have a large variety of well organized and active vocational training programs which it is hoped serve as a medium for nurturing emotional maturation. The education and vocational training unit chief assists the section chiefs in the design of training programs preparing patients for "payroll" jobs. The accomplishments of the patients in these programs are amazing when viewed in the light of their past vocational history or lack thereof. It demonstrates the unactivated potential for change that exists within these patients. Each month the vocational supervisor sends a report to the patient's administrative physician rating the patient

[16] Stanton, A. H., and Schwartz, M. S. The Mental Hospital. Basic Books, Inc., 1954.

on cooperation, attitude, interest, dependability, and progress in skill learning. Ratings have been found to be useful indicators of ability to adapt to living in the hospital. Toward the end of his hospitalization assistance in getting employment is provided.

For many of the patients narcotic drugs were the only source of pleasure in living. One source of pleasure for most people is recreation—reading, athletics, movies, television, bowling, music, etc. The hospital attempts to provide the patients with opportunities for developing interests in recreation as one facet of living. These patients are able to participate more readily in passive recreation or individual activities than in any endeavor that requires active cooperation as a team member. Recreation can serve as a vehicle for learning to live with other people and to accept the limitations of behavior imposed by the rules of the game.

Part of the patient's day and evening is spent in the dormitory with other patients. This presents many opportunities for constructive, destructive, and neutral associations. Since narcotic drugs were the central and sometimes the exclusive preoccupation of the patients before hospitalization, much time is spent in discussions on this subject. Until a few years ago the women patients were in a separate small building a short distance away from the main building. A frequent comment by the staff at that time was that the men spent so much time talking about drugs. Now the comment is that they spend so much time talking about women.

The aide on the dormitory has an important role in the hospital program. The responsibilities include helping the patients learn to live with other persons without more than the ordinary amount of strife; helping the patients to learn other adult patterns of living and, most important, the aide can listen to patients' problems and when indicated provide advice and encouragement. The dormitory aide can get assistance from his supervisor or if the problem is with regard to a particular patient then he can consult with the patient's administrative physician. A 12-month training program of classroom, demonstration, and supervised assignments is used to prepare aides for their work.

The social work service participates in the diagnostic studies and has the responsibility of identifying the social service needs of the patient. The principal activity is to provide casework services to patients. The problems presented range from personal problems of the patient in the hospital to family problems in a community many miles away. The staff does all the work related to parole and is the liaison with the probation officers.

Religion is an important part of the lives of many patients. The hospital has Catholic, Jewish, and Protestant chaplains whose duties include conducting services, individual counseling, and group discussions. The College of the Bible of the Christian Church operates a chaplain-training program at the hospital which is supervised by the Protestant hospital chaplain. The trainees work with patients as a part of their training.

Acting out behavior of persons with neuroses or character disorders is a problem whether at home, in the community, or in the hospital. For 20 years this hospital had a so-called adverse behavior clinic which has now been discontinued. Patients with problems are assisted by the staff members who have direct relations with them. When necessary, the supervisor, administrative physician, or a staff psychiatrist is available. Action that appears most helpful to the patient is taken.

When is hospitalization terminated? For the prisoner this is determined by the sentence received, the action of the Board of Parole, and earning of "good time." For some who demonstrate that they are unsuitable for treatment at the hospital it is terminated by transfer to a prison. Patients who are on probation or are committed by the District of Columbia courts remain until hosiptal treatment is completed. Voluntary patients can terminate their stay at any time.

Of the 350 infirmary ward beds, 150 are for nonaddict patients with mental disorders. Most of these patients are Merchant Seamen or United States Coast Guard personnel who have been transferred from other United States Public Health Service hospitals that do not have psychiatric services. The few addicts who are psychotic are admitted to these wards. About 85 beds are in the withdrawal wards for men and women. The medical and surgical wards have about 115 beds. The staff of the Addiction Research Center of the National Institute of Mental Health and about 30 consultants in the various medical specialties are available as consultants to the regular hospital staff.

It has been my intention to indicate that a great many persons have important roles in the treatment program at the hospital—the aide on the dormitory, the vocational supervisor, the physician, the social worker, and the consultant, to name some. It was also my intention to emphasize that completion of hospitalization is not completion of rehabilitation for the patient. This can only occur after the patient has left the hospital and has returned to his home community.

RESULTS

One way of describing results is in terms of the number of persons who were hospitalized and treated. From the time the hospital opened in 1935 until the end of fiscal year 1955, 23,625 addicts were admitted a total of 45,058 times. Voluntary patients accounted for 29,002 of the admissions and almost 24,000 of these occurred in the last 10 years. A study of 17,741 patients admitted from 1935–52 was made in 1955 to determine the number of times patients were hospitalized. There were 34,539 admissions in this period. Fourteen percent of the patients were admitted three or more times and accounted for 42 percent of the total admissions. Twenty-two percent were hospitalized twice and 64 percent were hospitalized once. (see graph, Number of Times Admitted.)

NUMBER OF TIMES ADMITTED
1935 – 1952 .

17,741 Addict Patients
U.S. Public Health Service Hospital
Lexington, Kentucky.

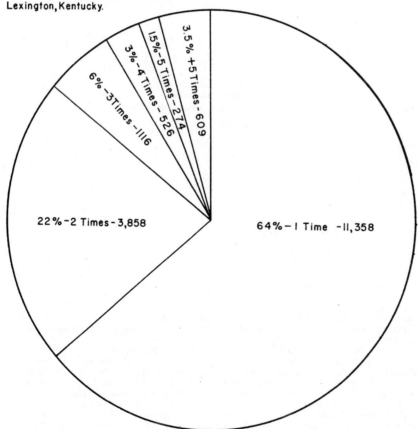

Another way of determining results is to ascertain how many patients stay in the hospital until hospital treatment is completed. A study of the 765 male voluntary patients discharged in January through June 1955 showed that 40 percent stayed less than 15 days and an additional 15 percent left by the end of 30 days. About 30 percent stayed until hospital treatment was completed. (See graph, Length of Stay, Male Addicts, Voluntary.)

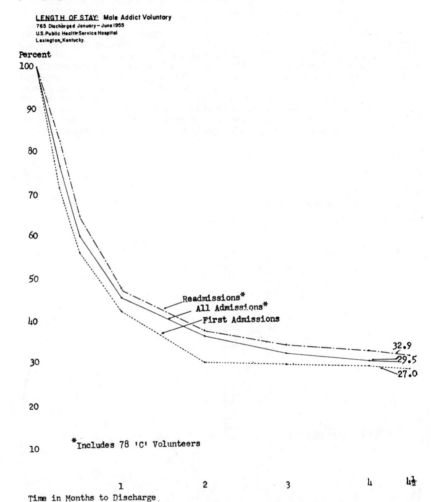

LENGTH OF STAY: Male Addict Voluntary
765 Discharged January–June 1955
U.S. Public Health Service Hospital
Lexington, Kentucky.

A study of 302 female patients discharged in the same period showed similar findings for the first 30 days but only 23.5 percent stayed until hospital treatment was completed. It should be noted that there was only a slight difference between the experience with first admissions and readmissions.

The results of hospitalization can be expressed by comparing the condition of the patient at the time of discharge with his condition at the time of admission. Patients are classified as "unimproved" if physical dependence is present at the time of discharge, or if there is no progress toward freedom from psychological dependence. "Hospital treatment completed" means that at the time of discharge there was freedom from physical addiction and enough progress toward freedom from psychological addiction had occurred so that discharge to the community is indicated. "Improved" is the status between these two.

In 1955 about one-third of the addict patients admitted stayed in the hospital for such short periods that their condition on discharge was "unimproved." These were voluntary patients. About one-third of the patients were discharged as "improved" and one-third reached the status of "hospital treatment completed."

The recovery from narcotic addiction is dependent upon many factors—the patient, what happens in the hospital, and what happens after he leaves the hospital. It would be interesting to know how many patients who were discharged did not become readdicted. While the results would not be related to hospitalization alone, it could be assumed, perhaps, that there was some relationship. Pescor[17] attempted such a study of 4,766 patients discharged in years 1936 through 1940. The followup information was obtained from four sources: first, the patient if readmitted; second, the arresting authority if the former prisoner or probationer's arrest was reported to the Federal Bureau of Investigation; third, probation officers, and fourth, letters mailed at 6-month intervals to former patients. Pescor felt that this method was crude and this opinion seems well founded since information was obtained on only 60.1 percent of the group even though 75 percent were prisoners and probationers. He did determine that 39.9 percent had relapsed in periods varying from 6 months to 6 years. It is interesting to note that paroled prisoners made the best record from the standpoint of abstinence. It was this group that received the most posthospital supervision and could not leave the hospital until there was a satisfactory plan for job, place to live, etc. An important item to remember is that parolees are a highly selected group and the results may be related to this as well as to what happened during and after hospitalization.

Rayport[18] studied 1,020 male patients consecutively admitted to the hospital to determine how many had first received narcotic drugs from a physician to the point of addiction, in the course of treatment for an illness. There were 141 such patients—137 white and 4 Negro, an incidence of 27 percent among the white patients and 1.2 percent among Negro patients. The average age of the whites was 47.4 years and the average duration of addiction 14.8 years. These 141 "medical addicts" were placed in three groups: those whose original illness was no longer present, 89 (63.1 percent); those who still had the original but reversible illness, 2; and those who had the original but essentially irreversible illness, 50 (34.7 percent). Treatment of the first group was similar to that of "nonmedical" addicts. Treatment of the second group required treatment of the original disease and of the addiction to opiates. All of the patients in group 3 were successfully treated for their physical addiction by the methadone substitution method and treated for their irreversible illness by the use of specific medication, non-narcotic analgesics and physiotherapy. After these patients had received no narcotics for about 100 days, 84 percent stated that they felt well or very well even though their cardiovascular, gastro-intestinal, pulmonary, bone and joint, or neurological diseases were still present.

DISCUSSION

There are a number of difficulties involved in the treatment of the patient with narcotic addiction. The patient must remain in the hospital if treatment of the physical addiction is to occur, yet 40 percent of the voluntary patients leave in less than 2 weeks.

If treatment of the psychological addiction is to be initiated, then the patient must have some motivation to live without narcotic drugs. There is little purpose in hospitalizing persons who do not have any desire to actively work toward this goal. To date medical science has discovered no way of artificially instilling this motivation. It has to be generated within the patient by the patient, or by persons in the environment who are important to the patient, or by the demands of society. There is no way known to measure motivation objectively. Its presence has to be inferred from verbalized attitudes and from actions.

Clinical and laboratory research has provided a very satisfactory method for treatment of physical addiction to opiates—the methadone substitution method— so this presents no difficulties if the patient is in a drug-free environment.

---

[17] Pescor. M. J.: Followup Study of Treated Narcotic Drug Addicts. Supplement No. 170 to the Public Health Reports, 1943.
[18] Rayport. M.: Experience in the Management of Patients Medically Addicted to Narcotics. JAMA, 156: 684–691 (October 16, 1954).

There have been some reports stating that chlorpromazine and reserpine are of value in the treatment of the acute opiate abstinence syndrome. To date the reports are based on clinical usage with poor or no controls and usually the reported intake of narcotic drugs in what the addict says he thinks he has been using. This information has no value. Fraser and Isbell[19] studied the effects of chlorpromazine and reserpine in patients who were in a rigidly controlled environment and who were administered known amounts of narcotic drugs for specified periods and in whom abstinence signs were measured by objective criteria. Neither chlorpromazine nor reserpine administered orally or intramuscularly reduced the intensity of the acute abstinence syndrome from morphine.

It is indeed unfortunate that the treatment of the psychological addiction to narcotic drugs is not as well developed as the treatment of physical addiction. Research has provided relatively less knowledge that is useful to the clinician. Psychological addiction is closely related if not a manifestation of a mental disorder and these same mental disorders occur in persons who are not addicts. One can expect then, that improved methods for treatment of the psychological addiction will become available as research on mental disorders progresses.

Completion of hospital treatment marks the beginning of community treatment and rehabilitation. While it is necessary to remove the addict from the setting in which addiction occurred to a controlled environment, if hospitalization has served its purpose it has prepared the patient for return to the community. Hospital treatment can start a patient on the way to recovery but it cannot provide a lifelong immunity that protects the patient against relapse. Hospital treatment can initiate rehabilitation but it must be completed after the patient returns to the community.

Senator LANGER. Thank you, Dr. Lowry.

We will recess until tomorrow morning at 10:30 in the District Committee Room. That is over in the Capitol.

(Whereupon at 4:15 p. m. the hearing was adjourned, to reconvene at 10:30 a. m. Tuesday, December 18, 1956.)

---

[19] Fraser, H. F., and Isbell, H.: Chlorpromazine and Reserpine: (A) Effects of Each and of Combinations of Each With Morphine, (B) Failure of Each in Treatment of Abstinence From Morphine. Accepted for publication, Arch. Neur. & Psych.

TREATMENT AND REHABILITATION OF JUVENILE DRUG ADDICTS

TUESDAY, DECEMBER 18, 1956

United States Senate,
Subcommittee of the Committee on the
Judiciary To Investigate Juvenile Delinquency,
Washington, D. C.

The subcommittee met, pursuant to recess, at 10:40 a. m., in room P–36, United States Capitol, Senator Estes Kefauver (chairman of the subcommittee) presiding.

Present: Senators Kefauver and Langer.

Also present: Ernest Mitler, special counsel and Peter N. Chumbris, associate counsel.

Chairman Kefauver. Call your first witness.

Mr. Mitler. Dr. Himmelsbach.

Would you give your name please?

TESTIMONY OF DR. CLIFTON K. HIMMELSBACH, MEDICAL DIRECTOR, CHIEF, DIVISION OF HOSPITALS, UNITED STATES PUBLIC HEALTH SERVICE

Dr. Himmelsbach. Clifton K. Himmelsbach.

Mr. Mitler. You are the Director of the United States Public Health Service.

Dr. Himmelsbach. No, sir; I am Chief, Division of Hospitals in United States Public Health Service.

Mr. Mitler. And what is the relationship of your department to the United States Public Health Service Hospitals at Fort Worth and Lexington?

Dr. Himmelsbach. Those are two of our systems of United States Public Health Service hospitals that deal with known indigents. We have 2 systems of hospitals, 1 for indigents and 1 for other beneficiaries. In the systeming of hospitals with which I am connected there are 16, 12 general medical and surgical hospitals and 4 specialty hospitals.

The 4 specialty hospitals are 1 for TB, 1 for leprosy, and 2 for neuropsychiatric disorders, the 1 at Fort Worth and the 1 at Lexington.

Mr. Mitler. Yesterday a portion of the hearing was devoted to the question of the need for followup program from Fort Worth and from Lexington and from any drug-treatment center, and could you tell us what the existing followup program is from these two hospitals that come under your jurisdiction? What provisions are made at the present time?

111

Dr. HIMMELSBACH. The position of the Public Health Service as enunciated by the Surgeon General last year is that the States and communities should be encouraged in and assisted in the development of followup programs for drug addicts that are treated either at our hospitals or elsewhere.

The Surgeon General emphasized this in the therapeutic program as it now exists. There is very little formal provision for going in and doing anything much in the way of treatment for the drug addict after he has left the hospital.

Mr. MITLER. Is there any prohibition in the law that would prevent from developing or having representatives in the major cities where drug addiction is most prevalent, is there any legal prohibition against their developing a followup program?

Dr. HIMMELSBACH. I would anticipate that the answer to that would be yes. There is no provision in law. I don't know whether there is any strict prohibition in law, there is no provision in law nor is there any provision in our budgeting for our program for drug addicts.

Mr. MITLER. What I had in mind in the question was whether the law would have to be changed in order to have a followup program or whether it could be done under existing statute.

Dr. HIMMELSBACH. The usual way the Public Health Service works with communities on community health matters is to aid the communities through grant-in-aid mechanisms under the Public Health Service Act and through furnishing counsel and assistance by sending to the States and communities people who have competence to aid them and assist them in the development of the community kinds of programs. The Public Health Service rarely except on a demonstration basis carries out community health programs.

Mr. MITLER. Assuming part and parcel of the function of the treatment program at Lexington and Fort Worth was having somebody just physically in the big cities, couldn't that be considered part of their inherent program?

In other words, wouldn't they just simply be branches of the hospital, completing the hospital program?

Dr. HIMMELSBACH. Yes, sir, it could be.

Chairman KEFAUVER. Doctor, what you mean is that you would have to have, you think you would have to have additional authorization in your basic statute plus of course a budget appropriation and budget approval?

Dr. HIMMELSBACH. Yes, sir. And I think it would get into Federal-State relations principles and that sort of thing, Senator.

We feel we do have a very clear responsibility in the assistance to States and communities through the treatment of the addicts they refer to us in our hospitals, because the development and management and operation of large hospitals for this purpose is perhaps a little too much for a municipality to undertake. But each community does have its own mental health facilities, its guidance clinics and that sort of thing which could be utilized for this purpose, its own public assistance, its own vocational rehabilitation and in the various community services that would be of tremendous assistance if focused on the drug addict that comes from that community. If you feel the Federal Government should step into this picture it would be a substantial departure from present relations and I feel I would have to discuss that with the Surgeon General before I could comment on it in any specific fashion, sir.

Mr. MITLER. The hospital has been there since 1935.

Dr. HIMMELSBACH. Yes, sir.

Mr. MITLER. Have any of the States in line with your encouragement of the States in developing such a program taken any affirmative steps?

Dr. HIMMELSBACH. Yes, sir.

Mr. MITLER. Where is there such a program working with your hospital?

Dr. HIMMELSBACH. The city of New York has a program which has been studied by the Public Health Service. Dr. Chapman is here who conducted the study and he can give you details on it. The city of Chicago has had such a program which has had enjoyable success and I am sure this committee has interviewed some of the folks from that committee.

The city of Detroit has had a program and I think it still has a rather good one. The city of Los Angeles has indicated some interest in such a program and I believe has made some steps in that direction. In addition to that some of the State health departments in what we call region 3—Kentucky, Virginia, West Virginia, North Carolina, and Tennessee, I believe—have made individual arrangements through the health departments with the medical officer in charge of our Lexington Hospital to voluntarily furnish counsel and guidance and assistance to those volunteer addicts coming from those States who request such service prior to their discharge.

The extent of their program at the present time, I am not aware of but it extends to them and naturally includes the prisoner patients because there is no prohibition against divulging information about them.

Mr. MITLER. Dr. Chapman is here and is familiar with those programs. Isn't it a fact that right now a volunteer when he leaves Lexington goes back into the community and there isn't any formal followup program in existence?

Dr. HIMMELSBACH. That's right.

Chairman KEFAUVER. That is generally true with the exceptions that you have named, is that true?

Dr. HIMMELSBACH. Yes, sir.

Mr. MITLER. What is your opinion about the value of that kind of program?

Dr. HIMMELSBACH. I think it would be essential to making additional inroads into the solution of the problem. I think that without that, without provision, adequate provision for followup assistance and guidance to the discharged addict following his hospitalization, the prognosis for making significant improvements in the treatment and cure of addiction is not very good.

Mr. MITLER. Yes, sir.

Chairman KEFAUVER. Doctor, how do you think some of these States—I think my State, Tennessee, has undertaken to do something about this in the way of a followup—just how far they have gone and what their program is I don't know in detail. But suppose you were given the job of setting up a followup program for those who have been treated for addiction in a State, just what would you establish, what would you do, what followup policy or program would you have?

Mr. MITLER. The program would differ for large cities and rural communities. Drug addiction today represents—let me start this over again. Excuse me. Our drug addicts today come from basically two kinds of communities, one, the large city, and two, the strictly rural southern community. A program directed at the large urban metropolitan city would be to utilize all of the existing resources within the community to mobilize them, to integrate them, to focus their energies in this direction, giving them what assistance was needed financially and by way of personnel. Actually they have the facilities and it is a matter of coordinating them and focusing their attention on this particular problem.

That I think can be done. I think they would be relatively simple compared with the problem of trying to create and to focus the utilization of community facilities that are needed in the post discharge rehabilitation of an addict in a rural southern community where you have one here, one there and one some place else.

The problem is more dispersed in the southern communities.

Now from the standpoint of the numbers of patients, we have I think about an equal number coming from the dense populations as from the rural populations. It would be difficult for me to plan and execute a program for it just as for the deserving individual from a small southern town as for hundreds coming from a large metropolitan center.

Chairman KEFAUVER. In any event they need medical or psychiatric consultation?

Dr. HIMMELSBACH. Yes, sir.

Chairman KEFAUVER. And they need also someone or some agency to help them with reemployment and guidance.

Dr. HIMMELSBACH. Yes, sir. And someone who is interested and concerned and who believes that these people are reclaimable and is willing to work hard at them and convince them that he is interested and to mobilize the community resources to the benefit of the individual.

Chairman KEFAUVER. You were present, I believe, yesterday when Mr. Neeb——

Mr. MITLER. He didn't come.

Chairman KEFAUVER. Are you familiar with the proposal that was explained by Mr. Neeb representing the Voluntary Commission in California? The legislation had passed the General Assembly of California but for some reason was vetoed by the Governor.

Dr. HIMMELSBACH. No, sir; I am not.

Chairman KEFAUVER. You are not familiar with it?

Dr. HIMMELSBACH. No, sir.

Mr. MITLER. I have no further questions.

Chairman KEFAUVER. Senator Langer?

Senator LANGER. You have ample authority now, do you not, to do that?

Dr. HIMMELSBACH. To treat people in the community?

Senator LANGER. Yes. It is just a matter of appropriation, just a matter of money.

Dr. HIMMELSBACH. I don't believe so; I am not sure. I can't answer that specifically.

Senator LANGER. You don't need more authorization?

Dr. HIMMELSBACH. To treat individuals in the community?

Senator LANGER. Yes.

Dr. HIMMELSBACH. I rather suspect we would.

I am not prepared to answer, Senator; I don't know. The question just hasn't been raised. It would require additional appropriations, obviously, but I don't know that we have the authority to go into the communities and to treat the drug addicts. On a demonstration basis I would assume that the National Institute of Mental Health would have; on a national going basis I don't know. Dr. Chapman might be better able to answer that than I because he works in the National Institute of Mental Health.

Senator LANGER. That's all, Mr. Chairman.

Chairman KEFAUVER. As I look at what might be done, with additional legislation or authorization and budget appropriation, the Federal Government, of course, could do it on its own.

Dr. HIMMELSBACH. Yes, sir.

Chairman KEFAUVER. Another method would be to grant aid to the States on a matching basis to enable them to carry on the program. That is true; it could be done 1 of 2 ways.

Dr. HIMMELSBACH. Yes, sir.

Chairman KEFAUVER. Have you made any study or any estimate of what the costs would be for the Federal Government of a followup program on either basis; that is, direct Federal followup and responsibility or a grant-in-aid to the States, comparable to what you do with the public health programs in the various counties?

Dr. HIMMELSBACH. No, sir; I have no working connection with that kind of program. My program is strictly the hospital side of our work and I am not really familiar with the costs or the character of programs in State aid.

Chairman KEFAUVER. But in any event if there were a good followup program, not only would those treated for addiction at Lexington and Fort Worth be helped, but you wouldn't have the recurrence or retreatment of the same people over and over again to such an extent as you do now.

Dr. HIMMELSBACH. That would be anticipated; that would be an expected result, I should think.

Chairman KEFAUVER. All right.

Mr. MITLER. I have no further questions.

Senator LANGER. Just one other question, if I may.

Chairman KEFAUVER. Yes, indeed, Senator Langer.

Senator LANGER. The Public Health Service has people in every State of the Union.

Dr. HIMMELSBACH. Yes, sir.

Senator LANGER. How many employees do they have?

Dr. HIMMELSBACH. I am going to hazard a guess. I think there are about 20,000 employees total in the United States Public Health Service.

Senator LANGER. Say in Tennessee or Montana or any of those States?

Dr. HIMMELSBACH. I would assume that there are from time to time. They are covered by the Bureau of State Services—services to States in assisting them in their health programs.

Senator LANGER. Are they divided in regions?

Dr. HIMMELSBACH. Yes, sir.

Senator LANGER. What region would Montana and Idaho be?

Dr. HIMMELSBACH. That would be of the Denver office, I should think. There is a regional office in Denver with a complete staff of public health physicians, sanitary engineers, and nurses, who would be working with those States, assisting them with their health problems.

Senator LANGER. It would be a comparatively simple matter, if you have these regions and have these employees, to carry it a step further and take care of these people?

Dr. HIMMELSBACH. The structure is there. Additional personnel will have to be added to render individual services to human beings. The services now provided to the States are assistive and consultative in helping the States do their jobs, along with finances, helping the State health program do their job perhaps a little better.

Senator LANGER. You have done a good job in wiping out venereal disease, for example?

Dr. HIMMELSBACH. Yes, sir.

Senator LANGER. You cooperate there with the State authorities?

Dr. HIMMELSBACH. Yes, sir.

Senator LANGER. Take, for example, Chicago, where they wiped it out entirely.

Dr. HIMMELSBACH. Yes.

Senator LANGER. It would be a simple matter to carry it a step forward without any new law. Except as for appropriations and budgeting, as Senator Kefauver said, you could carry it along in good shape; could you not?

Dr. HIMMELSBACH. Under the present Health Act.

Senator LANGER. Yes.

Dr. HIMMELSBACH. Is that correct, Dr. Chapman?

Dr. Chapman says it is. The present Mental Health Act would permit this.

Senator LANGER. It is just a matter of the Public Health Service giving it their attention?

Dr. HIMMELSBACH. I would think so.

Senator LANGER. Yes.

Chairman KEFAUVER. Well, what region is North Dakota in?

That is what we were getting around to.

Dr. HIMMELSBACH. It used to be in the Kansas City office. It used to be No. 7, I believe. The headquarters of the regional office at the time for North Dakota was in Kansas City. It might now be Chicago; things change from time to time.

Senator LANGER. When I was president of the State board of health for 4 years there, he would, he worked with Surgeon General Blue. We had no trouble getting any help we needed. They sent men out there whenever we wanted. We wiped out venereal disease where in World War I one National Guard unit went to the Mexican border and we had a terrific amount of venereal disease. In World War II after the fight that was put up through the cooperation of the Federal and State authorities, the first 2,700 men examined in World War II there were only 7 cases; that was less than one-fourth of 1 percent. I remember, Mr. Chairman, getting up on the floor of the Senate and calling it to the attention of the Senate, and Senator La Follette, young Bob La Follette got up and said that Wisconsin beat North Dakota because the first 2,700 examined there, there were only 6, and he said that that was partly due to the State legislation that had been passed by the State of Wisconsin dealing with this subject.

It seems to be a comparatively simple matter. You take this matter of drug addiction and carry it along the same line and wiping it out, just like you did with venereal disease.

You have a great record in TB. We have a TB place at San Haven, N. Dak., and you know that your Public Health Service is in there continually helping Dr. Loeb up these to treat these patients.

As a matter of fact, Dr. Dodd, one of the superintendents we had was the first doctor that invented I think you call it the method of blowing up a lung. He became famous all over the country. It was adopted afterward by the Public Health Service in wiping out TB. So I think, Mr. Chairman, you have a wonderful, already have a wonderful, groundwork here for just carrying it a step forward. You can take care of these drug addicts. I am surprised you haven't done it.

Chairman KEFAUVER. Maybe they feel like the Congress would not give them the money to do it. But I think it would be a fine thing if you would try us out and ask for the money.

Dr. HIMMELSBACH. There has been a long lean period, lack of interest in drug addiction. Then it has only been within the last few years that the public consciousness has been rekindled. Back in the late twenties there was a great deal of interest and we were given the job of creating and operating a couple of hospitals which we have been doing ever since.

I do agree with you that this is a remaining frontier, that something should be done about it, and I hope that whatever is done we will be able to do it, the part that you would wish us to do, sir.

Chairman KEFAUVER. I have observed in the 6 years that in one respect or another I have been serving on committees that deal with the problem of narcotics, beginning back in 1950 with the Senate Crime Committee, that the thinking of the American people has undergone a great change in the approach to this problem. First, back at that time, it was hush-hush, don't say anything about it, push it under the rug, don't face the problem openly, the least publicly said about it, the better. So, of course, that kind of an approach doesn't bring around the appropriations or doesn't result in the appropriations or the attention that is needed either to apprehend narcotic violators or to treat them when they are addicted or to follow up, to help them after treatment.

I am happy to note now that there is an entirely different approach. We consider it as a matter that the public must know about in order to secure the funds to enforce the law and also that these people should not be abandoned and considered as outcasts from society. They should be treated so that I hope in this next Congress that we can make recommendations which will secure the approval of the Public Health Service, the Bureau of the Budget and Congress itself to have some followup treatment.

Followup guidance in addition to the treatment at Lexington and Fort Worth.

Dr. HIMMELSBACH. I am most happy to hear that, sir. I am sure that is an excellent approach, one that will yield some good results.

Senator LANGER. You have had some considerable help from the Rockefeller Foundation, haven't you?

Dr. HIMMELSBACH. In this particular problem?

Senator LANGER. In connection with all the Public Health problems?

Dr. HIMMELSBACH. I think so, yes.

Senator LANGER. I might say, Mr. Chairman, that I remember on this very subject when I was Governor of my State, that the Public Health Service went into North Dakota and would hunt up marihuana, marihuana plant, they discovered the marihuana drug in Richland County. They found 1 field of some 25 acres that was planted in Richland County which would supply a large area and that was discovered by the Public Health Service of the United States Government.

Attention was called to that by the fact that one night in a restaurant, in a public place, there were a lot of young boys and girls who were smoking this marihuana and they all took off their clothing, stark naked, walking around that hotel. And they called in the Public Health Service of the United States, they sent men up there and they were experts and they went out looking for this field where there were marihuana plants, it is a kind of poppy.

Dr. HIMMELSBACH. It is hemp.

Senator LANGER. They cleaned it all up in wonderful shape so there has been some cooperation already.

Dr. HIMMEDSBACH. Yes.

Chairman KEFAUVER. You see you have bipartisan support for whatever you do from Senator Langer on the Republican side and me on the Democratic side.

Dr. HIMMELSBACH. That is fortunately true with respect to this problem. It is one that is nationally important and significant and we hope this committee will be able to do something to relieve it.

Chairman KEFAUVER. Anything else, Mr. Mitler?

Mr. MITLER. No further questions.

Chairman KEFAUVER. Thank you very much, Doctor.

Senator LANGER. I would like to ask one more question. Who has charge of your TB matters in Public Health? Why is it that the death rate among Indians is between 30 and 40 times as high as the white people?

Chairman KEFAUVER. From TB?

Senator LANGER. From TB.

Dr. HIMMELSBACH. It is due to many causes, one is the period of time they have been exposed to the disease. They have not developed a natural resistance, second the conditions of poverty, poor nutrition, and exposure and lack of an adequate public-health program for their treatment and management.

They are a little resistant to leaving their homes and going into a hospital for treatment, which means that open cases that are infectious would tend to expose other people than if those individuals were hospitalized.

That is just one factor. They do respond to the antibiotic drugs just as well as anybody else does. Their fundamental living conditions, their behavior patterns, their nutritional status and their genetic lack of as much resistance as we have acquired over several centuries are many of the factors.

Senator LANGER. When we were down in Arizona down there among the Indians investigating juvenile delinquency, we found that in the Papago Tribe the hospital had burned down in 1937. You only got in there in July. The death rate there according to Dr. Salisbury, head of the Public Health there who testified before Senator Kefauver and myself that out of every 100 babies born 17 died before they were a year old; 42 died before they were 6 years old; 52 died before they were 15 years old. Two of your men went down at the request of Dr. Salisbury. This committee couldn't find out why your man only stayed 3 hours in making any investigation. We got Senators Hayden and Goldwater and Senators Anderson and Chavez. Your department recommended that the hospital be rebuilt in the 1957 budget which would mean the hospital would be completed in 1959.

Senator Kefauver and I came back and took it up with Carl Hayden and the other Senators from New Mexico and Arizona. We got an appropriation of $250,000 to start the hospital at once. Three weeks later they started to build that hospital in, what town was that?

Mr. CHUMBRIS. Sells, Ariz.

Senator LANGER. It did seem as though they had been neglected and whoever had charge with them worked on it before and all did a good job, all the reports we have been getting since feel you have been doing a good job since you got the money in July. If you haven't money enough, get enough money to wipe out TB among the Indians. It is outrageous to think that 30 or 40 of them die for every 1 of the white men. I would like to get the man who has charge of that to get him up here because the situation is a disgrace.

Chairman KEFAUVER. Well, we will see if we can't get him up today.

Dr. HIMMELSBACH. Dr. James R. Shaw.

Chairman KEFAUVER. Mr. Mitler, will you try to get him up here.

I want to concur on what Senator Langer said about this hospital. Senator O'Mahoney helped us a great deal with it too.

I sometimes think in the matter of health, that many things you would like to do that you just feel that you don't want to ask for the money to do and I think you would find more interest and more appreciation of your work up here on the Hill than you would expect.

Dr. HIMMELSBACH. Thank you, sir.

Chairman KEFAUVER. So we want to encourage you to ask for more.

Dr. HIMMELSBACH. Thank you very much. We certainly will do that.

Chairman KEFAUVER. We want to ask Mr. David Strubinger, the Assistant Commissioner of Customs. You were here yesterday and we asked you to come back this morning. We don't want to hold you any longer than necessary.

You are the Assistant Commissioner of Customs?

TESTIMONY OF DAVID R. STRUBINGER, ASSISTANT COMMISSIONER OF CUSTOMS

Mr. STRUBINGER. Yes, sir.

Chairman KEFAUVER. How long have you been the Assistant Commissioner?

Mr. Strubinger. For the past 7 years.

Chairman Kefauver. Who is the Commissioner?

Mr. Strubinger. Mr. Ralph Kelly.

Chairman Kefauver. Mr. Mitler wants to ask you some questions with particular reference to the Mexican border. You may proceed, Mr. Mitler.

Mr. Mitler. Yesterday Mr. Neeb from California testified.

Did you learn about his testimony?

Mr. Strubinger. Just by telephone conversation with Mr. Mitchell of the Bureau of Narcotics. I don't know the details of it.

Mr. Mitler. He raised two points, one with respect to the authority of narcotics agents to search and seize on planes and boats. Could you tell us about that?

Mr. Strubinger. You mean whether or not the State authorities would have the right?

Mr. Mitler. Yes; do you know about that?

Chairman Kefauver. Whether first the Federal authorities, Federal narcotic agents have authority to search and seize and help the customs officers in trying to find and search for narcotics and, second, whether you can deputize State and local narcotic agents to assist and whether any additional legislation is needed in order to enable them to authorize to help you in searching for narcotics on the border or on planes coming in from other places?

Mr. Strubinger. The question as put to me covers 2 or 3 different aspects of narcotic and customs enforcement work. The Bureau of Customs under customs law does have all the authority we need for the search of vessels, planes, and other types of vehicles that might come across the border entering the United States, by air or by sea.

The Bureau of Narcotics, while they do not have similar authority in the statutes, do work with us and we very often team up together in making searches and seizures.

State authorities I am not sure whether they have authority or not. However, there have been many instances where they have given assistance to the Federal authorities. In New York City, as an example, the New York State Narcotic Bureau works very closely with the Bureau of Narcotics and with Customs on cases where we need assistance.

Mr. Mitler. Can a member of the narcotics squad of the city of New York board a vessel himself personally and assist one of your customs men in making a search?

Mr. Strubinger. They would not do it without a request from us.

Mr. Mitler. Can it be done or is it done?

Mr. Strubinger. I frankly don't know of any instances where we have requested assistance from State or municipal authorities for the searching of vessels. I might explain that in this way: The searching of vessels is really a very specialized job. It requires a lot of training and you need special equipment. So that we do have trained personnel and we are assisted I might say where we lack sufficient personnel in the Customs Service by the Coast Guard who have been trained in the searching of vessels.

We call upon the Coast Guard very often at various ports to assist us in searching a vessel where we feel we don't have a large enough squad.

The use of State or municipal enforcement officers for that purpose I doubt whether it would be very helpful, unless we had a special situation at a port where we did not have adequate personnel ourselves.

Mr. MITLER. Now, yesterday Mr. Neeb I think mentioned the border patrol. Of course, that is a branch of the United States Immigration Service.

Mr. STRUBINGER. That is correct.

Mr. MITLER. And that has nothing to do with the Customs, your division, except that you work with them, perhaps?

Mr. STRUBINGER. I might say that the immigration border patrol carry the additional designation as a customs border patrolman. So under that designation they have the same authority as a customs officer has.

Mr. MITLER. So they are your information or intelligence service?

Mr. STRUBINGER. No; actually the border patrol, it is what the name indicates. They are patrolling the roads. We had a border patrol until about 1948 along the Mexican border. It was discontinued for several reasons; one of which was the fact that the Immigration Service had a border patrol and we did not feel we should duplicate that patrol work down there. In addition through an intensive study of enforcement techniques we determined that a better approach to the problem of stopping narcotics was on the basis of—the smuggling of narcotics, that is—was on the basis of obtaining information rather than the physical control of a 2,500-mile border, which is impossible to do.

The immigration control is effective to this extent. They do not patrol the border itself. They patrol the roads back of the border and stop cars and question people. Our patrol to be effective had to be at the border itself.

We had about 225 people down in the Southwest patrol and while they were making seizures and arresting violators we felt that we could go on and do a better enforcement job by using the techniques of the purchase of information and developing information and developing informers and using more customs agents as investigators than just the physical patrol.

Mr. MITLER. Mr. Neeb yesterday testified about the border at Tijuana and there was testimony that a great many of the young people in California, especially southern California, secure their drugs in Tijuana, in that section of Mexico, and the question came up whether there were adequate numbers of customs men to be able control these young people coming back and to inspect them, because of the large number of people going back and forth at Tijuana.

Mr. STRUBINGER. We have a very different question at Tijuana.

Weekdays the traffic is under complete control at all times. On Sunday and holidays, they have races and bull fights, and also jai alai down at Tijuana. The result is that it is not unusual for six to eight thousand automobiles to come back from Mexico from 3 o'clock to about 6 o'clock in the afternoon, or try to get back during that time.

The result is that the inspection that we can give cars during Sundays or holidays has to be downgraded.

We cannot give those cars the same inspection we give them weekdays. The principal reason for that, however, is not the lack of manpower, it is the lack of the facilities, the lack of a proper facility.

Chairman KEFAUVER. I didn't understand. What do you mean by facilities?

Mr. STRUBINGER. The lack of a proper facility.

Chairman KEFAUVER. What do you mean?

Mr. STRUBINGER. The space in which the cars can be handled. What actually happens, Senator, is that even using all the men we can possibly use, in 8 lanes of traffic which is available to us, we back the traffic up for 2 to 3 miles.

A mile and a half is not unusual on a Sunday afternoon. It means that a person leaving the racetrack will be in the neighborhood of 2 hours or 2½ hours getting into the United States and that is using every bit of space we have to examine automobiles.

If we had three times as many men available we could not examine the cars much faster than we do, except we don't examine them at all.

Chairman KEFAUVER. Why don't you have more lanes; what is the trouble there?

Mr. STRUBINGER. We are. We have in progress a building program that will open when it is necessary, up to 19 lanes of traffic. And we feel that, well, when this new facility is installed, then we will be able to give a much better examination than we are giving at the present time. At the present time we are not satisfied with it, because there is little or nothing we can do about it except close the border on Sunday.

Mr. MITLER. Mr. Neeb brought up another question yesterday and that is about the reward that is given to a Mexican, I guess any informant, but is given in connection with against a person who secured drugs in Mexico.

Anyone who gives information to the Customs can get a certain reward, and he raised the question whether that might have some hazards connected with it.

In other words, encouraging somebody to sell in order to get the reward.

Mr. STRUBINGER. The reward is only payable when there is an arrest for seizure.

Mr. MITLER. The point is, isn't that kind of a reward also to a seller?

Mr. STRUBINGER. I don't quite follow you.

Mr. MITLER. Do you know what the amount of the reward is?

Mr. STRUBINGER. It would depend on what is involved. It is $500 for an ounce of heroin, a kilo of heroin, or a kilo of opium. That is a reward that we publish, we put it out in posters. However, in addition to that, we do purchase information and there is reward paid on seizures that is not a matter of advertisement. That is something under the statute we can do, and we do it all the time. We got this out because we felt people were, who would have knowledge, would come to us and give the information so we could stop this traffic.

Mr. MITLER. What Mr. Neeb was trying to say was, suppose I was selling in Tijuana, it might be an inducement for me to go ahead and sell and then tell somebody else to go to the Customs and tell them about it and then this somebody else could get $500 and we could split it.

Do you follow what I am trying to say?

Mr. STRUBINGER. Yes.

Mr. MITLER. The reward might be channeling it back to the seller.

Mr. STRUBINGER. That possibly could happen. We don't think it is happening because we, as you probably know, we do have men working under cover across the Mexican line.

They are pretty well informed as to who the drug dealers are both in marihuana and heroin and the rest of the drugs. We also have an extensive corps of informers who keep us pretty well informed as to what the traffic is over there.

Our difficulty, of course, is that we can't do anything about it in Mexico; we have to get them in the United States to do anything to them.

Many people we know are narcotic dealers in Mexico today, if we ever get them across the line we would put them in jail.

Mr. MITLER. Mr. Bobo and I were there, and it is amazing the way they were able to spot the people with drugs coming across, the terrific insight the officers had.

Mr. STRUBINGER. It is not as much insight as it is good information.

Mr. MITLER. Those are the questions that I thought Mr. Neeb brought up, Senator.

Chairman KEFAUVER. Well, Mr. Strubinger, are you sufficiently manned, do you have sufficient personnel in the Bureau of Customs to carry on your work, your assignment adequately?

Mr. STRUBINGER. Well, being a career employee I would have to say that I always think, I have felt for the last 5 or 6 years, we can use more people.

However, I do want to be very plain in this request. Congress had not in any way reduced our appropriations in the last 4 or 5 years.

Chairman KEFAUVER. Senator Langer, do you have any questions you wish to ask Mr. Strubinger?

Senator LANGER. No, thank you, Senator.

Mr. MITLER. Thank you.

Senator LANGER. I would like to ask you how many rewards have you paid in the last year?

Mr. STRUBINGER. In number, Senator, I don't think I can tell you. The amount of money we pay out in rewards over a year would run somewhere between thirty-five and fifty thousand dollars. It varies from year to year. But we have sufficient authority to go far beyond that if we have to.

Senator LANGER. Thank you.

Chairman KEFAUVER. All right, thank you, sir.

Before you leave and before the next witness, I am trying to find where Mr. Neeb testified about this. Here is the testimony. I can't find it. Mr. Strubinger, one other question. Both Mr. Cunningham and Mr. Neeb said that if visas or some kind of permits were required particularly of teen-agers going back and forth across the border that that would help in enforcement and would help prevent bringing in of narcotics. What is your thought about it?

Mr. STRUBINGER. It is really a matter that the Department of State would have to speak about and Congress would have to legislate on.

There are no passports or visas required to go to Mexico. I would imagine, and I am not sure about it, that it is something that would have to have legislation on it.

However the State Department may have ample authority at this time to require a person under a certain age to have some kind of a permit to leave the United States.

Mr. CHUMBRIS. Are you familiar with S. 959 which was introduced in the Senate last year in which minors had to get a permit to cross the border?

Mr. STRUBINGER. No; I am not familiar with it.

Mr. CHUMBRIS. From the Department of Justice.

Mr. STRUBINGER. I am not familiar with that.

Mr. CHUMBRIS. Isn't that what you have reference to, Mr. Chairman?

Chairman KEFAUVER. Either that or some other kind of permit. Of course, I know there is the problem of international relations with Mexico involved, but I was talking about purely from the enforcement problem if some system could be worked out to require permits or visas?

Mr. STRUBINGER. There would be one problem and that would be this: Unless we check them out we would be running into the difficulty when they came back when they didn't have a permit. At the present time we do not check people out of the country. We might be faced with a double-barreled job of checking them out and checking them when they come back. We are not staffed to do that. There would be additional expense involved if we were to try to check them out.

That would be necessary if you want to get the full effect of a law or regulation of that kind.

Senator LANGER. At the present time if you get a fellow with marihuana on him or other drugs in a car, can you confiscate that car?

Mr. STRUBINGER. Yes, sir.

Senator LANGER. How many have you confiscated during this year?

Mr. STRUBINGER. I would have to hazard a guess. We haven't our budget figures that we are going to present to Congress, and I am not sure, but I think in the neighborhood of a hundred. A good many of those cars are not worth much. The narcotic peddler and smuggler today is using old wrecks, so usually we seize them, for that, have them forfeited, and sell them for junk.

Senator LANGER. Have you confiscated an airplane?

Mr. STRUBINGER. Yes; we have. We have seized airplanes and we have seized and forfeited airplanes on occasions, not recently.

There have been airplanes seized and held under seizure for a period of a year or more by reason of the violation of the Munitions Act, that is either the attempt to export the plane for war purposes or it was carrying munitions of war.

Chairman KEFAUVER. Mr. Strubinger, Mr. Neeb's testimony is rather brief and it is not very clear about this reward business but here is what he said, "They simply go over the border and say 'We are Americans';" They simply come back and say 'We are Americans.' Very seldom is there any search and they can buy all the heroin and all the marihuana they want in Mexico. The thing that disturbs me out there is this: The Mexican Government apparently does very little if anything about these peddlers and we are sure they know them because our border guards give them money when they inform us as to who they sold to.

Mr. MITLER. Could you explain that, Mr. Neeb?

Mr. NEEB. Yes, our border guards apparently in an effort to do a good job—and I don't criticize them—I criticize the Mexicans for not clamping down on the peddlers, they have a standing offer of $500 of our money to any peddler in Tijuana who will inform and give the license number of the purchaser in Mexico. That applies to juveniles. I know cases where it is happening. They get paid for the heroin or the marihuana with American money and they get $500 from the border guard for giving the license number.

Mr. STRUBINGER. Well, very frankly there is a possibility of that happening. I don't believe that under this $500 award program that we have put up that we have made a dozen payments in the last year.

Mr. Emmerick, our Deputy Commissioner in charge of Enforcement tells me we haven't made any in Mexico.

Chairman KEFAUVER. In the last year?

Mr. STRUBINGER. At all, since it started. I am sure that must be true.

That program has not done a lot for us. We thought it would be more effective than it was.

Chairman KEFAUVER. I don't know what Mr. Neeb could be talking about. He is a very reliable man but he must have something else in mind.

Mr. STRUBINGER. I am afraid he has some information on something else. I am sure—as a matter of fact up until recently I had to personally approve the paying of every reward. I have no recollection of anything of that kind happening for the last year.

I have approved quite a few awards for the purchase of information generally but not under this particular program.

Chairman KEFAUVER. So you don't recall having paid any amount as a reward to anyone in Mexico?

Mr. STRUBINGER. Not to anyone in Mexico. No, sir.

We have paid awards. Rather we have—let me put it another way. We have paid informants for information with respect to the smuggling of narcotics acros sthe border quite a number of times. As a matter of fact, I would imagine that along the Mexican border the last year we paid in the neighborhood of $15,000 to $20,000 for that purpose alone. It hasn't been this type of award you are talking about. It has been paid to informers who are known by our people, who come to us with information, and that money is not paid unless there is arrest and seizure.

Chairman KEFAUVER. Are those Mexicans it is paid to?

Mr. STRUBINGER. It might be or might not be.

Chairman KEFAUVER. That is what he is talking about. He says he has information that a peddler will sell marihuana and heroin and then get the money for the sale and then come to you and give information and get an award.

Mr. STRURINGER. I would like for you to hear Mr. Emerick, who is our Deputy Commissioner in charge of enforcement. He is more familiar with our program than I am. Would you care to hear from him?

Chairman KEFAUVER. Yes, sir. Would you come around? You are Deputy Commissioner of Customs in charge of enforcement?

Mr. EMERICK. Yes, sir.

TESTIMONY OF CHESTER A. EMERICK, DEPUTY COMMISSIONER OF CUSTOMS IN CHARGE OF ENFORCEMENT

Chairman KEFAUVER. What about this informer method we are talking about?

Mr. EMERICK. We have three methods whereby we can pay an award of commendation. One is under section 619 of the Tariff Act, which is based on the amount of recoveries as a result of information furnished and is limited to $50,000 in any one case.

Another method is payment for information furnished; funds are available to make immediate payment. A third payment——

Chairman KEFAUVER. That second method—if you pay for information you pay for it regardless of whether there is a seizure or not?

Mr. EMERICK. We can on some occasions; yes. It may be general information of value that we hope that will eventually lead to seizures and arrests. The third method is the method that has been mentioned, and that is paying an award of $500 a kilo for heroin and opium.

The third method is only one. There has only been 1 payment made since that offer was published some 2 or 3 years ago.

And that was to a source of information at Hong Kong, British Crown Colony, that our agent there has developed. It has never been paid in connection with the Mexican-border traffic.

Chairman KEFAUVER. How about other payments?

Mr. EMERICK. Other payments are frequently made to sources of information in Mexico and along the border in the United States. They are anywhere from $25 up to $300, $400, possibly $500.

Chairman KEFAUVER. That is apparently what Mr. Nebb is talking about.

Mr. EMERICK. Yes, sir. It is customary for enforcement officers in all fields to make payments to informants for information. Now it isn't logical that a dealer in Mexico will inform on a good customer, because when that customer is apprehended and sentenced to 5 to 10 years in the penitentiary, he is no longer available to do business.

So we are of the opinion that the payment to a source of information in Mexico, which may not be an honorable person, would not in itself encourage narcotic traffic.

In fact, when we take this customer out of the business we are hurting the dealer in Mexico who makes his living by reason of the customers he has in the United States.

Mr. STRUBINGER. I think there are two classes of narcotic people we are talking about. We are talking about here the commercial peddler. I think the questions were originally directed to me and had more to do with the juveniles going across, and we would not pay anybody $500 for apprehending a juvenile with a dozen marihuana cigarettes, information of that kind.

There wouldn't be any such payment of that kind.

Mr. MITLER. There isn't any qualification in the offer of reward.

Mr. STRUBINGER. There isn't but our customs officers would not pay that kind of money for a case of that kind.

Chairman KEFAUVER. Of course, gentlemen, you know your business, but I think that what has been described here, that the kid or the customer going across—from the testimony here—that he may not deal with just one seller; it might be to the advantage of the seller financially to make a sale and give information and get paid twice.

Mr. EMERICK. To our knowledge, Senator, we do not know of having made payments to a narcotic dealer in Mexico.

Mr. MITLER. But he may tip somebody else off to give the information?

Mr. EMERICK. That is true.

Mr. MITLER. The money may channel back to him.

Mr. EMERICK. That is entirely possible.

Mr. MITLER. If there are a lot of customers, and perhaps one gets arrested, he has a fertile field with others coming through.

Mr. EMERICK. But the amount paid is governed by the person arrested and the quantities of marihuana or heroin seized.

As far as Tijuana and Mexicali are concerned, which Mr. Neeb is interested in of course, there is not an abundance of heroin there available for sale. The cases we make in that area are for the most part small cases, a few grams and an ounce or 2 or 3, we consider a very large case for that particular area.

There is opium available there in quite some quantities, there is some marihuana, but there again marihuana for the most part is grown south of Laredo and in that particular area of Mexico, down in the Monterey area. Tijuana itself, narcotics are available there, but they are not available in the large quantities as they are in some other places.

Our heroin for instance for the most part comes from Europe. It is a product of the raw materials that are obtained in the Near East and it is manufactured largely in France and smuggled across in the United States.

Mr. MITLER. Could I just ask this question? You spoke about money being paid to informants by narcotic squads. Don't you think there is a distinction after a man is arrested and a narcotics squad officer goes out in his presence and the person who is an addict makes a buy from a pusher and perhaps he gets a reward there in terms of money, don't you think that is a different situation than receiving information after a sale has been made and the money going to the informant afterward and perhaps sending back to the peddler himself?

Don't you think there is a big difference?

Mr. EMERICK. We don't know where the money goes after we pay it.

Mr. MITLER. But theoretically or logically, it could go to the peddler?

Mr. EMERICK. It is possible, yes, sir. But if we did not make payments for information, we wouldn't get very much information on the Mexican border.

Mr. MITLER. Isn't it really encouraging the peddler?

Mr. EMERICK. No, sir; we do not pay to the peddler.

Chairman KEFAUVER. What Mr. Mitler is getting at, if the peddler has a confederate, the peddler makes a sale and he tells his confederate he sold to a man wearing a yellow shirt with a certain license number, then the confederate tells your agent and your agent collects money for information.

You wouldn't have a very good way of preventing that from happening; would you?

Mr. EMERICK. The money we pay, Senator, the amount is so small that it wouldn't make it worth while for a dealer in Mexico to turn his customer to an informant who in turn would give the information to the customs. We are very careful in making payments and deciding the amount of payment which should be given in any given case.

Mr. STRUBINGER. I might add this: If that were a good way of operating, there would be more of it and I can assure you there is not an awful lot of it. There just isn't an awful lot of cases where we pay for information. So if it were a lucrative business, you can bet there would be more of it.

Chairman KEFAUVER. Are you gentlemen willing to make any comment relative to the testimony of Mr. Neeb that Communist China is a substantial source of heroin at the present time, what they are sending in is uncut, comparatively pure?

Mr. EMERICK. We have an office in Hong Kong, quite an active office. Narcotics are available in that area. They are also available at Macao, the Portuguese Crown Colony just 35 miles across the sound or the bay from Hong Kong.

We have advised the Macao authorities and Portuguese authorities of conditions there and we believe they have improved.

However, narcotics are available throughout the Orient but the cases we have made have been in the neighborhood of 5 or 6 pounds at a seizure, and we consider that a very good seizure of heroin from the Orient.

Now the heroin is laid aboard the vessels in Hong Kong, Singapore, Bangkok, and other places and ports in the Orient, but we have not had any information or have not made any substantial seizures such as have been made in the Atlantic seaboard from vessels coming from Europe.

Customs here last year made a seizure of over 21 pounds of heroin from a vessel in New York.

At Montreal about the same time 32 pounds of heroin were seized. Both of these vessels were French vessels. The information was that the merchandise had its origin in France.

Now, the raw materials no doubt originated in the Near East.

Chairman KEFAUVER. Then there was testimony that unusually large amounts were coming from Yugoslavia. Can you confirm that?

Mr. EMERICK. No, sir; I have no knowledge of that, sir.

Chairman KEFAUVER. Anything, Senator Langer?

Senator LANGER. What is the attitude of the Federal judges when you present a case to them? Do they hand out stiff sentences or don't they?

Mr. EMERICK. It is mandatory now that they do hand out stiff sentences. We have this problem, Senator: Many times we make seizures of a few marihuana cigarettes or a small quantity of marihuana for instance, and they were a little hesitant in invoking the Boggs Act in imposing sentences. They figured 5 years was a little bit too severe. Now they are required to; it is mandatory. However, some of these cases may be referred to the State authorities for prosecution, where it involves just 1 or 2 marihuana cigarettes and first offenders. I don't know just what attitude or what action the United States attorneys are going to take in their respective districts on that matter, but we are governed by the United States attorneys in regard to the prosecution of cases.

Mr. STRUBINGER. Generally speaking, Senator, we can say that the Federal judges do hand out stiff sentences on commercial smuggling of narcotics.

Chairman KEFAUVER. Do I understand from what your answer was to Senator Langer's question that you think some United States attorneys and judges rather than impose the severe penalty of the Boggs Act in cases that they think are relatively minor would rather defer to the State authorities and let them do the prosecuting?

Mr. EMERICK. That applies only to the United States attorneys and not to the courts.

Chairman KEFAUVER. Is that the reason they think they might be able to get a conviction where the penalty is so heavy?

Mr. EMERICK. That is in part true where the amount involved is so small and the person, the violator does not have a record, and other circumstances which may be in his favor.

Chairman KEFAUVER. Of course the Boggs Act does not require a penalty on the first offense.

Mr. EMERICK. That is true.

Chairman KEFAUVER. So it would have to be a second offense to come under what you are talking about?

Mr. EMERICK. The recent act, Marihuana Act, imposes quite a severe penalty for the first offense.

Mr. CHUMBRIS. Mr. Emerick, isn't one of the reasons why the States prosecute many narcotics cases is because of the searches and seizures clause in State constitutions is more liberal in favor of the State than the Federal prosecution?

Mr. EMERICK. That applies to traffic within the United States. But insofar as the customs barrier is concerned, we are not disturbed in that way.

Mr. CHUMBRIS. You are relating only to what came into the country?

Mr. EMERICK. The fourth amendment is not applicable until after you entered the United States. At the line the customs officer under section 1581, title 19, can conduct a complete examination of your person, papers and effects and even the clothing you are wearing without first obtaining a search warrant.

Senator LANGER. Have you agents in Hawaii?

Mr. EMERICK. Yes, sir.

Senator LANGER. What is your experience there at Honolulu?

Mr. EMERICK. Honolulu at the present time is very clean from the standpoint of narcotic traffic.

Senator LANGER. Is that true of all Hawaii?

Mr. EMERICK. Yes, sir.

Senator LANGER. It might interest you to know that some years ago a judge was nominated for a Federal position, a Federal judgeship in Hawaii, and the judiciary came in and refused to confirm him because he had been a lawyer for a lot of these people dealing with narcotics. Do you recall that case?

Mr. EMERICK. I don't recall them. But I think they were wise.

Senator LANGER. The Judiciary Committee wouldn't confirm him. Senator Kefauver was interested in that case.

Chairman KEFAUVER. Thank you very much. Mr. Mitler, our next witness?

Mr. MITLER. Mr. Rosenfeld.

Chairman KEFAUVER. Suppose we have a 5-minute recess before Mr. Rosenfeld testifies.

(Short recess.)

Chairman KEFAUVER. Dr. Schulz?

TESTIMONY OF DR. JOHN D. SCHULZ, CHIEF PHYCHIATRIST, DISTRICT OF COLUMBIA GENERAL HOSPITAL

Mr. MITLER. Would you spell your name, please, Doctor?

Dr. SCHULZ. John D. Schulz.

Chairman KEFAUVER. Chief psychiatrist, District of Columbia General Hospital, associate professor of psychology.

Dr. SCHULZ. Phychiatry. Associate professor of psychiatry at Georgetown.

Chairman KEFAUVER. At Georgetown University?

Dr. SCHULZ. Yes, sir.

Chairman KEFAUVER. All right, Mr. Mitler.

Mr. MITLER. Dr. Schulz, would you tell us about the civil commitment program that has been developed here in the District of Columbia? I think it is of value for other communities to know about. I understand that it is the only one of its nature in the country.

Civil commitment, of course, in connection with drug addicts.

Dr. SCHULZ. It has been in operation only a short while. I have a few figures for the record.

Mr. MITLER. Will you tell us what it is first?

Dr. SCHULZ. It is a civil act in three parts. Part 1 refers to the treatment of drug users. This is the section with which we at the hospital and here in the District of Columbia as physicians are most concerned.

Title 2 has to do with the regulation and control of certain drugs other than narcotics, this concerns largely pharmacies and pharmaceutical channels.

Title 3 is a miscellaneous section that covers various aspects of the laws particularly the vagrancy statutes as they might apply to addicts and redefines some of these.

Mr. MITLER. Apart from the law at the moment.

Chairman KEFAUVER. Let's get the statute. What is the statute and give us the number of it, when was it passed?

Dr. SCHULZ. This is Public Law 764 of the 84th Congress, chapter 674.

Chairman KEFAUVER. When was the program put into effect?

Dr. SCHULZ. Second session. It was approved and signed by the President July 24 of this year. In effective operation September 5. The reason for the delay was the necessity of setting up procedural channels.

Mr. MITLER. In effect what does the program do that would not have been done before?

Dr. SCHULZ. It makes treatment mandatory. It makes the addict committable through a civil process in the same sense that a mental patient is committable for treatment.

Mr. MITLER. An addict goes where in the District to have the benefit of the Civil Commitment Act?

Dr. SCHULZ. The District of Columbia General Hospital does the original screening, evaluation, determination of need, presentation of the facts to the United States attorney's office, so then the question of the need for commitment can be determined.

Mr. MITLER. And this is a voluntary kind of commitment?

Dr. SCHULZ. Oh, no, sir.

It is a commitment.

Mr. MITLER. What I mean to say is the person goes and asks initially to be committed.

Dr. SCHULZ. No, sir. Wherever an addict is known to the Health Department from any source of information to be a user of the drug, the Health Department must ask for the detention of the addict— this is involuntary from that point on. They may present themselves voluntarily at the hospital and the fact of their addiction is immediately known and then it immediately becomes involuntary.

Chairman KEFAUVER. The proceeding is in the nature of a civil commitment not a criminal commitment.

Dr. SCHULZ. That's right.

Mr. MITLER. After they first go to the District of Columbia General Hospital for a period of time what is the next step; where do they go next?

Chairman KEFAUVER. Let's take it a step at a time. Tell us your experience with it. How many commitments have you had? Give us your record.

Dr. SCHULZ. I asked the secretary this morning to tabulate our experience thus far. I have sufficient copies.

Chairman KEFAUVER. You have some copies which we will make exhibit 9 to the subcommittee hearing.

(The document was marked "Exhibit 9" and will be found in the files of the committee.)

Dr. SCHULZ. The act has been in effective operation only since September 5. The emphasis has been to process the cases that would be most likely to benefit from rehabilitation.

Chairman KEFAUVER. Has this report been made public, Doctor? Is there any reason why it should not be?

Dr. SCHULZ. I know of no reason why it should not be.

Chairman KEFAUVER. Do you have enough so the press could have copies?

Dr. SCHULZ. I have only one additional so if the committee could spare one of its copies.

Chairman KEFAUVER. Suppose you summarize for the press what your experience has been. You only had it in operation since September—September, October, November, and part of December here.

Dr. SCHULZ. There are certain limiting factors that have limited the number that have been processed. Our facilities are limited so we have tried to handle no more than 10 to 20 in the hospital at any one particular time. Also it is a matter of the prosecuting authorities available resources to process these cases and so on.

Therefore since September 5 the actual total of patients in the hospital has been 62. The top section shows the origins, whether they come from voluntary admission, police, or court, by months.

Chairman KEFAUVER. So during these 3½ months, you have 44 males and 18 females that have been placed in the hospital?

Dr. SCHULZ. That's right.

Chairman KEFAUVER. And then your discharges——

Dr. SCHULZ. Have been nearly the same. We actually have as of today in residence only three patients. We sent a large number to Lexington within the last 10 days. There are three still awaiting transfer with orders that we received from the court in the past week.

Chairman KEFAUVER. The chart shows that you sent 3 to Lexington in September, 3 in October, 6 in November and none in December up to the time this chart was prepared. How many have you sent since then?

Dr. SCHULZ. A total of 12 and 3 waiting or a total of 15 out of the 62 that we have had committed.

Chairman KEFAUVER. Can you project when the staff in the hospital and the prosecuting attorney's office and all the facilities necessary to put the act in actually full operation, the number that you would place in the hospital?

Dr. SCHULZ. We have attempted to do that, sir, and attempted to get various data together for our obvious needs in programing and have been unable to come up with anything very firm other than the fact that this probably represents a relatively small percentage of the total who could be processed.

Chairman KEFAUVER. What do you mean by relatively, 10 percent, 20 percent?

Dr. SCHULZ. I would say perhaps in the order of—there are at least 4 or 5 times this many that could be processed on the basis of what we think is available in the way of drug addicts in the District. Of course this is only for a period of 3 months really, which would mean about 50 patients a year.

The figures we have been using have been in the order of 150 to 200 per year as probably in the District needing treatment and could be rehabilitated and could be processed if they could be found, if they can be processed under the act, if the fact of their addiction can be shown with sufficient definition to warrant their commitment— there are many factors in other words that make the figure less than the total number of available addicts.

Chairman KEFAUVER. I am very interested in the fact that 31 of the 62 who have come into the hospital have done so voluntarily, is that correct?

Dr. SCHULZ. This is correct.

I might say that is partly influenced by the narcotic squad people who in some instances have suggested this to the individuals or they have suggested it to themselves at the time of an investigation and have said that they wanted treatment and would go into the hospital voluntarily and it is felt, by all concerned, since this is a civil process that the more the voluntary wishes of the individual can be brought to bear the better.

Chairman KEFAUVER. Mr. Mitler, you ask any questions you would like. I think it would be of great interest if you just explained whether this is working satisfactorily and you think it is a good plan.

Dr. SCHULZ. I think it is. Our emphasis is on rehabilitation. For that reason while we realize—I think the addict today, residual addict is a dangerous individual, should be confined. As a physician I am interested in those that can be treated. These represent in our recommendation those that are suitable for rehabilitation and can be helped if the facilities are available.

Mr. MITLER. This is a way of treating and helping the addict without making him a criminal, is that correct?

Dr. SHULZ. Yes, that is correct.

Mr. MITLER. Nonetheless, once they are committed, there is compulsion involved?

Dr. SCHULZ. That is correct.

Chairman KEFAUVER. You mean once they are committed they are required to stay for any given length of time?

Dr. SCHULZ. Yes. The act reads until rehabilitated. It is an indefinite commitment as I recall the exact wording of it.

Mr. MITLER. Certain of these persons go to the facility at Lexington, Ky.?

Dr. SCHULZ. Yes, that is correct; 15 since the act has been in operation.

Mr. MITLER. Do you know what the criterion is when they are dismissed from Lexington?

Dr. SCHULZ. No, I do not.

Mr. MITLER. But they stay at Lexington for a period of time and that is up to the judgment of the hospital authorities at Lexington.

Dr. SCHULZ. That is the way I understand it. The act reads.

Mr. MITLER. Dr. Chapman, is that correct?

Dr. CHAPMAN. Pardon?

Mr. MITLER. Is that correct that in the civil commitments from the District of Columbia law that the person stays at Lexington until they are certified for release by the hospital?

Dr. CHAPMAN. I believe the law reads up to a year and after that time they have to get special permission of the judge. Also prior to that time at the end of 6 months they may have to show due reason for keeping him for a longer period of time.

Mr. MITLER. The point I had in mind that is most constructive is that after their release from Lexington then do they remain on probation and some supervision when they return here to the district, some form of followthrough?

Dr. SCHULZ. They are required to report to a clinic for periodic evaluation. I might say, we do think the law has some deficiencies and it is in this connection.

Mr. MITLER. Would you want to state what they were?

Dr. SCHULZ. As we see the difficulties, partly that has to do with the fact that they go to Lexington, which is located at a great distance from the environment to which they will return, which precludes any evaluation of the environment while there or attempt to control the setting to which they will return.

When they return they are transferred from the hospital to a clinic that has not known the individual prior to that moment. In other words one physician starts the treatment, another physician completes the treatment.

This is not good medicine, in general. I realize it is good medicine under the circumstances. I am not being critical of the things that are being done. In other words our emphasis is that the followup evaluation is little more than a checkup and cannot be therapy in any real sense of the word, that a more graduated form of release would make more medical sense, which would require, however, that facilities be located nearer the residence of the individual.

Chairman KEFAUVER. Well, the transfer to Lexington and then back here, the fact that there is not the continuity of medical observation is not an insurmountable difficulty.

Dr. SCHULZ. It is not insurmountable; no. It is a factor that would require the greatest and closest liaison between the hospital and the subsequent followup and treating authorities. I can't speak to that. I don't know what has been developed there.

Mr. MITLER. I think the useful part to learn is the fact that here at least is a seed of a program in which the addict is treated constructively and he is kept on a long-range period of time under some kind of affirmative supervision.

Dr. SCHULZ. It is an excellent and very firm beginning, I think to a good treatment program. I think it is a beginning though.

Chairman KEFAUVER. You say it is a beginning and that is quite right. We would certainly like for this to be made a model for States to follow.

Dr. SCHULZ. Yes.

Chairman KEFAUVER. Or to consider. What is the length of supervision that you give a patient after having been discharged from the hospital or discharged from Lexington?

Dr. SCHULZ. I think the act reads 2 years.

Chairman KEFAUVER. Can you make it longer or shorter than that?

Dr. SCHULZ. According to the act, I don't believe so. I think again that is one of the criticisms I have of the act that these periods of time as Dr. Chapman has said in Lexington, if they are to remain over a year they must go back in court and justify the reasons for this. That seems to me to place somewhat of a burden on the treating authorities there and the length of time held in the clinic. These people have severe characters of disorders and most psychiatrists would say they are not significantly going to be changed in many instances in 3 years.

At least 3 years is perhaps a good minimum.

Chairman KEFAUVER. Then you would recommend that the 2 years be changed so as to give you authority to keep them under supervision?

Dr. SCHULZ. Indefinitely.

Chairman KEFAUVER. Say for years or as long as you think necessary.

Dr. SCHULZ. In mental cases the commitment is indefinite and the subsequent parole can be made indefinite. I don't know why these same considerations do not apply here. These are mentally sick people.

Mr. MITLER. With respect to the bottom portion of the chart which refers to discharges I assume that means where the people are discharged from the District of Columbia General Hospital.

Dr. SCHULZ. Yes.

Mr. MITLER. The first one is to self, the next one is to Lexington, narcotics squad, et cetera. Can you amplify what this means and what the criterion is?

Dr. SCHULZ. When the process has been completed those discharged to Lexington are discharged because they have been committed to Lexington. They are discharged for transfer to Lexington, that is 12 plus 3 that we noted at the bottom that are awaiting.

A total of 15 have been committed. Those discharged to self are those where it was felt either they are not a drug user sufficiently within the meaning of the act to justify their commitment; in other words, we are guided by the United States attorney's office in this.

He lets us know that he does not think, or our letter of findings is not sufficient to support a civil commitment act and I think he is on somewhat the conservative side in not prosecuting cases where there may be a great deal of controversy at least in the beginnings of the act.

Mr. MITLER. I have no further questions.

Chairman KEFAUVER. This first line, discharges to self. You started this operation of putting the act into effect in September and it seems that in the same month that you just discharged 9 people to themselves and in the second month you discharged 14, that would indicate that they did not get very much treatment.

Dr. SCHULTZ. That's right; they don't.

Chairman KEFAUVER. Do you think they were cured of the addiction in the short time or there is a legal technicality where the district attorney didn't think he could sustain the commitment?

Dr. SCHULZ. I think it is about half of each perhaps, that the first half consists of those that were sufficiently periodic in their use of durgs and used drugs in small amounts and could not be declared a drug user and the other half would be those where the United States attorney did not feel he had sufficient legal material.

Chairman KEFAUVER. These discharged to themselves, do they have to continue to report for any length of time?

Mr. SCHULZ. No. Again the difficulty with the act is in part that the hospital to which they are going to be committed and the only treatment facility is presently at Lexington, Ky.

Chairman KEFAUVER. Well, you have a clinic where they could be required to——

Dr. SCHULZ. Not under the act. One of the things I spoke about when this act was being considered is the fact that the treatment must be confinement until cured. I think it reads something to that effect "Confined there for rehabilitation until released." In other words, they must be according to the act treated in confinement. It does not provide for any kind of graduated release or partial confinement as is done with mental cases. My feeling would be that we would be in a stronger position presuming a local facility were available to release them 8 o'clock in the morning to go to work and they returned to the hospital at 8 o'clock in the evening, as is done with other mental cases.

They are only out of the hospital for a specific purpose and for a specific period of time and having accomplished that purpose they return to the confinement of the hospital.

Under this act it would be impossible even if they were under local care. That is the way I read it.

Chairman KEFAUVER. Even if they didn't return to the hospital, might it not be of value if once a day or certain specified times they could return to be interviewed and talked to by a psychologist or a psychiatrist.

Dr. SCHULZ. Yes, indeed; very definitely.

Chairman KEFAUVER. There is no provision for that.

Dr. SCHULZ. No; there seems to be an abrupt transition, confinement until cure and then released to be watched, that is the emphasis.

Chairman KEFAUVER. You spoke about after they came back from Lexington they report to a clinic in the District of Columbia. What clinic is that?

Dr. SCHULZ. That is a clinic operated by the Health Department, it is a legal psychiatric service to the courts and that is it has been assigned this followup responsibility.

Chairman KEFAUVER. Why couldn't that clinic do some followup work with those people released directly here?

Dr. SCHULZ. As I undestand it, the act, that could not be made compulsory.

Chairman KEFAUVER. I know you are the chief psychiatrist.

Dr. SCHULZ. As I understand the act I don't think that could be accomplished under it. Perhaps it could. It would be an interpretation that I don't think most people would make.

Chairman KEFAUVER. That would be of some help even if there were just clinical followup.

Dr. SCHULZ. Very definitely; yes.

Mr. MITLER. Suppose on the probation someone does not turn up, as I understand quite a few don't, when they come back, are there teeth in the law that compel them to come in?

Dr. SCHULZ. Yes; there is. They can be picked up immediately and brought back in for reexamination and determination, whether they are a user or not.

The way the act reads, this implies more of a checkup rather than treatment.

To answer again your question, Senator, before they could be compulsorily required to go to the clinic they would have to be committed. Those discharged to themselves have not been committed. They are the same again as mental cases where commitment action is not found to be necessary, desirable, or possible, and then we have no authority, we can recommend but we have no authority to require without a commitment process attendance at a clinic. I agree that should be so. It might be desirable to require clinical attendance rather than hospital attendance at all.

This would be a question of medical opinion.

Mr. MITLER. Aren't some discharged because determination is made that treatment would not benefit them? I learned of a case where a girl went to Lexington several times and they discharged her because they gave up in despair?

Dr. SCHULZ. Yes; this is a treatment act and not a punishment act and for that reason the clinic users were we feel at least under the presently available facilities they cannot be held, we have not committed them.

Mr. MITLER. So they go back into the community and the merry-go-round goes on.

Chairman KEFAUVER. The third line under discharges, discharges to narcotic squad, you seem to have none, until November when you had six. Does that refer to the District of Columbia narcotics squad?

Dr. SCHULZ. Those are vagrancy cases who are brought in under title 3 of the act and cannot be committed under the civil portion of the act which excludes any with any criminal charges pending against them. They are discharged back to the squad for prosecution under those criminal aspects and this was what has been done in some of the chronic cases in order to confine them.

Chairman KEFAUVER. So that that means because there are criminal charges pending they cannot be kept in the hospital and they are discharged back to the narcotics squad for prosecution or whatever may be done?

Dr. SCHULZ. That's right.

Chairman KEFAUVER. Then is the same rule applicable to the District police?

Dr. SCHULZ. Yes. Actually police and narcotic squad there is more of a technical difference.

Chairman KEFAUVER. It does not mean the narcotics squad or police is supervising them for rehabilitation, only for the purpose of prosecution.

Dr. SCHULZ. That's right. Presumably they are then prosecuted.

Chairman KEFAUVER. So actually you have no followup after they are discharged?

Dr. SCHULZ. No; none whatsoever.

Chairman KEFAUVER. And that is an apparent weakness, one of the weaknesses of this act?

Dr. SCHULZ. I think so.

Chairman KEFAUVER. Well, sir, I assume that you and others who are interested and have charge of the administration of this act will make appropriate recommendations to the Congress for improvements in the light of your experience thus far.

Dr. SCHULZ. Yes; that has been very brief thus far. I think even as we had it given to us, we saw some possibilities for change. Perhaps our beginning experience is already sufficient to warrant some change.

Chairman KEFAUVER. I certainly hope you will as soon as possible, in the early part of the Congress, make such recommendations. It will be not only helpful to the treatment of victims here, but I think if there could be developed into a model treatment and followup law and procedure it would be very helpful to the many States that are also struggling, looking for some remedy.

Dr. SCHULZ. Yes, because there is very little of this so far. I would be very glad to get together with the other colleges working with this and initiate other recommendations as we now see it.

Chairman KEFAUVER. Who has the prime responsibility for the administration of this act?

Dr. SCHULZ. The District Commissioners, and through them the Health Department in the sense that they are the ones charged with the responsibility for initiating the action. Of course, in conjunction with the United States attorney who does the actual processing of the commitment.

Chairman KEFAUVER. I hope you will tell them of our great interest in this and solicit suggestions.

Mr. MITLER. Do you mean in these situations the United States attorney is declining to prosecute? What is the situation?

Chairman KEFAUVER. Planning not deliver, not to prosecute but to——

Dr. SCHULZ. We release them on information from the United States attorney. Obviously his decision is based in part on the medical findings. If we find the individual a drug user and so report, to my knowledge he has prosecuted all of these. If we are medically equivocal about it in the sense that we cannot say the person is a drug user within the meaning of the act, then it has to be a matter of his judgment as to whether what we do say is sufficient to warrant commitment proceedings or not.

In some instances we have had to say there is no medical evidence that the person is at this time a drug user. Most of the instances where there has not been prosecution there has been a matter of no withdrawal symptoms, nothing showing at the time, either the person has been withdrawn or is using it in such small quantities that he does not show immediate signs even though he has a history of purchasing or taking it.

So he had nothing but that information to go on.

Chairman KEFAUVER. Where they are committed and turned back to the narcotics squad or to the police for prosecution, presumably some of these people are tried on criminal charges. Then what happens to them?

Dr. SCHULZ. I don't know. I haven't any followup information on that; we have only had them very recently.

Chairman KEFAUVER. I assume they might even be sentenced in a penal institution or sent to Lexington according to the judgment of the court.

Dr. SCHULZ. Yes. Title 3 definitely stiffens the statute. Someone with legal information would have to comment on that.

It gives them an opportunity to confine them, I think, up to a year. I am not sure.

Chairman KEFAUVER. What is the budget for the operation of this program?

Dr. SCHULZ. The Public Health Service has agreed to take up to 200,000—I am not sure of that exact figure—at one time at Lexington. So far as facilities are concerned it is adequate to accommodate what we anticipate what might be the maximum load.

Chairman KEFAUVER. I know. But I mean for the District of Columbia, what is the budgetary amount designated for this program?

Dr. SCHULTZ. I don't have a figure. I break that down—moneys were made available in a limited amount for the team that does the actual processing, largely additional nursing personnel. As of the present I would not say that we require greater budgetary allocation for processing under the commitment phase.

My major recommendation would be for considerable expansion of the treatment phase, particularly the clinic aspect. I would question whether Dr. Griffin's clinic would absorb any large amount of treatment potentially. I would doubt it very much.

It would mean, in other words, expansion of clinic treatment facilities and local hospital treatment facilities if that should be desired.

And the act implies this: This allows the District to use the facilities at Lexington for 2 years at which time they are then presumably going to have facilities that will permit treatment locally. That is the hospital phase.

Chairman KEFAUVER. Who prepared the recommendation for this act; who worked up the procedure?

Dr. SCHULZ. Senator Daniels' committee largely.

Chairman KEFAUVER. I mean in the District of Columbia.

Who advised them?

Dr. SCHULZ. A great many persons were involved. The Health Department.

Chairman KEFAUVER. District attorney?

Dr. SCHULZ. Yes, United States attorney, narcotic people.

Chairman KEFAUVER. It is certainly a very wholesome step in the right direction. We certainly hope that that will be carried on and improved and enlarged to be put into full operation and also to the most useful operation.

Dr. SCHULZ. Our impression is that it has no negative aspects that we should not be in. It perhaps lacks things that could be added as additions.

Chairman KEFAUVER. Senator Langer?

Senator LANGER. No questions.

I understand that our witness is here that we sent for about the Indians.

Chairman KEFAUVER. We thank you very much, Dr. Schulz.

I believe we had one witness before, we had Mr. Rosenfeld who has to get back to a radio program.

TESTIMONY OF JOE ROSENFELD, JR.

Mr. MITLER. Your name, sir?

Mr. ROSENFELD. Joe Rosenfeld, Jr.

Mr. MITLER. What is your occupation, Mr. Rosenfeld?

Mr. ROSENFELD. I am a radio broadcaster.

Mr. MITLER. Very briefly, Mr. Rosenfeld, you have——

Chairman KEFAUVER. Let's get a little bit more about Mr. Rosenfeld. Big Joe's Happiness Exchange Foundation, Inc.

Mr. ROSENFELD. Yes, sir.

Chairman KEFAUVER. Is that the sponsorship of your program?

Mr. ROSENFELD. That is the title of the foundation. It is called on radio the Happiness Exchange.

Chairman KEFAUVER. This is a nonprofit tax-exempt foundation.

Mr. ROSENFELD. Yes, sir.

Chairman KEFAUVER. Which collects money and gives information for rehabilitation of narcotic addicts and others?

Mr. ROSENFELD. Yes.

Chairman KEFAUVER. I believe you married a girl from Tennessee, is that correct?

Mr. ROSENFELD. Chattanooga. My home is in Tennessee. I was born in Clarksville, Montgomery County.

Chairman KEFAUVER. It is good to have a Tennessean testify here, Senator Langer.

Senator LANGER. Off the record.

Chairman KEFAUVER. All right, we are glad to have you here, Mr. Rosenfeld, particularly with your good Tennessee background.

Mr. ROSENFELD. Thank you.

Chairman KEFAUVER. Will you proceed, Mr. Mitler?

Mr. MITLER. What we are particularly interested in is the fact that you have embarked in a personal way in helping many of the people who have been released from Lexington. Would you tell us about what you have done and what the results have been of this project of yours?

Mr. ROSENFELD. I think I can best explain how it happened as well as what has happened. It was through my own association with Alcoholics Anonymous that I felt that narcotic users could be kept free from drugs by the same identical 12 steps.

I have been a member of Alcoholics Anonymous successfully—it will soon be 12 years. We suggested that anyone who had a narcotic problem come to see us; we might be able to help them. And, in the past 5 years, we have sent over 300 drug addicts to Lexington. We have some who have been free from drugs 2, 3, 4, and 5 years.

Mr. MITLER. Some of them were under 21 years of age?

Mr. ROSENFELD. No. We have sent some who were—well I have known many. We have not sent any under 21. They may have been 20 or 21.

Mr. MITLER. But you have had contact with those in the under 21.

Mr. ROSENFELD. I am in contact with them because their parents bring them in to see me. We have been fairly successful only through a personal rehabilitation program.

I am sure that you gentlemen know the entire situation at Lexington. When you——

Mr. MITLER. Would you tell us what happens? What is the work that you do when they leave Lexington?

Mr. ROSENFELD. The work we do first is that we sent them there. My listeners send in contributions to help us help them. We provide them with a railroad ticket. We give them bus fare from the station or taxi fare. We tell them that if they will let us hear from them we will send them $2 or $3 a week commissary. When they come home, if they will get off the train and come directly to my studio, we will provide them with a week's rent, we will provide them with food. We will provide them with clothing, and we will give them a job and give them something to hold on to, which no one else has been able to do.

I have found—and I don't mean—I have had contact with some 800 to a thousand drug addicts, and the only way that I have found is to give that person a confidence in themselves, something that they know you believe in them.

In my opinion it is only a personal thing. A narcotic user is different than an alcoholic. They are different than any other form of addiction or habit, and unless some personal interest is shown in that particular person, their chances are not one in a million, because when they come back many of them as you know get off the train in Cincinnati. They take their first fix in Cincinnati, immediately when they get out. Some of them have people waiting for them when they get off the train in New York, even though they have been there 3 or 4 months.

Chairman KEFAUVER. What do you mean "people"?

Mr. ROSENFELD. Pushers and their friends. They only have $3 when they come back from Lexington. That money is used on the train for food. If it is a woman, she has no place to sleep. Her life has been completely ruined by drugs. She has no friends except narcotic users. She doesn't have a place to go that night. She does not know where she will get money for supper. She is immediately forced either into prostitution or to find the man who had been supplying her with drugs, and she can't stay off drugs.

If it is a man, he has to start stealing immediately, because no one will give him a job. He hasn't worked in from 2 to 10 years. He has no recommendations. He doesn't have anybody to give him a helping hand or to put out a hand and say, "I'm willing to help you."

He doesn't know anyone that is worthwhile, and he just doesn't have the chance, and we have found that the only way that we can help them—and we have, and I can produce approximately 40 addicts, and their term of using was from 5 to 20 years, but by giving them some decent clothes, giving them decent food, showing a personal interest in them, and giving them something to look forward to, you can help them.

But that in my opinion, and from what experience has been in 5 years—and I do feel that I have had sufficient experience to know this; that is the only way that you can rehabilitate a drug addict.

Mr. MITLER. In other words, you feel that only part of the job is done at the hospital and that the followup part is essential.

Mr. ROSENFELD. It is more than essential. It is an absolute necessity, and, if I might say, I don't want to fatten my part, but when a person goes to Lexington, if they have used drugs for a year or 2 or 5, 3 months is not sufficient time. It is from the standpoint of being through with the drugs physically, but not mentally. There should be at least 6 months, and the last 3 months should be a mental thing, giving the person a career, or teaching them typing or teaching them bookkeeping or teaching them selling, teaching them something that will be useful to them when they get out, and to have a job for them when they get out—and to have that, you could help instead of 2 percent, you could help 20 to 30 percent. If there were a positive means of that person not having to worry where their next meal is coming from.

Chairman KEFAUVER. What is the discharged addict from Fort Worth given in the way of money, transportation, et cetera?

Mr. ROSENFELD. $3 and a ticket back to where they came from.

Chairman KEFAUVER. And a ticket back to where they came from?

Mr. ROSENFELD. Yes, sir.

Chairman KEFAUVER. As far as you know—and I think it is correct—there is no program for finding them employment or giving them supervision or trying to see that they have a new environment, operated by the Federal Government?

Mr. ROSENFELD. I have not heard of it, and no one has ever mentioned it to me, nor has it ever been suggested by any of the addicts that there would be a place for them to go.

Chairman KEFAUVER. Your studio is in New York, and you told what you do for the ones who are discharged from Lexington. Does that apply only to those who come to New York?

Mr. ROSENFELD. No, sir; we have sent addicts from Maine, Connecticut—our station is a 50,000-watt station, and it reaches even into Canada. We have helped one man from Canada. We have helped people in Massachusetts. And I also have sent approximately 150 persons to Riker's Island, which is a voluntary thing in New York, a prison, to which a person, a man—it is for men only—can go to the criminal courts building and admit that he is a narcotic user, and he is sentenced to 30 days cold turkey, without even an aspirin tablet.

I have found when a man, a person is willing to do this, he has a much greater desire—and this is the one thing that I have not heard touched on here nor have I read—unless there is a desire in the person's mind that they do not have it, the law, a penalty of death, nothing can keep an addict off drugs unless the desire to be free is implanted in that person's mind.

And this is the great failing that this desire has not been put in the people's minds when they go to Lexington or Forth Worth or Riker's. Women are thrown into the House of Detention in New York, and the treatment there would startle you.   I am talking too much.

Chairman KEFAUVER. One or two other questions.   You have been carrying on this program since May 1949, is that correct?

Mr. ROSENFELD. That is when I went to New York.   I have been broadcasting there for 7½ years, 7 years and 8 months.   I have been working with the narcotics for 5 years.

Chairman KEFAUVER. How many have you been responsible for sending to Lexington or Fort Worth?

Mr. ROSENFELD. None to Fort Worth.   Approximately 250 to 300.

Chairman KEFAUVER. How many have you assisted upon release?

Mr. ROSENFELD. All that came back to us.   That would be roughly 50.   The rest——

Chairman KEFAUVER. That is only a small percentage of the number that are released from Lexington.

Mr. ROSENFELD. That is about 15 percent of them.   That is about the biggest percentage that has ever been shown—I am not boasting of our percentage.

Chairman KEFAUVER. A large number of them just don't have anybody to help them or don't avail themselves of any help after they release them.

Mr. ROSENFELD. Yes, that's right.

Chairman KEFAUVER. How much have your radio listeners sent in to carry on this work?

Mr. ROSENFELD. For narcotic addicts?

Chairman KEFAUVER. Yes.

Mr. ROSENFELD. The first 2 years we spent $36,000.   It is over $50,000.

Chairman KEFAUVER. Have you written a book about this matter?

Mr. ROSENFELD. No.   I have an autobiography in which there are several chapters about what we have done with narcotics.

Chairman KEFAUVER. As a matter of information, what is the name of the book?

Mr. ROSENFELD. The Happiest Man in the World.   That is an autobiography.   I did not come here to talk about my book or the radio program.   I came here because I have been helped——

Chairman KEFAUVER. You can't help my asking you about it.

Mr. ROSENFELD. No, sir.   And I apologize.   I did not mean it in that way.

Chairman KEFAUVER. I know you didn't come here to promote your own cause, but I thought as a matter of information I would ask you.

Mr. ROSENFELD. Thank you.   May I also tell you that Doubleday published the book?

Chairman KEFAUVER. All right, Mr. Mitler.

Mr. MITLER. Mr. Rosenfeld, you have spoken of course as we know to a great many people who have been at Lexington.   As a result of these conversations what can you say about the wisdom of the mixing of the small group of younger people that are with older addicts there?

Mr. ROSENFELD. I think it is criminal.

Mr. MITLER. For what reason?

Mr. ROSENFELD. To put a teen-ager or a person who has only been using drugs for 1 or 2 years together with men or women who have been incarcerated many times, who are 3- or 4-time losers. It makes of this teen-ager or young person a hardened criminal. The oldtimers teach them every way in the world to what they call boost and hussle and steal. They learn everything about how to break the law. They are taught everything.

They are taught even in there to crush aspirin tablets and put them in cigarettes, to use lighter fluid or anything. They are taught things that they never knew before. This they might find with other teen-agers but to me it is just putting, it is just giving them the worst chance in the world.

They have no chance when they are put in with these oldtimers who have been beating themselves to death for 15 or 20 years and who know all of the angles.

I personally think it is the worst thing that could possibly be done.

Mr. MITLER. You are not saying that Lexington isn't worthwhile, were you. It is your suggestion that they be segregated?

Mr. ROSENFELD. Lexington is wonderful, it is the only place you can, it is marvelous because it is the only place. There are certain things I feel—I am only a layman although an experienced layman— that could be added to Lexington to make it twice as efficient. I think it is marvelous that we have a place like that. My only complaint is that when you spend—I don't want to quote this as a fact but it would occur to me that it costs $2,500 to $3,000 to treat a narcotic addict.

I don't know what the budget is there but the number of addicts they put there in a year, I would say the least they can take care of an addict for is $2,500 and then to turn the man loose and give him $3 and say, go make a living and stay free from drugs, this to me is just horrible.

In regard to the young people, your chances of saving young people are very small because they haven't had enough arrests. They haven't had enough lumps, they haven't had enough heartbreaks, they haven't broken their mother's and father's heart. They haven't stolen everything that their parents had. They haven't robbed. They have just been arrested or someone has persuaded them to go to Lexington against their will.

They are not ready to quit drugs. But putting them in with these oldtimers you couldn't save one out of a hundred thousand, even if you brought him back and gave him a job and did everything I say, until such time he has proven to himself how low he can sink, he is not ready to quit.

An addict is ready to quit when he has sunk so low that there's nothing lower.

Mr. MITLER. I have no other questions.

Chairman KEFAUVER. Senator Langer?

Senator LANGER. No questions.

Chairman KEFAUVER. I think it is very important to consider a point you brought out. We all would know about it if we thought it through. That is that the average addict coming out of Lexington and somewhere else, he is not likely to have many friends, if any, who would be wholesome friends. By virtue of his addiction he would have lost most of the worthwhile friends, so that he naturally——

Senator LANGER. I might add, Mr. Chairman, in the National Penitentiary Committee a murderer coming out of the penitentiary can get $200 and a suit of clothing. Certainly the provision should be made to take care of these addicts and give them a start when they get out.

Chairman KEFAUVER. That is something new we got by in the last Congress, this $200.

Senator LANGER. Yes.

Mr. ROSENFELD. If I might make some suggestion. Years ago a jurist in Denver, Colo., his name was Judge Ben Lindsey, who did more with delinquency and young people than if under the Public Health Service System there would be one person in each city to which an addict could go.

If that would be a person whose confidence the addict could have, if he could go to this person, one person, you would have a whole lot less of the habitual narcotic users.

Senator LANGER. Don't you think the church ought to take an active interest in it, go to the Presbyterian minister, or Catholic priest or Jewish rabbi or Protestant minister?

Mr. ROSENFELD. I can only say this, that a plumber could not talk to an electrician. An electrician couldn't speak to a bricklayer. Unless a person has been an alcoholic he can't talk to another alcoholic. Unless a person has been a drug addict or has worked with them and knows the thoughts of the addict it is an impossibility.

You could not get anyone. They can't quit for their mother. They can't quit for their father. They can't quit for their children. They can't quit for God. They can only quit for themselves and this must be put into them until such time as they want to quit for themselves. They have denied God. They don't thing of God. They think of nothing but that next fix. That is the only thought in their minds and until such time as they have hit their bottom, and until such time as they want to quit for themselves, they will never quit.

There is only one way to put that in their mind and that is to show them the advantages of quitting.

Chairman KEFAUVER. At least the rabbi or the priest or the minister would have contacts to help them secure employment and be someone to take an interest in them?

Mr. ROSENFELD. If they will.

Chairman KEFAUVER. So I think there is a lot of validity in Senator Langer's suggestion.

Mr. ROSENFELD. I certainly do. I know of one priest in New York who also was an addict. This man can talk to them. He was an addict and he whipped drugs and he is now 25 years. It happens that he is a priest. He can help because he knows what he is talking about.

Chairman KEFAUVER. All right, thank you, Mr. Rosenfeld. I want to say that we appreciate the work you are doing.

Mr. ROSENFELD. Thank you. I brought that for you.

Mr. MILTER. Mr. Rosenfeld had a lady with him. We heard her in executive session just a little earlier and we have that on the record, her testimony which is helpful.

Chairman KEFAUVER. Yes; I know. Senator Langer told me. We thank you very much.

(Discussion off the record.)

Chairman KEFAUVER. We will stand in recess until 2 o'clock.

(Whereupon, at 12:55 p. m., a recess was taken until 2 p. m. of the same day.)

AFTERNOON SESSION

Chairman KEFAUVER. Mr. Rufus King, will you come around, please.

STATEMENT OF RUFUS KING, PARTNER IN THE LAW FIRM OF RICE & KING, WASHINGTON, D. C.

Mr. MITLER. Your name is Rufus King?

Mr. KING. Rufus King.

Mr. MITLER. Would you state your occupation?

Mr. KING. I am a partner in the law firm of Rice & King in Washton, D. C., a member of the New York, Maryland, and District of Columbia bars.

Mr. MITLER. What is your background in connection with this problem that the committee is having hearings on?

Mr. KING. Well, I had the honor and privilege of serving with the chairman and Senator Wiley with the Senate Crime Committee. I was then counsel to a subcommittee of the Senate District Committee investigating crime and law enforcement in the District of Columbia, which made an extensive study of the narcotics situation locally here in the District.

I served as a consultant to the commission on organized crime of the American Bar Association. I have been secretary of the criminal-law section of the American Bar Association for the last 3 years; chairman of its committee on narcotics and alcohol; and I am presently serving as chairman of a joint committee of the American Bar Association and American Medical Association, which is engaged in making a thorough reappraisal of the attitude of the two professions and their responsibilities toward this whole field of narcotic-drug addiction, and the policies and problems relating to it.

Mr. MITLER. Would it be possible for you to first make a statement with respect to the juvenile problem? I think that would be helpful, if you could touch on that.

Chairman KEFAUVER. Before you start, Mr. King, I would like for the record to show that the chairman appreciates his long acquaintance with Rufus King, dating back over a period of many years. Mr. King served capably and unusually well as associate counsel of the Senate Crime Investigating Committee; and in these other capacities which he has mentioned, it has been very gratifying to me to find he has a continuing active interest in committees of the American Bar Association and other associations interested in improving law enforcement, giving young people a better chance.

All too often, people who do have some official connection with committees such as we have had here in Congress, lose their interest as soon as they get out. Rufus King has given strenuously of his time in helping us frame legislation, and supporting it with testimony, and we are very grateful for your interest and your help to us.

Mr. KING. Thank you, Senator, and I would certainly like to observe that from my association with the work of the bar association and with other groups interested in improving law enforcement, that from the beginning of the work of the Crime Committee to the present, we have always looked on Senator Kefauver as our stanchest and most devoted friend and ally and associate in this type of endeavor.

To refer to the relation of young people to this problem will take me to perhaps the most important single point that I want to make, and I shall approach it right at the outset, and that is to urge this committee to give the most serious weight and consideration to the proposals and the views that you have heard and are about to hear with respect to treating the narcotic addict as a sick person, as a person with a medical affliction rather than as a criminal.

For some 40 years past, we have been dedicated to the proposition that the narcotics traffic and everything and everyone related to it is a criminal activity and a criminal endeavor, and this attitude has reached its culmination in the last few years with the enactment at the Federal level of mandatory minimum sentences of great severity, out of all proportion to the penalty structure that supports other similar Federal legislation.

This has cut the narcotics addict himself, the afflicted person on whom this traffic feeds, this has cut him off from any possibility of making a bargain with society for his own comfort or salvation. It has driven him into the arms of the peddler. He is unable to deal with public-health authorities. He is unable to deal with the medical profession in solving this problem.

He has only the peddler, and I certainly concur with everything that has been said in these hearings about what a vicious, predatory type of criminal the nonaddicted peddler who preys on these people is.

I think that this point is of greatest importance with respect to the young people who become involved with the peripheries of this traffic. The type of addict that perhaps has drawn most of this opprobrium from the press and the public and the severe legislation, is the old, confirmed addict who has been through several cures, who has had to resort to crime to support his addiction.

The person with whom society should begin to treat and deal is the youngster who is on the threshold of this. It is my opinion, and I am going to allude briefly to the reasons why I hold to that opinion in a minute, it is my opinion that the medical profession should assume primary responsibility for the handling of this problem.

In the interim, until we perhaps reach a point where medical doctors are able to begin the treatment of narcotics addicts, I think it is imperative that some increased provisions be made to enable the public-health authorities to establish treatment facilities and treatment programs. And again I come back to the importance of this kind of program for the youngster who is just starting.

We have had something of an "iron curtain" over this area. We have had a little, very little, understanding of the problems involved. And specifically—well, there is an interim stage of addiction which is easily curable, where the victim is salvageable.

Many of the youngsters who have been brought to light in some of these studies have had actually a needle habit. They have had so little actual narcotics ingested that simply stopping the injection process cures them of their addiction.

So, I would try to summarize this point that I am trying to make, that some kind of facilities recognized by society, whether it is called a clinic, a public-health establishment, a doctor's office somewhere, where a young person who is either embroiled in the edges of this affliction or embroiled with associates who are involved in it, can go and sit down across a desk from a man with a white coat, discuss the problem, be given guidance, be given such treatment, rehabilitation, therapy, employment assistance, help in working out whatever the other problems that are involved are—this is the imperative first step.

And I think that if your committee could make it possible for some such establishment to be created on at least an experimental basis, perhaps a narcotics information center would be a sufficient formulation, but something where these youngsters who still realize only that this is on the edge of a profound kind of criminality, can still reach across to society, reach across to the authoritative medical man or public-health officer, and discuss the problem and work it out, and undertake some kind of curative treatment at the outset.

Mr. MITLER. Excuse me, Mr. King. What is your—you are familiar with the situation in the District of Columbia?

Mr. KING. Yes.

Mr. MITLER. What is the available program for youngsters in the District of Columbia? Would you comment on that?

Mr. KING. Well, to my knowledge, there is nothing of the kind of facility that I have in mind, nor is there anything that approaches the kind of atmosphere that I am speaking toward in the District of Columbia.

In the District of Columbia, the narcotic addict is subject either to imprisonment if he is caught in possession of narcotics, under the Federal narcotics laws, as a criminal, or he is subject to imprisonment under the recently revised Civil Commitment Act, which now permits an officer to take him into custody, to deprive him of his liberty, on suspicion he is an addict.

And perhaps this is even a better way to point out what I am trying to say. This dual approach of criminal law enforcement directed at the addict to the fullest possible extent, if you can make a possession case or get him for vagrancy or loitering or peddling on the one hand, and involuntary commitment for the mere fact of addiction on the other hand, is the ultimate way in pushing the addict into the underworld community.

So that I would say that the situation here is similar to the situation in most other communities, with the exception of New York, where they have done some very fine pioneering work, and I believe California, where some attempt under their Youth Authority Act has been made to approach the potential delinquent in this narcotics area before he becomes deeply involved, as actually similar efforts have been made to approach him in the predelinquency phase in other areas.

Mr. MITLER. In New York, you mean the Riverside Hospital on North Brothers Island?

Mr. KING. Yes.

I should add, also, that I believe similar work has been undertaken in Chicago, where there is a narcotics facility which has made considerable efforts to approach salvageable addicts, if that is a fair word, before they are embroiled with the law.

Mr. MITLER. The Northwestern Clinic, is that the one?

Mr. KING. Yes.

I have led to this conclusion which follows from the main point I wanted to make before the committee.

Mr. MITLER. Surely.

Mr. KING. If I might very briefly return to that now.

I have already stated that the basic philosophy which I bring to bear on this from my studies of it, is that the problem of addiction itself is a medical problem. It is a health problem. I believe that back in the 1920's, we made the disastrous mistake of converting what was in effect a tax measure, the Harrison Act, into a law-enforcement measure, and then the further mistake of wiping out any distinction between the addict who is the victim of the traffic, and the peddler who is exploiting him.

And the point that I wish to emphasize and leave on this committee's record is that in my opinion as a lawyer, and based on my studies of the Harrison Act and its history, this entire position is not soundly grounded in the original legislation, and it is not consistent with the direct pronouncements of the Supreme Court on the subject.

The ruling case on the interpretation of the Harrison Act with respect to its impact on the relations between narcotics addicts and the medical profession, is the case of *United States* v. *Linder*, which was decided by the Supreme Court by a unanimous court in 1925, and this language, a very brief quotation which I would like to read into the record, is the Court's pronouncement on the subject at that time, and it is still the law of the land.

Referring to the Harrison Act, the Court said, and I commence the quotation:

The enactment under consideration levies a tax, upheld by this Court, upon every person who imports, manufactures, produces, compounds, sells, deals in, dispenses or gives away opium or coca leaves or derivatives therefrom, and may regulate medical practice in the States only so far as reasonably appropriate for or merely incidental to its enforcement. It says nothing of "addicts" and does not undertake to prescribe methods for their medical treatment. They are diseased and proper subjects for such treatment * * *.

And then the opinion goes on to discuss an earlier case, the case of *United States* v. *Behrman*, on which the then enforcement authorities had based their law-enforcement activities with respect to the medical profession, and of this Behrman case the Supreme Court says:

The opinion cannot be accepted as authority for holding that a physician who acts bona fide and according to fair medical standards, may never give an addict moderate amounts of drugs for self-administraiton in order to relieve conditions incident to addiction. Enforcement of the tax demands no such drastic rule, and if the act had such scope it would certainly encounter grave constitutional difficulties.

That is the end of the quotation.

I have made an extensive analysis of these cases, and the quotations that I was reading from are from this rather lengthy analysis which I would like to submit for the record, if I may.

Mr. MITLER. Yes; I ask that it be made subcommittee exhibit No. 10.

Chairman KEFAUVER. Let it be made a part of the record.

(The document referred to was marked "Exhibit No. 10," and is as follows:)

The Narcotics and the Harrison Act: Jailing the Healers and the Sick

By Rufus King*

At last there are faint stirrings to suggest that this Nation's policies toward its narcotic drug traffic may soon be exposed to a full critical reexamination and review.[1] Nearly 40 years have gone by since Congress passed the Harrison Act,[2] intended partly to carry out a treaty obligation,[3] but mainly to aid the States in combating a local police problem which had gotten somewhat out of hand.[4] In other areas of law enforcement, when Congress has thrown Federal power into the balance, these local problems have usually diminished or disappeared.[5] In the case of narcotics control, however, the indications are all quite to the contrary.

It must be conceded that there are large gaps in what we know about narcotics addiction and the illicit traffic. The comment elsewhere in the Journal[6] presents a dispassionate collection of information and authorities. Yet there is simply not much to go by. When the Federal authorities took over, we entered a 40-year eclipse; for years on end there has been nothing but the "official line" for those who wished to inquire into the subject. But enough information is available to convince this writer; along with a handful of other protestants,[7] that the United States—alone among civilized nations—has driven relentlessly down the wrong road ever since the end of World War I. This article (which is not dispassionate) will relate the episode in our legal history which propelled our enforcement agencies along this road. But first it may be helpful to set forth a brief history of the relationship between the addict and his Government.

Our grievous error was in allowing the narcotics addict to be pushed out of society and relegated to the criminal community. He isn't a criminal. He never has been. And nobody looked on him as such until the furious blitzkrieg launched around 1918 in connection with the enforcement of the Harrison Act.

That act was a tax measure, designed and intended to bring the domestic traffic in narcotics into the open under a licensing system, so that the sloppy dispensing practices of the day could be checked. It said nothing about "addicts" (partly because the word had not achieved its wide current usage), and specifically exempted the "patient" in bona fide doctor-patient relationships.[8] Narcotics users were "sufferers" or "patients" in those days; they could and did get relief from any reputable medical practitioner, and there is not the slightest suggestion that Congress intended to change this—beyond cutting off the disreputable "pushers" who were thriving outside the medical profession and along its peripheries.

Two things, very likely related, distorted this intent. The act was assigned, for enforcement, to the same righteous zealots who were undertaking another national mistake—enforcement of our then new prohibition laws;[9] and, secondly,

---

*Special counsel, subcommittee of House Committee on the Judiciary to investigate the Department of Justice; special counsel, Investigations Subcommittee of Senate Interstate Commerce Committee.

[1] See note 70 infra. See also S. Rept. No. 725, 82d Cong., 1st sess. (1951); hearings before Special Committee To Investigate Organized Crime in Interstate Commerce, 82d Cong., 1st sess, pt. 14 (1951); Goldstein, Narcotics, a Report by the Attorney General to the Legislature of the State of New York (Legislative Doc. No. 27, 1952).

[2] 38 Stat. 785 (1914), 26 U. S. C., sec. 2550 (1946).

[3] The United States adhered to the Hague Opium Convention on January 23, 1912 (38 Stat. 1912 (1912)); this obliged adherents to control the manufacture, sale, use, and transfer of "morphine, cocaine, and their respective salts."

[4] See H. Rept. No. 23, 63d Cong., 1st sess. 2 (1913).

[6] Comment, Narcotics Regulation, 2 Yale Law Journal 751 (1953).

[5] See, e. g., 31 Stat. 188 (1900), 18 U. S. C., sec. 43 (1946) (poaching); 41 Stat. 324 (1919), 18 U. S. C., secs. 2312–13 (1946) (transportation of stolen vehicles); 47 Stat. 326 (1932), 18 U. S. C., sec. 1201 (1946) (kidnaping).

[7] See, e. g., remarks of Hon. John M. Coffee, 83d Congressional Record 2607 (1938); Stevens, Make Dope Legal, Harpers Magazine, November 1952, p. 40; statement of Representative Cleveland M. Bailey, member of House Interstate and Foreign Commerce Committee, March 23, 1953.

[8] The exempting language, relieving from the duty to use Treasury-prescribed order forms, 38 Stat. 786 (1914), 26 U. S. C., sec. 2554 (c) (1) (1946), is:

"Nothing contained in the section * * * shall apply * * * [t]o the dispensing or distribution of any of the drugs mentioned * * * to a patient by a physician, dentist, or veterinary surgeon registered under sec. 3221 in the course of his professional practice only. * * *" [Emphasis supplied.]

Those who avail themselves of this exemption must keep records of each transaction for a prescribed period.

[9] Schmeckebier, The Bureau of Prohibition, in Service Monograph 57, Institute for Government Research, Brookings Institute 3 (1929). The Narcotics Division was merged into the Prohibition Unit of the Treasury Department in 1920, and carried into the Prohibition Bureau when the latter was created in 1927. Since 1930 it has been a separate entity entitled "The Federal Narcotics Bureau."

a great public hullabaloo about the "dope menace" swept the country.[10]   The
narcotics user suddenly became a "dope fiend."   Official estimates of the addict
population leapt to the fantastic figure of 1 million—mostly young folk, many
"under the age of 20." [11]   The good people of our land were terrified.   The
Narcotics Division of the Treasury Department came charging to the rescue;
our prisons began to fill, not with illicit peddlers only, but with addicts—and
reputable medical men who had tried to help them.[12]   And there has been no
surcease from that day to this.

In sum, the Narcotics Division succeeded in creating a very large criminal
class for itself to police (i. e., the whole doctor-patient-addict-peddler community), instead of the very small one that Congress had intended (the smuggler
and the peddler).   Subsequent Division officials have sustained the enforcement-
oriented propaganda barrage: the addict is a criminal, a criminal type, or laden
with criminal tendencies;[13] addicts can only be dealt with by being tracked down
and isolated from society in total confinement;[14] the cureall is more arrests and
stiffer criminal penalties for all narcotics offenders;[15] and anyone who raises a
dissenting voice is most likely a bungling "do-gooder" [16] or one who wants to
undermine the foundations of our society.[17]   The States have been pushed and
swept along this same vindictive line of approach,[18] with very few dissents.[19]
And the present campaign is as vigorous and formidable as ever.[20]   To this cam-

[10] See New York Times, April 10, 1919, p. 1; U. S. Treasury Department, Report of
Special Committee To Investigate the Traffic in Narcotic Drugs (April 15, 1919) (quoted
in U. S. Treasury Department, The Traffic in Habit-Forming Narcotic Drugs (1923)).
[11] U. S. Treasury Department, The Traffic in Habit-Forming Narcotic Drugs (1923).
It is noteworthy that as soon as the Narcotics Division turned to reporting its enforcement
achievements, this estimate dropped to 100,000 and remained at that figure until World
War II.
[12] As of June 30, 1928, of the 7,738 prisoners in Federal penitentiaries, 2,529 were
sentenced for narcotics offenses, 1,156 for prohibition law violations, and 1,148 for stolen-
vehicles transactions.   Data are not available for approximately the same number in
State institutions at this time.   Schmeckebier, supra, note 9, at 143.
[13] See, e. g., Federal Narcotics Bureau, Memorandum Regarding Narcotic Clinics, Their
History and Hazards, 6 (1938) :
"With regard to the plan which is in effect in Formosa, we have a valuable and informing
contribution to our knowledge on the subject by Dr. Somei To of the Health Commission of
Formosa.   After classifying 57,073 crimes committed during 7 years by natives of
Formosa, his records show that based upon the relative proportion of opium users to
nonusers we find *70.83 percent criminality among opium users as against 29.17 percent
criminality among nonusers.*   In Formosa, opium smoking is licensed and the cost of opium
is very small.   UNDER THESE CONDITIONS THE ONLY ATTRIBUTABLE CAUSE
FOR GREATER CRIMINALITY AMONG NARCOTIC ADDICTS THAN NONADDICTS
IS THE DIRECT EFFECT OF THE USE OF NARCOTICS UPON THE CHARACTER
OF THE USER.   Dr. To gives us the answer.   It is because drug addiction causes a
relentless destruction of character and releases criminal tendencies."   [Emphasis as in
original.]
[14] Id., at 4 :
"Medical authorities agree that the treatment of addiction with the view toward effecting
a cure, which makes no provision for confinement while the drug is being withdrawn, is a
failure, except in a relatively small number of cases where the addict is possessed of a
much greater degree of will power than the average addict."
[15] See testimony of Commissioner Harry J. Anslinger, Federal Bureau of Narcotics, in
hearings before Special Committee to Investigate Crime in Interstate Commerce, 82d Cong.,
1st sess., pt. 14, pp. 426–432 (1951).
[16] See, e. g., McCarthy, A Prosecutor's Viewpoint on Narcotics Addition in Fed.
Prohib. Q., October 1943 (reprinted and distributed by the Federal Bureau of Narcotics in
1945).
[17] In the Chicago Daily News, December 15, 1952, the last argument in extremis was set
forth by local public officials of that city : proponents of clinic treatment for narcotic addicts
are obviously Communists or Communist-inspired, seeking to destroy the integrity of the
American people.
[18] Illinois Legislative Council, Disposition of Narcotic Law Offenders and Addicts,
12–19 (1951).   A careful distinction must be made between incarceration per se, and programs which place true emphasis on treatment and rehabilitation.   The Federal hospitals
at Lexington, Ky., and Fort Worth, Tex., are admirable examples of the latter.
[19] Governors Green and Stevenson both vetoed incarceration laws for the State of Illinois
because no provisions for adequate treatment had been made.   Veto messages, July 24,
1947, and August 9, 1949, respectively.   In the words of Governor Stevenson :
"It appears that the provision in this bill authorizing imprisonment may have been
intended only as a threat to compel the addict to undergo treatment, but whatever may
have been the intention in this regard, the bill does authorize imprisonment for a condition
which it is admitted does not constitute a criminal act."
[20] The Narcotics Bureau is pressing a bill, H. R. 3307, 83d Cong., 1st sess. (1953), which
would provide incarceration for all addicts in the District of Columbia.   The worst feature
of this bill—in the light of the full problem—is a "sneaker" in the recitation of its
purpose, which reads:
"The Congress intends that Federal criminal laws shall be enforced against drug users
as well as other persons. * * *"
This may prove as effective, and as tricky, as the "rigged" indictment to which this
article is principally addressed.

;paign, the judiciary made its own contribution in a series of decisions rendered in the 1920's and to which we now turn.

THE NARCOTIZATION OF THE HIGH COURT

Dr. Behrman and his predecessors

Before the Narcotics Division could really turn the Nation into a happy hunting ground, stocked with addicts as fair game, it had to drive the medical profession out of the way. As has been noted, section 2 of the Harrison Act exempted the prescription of drugs "to a patient by a physician * * * in the course of his professional practice only." [21] This was unrevealing draftsmanship,[22] and many doctors felt that the agonies of unrelieved addiction were as much encompassed in their Hippocratic Oath as any other human suffering.

The division's assault on this expression of the physician's conscience started in the courts. The Government aimed for a construction which would exclude from the Harrison Act exemption a doctor's dispensation of narcotics to ease an addict's craving. The attack had two objectives: to end all so-called ambulatory treatment [23] (including the clinic system for controlled distribution of drugs to addicts [24]); and then, if possible, to drive the profession away from the addict altogether. It succeeded in both goals—for a brief period. But its short-lived success was enough, as we shall see. Government victories in the Supreme Court, culminating in *United States* v. *Behrman*,[25] pose two problems that are broader than the subject matter of this discussion. To what extent is it morally justified for an administrative agency to select the cases it feeds our appeals courts in order to gain some desired interpretation or result? And how far ought the rule of stare decisis be extended into successive administrative actions and interpretations—particularly when the court decision underlying the original action has meanwhile been effectively overruled?

The Harrison Act came through its first constitutional test by a 5-to-4 margin.[26] On the same day the Court decided *Webb* v. *United States*,[27] a physician case under the exemption in section 2. The facts showed flagrant abuse; the doctor had sold prescriptions—4,000 of them in 11 months—indiscriminately to anyone for 50 cents apiece. The issue was presented in a certified question:

"If a practicing and registered physician issues an order for morphine to a habitual user thereof, the order not being issued by him in the course of professional treatment in the attempted cure of the habit, but being issued for the purpose of providing the user with morphine sufficient to keep him comfortable by maintaining his customary use, is such order a physician's prescription under exception (b) of § 2?" [28]

The Court replied:

"[T]o call such order for the use of morphine a physician's prescription would be so plain a perversion of meaning that no discussion of the subject is required."[29]

Note how the question was loaded: "sufficient to keep him comfortable by maintaining his customary use" is not a description of the facts of the case; it not only blankets the outright peddling involved in the case before the Court, but it also reaches toward the bona fide administration of drugs for the relief of a patient-addict.

---

[21] See note 8 supra.

[22] The legislative history of the provision sheds little light. The original draft required that the physician "shall personally attend upon such patient." H. Rept. No. 23, 63d Cong., 1st sess. 3 (1913). The Senate proposed changing this to: "shall have been specially employed to prescribe for the particular patient receiving such drug: And provided further, That such drug shall be dispensed in good faith and not for the purpose of avoiding the provisions of this act." S. Rept. No. 258, 63d Cong., 2d sess. 4 (1914). The ensuing conference adopted the present language without edifying comment, merely noting that the requirement of personal attendance had been dropped and that the dispensing physician, etc., would be required to keep records. H. Rept. No. 1196, 63d Cong., 2d sess. (1914).

[23] There is a much-neglected distinction between prescription of narcotics to an addict for self-administration, and direct administration by the physician. The former is the subject of valid criticism, i. e., it does remove all restraints on consumption by the addict, and the drugs prescribed may be resold in the illicit traffic. There is merit in the suggestion, made from time to time, that all self-administration of narcotics should be made illegal. The "official line" has always ignored this distinction, equating prescription for self-administration with direct or supervised administration, and attacking both as "ambulatory treatment."

[24] See notes 70, 72, infra; Comment, Narcotics Regulation, 62 Yale L. J. 751 (1952).

[25] 258 U. S. 280 (1922). See pp. 741–744, infra.

[26] *United States* v. *Doremus*, 249 U. S. 86 (1919).

[27] 249 U. S. 96 (1919).

[28] *Webb* v. *United States*, 249 U. S. 96, 99 (1919).

[29] Id., at 99–100.

The next case, *Jin Fuey Moy* v. *United States*,[30] was likewise flagrant on its facts. The doctor had prescribed morphine to strangers indiscriminately, in bulk, 8 to 10 grams at a time for $1 per gram. The Court, this time apparently choosing its own wording, said:

"Manifestly the phrases 'to a patient' and 'in the course of his professional practice only' are intended to confine the immunity of a registered physician, in dispensing the narcotic drugs mentioned in the art, strictly within the appropriate bounds of a physician's professional practice, and not to extend it to include a sale to a dealer or a distribution intended to cater to the appetite or satisfy the craving of one addicted to the use of the drug." [31]

Again, the language goes beyond the facts of the case. It separates "professional practice" from any administration whatsoever "intended to cater to the appetite or satisfy the craving" of an addict.

Now the stage was set for Dr. Berhman. For purposes of finding the doctor a peddler for profit, the case presented an ideal set of facts. He was arrested in New York for giving one addict, at one time, for use as the addict saw fit, prescriptions for 150 grains of heroin, 360 grains of morphine, and 210 grains of cocaine.[32] Again the question posed was whether this was "in the course of his professional practice only." The Government, however, drew up a trick indictment, alleging not that the prescriptions were incompatible with approved and proper therapeutic treatment, but instead alleging that, in effect, the drugs were given in a good faith attempt to cure the addict.[33]

Behrman demurred. The district judge delivered a brief tirade against "ambulatory treatment," but reluctantly sustained the demurrer, referring to a decision in another trick-indictment case,[34] and closing with an inviting conclusion: "For the sake of uniformity in this district, however, I am disposed to follow precedent until the question is concluded by a decision of the Supreme Court." [35]

The Government appealed the case directly to the Supreme Court [36] and promptly moved to advance it, stating in support of its motion:

"[The case involves] a matter of general public interest, viz. * * * what is the meaning of the words 'in the course of his professional practice only' in that

---

[30] 254 U. S. 189 (1920).

[31] Id., at 194.

[32] Enough, as the Supreme Court noted, for over 3,000 standard injections. *United States* v. *Behrman*, 258 U. S. 280, 289 (1922).

[33] After reciting the delivery to the addict, one Willie King, the indictment alleged:
"That on said date the said Willie King was a person addicted to the habitual use of morphine, heroin, and cocaine and known by the defendant to be so addicted; that on said date the said Willie King did not require the administration of either morphine, heroin, or cocaine by reason of any disease or condition other than such addiction, and the defendant did not dispense said drugs or any of them to said Willie King for the purpose of treating any disease or condition other than such addiction; that none of the said drugs so dispensed by the defendant was administered or intended by the defendant to be administered to the said Willie King by the defendant or by any nurse or person, other than the said Willie King, acting under the direction of the defendant, nor were any of said drugs consumed or intended by the defendant to be consumed by the said Willie King in the presence of the defendant, but all of said drugs were put in the physical possession and control of the said Willie King with the intention on the part of the defendant that the said Willie King would use same by self-administration in divided doses over a period of several days, the amount of each of said drugs dispensed as aforesaid being more than sufficient or necessary to satisfy the craving of the said Willie King therefor if consumed by him all at one time: that said Willie King was not, at the time and place aforesaid, nor was he intended to be, during the period in which the drugs dispensed as aforesaid were to be used by him, under the observation and physical control of the defendant or of any nurse or other person acting under the direction of the defendant, nor was said Willie King in any way restrained or prevented from disposing of said drugs in any manner he might see fit; that said drugs dispensed by the defendant to the said Willie King as aforesaid were not mixed with any other substance, medicinal or otherwise, but were in the form in which said drugs are usually consumed by persons addicted to the habitual use thereof to satisfy their craving therefor and were adopted for such consumption; against the peace * * * etc." (transcript of record, pp. 2–3, *United States* v. *Behrman*, 258 U. S. 280 (1922)).
For a rather complete paraphrase of the indictment, see *United States* v. *Behrman*, 258 U. S. 280, 286–287 (1922).

[34] *United States* v. *Balint*, C. 28/136, S. D. N. Y., June 28, 1921, in transcript of record, pp. 4–5, *United States* v. *Balint*, 258 U. S. 250 (1922), in which the indictment alleged violation of sec. 2 of the Harrison Act without including the word "willfully." Defendant's demurrer to the indictment was sustained, and the indictment dismissed. Ibid. The dismissal was ultimately reversed by the Supreme Court, *United States* v. *Balint*, supra, which ruled that it was not necessary that defendant have knowledge of the fact that the product sold was a drug whose sale was regulated by the act.

[35] *United States* v. *Behrman*, C. 28/425, S. D. N. Y., September 21, 1921, in transcript of record, pp. 5–6, *United States* v. *Behrman*, 258 U. S. 280 (1922).

[36] Under the Criminal Appeals Act, 34 Stat. 1246 (1907), now as amended, 18 U. S. C. sec. 3731 (Supp. 1951).

portion of the act which exempts from its provisions the dispensing or distribution of the drugs to a patient by a physician 'in the course of his professional practice only.'

"The practical administration of the Harrison Narcotic Act is dependent, to a very large extent, upon the decision which this court may render in [this case]." [37]

In the Behrman brief, Solicitor General Beck made no attempt to gloss over what was being sought, apparently relying—rightly, as the outcome proved— on the flagrancy of the case and the prevailing temper of the times: [38]

"The purpose of this indictment and of the present writ of error is to raise for the determination of this Court the following questions, viz., whether the so-called 'ambulatory treatment' of drug addicts by a physician is or is not, as a matter of law, prohibited by section 2 of the Harrison Narcotic Act. * * * By the term 'ambulatory treatment' is meant the treatment by a physician of a drug addict, for the alleged cure of his drug addiction, by giving to him a prescription for the amount of the drug which the physician, in good faith, believes to be necessary in the condition of the drug addict at the time the prescription is given, for his use as one dose or over a period of time, and allowing the addict to take the prescription and to use it in any manner he may see fit, without any supervision or control of the doctor over him in any manner or form whatsoever.[39]

* * * * * * *

"The theory of the indictment is that this action upon the part of the defendant was, not a question for the jury, either on the defendant's intent, or as to what constituted the legitimate practice of his profession, but a violation of the Harrison Narcotic Act as a matter of law. * * *

"In order that the matter may be made perfectly clear, it should be again insisted that, according to the indictment, the so-called 'patient' in this case was suffering from no disease whatever except drug addiction. It must be admitted, for the purpose of the case at bar, that drug addiction is a disease, and that the defendant intended by his method of treatment to cure the same, and honestly believed that he could cure the disease by this method. Nevertheless, it is a well known fact, of which this court has taken notice, that drug addicts as a class are persons weakened materially in their sense of moral responsibility and in their power of will, and this court also knows, as a matter of common knowledge, that, in any community where drugs are prescribed, there will be a large number of physicians to whom any construction of section 2 of the Harrison Narcotic Act will be applicable. The question therefore, is whether every physician licensed and registered under the Harrison Narcotic Act, is at liberty, if he honestly believes such a course to be proper, to furnish to persons of the character of the drug addicts the means to obtain drugs without any supervision upon the part of the various doctors involved of the manner or time of taking the drugs or whether, indeed, the drugs are ever taken by the addict at all.

* * * * * * *

"It is true that in the Doremus, Webb, and Jin Fuey Moy cases it was assumed that the physician * * * did not honestly intend to effect a cure of the drug addiction and did not honestly believe that his method would effect a cure, but was merely administering the drug to satisfy the cravings of the addict; and that this court is asked in the case at bar to go beyond these decisions, and to hold that, irrespective of the physician's intent or belief, the act is violated where the drugs are placed by him in the sole control and subject to the unrestricted disposal of the drug addict."

Justice Day and five of his associates sustained the Government's position, reversing the district court and thus putting the stamp of approval on the Behrman indictment. That the majority of the Court did not see clearly what they were doing—notwithstanding the Government's candid brief—is apparent from the fact that they relied heavily on the mere amount of the prescriptions,[40] apparently without realizing that the doctrine they were setting would make volume—and good faith, as well—irrelevant. The other three Justices, Holmes, Brandeis, and McReynolds, were more clairvoyant. Justice Holmes wrote for them:

[37] Motion to advance, p. 2, *United States* v. *Balint,* 258 U. S. 250 (1922), *United States* v. *Behrman,* 258 U. S. 280 (1922).
[38] Brief for United States, pp. 7–8, 12–13, 18, *United States* v. *Behrman,* 258 U. S. 280 (1922).
[39] This description was far from precise. See note 23, supra.
[40] *United States* v. *Behrman,* 258 U. S. 280, 288–289 (1922).

"It seems to me wrong to construe the statute as creating a crime in this way without a word of warning. Of course, the facts alleged suggest an indictment in a different form, but the Government preferred to trust to a strained interpretation of the law rather than to a finding of a jury upon the facts. I think that the judgment should be affirmed." [41]

After Behrman

If some members of the Court were not fully aware of what they were giving in the Behrman holding, the Narcotics Division nonetheless saw perfectly clearly what it had received. Manifestly, if a Behrman indictment was unassailable when it charged the dispensing of shocking amounts of drugs, it was no less unassailable when it charged a minute quantity only. The Division had what it wanted. Any doctor who prescribed any narcotic drug to any addict could be threatened with prosecution or packed off to prison—and good faith was no defense. Immediately there commenced a reign of terror.

The medical profession was shamelessly bullied and threatened, until it withdrew, totally and irrevocably, as the addict's last point of contact with society.[42] The narcotics clinics, which had been established in a number of States to alleviate the situation, were closed—in some instances as a direct result of threats by Division agents.[43] In 1924 a special committee of the American Medical Association docilely reported its "firm conviction" that ambulatory treatment of narcotics addicts "begets deception, extends the abuse of habit-forming narcotic drugs, and causes an increase in crime." [44] An earlier version of this report (prior to its adoption by the A. M. A.) had been reprinted by the Division (a practice, as to "approved" materials, that continues to this day) and had been widely circulated as an officially endorsed pronouncement.[45] Doctors went to prison.[46] The hunt for addicts was pressed relentlessly.[47] Prices rose, prisons filled, dope rings throve. The United States acquired the renown of being the world's best market for illicit narcotics—a reputation which stands unchallenged to this day.

When the Supreme Court was jolted into further action, it was too late for the Justices to alter the situation. They spoke firmly, but to no avail.

Dr. Linder's case: A theoretical reversal

The jolt took the form of the next Behrman indictment case to reach the Supreme Court.[48] The facts in this case were fully as outrageous as in Dr. Behrman's case, but invoked the opposite alinement of sympathy. Dr. Charles O. Linder was a long-established practitioner in Spokane, Wash., with a large practice. At 4 o'clock one Saturday, while he was examining a female patient, with other patients waiting for him, four Narcotics Division agents burst :n upon him, and "boisterously and in an ungentlemanly and forcible manner, took charge" of his office. When he protested, the agents showed their Treasury Department badges and told him, "This is sufficient." After a rowdy search they took him off to jail.[49]

Dr. Lindler was indicted in a word-for-word repetition of the Behrman indictment, only this time the amount was 3 small tablets of cocaine and 1 of morphine. These had been given to an "addict stool pigeon," who was working for the agents. She claimed she had told him she was an addict; in his version he had represented that she had a painful stomach ailment and that the doctor who regularly treated her was out of the city.[50]

---

[41] Id., at 290 (dissent).
[42] It is noteworthy, for its bearing on the addicts-are-criminals argument, inter alia, that addiction among doctors themselves has always been a problem, alluded to by the narcotics authorities year after year in their annual reports. See, e. g., U. S. Treasury Department, Traffic in Opium and Other Dangerous Drugs, 3 (1926) ; id. at 3 (1927) ; id. at 4 (1928).
[43] See New York Times, June 23, 1920, p. 8 ; Stevens, supra, note 7, at 43.
[44] Rep. Ref. Committee on Legislation and Public Relations (1924), reprinted in 82 American Medical Association Journal, 1967 (1924).
[45] Stevens, supra, note 7, at 43.
[46] See *Simmons* v. *United States*, 300 Fed. 321 (6th Cir. 1924) ; *Hobart* v. *United States*, 299 Fed. 784 (6th Cir. 1924) ; *Manning* v. *United States*, 287 Fed. 800 (8th Cir. 1923).
[47] For many years the Division reported its "score" (in a column with other statistics) by the number of years in sentences imposed : e. g. (1926) 10,342 violations, 5,120 convictions, 6,797 years, 11 months, 10 days ; (1928) 8,653 violations, 4,738 convictions, 8,876 years, 4 months, 28 days ; (1933) 3,468 violations, 1,694 convictions, 3,248 years, 10 months, 18 days. See U. S. Treasury Department, The Traffic in Opium and Other Dangerous Drugs (1926) and subsequent yearly reports.
[48] *Linder* v. *United States*, 268 U. S. 5 (1924).
[49] Motion to quash search warrant, transcript of record, *Linder* v. *United States*, 268 U. S. 5 (1924).
[50] Transcript of trial, *Linder* v. *United States*, 268 U. S. C. 5 (1924).

Linder was convicted,[51] the ninth circuit affirmed,[52] and he petitioned for certiorari, arguing:

"The [Harrison] act * * * was not intended to trench on the police power of the States, and ought not to be given an interpretation which would bring within its purview an act the cognizance of which properly belongs to the States. '* * * [T]he lower courts almost uniformly try these narcotic cases on the theory that the purpose of the statute was to punish physicians and others dispensing morphine or other narcotics to satisfy the cravings of drug addicts, even where all the revenue features of the act have been complied with, as registration, payment of the tax, and the making and keeping of the records required by the act. We submit that the United States has nothing to do with such acts. Whether the health and morals of their people require that such practices be repressed by penal sanction is for the States alone to determine."

* * * * * * *

"Now what is the nature of the act charged in the indictment, giving the indictment the widest scope claimed for it? Simply that the defendant, being a registered physician, dispensed a small quantity of narcotic drugs to gratify the appetite of an addict." [53]

When the petition was granted, Solicitor General Beck disposed of the merits, in the Government's brief, in a pithy five-page statement that attempted merely to pin the Court to its earlier declared position:

"Petitioner contends in substance that if the indictment and the statute upon which it is founded, be construed as charging the administration of drugs merely to gratify the appetite of an addict, such an offense is beyond the power of Congress to create. * * *

"This is precisely what the indictment and the statute cover, and what the court intended to uphold in *U. S.* v. *Behrman* (258 U. S. 280, 287, 288). * * *

"The indictment in the case at bar is framed in the same language as the indictment in the above-mentioned Behrman case, except for the amount of the drug alleged to have been sold or distributed otherwise than in the course of professional practice. No distinction, however, can be made between the two cases on the ground merely of the difference between the amounts of drugs which are charged in the two indictments. In the Behrman case, supra, this court had before it only the strict allegations of the indictment, and for that purpose the amount of the drug becomes immaterial in determining whether the indictment actually and sufficiently charges it to have been unlawfully sold or distributed.

* * * * * * *

"Petitioner also contends that the indictment is capable of the construction, in substance, of charging that the drug was given in the professional treatment of the addict. The Behrman case, supra, must be held to dispose adversely of such claim, for if the indictment there, of which the indictment at bar is a duplicate in allegation, had been capable of such construction, this court would have said so." [54]

The Court's opinion, handed down in 1925, was written by Justice McReynolds, and was unanimous. Dr. Linder's conviction was reversed, and the opinion is as emphatic in tone as circumstances could permit:

"The enactment under consideration levies a tax, upheld by this Court, upon every person who imports, manufactures, produces, compounds, sells, deals in, dispenses, or gives away opium or coca leaves or derivatives therefrom, and may regulate medical practice in the States only so far as reasonably appropriate for or merely incidental to its enforcement. *It says nothing of 'addicts' and does not undertake to prescribe methods for their medical treatment. They are diseased and proper subjects for such treatment,* and we cannot possibly conclude that a physician acted improperly or unwisel y or for other than medical purpose solely because he has dispensed to one of them, in the ordinary course and in good faith, four small tablets of morphine or cocaine *for relief of conditions incident to addiction.*" [55]

Of the Webb case,[56] the Court said:

---

[51] His sentence: $1,000 and 2 months in jail. Transcript of record, pp. 25, 26, *Linder* v. *United States*, 268 U. S. 5 (1924).
[52] *Linder* v. *United States*, 290 Fed. 173 (9th Cir. 1923).
[53] Brief in aid of petition for writ of certiorari, pp. 9–11, *Linder* v. *United States*, 268 U. S. 5 (1924).
[54] Brief of United States, pp. 3–5, *Linder* v. *United States*, 268 U. S. 5 (1924).
[55] *Linder* v. *United States*, 268 U. S. 5, 18 (1925). [Emphasis added.]
[56] *Webb* v. *United States*, 249 U. S. 96 (1919).

"The answers thus given must not be construed as forbidding every prescription for drugs, irrespective of quantity, when designed temporarily to alleviate an addict's pains, although it may have been issued in good faith and without design to defeat the revenues. [57]

Of the Jin Fuey Moy case: [58] ʹ

"The quoted language must be confined to circumstances like those presented by the cause." [59]

And of the Behrman case [60] itself:

"This opinion related to definitely alleged facts and must be so understood. * * * The opinion cannot be accepted as authority for holding that a physician who acts bona fide and according to fair medical standards, may never give an addict moderate amounts of drugs for self-administration in order to relieve conditions incident to addiction. *Enforcement of the tax demands no such drastic rule, and if the Act had such scope it would certainly encounter grave constitutional difficuities.*" [61]

The lower Federal courts have since been fairly true to this corrected interpretation of the Harrison Act, when they have had opportunities to express themselves. [62] But there have been few significant cases. The doctors are still in retreat. And the Federal Narcotics Bureau has been undeterred in its own lusty applications of the act. Its regulations under section 2 [63] still provide (paraphrasing the loaded question in the discredited Webb case [64]):

"An order purporting to be a prescription issued to an addict or habitual user of narcotics, not in the course of professional treatment but for the purpose of providing the user with narcotics sufficient to keep him comfortable by maintaining his customary use, is not a prescription within the meaning or intent of the act: and the person filling such an order, as well as the person issuing it, may be charged with violation of the law." [65]

CONCLUSIONS

It wasn't many decades ago that sufferers from tuberculosis, sub nomine consumption, were regarded as unclean, and shunned by society. We have stopped treating our insane population as felons, raised the ancient stigma from leprosy and epilepsy, and transformed our penal philosophy from one of vengeance to one of rehabilitation. We have shown growing interest in large-scale attempts to salvage the victims of alcoholism; we caught up with most of our error vis-a-vis the liquor drinker 15 years ago. [66] And we have made venereal afflictions the subject of wholesome programs and campaigns. But we have not shown comparable understanding of the addict's problems.

The true addict, by universally accepted definitions, is totally enslaved to his habit. He will do anything to fend off the illness, marked by physical and emotional agony, that results from abstinence. So long as society will not traffic with him on any terms, he must remain the abject servitor of his vicious nemesis, the peddler. The addict will commit crimes—mostly petty offenses like shoplifting [67] and prostitution—to get the price the peddler asks. He will peddle dope and make new addicts if those are his master's terms. Drugs are a commodity of trifling intrinsic value. All the billions our society has spent enforcing criminal measures against the addict have had the sole practical result of protecting the peddler's market, artificially inflating his prices, and keeping his profits fantastically high. [68] No other nation hounds its addicts as we do, and

---

[57] *Linder* v. *United States,* 268 U. S. 5. 20 (1925).
[58] *Jin Fuey Moy* v. *United States,* 254 U. S. 189 (1920).
[59] *Linder* v. *United States,* 268 U. S. 5, 20 (1925).
[60] *United States* v. *Behrman,* 258 U. S. 280 (1921).
[61] *Linder* v. *United States,* 268 U. S. 5, 22 (1925).   [Emphasis added.]
[62] See *United States* v. *Brandenberg,* 155 F. 2d 110 (3d Cir. 1946).
[63] See note 8, supra.
[64] *Webb* v. *United States,* 249 U. S. 96 (1919).
[65] U. S. Treasury Department Narcotics Bureau Reg. No. 5, art. 167 (1949), 26 Code Fed. Regs., sec. 151.167 (1949).
[66] This analogy goes further. It was in the heyday of the bootlegger that organized crime, as we know it today, got its start. Revenues from the illicit narcotic traffic are, next to gambling, the largest current source of underworld wealth. Quite apart from humanitarian considerations, we should end this billion-dollar-a-year subsidy to the Nation's real criminals.
[67] See comments, Shoplifting and the Law of Arrest: the Merchant's Dilemma, 62 Yale Law Journal 788, 791, note 36 (1953).
[68] At frequent intervals the Feederal narcotics authorities publish tables of the going rates for illicit drugs. See, e. g., U. S. Treasury Department, Traffic in Opium and Other Dangerous Drugs 26 (1930). In this issue the Narcotics Division notes a "marked general increase in the prices of narcotic drugs. * * * This is a fair indication of the relative scarcity of narcotic drugs in the illicit market, due to increased efficiency of narcotic-law enforcement."

no other nation faces anything remotely resembling our problem.

Where does the solution lie? Out of reach, for the moment, because we shall not undo 40 years of carefully wrought error overnight. Out of sight, also, at least in precise detail, because we have little reliable data to guide us. But— at least until they are fully explored—the road would seem to lead toward the following areas: (1) relief from persecution for the addict; (2) therapy programs through institutions,[69] clinics,[70] and aftercure followups;[71] (3) provisions for incurables, through clinics or the individual practioner or both;[72] (4) a forthright out-of-the-dark educational program on narcotics; and (5) a vigorous assault, with all the enforcement resources we can muster, on whatever is left of the peddlers' empire after we have freed the addict from his present bondage to it.

Sooner or later some responsible appraiser, probably Congress, will have to take a clear look at our narcotics problem and the plight of the addict. It is to be hoped that retelling this tale, of Dr. Behrman, who was rightly punished for the wrong reasons, and Dr. Linder, who was vindicated in vain, may hasten the advent of that happy day.

Mr. KING. In this context, then, again, and more broadly, I would urge that consideration be given to those persons and views that have been presented to the committee here tending to support a liberalization of the underlying law-enforcement pattern which will permit ultimately the medical profession to treat more directly with narcotic addicts, and as an interim measure that necessary liberalization in the law, and necessary appropriations and directives from Congress, be considered, to permit the public health authorities, both at the State and at local levels, to establish direct consultation and treatment facilities to the widest possible extent, to deal with the addict as a medical problem.

Now, this leads to the last point that I want to touch very briefly on.

You have already asked me to comment on the involuntary commitment pattern here in the District, and its relation to juveniles. I believe on the basis of the analysis I have submitted, that the entire philosophy underlying involuntary commitment may need reappraisal, but in any event, I would like to caution the committee strongly against something that seems to have happened in recent years, and that is the enthusiastic passing of voluntary—involuntary commitment acts through the country, with the support, not of the health authorities, but of the law-enforcement people, without any commensurate provision of treatment facilities.

So that, in effect, these laws—and I beg to differ strongly with the witness who stated earlier that the act we have in the District is unique or a model. Some 35 States have such laws, and some of them go back to the 1890's.

These laws have recently been used, and have been enacted to be used, as alternative ways to hound the addict off the streets, to imprison him in facilities that have no relation to treatment.

[69] Such as the Federal hospitals administered by the U. S. Public Health Service, 58 Stat. 698 (1944), 42 U. S. C., sec. 257 (1946), the North Brother Island Hospital experiment in New York, and the proposed Seabrook Farm Unit in New Jersey.
[70] A bill to create a Federal Bureau of Clinics, to develop this approach to the problem, is now pending in Congress: H. R. 2449, 83d Cong., 1st sess. (1953). The bill also includes alcoholics as beneficiaries of the same program. For discussion of clinic system merits, see Comment, Narcotics Regulation, 62 Yale Law Journal 751, 784–787 (1953).
[71] This would perhaps be another function of narcotic clinics; it is contemplated, in connection with H. R. 2449, supra, note 70, that other Federal agencies, such as the U. S. Employment Service, would be called upon to cooperate in placing and rehabilitating addicts.
[72] See Stevens, Make Dope Legal, Harpers Magazine, November 1952, p. 40.

So that if the committee does urge and favor involuntary commitment, then it certainly should emphasize and stress at the same time the importance of backing any commitment laws with complete and adequate programs for therapy.

Lastly, because some question might arise from what I have just said, I would like to add that I have been at both the installation at Lexington and at Fort Worth, and I regard those as model institutions. I think that the work they are doing there, within the limitations imposed on them, the primary limitation being that they do impose a prision—they do impose incarceration conditions, is absolutely superb.

Mr. MITLER. In other words, simply saying an addict is going to be sent somewhere for treatment doesn't establish they are going to get treatment. It is contingent on what happens when they get there.

Mr. KING. Precisely.

Mr. MITLER. In other words, a lot of the—as you have observed, do you know a lot of the so-called treatment centers just bear that title, but when they get there nothing happens?

Mr. KING. Well, some 35 States, I believe Dr. Chapman can give you the precise number, have involuntary commitment statutes for noncriminal addicts. I have here a summary made by the Council of State Governments as of November 1956 of the treatment facilities that are available in these States, so that on the one hand you have, say, 35 States with laws which pull the addict into involuntary—into confinement for treatment; only 7 States purport to have any kind of treatment programs for narcotics addicts as such, actually 6 States and the Territory of Hawaii. The six States are Illinois, Maryland, Michigan, New York, Pennsylvania, and West Virginia.

Fourteen States have provisions of some sort for the incarceration of mental—of narcotics addicts in their mental hospitals.

Now, understand this means not special treatment for narcotics addicts necessarily, but incarceration facilities in mental hospitals rather than in jails.

Those States are California, Connecticut, Delaware, Indiana, Kansas, Minnesota, Mississippi, New Hampshire, North Dakota, Ohio, Oregon, Texas, Washington, and Wisconsin.

Two other States, Florida and Massachusetts, permit noncriminal addicts to be sent to the State prison hospitals, in other words, to hospital facilities in connection with the prisons.

I think those figures, plus the fact that 23 States have no provisions, are a very important conditioning factor when you look at the involuntary commitment laws of the States.

Mr. MITLER. I have no further questions, Mr. Chairman.

Chairman KEFAUVER. Mr. King, I hope that the American Bar Association is continuing its interest in all of these related subjects. Can you tell us if it is?

Mr. KING. Well, this study that I mentioned, Senator, is a joint study which we hope will determine a position for both the American Bar Association and the American Medical Association, both professions.

As a result of the fine work that has been done here on Capitol Hill, they have been made increasingly aware of the importance of this problem and of the deep responsibility that both the doctors and the lawyers have for assisting in finding a solution; and it is our hope that the work of this committee, which will ultimately report back to the board of governors of the American Bar Association and the board of trustees of the American Medical Association, will lead to some kind of joint position and clarification on the part of the two associations.

I believe that specifically this narcotics problem and, in more general terms, problems relating to law enforcement, are of major interest to the American Bar Association, and I certainly would hope this is an interest that will never flag.

Chairman KEFAUVER. We are certainly very grateful to you, Mr. King, for your interest and help.

Mr. MITLER. Thank you very much.

Mr. KING. Thank you.

Mr. MITLER. Dr. Kolb?

STATEMENT OF DR. LAWRENCE KOLB, FORMER MEDICAL OFFICER IN CHARGE, UNITED STATES PUBLIC HEALTH HOSPITAL, LEXINGTON, KY.

Chairman KEFAUVER. Dr. Kolb, we are very grateful to you for being here with us. We are sorry that we have delayed your testimony so long.

Dr. KOLB. That is all right.

Chairman KEFAUVER. We consider you one of our most important witnesses in this entire hearing.

You are Dr. Lawrence Kolb?

Dr. KOLB. Yes.

Chairman KEFAUVER. Speak louder, Dr. Kolb.

Mr. MITLER. Could you give us your background, Dr. Kolb?

Dr. KOLB. Well, I entered the Public Health Service in 1909. I became a psychiatrist in the Service in 1915, served in various capacities.

In 1920, I opened up a mental hospital for the Service in Waukesha, Wisc., for the treatment of mental cases. At this hospital we had a few addicts, not many.

In 1923, I was called to Washington to what is now the National Institute of Health, to study drug addiction for the Service. I studied drug addiction in the laboratory and in hospitals, in treatment, and I traveled throughout the eastern part of the United States to various places where there were addicts, to study them.

I studied at that time very carefully about 700 or 800 addicts.

In 1928, I was relieved of that duty and went to Europe on a special mission for the Service; but while there, as a side issue, I studied the situation of drug addiction as it was handled in Europe, and I was rather amazed to find out the difference between their methods and our methods.

Mr. MITLER. What are the differences?

Dr. KOLB. The difference is that in Europe the addict is known to be a sick man, especially those addicted to the opium drugs like heroin and morphine, and the doctors are not harassed thereby when they prescribe for such addicts, nobody tries to put them in jail for it.

There is no sneaking an informer in, trying to get them to prescribe for a fictitious addict, as is done here, and by which means so many of our doctors in this country have been sent to prison for doing that.

And, of course, in doing that here, they have become so terrorized at prescribing narcotics, the opiate drugs especially, that they have just shoved the thing aside, and it has become wholly a police problem here; whereas, as a matter of fact, it is 90 percent a medical problem.

Mr. MITLER. Doctor, I didn't let you complete your background. Forgive me. I started to ask you a question.

Would you bring us up to date?

Dr. KOLB. On background, I returned to the United States and was for 2 more years associated at the Bureau of Public Health Service in mental health work; and then I went to Springfield, Mo., to open up the Department of Justice medical center, which was a new thing, and I opened up and operated that for 18 months.

They had some addicts there, but they were criminals, and it was not a major issue; mostly the treatment of criminally insane people.

In 1935, I went to Lexington, Ky., to open up and to conduct the hospital that was opened there for the treatment of narcotic addicts. I did that for 3 years, and I was relieved from there in 1938 and came to Washington as Assistant Surgeon General in the Surgeon General's cabinet to be over the mental-hygiene program, and to have administrative control of those two hospitals.

Since that time, the administrative control has somewhat changed.

I retired from the Service in 1945 early, and went to California and conducted there—I was over the State mental hospitals as deputy director of the department of hygiene for 7 years.

Since that time, I have continued my interest in psychiatry, but I have more or less retired except for a short detail in Pennsylvania at a mental hospital.

Mr. MITLER. And you also wrote a recent article for the Saturday Evening Post?

Dr. KOLB. I wrote a recent article for the Saturday Evening Post in order to acquaint the general public with the facts about drug addiction, in order to point out here I think our policy has been entirely wrong, and has resulted in disease and death and crime that otherwise would not occur if we had what I think is a more rational and medical approach to the problem.

Mr. MITLER. Would you give us the highlights of your view?

Dr. KOLB. Well, I wrote it up——

Chairman KEFAUVER. How long is the article?

Dr. KOLB. This is 1,500 words. I wanted to offer it for the committee if you wish to have it.

Mr. MITLER. Because there is a lot in here about juvenile addiction, too.

Chairman KEFAUVER. Let's make it exhibit 11, I believe, and it will be printed in the appendix to the record.

(The article referred to was marked "Exhibit No. 11," and is as follows:)

LET'S STOP THIS NARCOTICS HYSTERIA!

(By Laurence Kolb, M. D.)

Drug addiction should be treated as an illness, not a crime, says this doctor, who offers a bold minority report on what he calls "the so-called drug menace."

Many years ago, when I was a stripling, I sat listening to a group of elderly men gossiping in a country store. They were denouncing the evils of cigarette smoking, a vice that was just coming in.

This store had on its shelves a jar of eating opium, and a carton of laudanum vials—10 percent opium. A respected woman in the neighborhood often came in to buy laudanum. She was a good housekeeper and the mother of two fine sons. Everybody was sorry about her laudanum habit, but no one viewed her as a sinner or a menace to the community. We had not yet heard the word "addict," with its sinister, modern connotations.

Since those days, public opinion has done a complete about-face. The "sin" of smoking cigarettes, in 50 years' time, has become a socially acceptable habit, while drug addiction has been promoted by hysterical propaganda to the status of a great national menace.

As an example, one prominent official has said that illegal heroin traffic is more vicious than arson, burglary, kidnaping, or rape, and should entail harsher penalties. Last May 31 the United States Senate went even further, in passing the Narcotic Control Act of 1956. In this measure, third-offense trafficking in heroin becomes the moral equivalent of murder and treason; death is the extreme penalty, "If the jury in its discretion shall so direct," for buyer and seller alike, whether addicted or not.

In my opinion, the lawmakers completely missed the point. For drug addiction is neither menace nor mortal sin, but a health problem—indeed, a minor health problem when compared with such killers as alcoholism, heart disease, and cancer.

I make that statement with deep conviction. My work has included the psychiatric examination and general treatment of several thousand addicts. I know their habit is a viciously enslaving one, and we should not relax for a moment our efforts to stop its spread and ultimately to stamp it our completely. But our enforcement agencies seem to have forgotten that the addict is a sick person who needs medical help rather than longer jail sentences or the electric chair. He needs help which the present Narcotics Bureau regulations make it very difficult for doctors to give him. Moreover, no distinction has been made, in the punishment of violators, between the nonaddicted peddler who perpetuates the illicit traffic solely for his own profit and the addict who sells small amounts to keep himself supplied with a drug on which he has become physically and psychologically dependent.

The Council of the American Psychiatric Association, in a public statement issued after the Senate passed its bill, declared that this and a companion measure introduced in the House, "represent backward steps in attacking this national problem." The association, after listing some of the points I have just made, concludes by remarking that "additional legislation concerning drug addiction should be directed to making further medical progress possible, rather than discouraging it. The legislative proposals now under consideration would undermine the progress that has been made and impede further progress. Thus, they are not in the public interest."

I was launched in this field of medicine in 1923, when the United States Public Health Service assigned me to study drug addiction at what is now the National Institute of Public Health. In 1935 I opened the Service's hospital for treatment of addicts at Lexington, Ky. Three years later I become Chief of the Division of Mental Hygiene, overseeing administration of the Lexington hospital and a similar institution at Fort Worth, Tex. And after retiring from the service in 1944, I continued to be active in psychiatry. So I know a great deal about addiction, and how perverse our attitude toward it has become.

Most addiction arises from misuse of marihuana, cocaine, alcohol, opium or opium's important preparations and derivatives—eating opium, smoking opium, laudanum, morphine, and heroin. Alcohol is a yardstick with which to measure the harm done by other drugs. The are 4,500,000 alcoholics in this country, and about 700,000 of them are compulsive drinkers who are on "skid road" or headed for it—gripped like opium addicts by psychological forces they cannot control.

Until recent times, millions of people in Asia and Africa were habitual users of opium. Dr. C. S. Mei, a physician and Chinese Government official, told me in 1937 that there were about 15 million opium smokers in China. He was interested in the antiopium campaign because the slavish habit was lowering users' diligence and industry. But he remarked that opium smoking had little or no effect on health and no effect whatsoever on crime.

Addiction is far less common among Western peoples, chiefly because of our preference for alcohol. At the highest point of drug addiction in the United States, 1890–99, when all kinds of opiates could be bought as freely as candy or potatoes, there was only 1 opium addict for every 300 of the population. Today we have about 60,000 addicts in the United States—that is, about 1 in 2,800 of population. About 50,000 of them are addicted to opiates, mostly heroin, about 5,000 to opiumlike synthetic drugs, and about 5,000 to marihuana. Cocaine, once widely used, has practically disappeared from the scene.

Lawmakers may feel that addicts as well as sellers deserve death, but few doctors would agree. I have in mind particularly a report issued in June, 1955, by a group of prominent New York physicians, appointed by the New York Academy of Medicine to study the addiction problem. The gist of their report is that drug addiction is not a crime, but an illness, and that the emphasis should be placed on rehabilitation of addicts instead of on punishment.

This committee deplores the fact that addicts are forced into crime by unwise suppressive methods. It recommends that, under controlled conditions, certain morphine and heroin addicts be given the drug they need while being prepared for treatment. For certain incurable cases, the committee advocates giving the needed opiate indefinitely at specially regulated clinics, although many physicians oppose using clinics in this way. My own proposal, which I shall go into later, would be to have such cases evaluated by doctors appointed for their competence in this field. The New York committee also recommends counseling services for patients after withdrawal treatment, to help them resist the temptation to return to the drug when stress situations arise.

A key fact to bear in mind is that the man addicted to an opiate becomes dependent on frequent regular doses to maintain normal body functions and comfort. If the drug is abruptly withheld he becomes intensely ill. In rare cases he may even collapse and die.

I once saw a woman who had come here from abroad, where she had been taking eight grains of morphine daily. Cut off from her supply, she got into an American hospital where suppression of the drug menace was more important than the relief of pain. She died in 2 days, due to sudden stoppage of the drug. There was nothing in the law to forbid giving this woman morphine to relieve her suffering, but propaganda about drugs had clouded the judgment of someone in authority.

The effect of opiates on the general health of addicts is not definitely known. There is a lack of positive evidence that a regularly maintained opium habit shortens life, but it probably does so, especially when large doses of morphine or heroin are used. The few reports that indicate harm are based on death statistics of groups of addicts, mostly opium smokers, many of whom started using the drug to ease already existing illness. Addicts in American jails undoubtedly have a high death rate. Some are repeatedly ill due to many periods of forced abstinence. Others, unable to buy enough food after paying for needed drugs, arrive at the prison gates half starved and a prey to infections.

In the 1920's the average American addict was taking 6 grains of morphine or heroin daily. It was impossible to find harmful effects among those who got their dose regularly. I have known a health, alert 81-year-old woman who had taken 3 grains of morphine daily for 65 years. The well-fed opiate addict who regularly gets sustaining doses is not emaciated or pale, nor does he have pinpoint pupils, as is popularly supposed. He cannot be recognized as an addict on sight.

Cocaine is another story. It is fortunate that cocaine addiction is seldom seen nowadays, for excessive use of this drug causes emaciation, anxiety, convulsions, and insanity. Neither cocaine nor marijuana has the merit of making some neurotic people more efficient, as is the case with opiates. And the use of marijuana or cocaine can be discontinued abruptly without bringing on uncomfortable or dangerous withdrawal symptoms. When cocaine is suddenly denied a large user, he simply goes into a deep and very prolonged sleep. Therefore there is no reason why any cocaine or marijuana user should be allowed to have his drug, even for a short time.

While cocaine causes anxiety, opium relieves it. In fact, opium is such a soothing drug that it makes the addict less likely to commit a crime while under its influence. Addicts do commit crimes, of course, since most of them are emotionally unstable people to begin with. Among these are psychopaths who were criminals before becoming addicts, and continue to be. Then many respectable people who become addicts will steal, forge prescriptions, pass bad checks, and commit other petty crimes to support their habit. Most crimes of drug addicts are in this class. They are law-induced crimes.

One of my earlier studies showed that heroin, like other opiates, repressed aggressive criminal impulses. In the words of heroin addicts, "You have no guts, it brings out the yellow in you, and a man can slap you in the face and you won't resent it: but you do things there are no risks in."

In contrast, alcohol is the direct cause of many crimes. Ralph S. Banay, reporting in 1942 on a survey of Sing Sing prisoners during the period 1935–40, showed that 107 of 651 prisoners convicted of homicide had been intoxicated when they committed their crimes; so were 114 of 508 prisoners convicted of sex offenses.

Opiates do not, in my opinion, impair motor control or critical judgment. Consequently, there are no traffic accidents due to opium addiction. But alcohol and driving don't mix, as everyone knows. In Los Angeles, one of the cities said to be imperiled by juvenile drug addiction, 400 persons 17 years of age or under were arrested in 1954 for drunken driving. Such offenses seldom make headlines, but the arrest of a few teen-agers caught experimenting with a narcotic is featured as evidence of a deadly peril.

Insanity caused by opium addiction is extremely rare and almost always of short duration. Yet hospitals treating mental diseases in this country have more than 18,000 admissions for alcoholic insanity each year, and thousands more for serious chronic alcoholism. Among several thousand insane people whom I have seen, there were only two whose psychosis was due to opium. After many withdrawal treatments, they had developed hypomania. In a few months both patients resumed the use of morphine and recovered their mental balance. Only disaster could result from attempts to rid such patients of their addiction. Without the necessary opiate, they become troublesome derelicts or inmates of mental institutions.

In an earlier period, opiates could be bought anywhere in America without restriction, and many people became addicted. Still, they worked about as well as other people and gave no one trouble. Only the physicians were concerned. They saw that the cocaine user and 60-grains-a-day morphine addict were injuring their health. More important, they saw thousands of unhappy opium eaters, opium smokers, and laudanum, morphine, and heroin users seeking relief from slavery, and often failing to get it.

Distressed by the evil, physicians advocated laws to prohibit the sale of opiates without prescription. By 1912 every State except one had laws regulating in some way the prescribing or sale of opiates and cocaine. As a result, the number of addicts fell from 1 in 300 of the population during the decade 1890–99, to 1 in 325 during the next decade. And after 1909 a ban on smoking opium caused a further decline in addiction.

Until 1915, however, addicts who needed opiates to continue their work in comfort could get their supplies legally without much trouble or expense. Then the Harrison Act became effective. This important Federal law had both good and bad effects. Unable to get opiates, hundreds of addicts were cured by deprivation. These were mostly normal or near-normal people who were not seriously gripped by the psychological forces which hinder treatment of neurotic addicts and drunkards.

The bad effect came through unwise enforcement of the law. Physicians thought they could still prescribe opiates to addicts who really needed them for the preservation of health or to support the artificial emotional stability which enabled so many addicts to earn their living. However, physicians prescribing for such people wound up in the penitentiary. Inability to get opiates brought illness to many hard-working citizens, and illness cost them their jobs. Some of them committed petty crimes to procure narcotics.

To remedy the situation, narcotic clinics were established throughout the country, where addicts could get needed drugs. Practically all of these clinics were forced to close by 1923. They had not been well run, but the chief reason for closing them was that addiction had become a crime, by legal definition.

The arrests of physicians, some of which were justifiable, and the sending of hundreds of addicts to prison, brought about a perversion of commonsense unequaled in American history. Uncritical observers concluded that opium caused crime. The sight of so many law-abiding citizens applying to the clinics for help, instead of arousing public sympathy, was interpreted as evidence of moral deterioration, calling for increased penalties. The stereotype of the "heroin maniac" was born.

The number of addicts continued to decline. In 1924 the United States Public Health Service reported there were only 110,000 of them. By 1925, however, propaganda had led people to believe that there were 4 million addicts in the country, and our fancied heroin menace was in full swing.

An ex-Congressman appeared before the Senate Committee on Printing in 1924 to urge publication of 50 million copies of an article entitled "The Peril of

Narcotics—A Warning to the People of America." He wanted a copy in every home.

Among other strange things, the article warned parents not to allow their children to eat away from home. If they did, it was said, some other child—a heroin maniac—might inject the drug into an innocent-looking tidbit; whereupon the child eating it might instantly become an addict and join in a campaign to promote heroin addiction among other children. A Public Health Service physician persuaded the committee that this was nonsense, but propaganda about the heroin menace continued.

It was said that thousands of schoolchildren in New York were heroin addicts. An investigation was made, and in 1927 Dr. Carlton Simon, deputy police commissioner in charge of the narcotics bureau, stated that a thorough survey had failed to reveal 1 case of heroin addiction among 1 million New York City schoolchildren.

When American physicians advocated laws regulating narcotics, they had in mind the kind of laws in force in most Western European countries. What our physicians did not foresee was that they would be bound by police interpretations of the regulations; and that doctors who did not accept police views might be tricked into giving an opiate to an informer, who pretended to need it for pain or disease. Conviction meant that the physician went to prison.

Europeans regulate narcotics, as we do, but they are not alarmed by addiction, as we so obviously are. They have never lost sight of the fact that, as a great English physician wrote in the 19th century, "Opium soothes, alchohol maddens."

An English doctor is free to prescribe narcotic drugs, exercising his professional discretion, when it is found, after prolonged attempts at cure of addiction, that the opiate cannot safely be discontinued or when it is demonstrated that the patient can lead a useful, normal life when a certain minimum dose is given regularly, but is incapacitated when the drug is entirely stopped.

Under this system England's addiction problem is far milder than ours. There, and in Western Europe, too, the addicted old men, the dying women and the neurotic workmen who need an opiate to keep going are allowed to have it. No one in those countries advocates sending such people to prison, and no one feels that in doing so they would be breaking up nests of sin and crime.

In 1954 England controlled the illegal narcotic traffic with the conviction of only 214 persons, 74 for opiate violations, 140 for violations involving marihuana. In the same year 12,346 persons were convicted in the United States for similar offenses. Allowing for differences in population, we had about 14 times more convictions than the English. Prison sentences meted out here ran into thousands of years—a fact that zealots boast about. In England light sentences sufficed to discourage illegal traffic—28 days to 12 months for opiate offenses, 1 day to 3 years for marihuana violations.

England's sensible, effective policy is in sharp contrast with what goes on in the United States. I became well acquainted at the hospital in Lexington with a paralyzed, bedridden man who had been sentenced to 4 years for a narcotic violation. Just how he could be a menace to society was never clear to me. In Europe he would have been allowed to live out his last days in comfort. Only in the United States must addicts suffer and die or deteriorate in prison.

After World War II, it was found that some teen-agers in a few large American cities were becoming addicted to heroin and marihuana. Although the addiction was not widespread—it was found mostly among deprived classes in neighborhood gangs—there was a loud outcry. A statewide survey conducted by Pennsylvania officials, reported in the January 1952 issue of Pennsylvania Health, disclosed no positive case of teen-age addiction in Pennsylvania schools. The "up-surge" was a myth; there are actually fewer teen-age addicts in the United States now than there were in the 1920's.

Marihuana has been used as an intoxicant for about 3,000 years that we know of, mostly in Asia and North Africa. Like alcohol, marihuana in large doses releases impulses to irresponsible action. In 1938, much talk about the addiction of school children to marihuana, and of crime due to the drug, led the mayor of New York City to ask the New York Academy of Medicine for advice. On recommendation of the academy, a committee was formed to make a thorough survey.

The committee report showed considerable marihuana addiction among certain groups in New York. It was shown that marihuana had effects on behavior which might lead to acts of violence, but no association between marihuana and crimes of violence was found in New York. Further, the committee reported that there was no organized traffic in marihuana among New York schoolchildren. This valuable scientific paper was severely criticized by "drug-menace" extremists. Yet there have been 4 other studies in this country and 2 in Mexico which failed to show a connection between marihuana and crime.

Unreflecting and sometimes unscrupulous people—and newspapers too—have contributed to the hysteria about drug addiction. News items reporting the seizure of "dope" frequently exaggerate the contraband's value. One "$3 million seizure" of heroin which made headlines was actually only enough to last seven 6-grains-a-day addicts for a year. To justify the $3 million figure, heroin would have to bring $196 a grain.

One citizens' advisory committee on narcotics, reporting to the State's attorney general, placed the value of a pound of heroin in the illegal market at from $768,000 to $1,228,000. This would be from $100 to $160 a grain, and would place addicts with 6-grain habits in daily expense brackets of $600 to $960. The absurdity of such spending by starving, out-at-elbows addicts is self-evident. Some addicts do spend from $5 to $10 a day on the habit, but few can afford it; hence the sickness and stealing.

Distorted news has prepared the public to support extreme measures to suppress imagined evils. When legislators undertook last spring to do something about the so-called drug menace, Federal law provided 2 years in prison for a first-time narcotic-law offender. The minimum for a second offense was 5 years, and for a third, 10 years, with no probation or suspension of sentence for repeaters. The Narcotic Control Act of 1956 proposed increasing penalties for heroin trafficking to a minimum of 5 years for the first offense, 10 years for the second offense, life imprisonment or death for the third offense.

What happens under such laws? In one case, under the old law, a man was given 10 years for possessing 3 narcotic tablets. Another man was given 10 years for forging three narcotic prescriptions—no sale was involved. And another 10 year sentence was imposed on a man for selling 2 marihuana cigarettes, which are just about equal in intoxicating effect to 2 drinks of whisky. Extremists have gone on to demand the death penalty. They would do away with suspended sentences, time off for good behavior, the necessity for a warrant before search. They want wiretapping legalized in suspected narcotic cases, and they would make the securing of bond more difficult.

Existing measures and those which are advocated defy common sense and violate sound principles of justice and penology. There is nothing about the nature of drug addicts to justify such penalties. They only make it difficult to rehabilitate offenders who could be helped by a sound approach which would take into account both the offense and the psychological disorders of the offender.

Drug addiction is an important problem which demands the attention of health and enforcement officials. However, the most essential need now is to cure the United States of its hysteria, so that the problem can be dealt with rationally. A major move in the right direction would be to stop the false propoganda about the nature of drug addiction and present it for what it is—a health problem which needs some police measures for adequate control. Our approach so far has produced tragedy, disease and crime.

The opinion of informed physicians should take precedence over that of law-enforcement officers, who, in this country, are too often carried away by enthusiasm for putting people in prison, and who deceive themselves as well as the public about the nature and seriousness of drug addiction.

We need an increase in treatment facilities and recognition that some opium addicts, having reached the stage they have, should be given opiates for their own welfare and for the public welfare too.

Mandatory minimum sentences should be abolished, so that judges and probation and parole officers can do what in their judgment is best for the rehabilitation of offenders.

Medical opinion should have controlling force in a revamped policy. This is not to say that every physician should be authorized to prescribe opiates to addicts without restrictions. Some would be dishonest, others would be indifferent to consequences. Neither should the old type of clinic be reestablished. A workable solution would be to have the medical societies or health departments appoint competent physicians to decide which patients should be carried on an opiate while being prepared for treatment and which ones should be given opiates indefinitely. Physicians would report individual cases to local medical groups for decision. And that decision should never be subject to revision by a nonmedical prosecuting agency.

The details of a scheme of operation should be worked out by a committee of physicians and law-enforcement officers, with the physicians predominant in authority. The various States could make a start by revising their laws to conform to actual health and penological needs. The medical profession could help by giving legislators facts on which to take action.

It should be stressed that it is easy to cure psychologically normal addicts who have no painful disease. Even the mildly neurotic addict is fairly easy to cure. Severe withdrawal symptoms pass within 5 days, although for several months there are minor physical changes that the patient may not feel or even know about, but which increase the likelihood of his relapse. The reason for the apparently large relapse rate among addicts is that a difficult group remains to be dealt with after the cured cases have been dismissed. The most difficult cases, perhaps, are neurotic addicts who suffer from migrane or asthma. Neurotics who have a painful disease are liable to have a psychic return of pain when their drug is withdrawn. When several treatments fail, such persons should be allowed to have the drug they need.

Thomas Jefferson, distressed over the ravages of alcohol, once said that a great many people spent most of their time talking politics, avoiding work and drinking whisky. One wonders what he would say today if some muddled citizen warned him that opiates were rotting the moral fiber of our people. I suspect that the would advise his informant to take care, in walking down the street, lest he stumbled over one of our 4,500,000 alcoholics and break a leg.

A JUDGE SPEAKS OUT

John M. Murtagh, Chief City Magistrate, City of New York

The narcotics problem is not being solved by sending drug addicts to prison, and the futility of penal sanctions is most evident in New York City. Here thousands of addicts are paraded before the courts in an endless revolving-door process. Thousands of others, driven to petty crime to support the habit, add to the congestion of our calendars. Last year, over 1,100 desperate victims voluntarily committed themselves in our court. Only when we recognize that this problem is basically a social and medical one will progress be made.

In this field, Dr. Laurence Kolb speaks with authority. He has devoted a lifetime to the study and treatment of addiction, and for years pursued his speciality as Chief of the Division of Mental Hygiene, United States Public Health Service. His views, presented here, should lead to a reevaluation of the penal approach to narcotic addiction.

Dr. KOLB. Now, as to juvenile addiction, I have written up a four-page statement here, and I don't need to read it.

Mr. MITLER. Would you give the highlights of it?

Dr. KOLB. I will give you the highlights.

Chairman KEFAUVER. Let's have it printed as your statement, and you give us the highlights.

Dr. KOLB. Yes.

(Dr. Kolb's prepared statement is as follows:)

STATEMENT BY DR. LAWRENCE KOLB

Drug addiction is a minor and very unimportant phase of the general problem of juvenile delinquency. A few delinquent children among certain deprived groups in several of our large cities experiment with drugs. The Children's Bureau estimates that 500,000 children age 10 to 17 come to the attention of the juvenile courts each year. During 1953 and 1954 fewer than 400 addicts of school age come to the attention of the authorities. According to the Department of Education there are 38,149,000 school children in grades from kindergarten through the eighth grade in the United States and 7,919,000 in grades 9 through 12. The total number of addicts under 21 that came to the attention of the authorities in 1953 and 1954 was 3,125. Nearly 88 percent of these were 18 or over. Juvenile delinquency as expressed by narcotic indulgence is in practically all cases evidence of an unstable personality. In the deprived groups this expression occurs in insecure individuals seeking to express themselves in ways that promise excitement, unusual sensations, and the thrill of defying authority. In the group that become addicts there are a few who have a normal personality.

There is no problem about curing these normal persons. They become frightened. They want to be cured and get cured with or without hospital assistance and as a rule do not relapse. The mildly unstable juveniles as well as older persons of this type who become addicted also get panicky, seek cure and achieve it as they always have but more of these relapse. The most unstable become chronic addicts and are extremely difficult to cure. It is this unstable group, many but not all of whom were delinquent before they became addicts, who give some people the impression that drug addicts are never cured.

The chronic addict to the opium drugs, including morphine and heroin, and to the synthetic drugs, methadone and demerol, is in the same situation as to cure as the chronic compulsive alcoholic who is extremely prone to relapse. Nevertheless, I have seen cure of an alcoholic who had been in jail 167 times for drunkenness. I have also seen an addict cured after 40 years of morphine indulgence. Therefore, hope of cure should not be abandoned in either condition.

The juveniles who become chronic addicts are always decidedly unstable and are usually delinquent before they become addicts. The impulse to commit delinquent acts is not increased by morphine, heroin, or other opiate drugs or by methadone and demerol. The direct effect of these drugs is to decrease aggressive crime, but addicts to these drugs do commit crimes in order to get drugs to ward off the suffering that follows forced abstinence. The crimes are violations of narcotic laws, stealing, forging prescriptions, etc., and more serious crimes in the case of original aggressively inclined criminals.

Rape, a common crime among juveniles, is less likely to be committed by a juvenile morphine or heroin addict, both during sustained addiction and the distressing withdrawal period. During sustained addiction the sex impulse is decreased by the drugs and during withdrawal the physical distress siphons his attention away from sex.

Heroin is no more harmful as an addicting drug than morphine. There is no reliable medical evidence to sustain the popular conception about the special sinister effect if this drug. Heroin is more toxic; however, like morphine and some other opiates, it quickly causes physical addiction if used daily.

The physical addiction caused by opiates and related drugs is the only effect of these drugs that justifies special measures to control their use beyond the usual measures applied to other dangerous drugs, such as forbidding purchase except on prescriptions and forbidding the refilling of prescriptions. The opiates are usually more effective tranquilizers and always less harmful to the physical and mental well-being of patients than the tons of tranquilizing drugs now being taken all over the United States. This is the reason why the Public Health Service should continue its efforts to develop a pain relieving, tranquilizing opiate that does not cause physical addiction.

The physical addiction to opiates causes such a severe and distressing type of slavery that every effort should be made to cure it at an early stage before developing habit patterns intensify and add to the original psychological reason for the addiction. Hospitalization with adequate followup, not by police, but by social workers and mental-health clinics to which addicts can go both before and after hospitalization is the answer. Hospitalization for voluntary patients especially juveniles is important. Hospitalization for addicts caught violating a narcotic law should be on a commitment or probation basis. The recidivist criminal who is an addict because he is a criminal may as well be sent to jail. Very few persons under 21 fall in this class.

Marihuana addiction is more serious from the mental, physical, and social standpoint than opiate addiction, but less serious in that there is no physical addiction. Marihuana addiction does not lead to heroin addiction because of the marihuana, but most members of the unstable sidewalk juvenile groups who experiment with both marihuana and heroin are apt to become heroin addicts because of the physical dependence that heroin produces. One marihuana cigarette produces about the same degree of intoxication as 1 ounce of whisky. Juveniles should therefore be protected from it especially as like alcohol intoxication, marihuana intoxication may lead aggressively inclined persons to commit aggressive crimes. However there are fewer than 5,000 marihuana addicts in the United States as against the 68 million drinkers. Well known authorities have estimated that there are 200 million marihuana users in the world.

In summary, drug addiction is of only slight importance in juvenile delinquency. It is believed that most of the addiction proceeds from delinquency and that most juveniles who experiment with narcotics will discontinue the experiment before they become seriously addicted. Treatment divested as far as possible from police action should be provided for them.

In the event that the United States should adopt a policy of dealing with addicts based on the British method of giving maintenance doses of opiates to chronic addicts so that they can continue at work and in good health and not commit crimes, the method adopted should not result in giving maintenance doses to juveniles. Several efforts should be made to cure juveniles before maintenace doses are thought of as a remedy. They would then be beyond age 21.

The British method is explained in the Home Office Regulations DD101 (6th edition) February 1956 entitled "The Duties of Doctors and Dentists Under the Dangerous Drugs Act and Regulations."

Dr. KOLB. Now, drug addiction is a very minor factor in juvenile delinquency. For instance, I get from the children's bureau they have 500,000 children each year before the juvenile courts.

Now, the President's Committee on Drug Addiction found out that over a 2-year period, 1953 and 1954, there were only 400 addicts of school age in the United States—this was up to age 18—and according to the Department of Education, there are 38 million schoolchildren of that age; and from there on, from the 9th to the 12th grade, there are 7,919,000 additional schoolchildren.

Well, in that entire age group, the President's Committee found that there were 3,125 addicts, and that makes over 40 million children, so you can see really how small the problem is. But there is a problem, and it should be attended to.

Now, juvenile delinquency as expressed by these children who become chronic addicts, is a problem of an emotional disturbance. I have found, and other researchers in this field have found, that with practically all of these children, there is some sort of an emotional disorder to begin with. It is not an absolute rule in all cases.

In our large cities at the present time there are some addicts among the juveniles who probably are normal and near-normal, and I want to say about those addicts you needn't worry about them, they are going to get cured, because along with other addicts they get panicky as soon as they become addicted to a thing like heroin, they ask for a cure, and a lot of them get cured, even without going to a hospital. They get cured just by stopping the drug themselves or by a private doctor who doesn't give them any drug or, if they go to a hospital like Lexington, that group will remain cured.

We had from Dr. Lowry yesterday the fact that 61 percent of the people who came to Lexington, you never heard of them before. One reason why, I found out, you don't hear of those people through the years any more, is that they don't go out and advertise the fact they were addicts, because addiction is a thing that is looked upon with such extreme disfavor by all strata of our society.

Now, the chronic addict to all—whether he is an adult or whether he is a juvenile, the chronic addict to such things as morphine and heroin, and the synthetic drugs, methadone and demerol, is always a disturbed person emotionally.

We don't have any more in the country, chronic addicts, who are normal from a nervous standpoint.

I would point up that in the United States we have 9 million people who are somewhere mentally disturbed. It doesn't mean we need to be in a mental hospital or jail or anything like that. We are just distressed about some emotional problem, but we probably never tell anybody about it.

But that is the group of people from which the chronic addict is recruited. Those persons who, unfortunately, get started onto this thing and who, because of the magnitude of their emotional problems, get so much relief from it, when they get cured and they meet another distressful situation they go back to solve it the same way; and I always explain this matter, in order that the layman might understand it, in terms of chronic alcoholism.

The chronic drug addict is exactly the same thing, emotionally, as the chronic alcoholic. That is the problem alcoholic who can't be cured; who swears off from drinking and who goes home, and gets drunk on the way home.

That same thing happens to the chronic drug addict. But even these people, some of them, are cured. I have seen a chronic alcoholic of this kind cured after 167 times in jail; and I have seen a drug addict cured, of this type, after 40 years of addiction. So it isn't absolutely a hopeless thing.

Now, what we hear about people saying drug addicts can't be cured just comes from this situation: We are constantly curing those that are curable, that is, easily curable, and they never advertise any more, and we get left over a type that are like the "skid row" alcoholics, the cure of them is extremely difficult because of emotional problems, not because of any particular thing that the drug itself has done for them to make them deteriorated, or anything like that.

The fact is that there is no deterioration associated with the taking of morphine or heroin or any other opiate, unless you get into very large doses. All of this stuff you read in the public newspapers about the terrible effect of heroin is just pure hogwash. There is nothing to it, and there is no medical opinion anywhere to support it.

I have studied this thing carefully, and other people in this country have studied it carefully, and it has been studied carefully abroad. There is no deterioration from the taking of morphine or heroin within, but some of these people appear to be deteriorated, for the reason they appear to be deteriorated from the emotional standpoint, criminals and addicts.

And the association these addicts have to keep to continue the habit, the secrecy of the habit, does have a deteriorating effect on personalities, in being arrested and being associated with criminals; but the drugs themselves, morphine and heroin, never cause any deterioration.

There is an interesting thing that I might mention right here.

Mr. MITLER. Are they violent people?

Dr. KOLB. How is that?

Mr. MITLER. Are drug addicts violent people?

Dr. KOLB. No.

Mr. MITLER. You always hear about that.   What is the fact?

Dr. KOLB. No.   I will stop now and say during the 5,000 years that opium has been used, that there hasn't been one violent crime committed by anybody because of the effect of this drug.   The exact effect of all types of opiates is to soothe people and make them less likely to commit crime.

But drug addicts do commit crimes; they commit crimes if they were criminals before; the addiction doesn't quite cure them, and of course they commit crimes to get the drug for this reason: The opiate drugs, and the two synthetic drugs, have an effect that no other drugs have to the same degree.   They create a dependence.   You get tolerant.

One can take as much after they get well—they can take enough at 1 does that will ordinarily kill 5 or 6 people who are not addicted, and they won't feel anything special from it.   In fact, it is almost impossible to poison with morphine or heroin a well-addicted addict.

Well, when you take that drug away from them, they suffer intensely.   They even—they get extensively sick, and some of them die unless they are properly treated, just from the withdrawal symptoms, and I have seen that happen, and it happened due to the enforcement of these laws, because doctors get scared off, and I can cite cases where the doctor could have given drugs and has been scared off by narcotics inspectors, and let the people go, and you have got a death, and they are fine people.

But there is a lot of crime in drug addiction, and 90 percent is not due to the drugs they have taken, but to the impulse they have to keep up this habit, to keep from being intensely sick, and so they violate narcotic laws and they get—lots of them, to begin with, are unstable people, and they get to committing these petty crimes like stealing, and things of that kind, forging prescriptions, and those who were criminals before then will occasionally commit a violent crime like an armed robbery, and they even might commit murder.

But it is not because of the drug in them, but it is because of their original state, and it is because they are suffering intensely from this thing, and will do most anything to get this drug.

Chairman KEFAUVER. Doctor, isn't your testimony contradictory to the great mass of professional evidence on this subject?

Dr. KOLB. It is not contradictory to the great mass of professional evidence on this subject.

Chairman KEFAUVER. I had always understood——

Dr. KOLB. Let me say what I mean by "professional evidence."   I mean informed professional evidence.   You can talk to physicians throughout the country now, and they have absorbed their ideas on drug addiction from newspapers through inflammatory articles, and magazine inflammatory articles, because they won't handle drug addicts and don't handle them.   And when they hear in the newspaper that heroin is the atomic bomb type of thing, they believe it.

I have talked to doctors who believe it.   I think if you ask the Lexington people about it, and if you ask Dr. Chapman about it, and any other person who has treated drug addiction, you will find, just as I say, it is a soothing drug.

I want to come to the English situation here.

Chairman KEFAUVER. Let me ask you another question.

I suppose, like alcohol, that if you drink a certain amount of alcohol, basically that does not ruin your body, but it is generally believed that it might deaden your senses or lessen your responsibilities so that you do things that you would not otherwise do, and commit crimes that you would not otherwise commit.

So I always understood it was, to a greater degree, with heroin and drugs.

Dr. KOLB. It is just exactly the other way around, and I will show you why.

Heroin and morphine give the soothing effect that people get from alcohol, and why they become drunkards through alcohol. But the person who takes heroin and morphine does not get intoxicated in that sense. He maintains his judgment in perfectly good form. That is very well known.

Now, alcohol, as I have written about in that article, does, I think, a couple of thousand times more harm in the United States in a year than the narcotics do, because thousands of people do become insane, 18,000 are in our hospitals every year from alcohol, and I would guess right now not one enters from narcotic drugs. And that is the difference.

Chairman KEFAUVER. Well, all of these police officials couldn't be wrong in saying that things happen at marihuana parties and heroin parties that certainly normal people would not do.

Dr. KOLB. No; they wouldn't be wrong when they are talking about marihuana, but the police have got this police attitude. The thing has been turned over to them, and they know these drug addicts commit crimes to get their drugs, and they testify to that effect. But it is not because of the effect of the drug, morphine or heroin, on them; it is because they cannot get it, and they are suffering, and because, as I said before, they were recruited from an unstable type of people.

I am absolutely sure if you made every violent criminal in the United States an addict, and they wouldn't like it, I am sure, and would give them the drug that they needed, that violent crime would be decreased tremendously.

It is different with alcohol. Alcohol is one of the most important causes of crime—that is very well authenticated—and also of disease, insanity. I have only seen two cases of insanity due to drug addiction. These people had been addicted for about 40 years. They tried to get cured. They had been taking 5 or 6 treatments. When they got off, they got hypomania; that is, having been compelled to do without that sedative, they got excited, talked too much, some foolish action, and when they got back on the drug again they were cured in less than half a day. They needed that sedative that they had gotten used to throughout the period of years.

Now, alcohol, as you said, there are millions of people, there are about 55 million people in the United States who drink alcohol without any harm. But—there is a total of 68 million people who drink alcohol, and from that 68 million people we have got 4,500,000 alcoholics who are marching on their road to the grave or to the insane asylum or to the gallows for killing somebody.

And, of course, among that number are a certain number of persons who get drunk and irresponsible and have all these automobile accidents. Automobile accidents don't go along with morphine or heroin addiction, because it doesn't have that loss of motor control from taking morphine or heroin.

Chairman KEFAUVER. Marihuana is a stimulant?

Dr. KOLB. Marihuana is as bad as alcohol, no worse, no better.

Chairman KEFAUVER. Cocaine is a stimulant?

Dr. KOLB. Cocaine is a stimulant which, from the standpoint of health, is worse than any of these drugs, but cocaine isn't quite as bad from the standpoint of crime as marihuana would be, or alcohol would be, because the man who gets cocaine gets extremely anxious, and he develops a paranoid type of psychosis, and he stops. in that psychosis, he could commit a crime.

Mr. MITLER. He sometimes thinks people are coming through the keyhole, and detectives are coming after him.

Dr. KOLB. I have seen cocaine addicts—we don't see many now— I saw one who, after walking around the city, saw a policeman walking behind him, and he attacked a laundry bag, attacked it with a bar, thinking it was a man.

Cocaine is really a destructive drug taken excessively, and it fortunately isn't today.

Marihuana is a dangerous drug, but it isn't anywhere near as dangerous as it is put up to be.

For instance, there are 200 million, estimated 200 million, marihuana addicts in the world. I don't know whether that is right. I rather think it is large now. There are about 5,000 in the United States.

Now, illustrating the hysteria in the United States about addiction, how we advertised our plight, marihuana has gotten to be known in Europe as an American vice because of our good advertising policy of a distressful situation we are in from addiction. Of course, it would be a terrible thing if we should get 68 million people in the United States smoking marihuana; then it would be an accentuation of crime. But there is no danger of that, even if you turn it loose, because it is not a destructive thing and it has no social usages like alcohol does; and even if we didn't have any laws, I doubt if we would ever get more than 50,000.

Did you want to ask a question?

Mr. MITLER. I just wanted to ask you what your recommendations were for an improved treatment program.

Dr. KOLB. I would like to finish answering the question that Senator Kefauver asked.

Mr. MITLER. Surely. I am sorry.

Dr. KOLB. That is about the medical opinion about this opium and heroin.

Now, in 1898, a great English psychiatrist and physician wrote a book on narcotics, and he coined a phrase there which is true and which is followed all over Europe, that is, "Opium soothes; alcohol maddens." It just expresses the difference between those two things, and they go after the alcoholic in Europe much more than they do after the addict, because they know that the opium and morphine addict is not harming anybody.

They do, however, attempt to cure these addicts. Now, morphine and heroin and opium addiction is a terrible thing because of this physical dependence that people get; not because of the harm that it gives to a person who has taken 5 or 10 grains a day, but that person has got to have his dose 4 or 5 times a day or he gets sick. It makes a slave of a person; and practically every addict I ever saw, except some of the very psychopathic, wanted to get cured, and they make an attempt to get cured over and over again, and they flunk on it just as the alcoholics do when they are of the psychopathic type of people.

So the world agitation against the opium drugs is very well based. It is based, not on the fact that these drugs are making people commit crimes, but on the fact that these people become slaves, and on the fact also that if you do get up to 30 or 40 grains of morphine or heroin a day, I personally think that it is physically harmful, because I did a lot of experiments with monkeys on—more with morphine than heroin, and found when I got to giving them up to what in a man would be the equivalent to 60 grains a day, that they very definitely suffered in health.

And while we are talking about withdrawal symptoms, one of these monkeys when I suddenly took the drug away from him, just died in the withdrawal period.

Did you want to ask me a question?

Chairman KEFAUVER. Then as I understand it, you feel as to heroin and morphine, that while in large amounts they may be harmful to the person, the chief crimes that come from them are that you become tolerant and addicted, and you must have your dose, and you go out and steal or do anything else in order to get the money?

Dr. KOLB. That is right.

Chairman KEFAUVER. In order to carry on this nefarious habit.

Dr. KOLB. That accounts for at least 95 percent of the crimes that the drug addicts commit. The other 5 percent are violations, and from the fact of the nature of these people beforehand, that they were criminals anyhow, and the drug addiction——

Chairman KEFAUVER. Of course, is it not well known that a morphine or heroin addict's appetite for food diminishes, he does not take nourishment, and he does not eat normally?

Dr. KOLB. No; that is not well known. When you get tolerant to drugs, the tolerance implies that your physical functions are acting normally; and if a morphine or heroin addict taking 5 to 10 grains a day is given all the food he needs, he will eat it and he won't be emaciated, and I defy anybody in the world to pick out an addict just to look at him, a nourished addict, who is getting his dose.

Now, you can go around to jails and prisons when they first come in, and station houses when they brought a lot of people in, and pick one out and say, "That fellow is an addict," because he will be emaciated because he starved to death and spent all his money for morphine or heroin, and also because he has not been able to get enough of the morphine or heroin in between. He has been sick in between, say, 1 day sick because he hasn't got it, and the next day too much. And he gets to vomiting and has diarrhea, and he doesn't eat. That is what brings about emaciation.

Cocaine is the thing, if you take it in large doses, you will get emaciated from it, sort of an anesthetic effect on the stomach, and it is a terrible drug.

Chairman KEFAUVER. Well, morphine and heroin are given to people to quiet them, are they not, in hospitals?

Dr. KOLB. They are.

Chairman KEFAUVER. And you say that putting them to sleep and the effect when it has been given in hospitals, does not adversely interfere with their normal——

Dr. KOLB. Well, the one dose will. The one dose—if some of us here should take, say, a half a grain of injection of morphine now, we probably would be sick, we might be vomiting. But if you kept on giving it to us for 2 months, we would have to have that thing just to keep from being sick; that is the difference.

But the first dose of morphine is liable to make a person sick, and often does; and in that time it will have cut down the appetite, cut down digestion, too, and will make you constipated, and all that type of thing.

But when you get tolerant to that type of thing, that is what builds up a person—you can build up a quarter of a grain a day, and in the course of 2 months, you can build them up in 2 months to taking 10 grains a day, where you will absoluely be in need of it, and he absolutely has to take it, and he will be sick if he doesn't take it.

And that is what makes the opiate drugs such dreaded drugs. I am talking about alcohol. I would rather be a drug addict, that is, if it weren't for our severe laws, rather than be an alcoholic, if I was sure I could stay out of crime with drugs and could stay out of the gutter.

Now, these 4½ million alcoholics we have in the United States are not all in the gutter; some of them are functioning all right, and some of them are just killing themselves. And they didn't get so they have got to have that alcohol in order to keep from being sick. They built up an emotional attitude for it, but there is a different type of emotional withdrawal from alcohol. You can build up a withdrawal, brilliantly proved down at Lexington, by giving large amounts of alcohol to people, in 6 weeks they have had just as bad withdrawal symptoms as morphine and heroin, but that was amounts of alcohol that very few people take.

A fellow who takes 4 or 5 or 6 drinks a day isn't going to get any withdrawal symptoms. He can stop, and might be functioning perfectly normally. That is the difference between these drugs. And the terror that people have of becoming addicts, physical addicts, is what has caused all of the agitation throughout the world to stop the addiction.

Now, these tranquilizing drugs that are now being given to so many of the insane people and to the neurotic people are physically, every one of them is physically, more harmful than morphine or heroin. They cause dysphasias, they cause stomach and liver disorders and death.

Chairman KEFAUVER. What kind of drugs are they?

Dr. KOLB. The so-called tranquilizing drugs that you hear so much about in the newspapers, that are curing all the mental patients. Of course, it is not curing them, but it is quieting them down, and it may be curing some of them; I don't know.

But the morphine and heroin are much better tranquilizers, but of course they wouldn't be used because, if you used them right along, those people would become slaves to it and users. But those drugs are doing much more physical harm.

Chairman KEFAUVER. What is the makeup of the tranquilizing drugs?

Dr. KOLB. I couldn't give you the chemical formula.   One of them is called chlorpromazine; one is reserpine—it comes from an old Chinese plant, I believe; and another one is called Milltown; and there is one called frenquil.   And they are being given by the tons now to nervous people.   In fact, the medical profession is getting disturbed about it, because every doctor has become a psychiatrist.   If anybody has become anywhere nervous, they give him tranquilizing drugs.

I attended a meeting here in Washington 2 months ago that was called just because they were disturbed about this thing, and it came out there that 30 percent of all the prescriptions issued by physicians in the United States are issued for these tranquilizing drugs.

Of course, this is not a thing that any police need to get in on.   The doctors will solve this eventually in their own way, and will use these things as they should be used.

But I merely brought up the effect of the tranquilizing drugs. They say it is the same thing that morphine and heroin do.

The Public Health Service has been trying for years to find an opium drug, a drug that would act like morphine, that wouldn't have the physical addicting properties of morphine.   I don't think—I don't know whether they are ever going to succeed in it or not, but if they do, it would be the greatest boon to mankind, because these opium drugs are tranquilizers; they cure a lot of things.

There was one time in the world when morphine was practically given for everything, or opium, because it is a soothing, pain-relieving thing, but always we had this thing, that physical addiction.   And in legislating we should remember this one thing: The only reason we need to stop, we need to regulate, the opium drugs at all, morphine and heroin, is the physical addiction.   It is not crime producing; it is nor character deteriorating.

We got off on the wrong foot in this country in contrast to what they did in England, and made it a criminal problem, and this is how it came about:

They began arresting doctors for violating this law, Mr. King told you about that, and sent them to the penitentiary, often for giving drugs to cure patients and to save their lives.

I have seen a drug addict, a woman, who wanted to come to Lexington.   The doctor had been scared off.   She died.   She was a fine mother of children.   It was because of this one thing.

Now, this hasn't happened once, it has happened dozens of times. I have seen a woman commit suicide who in England would have been given her drugs.   She was a nurse.   I advised her to go to Lexington; she couldn't go.   The police went after her.   She committed suicide. In England she would have been doing a good day's work, and would not have been disturbing anybody.

Now, the idea that the addicts try to create addicts is another fallacy that has gotten into this business.   My own experience has been that the addicts advise their friends to stay away from this drug and to get cured.

The reason why I bring this up is that they state that every addict— and I have heard it stated from a reasonable source—every addict creates four addicts.   That has been given, not by a doctor, but by a law-enforcement official of high standing.

Well, I figured out what this would come to. I knew it was absurd from my own experience, but I got a statistician to work out what would happen. Well, if every addict, starting with our 60,000 in the United States, made 4 other addicts, and assuming no deaths, in 30 months there would be 187,500,000 addicts in the United States.

So now there is an illustration of the absurd things that are said about drug addiction, and which gets the public so stirred up that they will support any sort of ridiculous legislation that is proposed.

We heard, I believe yesterday you said something about the California report. I don't know what it is, but I think I have seen the report, the report to the Attorney General, and it has some good points in it.

But it has one thing in it of extreme absurdity which I would like to point out to you.

Chairman KEFAUVER. Let's let the record show at this point that the doctor is talking about the report brought out in testimony of Mr. Neeb, which is called the report of the Citizens Advisory Committee to the Attorney General.

Dr. KOLB. Well, I haven't read that report for some time, but I thought yesterday that was it. But in that report, this statement is made about the illegal market: One pound of heroin sells in the illegal market—let's see, I put it down here; I looked it up again this morning—for $768,000 to $1,228,000, and people grab that.

Those kind of foolish statements are being made in newspapers right along.

Well, figuring that out, it means that a 6-grain-a-day heroin addict would have to spend $900, from $600 to $900, which is, of course, to anybody who ought to know, an absolute absurdity.

But these statements are made repeatedly in newspapers about this $1 million, $2 million, $3 million seizure, and if I read them all, it makes me a little bit mad because it is so absurd, and find out that just this thing is what would happen.

Of course, the heroin and morphine addicts do pay a lot. They pay up to $10, maybe some $15, a day, and they haven't got it; that is why they commit a crime.

Chairman KEFAUVER. Well, but are you taking into consideration the fact that when they talk about these large payments, that when you translate it down to the individual dose, that the pure heroin or morphine is cut many times before it finally reaches the consumer.

Dr. KOLB. That is right. It is cut more times; and even that $1,800,000–$200,000 there, if a man got the equivalent of the 6-grain-a-day habit, that is what he would have to pay.

Now, the 6-grain-a-day I found out in 1924 was the average addiction-day habit at that time. And it was a reasonably moderate habit. They would have—I also discovered in my studies at the time, if the average addict had his way about it, he would be taking 15 grains a day, but I have seen people—I saw 1 woman who had been on morphine for 65 years, and she was taking 3 grains a day— I think she was in Tennessee, Bristol, Tenn., or Virginia. And she was perfectly healthy, the mother of six children, and nobody was after her.

In the present day they would have gotten after her, and she probably would have died from withdrawal or would have been intensely miserable from the thing; or, if they had gotten her soon enough, she would have been cured. But she would never have been hurt all during those years from taking that amount of drug.

To return—I want to say——

Chairman KEFAUVER. Before you return, we were talking about tranquilizing drugs.

Dr. KOLB. Tranquilizing drugs; yes.

Chairman KEFAUVER. What is the makeup of any of the so-called tranquilizing chemicals or ingredients in various types of barbiturates, sleeping pill tablets?

Dr. KOLB. Well, a barbiturate is the salts of barbituric acid. I can't give you the chemical formula for all of them; I have it in the book. But there is a very large group of barbiturates that people take for sleeping, and, of course, sometimes you hear of people taking those things for suicide.

Chairman KEFAUVER. Are they made of the same kind of ingredients as tranquilizing drugs?

Dr. KOLB. No; they are different. The tranquilizing drugs are a different chemical composition. I don't know enough about chemistry and pharmacology to give you that.

Of course, I have it in books and things. But they are entirely different in chemical composition from the barbiturates, and entirely different from the opiates in chemical composition.

Chairman KEFAUVER. All right. Thank you.

Mr. CHUMBRIS. Doctor, you mentioned if you could discover a formula, it would be a saving to mankind. Let me ask you this: How much money is going into research along that line?

Dr. KOLB. Well, I will tell you about this program. This program of finding out, trying to discover a different opiate drug that wouldn't have the physical properties, was started as a joint project between the Public Health Service and the University of Michigan and the University of Virginia.

That program came to an end in, well, I think 1937 or so, when the Public Health Service took it over because the other people ran out of money; and they were working on it on a grant.

The Public Health Service took that over, and took some of the personnel over, the pharmacologists and the chemists, who were trying to develop that drug, and they have since been pursuing that.

But I understand from a chemist who is in that thing that they are not supporting it quite as much as they did before, perhaps because they think maybe this thing is not going to pan out to anything.

Now, they have actually made numerous, perhaps 50, different opiate derivatives, but every one of them has had the physical-addiction properties; and that is something that the addiction research center at the Lexington Hospital finds out; they try these drugs out to see whether they do have the physical-addiction properties. If they do, they tell them, and they are not released to the public.

I think there are only about two of the drugs that have been discovered in this thing that are in use now, than can be prescribed. I don't know what they are, but they are physically addictive, so it doesn't amount to anything.

Senator KEFAUVER. All right.

Mr. MITLER. Do you have some affirmative recommendations about what a good treatment program would be in the United States?

Dr. KOLB. Yes. We, of course, should have more hospitals for treatment of drug addicts. But it should be treated entirely as a medical problem.

Now, I don't believe in forcibly arresting people as has been so much done now and then, forcing them into treatment like is done under this new law that was passed in the District of Columbia. I don't agree with that law, and Dr. Chapman, I believe, will tell you later on how many States have commitment laws that are not on that basis; but we should have hospitals to which patients should go, either voluntarily or by commitment, depending on where the hospital is and whether it is by a State or a city.

Chairman KEFAUVER. How are you going to commit them unless you have compulsion?

Dr. KOLB. I would only commit people who are found violating a law, and who come to the attention of the police that they are addicts. I wouldn't go out hunting for them. And the reason I wouldn't do it is because I have found by studies in Europe that it is not done there, anyway. They know that this opium addict out in the public is not hurting anybody and is not going to commit any crime because of his addiction, so they don't go after him to commit him to a hospital.

I don't say we shouldn't do it here. If we come across this addict, and he comes to the attention of the police because of some violation, or if his family will make a complaint against him as they do when he becomes mentally ill, they say, "He is an addict; we would like to have him treated," then I would go in for the commitment.

I would have hospitals for treatment, and I would repeal these, what I consider more or less extreme laws, whereby an addict cannot be put on probation.

The thing I think we should have or what the original narcotics law had when Lexington and Fort Worth were established—judges could put addicts, violators, on probation and send them to Lexington or Fort Worth, on the condition that they go there and stay until they are cured.

Now, the probation feature at Lexington has fallen down because we have got these extreme laws, partly because of that, whereby the judge is forced to give a prison sentence, and prison sentences which are, to my mind, excessive.

Well, we should have hospitals to treat these people, and there should be commitment procedures to hospitals like the Riverside Hospital in New York; they have it in New York. Being a State institution, they can commit to them or put them there with some little police pressure. That is all right. And they should stay until they are cured.

Now, it is very important that when they come out, that there should be some followup, but not by police. That is a destructive thing, and the thing where we have gone so far wrong.

I would like to digress a little bit here, just to say what this has done. I have seen a fellow come back to Lexington in tears. We cured him, got him a job, and the police came around and said to his employer, "You know, that fellow is an addict."

What happened? The employer gets distressed. He thinks, "Well, there is a terrible criminal here," and he isn't anything of the kind, "and besides, I might be violating some law."

And so the fellow, he discharged him. The fellow couldn't get a job, and he got into a distressful situation without any employment, and he relapsed to drugs, and he comes back again.

This has happened over and over again. That is why the police should never follow these people.

Now, the followup that I would recommend for people coming from Lexington and Fort Worth would be, in the big cities, for the Public Health Service, big cities like Washington or Chicago or New York, Detroit, Los Angeles, where they have most of the addicts, to have a clinic there to which these people would be asked to go and report from time to time, and the clinic would be run by trained psychiatric social workers, perhaps, with a psychologist, where we could get one, and with some psychiatric consultants where these people could go from time to time to get their emotional problems straightened out, and some assistance from the social workers in getting them into jobs and, when necessary, to refer these people to psychiatrists to get them to help to unravel their emotional disturbances so that they could stand stresses more than they ordinarily can, and would not relapse too much.

I doubt whether it would be feasible to have a program to follow every addict who might go to rural regions and to all the small cities in the United States. It would be more expensive, and the results wouldn't justify it.

Chairman KEFAUVER. Then in that followup program, you said that you don't know about the smaller cities; but most cities, and also counties, have some kind of public health service, and cities the size of Knoxville and Chattanooga certainly have psychiatric physicians to be of service.

Dr. KOLB. Yes, sir, but I don't think from Knoxville and Chattanooga you will get very many addicts going to Lexington and Fort Worth. I don't know just what the figures are. They are getting the biggest numbers from New York, Chicago, Philadelphia, Washington, Detroit, Los Angeles.

Chairman KEFAUVER. Would it not also be helpful if the employment service, for instance, could help in making a special problem of employment for these people?

Dr. KOLB. It would be very helpful if they did that, because that is one thing that causes addicts to relapse, to go out, and they are more or less shunned; and if they are known about, people avoid them. They are afraid they are criminals, and they are not necessarily criminals at all. They are just weak people.

And there are thousands of them around here working, of the same type of person except they haven't been unfortunate enough to become drug addicts.

Now, the thing that Mr. Rosenblum said here today, I believe that was his name, who has that followup thing in New York, I think that is very good, sort of a AA type of followup where they go to those people——

Chairman KEFAUVER. His name is Rosenfeld.

Dr. KOLB. The program he had there was a very good program for those people, and it has been a very good program, like Alcoholics Anonymous for alcoholics.

Of course, he said a lot of things about the nature of curing them with which I don't agree, but that is not important.

Chairman KEFAUVER. He is a layman.

Dr. KOLB. But he is doing a splendid job there, I can see very well. That type of followup is a very good thing for drug addicts.

Mr. MITLER. Could I clarify just one thing, Doctor. In your speaking about these laws, you are not making reference to the non-addict pusher, the man who just goes out coldbloodedly and sells?

Dr. KOLB. I don't care what they do with a fellow who is not an addict.

Mr. MITLER. In other words, the law should be severe for that?

Dr. KOLB. I think about 95 percent of the fellows who are selling them and are arrested for selling are addicts who are selling a little in order to get more money to support their own habit, and those are the kind of people I would treat as addicts, and not as a pusher like people such as Lucky Luciano and other people. They are the terrible criminals who ought to be dealt with in a severe way, and it doesn't make any difference.

But for the ordinary addict-pusher, he should be treated usually in a probationary way in a hospital like Lexington and Fort Worth, and stay there until the doctors think he is all right.

Now, in the case of probationers, people who have been sentenced, when they go out and they are followed by the probation officers, that is all right. But for the voluntary addict, he should never be followed by any police at all, because it will inevitably happen they will be, with perfectly good intentions, the police will make raids on them and arrest them, and they will get into the criminal class, and we will have these headlines about 300 or 400 people being brought in, and you find out that two-thirds of them are nothing, they are just raiding people, and it adds to the excitement.

I did intend to say something about the British system as I found out about it when I was over there, and as I have later on studied about it.

Now, in England especially—I will refer to England because I especially studied it there, and since I have studied it, and it applies also to countries like Germany, Italy, and Denmark. In England, the doctor is never disturbed in his prescribing for narcotics. Dr. Lindesmith yesterday gave you a very good example of what is going on in England.

I don't think any doctor in England ever has been sent to jail because he prescribed for an addict. But they do prosecute a doctor in England if he prescribes for himself.

What happens there, and I will go over it again, is this: that there are people on the panel in England, doctors; they write prescriptions for an addict if they think he should be carried on a maintenance dose, and they noted it on the panel. And a regional medical officer will go around and see the doctor about it, and consult with him and suggest to him, "Now, maybe you should cut this fellow down" or "maybe you should have a consultation with another physician before you continue to carry on with him."

Mr. MITLER. That was the system Dr. Lindesmith described.

Dr. KOLB. That was the same system he described in England.

Mr. MITLER. In other words, your observations are the same as his.

Dr. KOLB. My observations are the same as his.

Mr. MITLER. Do you have an account there?

Dr. KOLB. I have here——

Mr. MITLER. We will put that in the record.

Chairman KEFAUVER. Let him explain what it is.

Mr. MITLER. I am sorry.

Dr. KOLB. The reason why I brought this down here is that people in this country, in perfect good faith, say that the English don't do the thing any different from what we do. And I have heard it said over and over again—it is surprising what intelligent people will allow their their emotions to carry them on to say, or how they can get blinded to facts. I will just read the 2 lines in this thing that they go by, in this 15-page thing. This line is:

The continued supply of dangerous drugs to a patient solely for the gratification of addiction is not regarded as medical need.

Now, that is in there, and the English don't indiscriminately give opiates to addicts, and this shows it.

In 1924, a committee that was called the Ralston committee in England was appointed to advise the Government what to do about this, and they made a report which has been English law ever since; and in these instructions to doctors and dentists under the Dangerous Drugs Act and Regulations, revised by the Home Office in 1956, it very definitely tells you how the doctor can go about these things and what he should do, and I would like to read perhaps just what is the law, and with the various modifications which Lindesmith and I told you about.

They carry an addict, when they find out that he is an addict and they can't cure him, they carry him on drugs indefinitely with the minimum dose. Here is what they do, I would like to read this:

In the preceding section, the conclusion has been stated that morphine or heroin may properly be administered to addicts in the following circumstances, namely, (a) where patients are under treatment by the gradual withdrawal method with a view to cure—

that is not allowed in the United States. Doctors have gone to jail for trying to do that here—

(b) where it has been demonstrated, after a prolonged attempt at cure, that the use of the drug cannot be safely discontinued entirely, on account of the severity of the withdrawal symptoms produced, (c) where it has been similarly demonstrated that the patient, while capable of leading a useful and relatively normal life when a certain minimum dose is regularly administered, becomes incapable of this when the drug is entirely discontinued.

Now, these people are carried in England on maintenance doses as long as they live. They continue with their work, they never disturb anybody because of addiction.

But in their regulations, if one of these men getting narcotics from one doctor goes to another doctor and gets one, then they punish him and they give him a short jail sentence and put him back on the thing.

Mr. MITLER. That is the gist of Dr. Lindesmith's statement.

Dr. KOLB. That is the gist of the whole thing, and that thing put in regulation here would wipe out 90 percent of our crime overnight because of drug addiction.

The thing I would do here, I wouldn't be quite as liberal with it as the English are, because we are a little bit different culture; I would have this thing policed by doctors, not by policemen, not by narcotics enforcement people. I would have the law so changed that people could be sent to penitentiaries up to 10 years, that is what they can do in England, but always within the discretion of the judge.

This idea of not having probation and parole is simply a fantastic bit of thing that there is no sense in at all, because the crimes are not severe.

And then I would have it so that in each State there would be a group of doctors appointed by the State health authority to decide on each addict. When a doctor found he had an addict he thought needed treatment, he would refer the case to that group of doctors. They would examine it, and they would say "Go ahead" or "Try to treat him." But there wouldn't be any question, as there is now, of sneaking in with a policeman to try to get this doctor to do something that they can put him in the penitentiary on, and the rest of it. That never has happened in England. And this would clear up our addiction.

And I want to say this: that drug addiction has decreased in the United States since 1900, even before we had it in America, and it would have decreased just as much if you had this law as if you had these extreme laws. The experience in Europe proves it.

Mr. MITLER. Those are your recommendations?

Dr. KOLB. Those are my recommendations. You would wipe out the crime, and you would wipe out the deaths.

The tragic thing about this, Senator, is this: There are lots of people who could work and who do work under drug addiction. Some years ago I studied a couple of hundred addicts just with this view in mind. That was before the law clamping down on them too severely was passed.

Seventy-eight percent of those addicts were working as well as anybody, obeying all the laws and not hurting anybody.

But the law was beginning to close down on them, and I have no doubt but that most of them found their ways—they were getting their drug from doctors.

I might say that in Bristol, partly Tennessee and partly Virginia, I saw a lot of that.

Chairman KEFAUVER. Doctor, you have spoken of Bristol two or three times. What was your connection with Bristol?

Dr. KOLB. I went down there merely to study the addicts, because I was in good rapport with the Narcotic Division, I asked them to tell me where I could find addicts, and they knew about it.

I went from Maine to Albany studying drug addicts. I studied a lot of them in Bristol, and a lot in Atlanta and some other places in the South. There was more in the South then than there was in the North, for this reason: When we didn't have narcotics laws, when we could go and buy this stuff like you could candy and potatoes, laudanum was a very addicting drug.

Chairman KEFAUVER. What was that drug?

Dr. KOLB. Laudanum. It is a 10 percent opium or 10 morphine, I forget which, but anyhow it was an opium drug, and people would take it for diarrhea. There was more diarrheic disease in the South because it was a warmer climate, and they had not developed their water system to the same extent they had in other parts of the country. People got a diarrheic disease, people started to take laudanum for diarrhea, and would keep on taking it for a month, and they would become slightly addicted and take some more, and they would be addicted, not because of diarrhea, but because of the drug. They would wake up and within a year they were addicted.

Maybe they were getting opium because you could buy this in stores, too. At that time addiction was more prevalent in the South than in the North, except for a few large cities in the North that got into the underworld, and these people in the South were just as good as anybody else.

I don't know what happened to them. In Bristol, Tenn., I wanted to say, I examined a lot of addicts there. A doctor there who was prescribing—and I got access to them during the early days through the Narcotics Division, and I found that a lot of them were just this way, and some of them were fellows paying for their house like a fellow now, and working every day, and he was getting a drug.

I don't know what happened to them afterward, but I did have somebody mad by a report I made; perhaps I shouldn't have done it. I made a report saying the ones I thought should be cured and the ones I thought should continue to take drugs, and the narcotics inspector for that district got sore about that, but I gave it to him.

I think I gave it to a doctor who was taking care of those drug addicts, too. But that was all right; so far as the Narcotic Division in Washington was concerned, it was all right with them. They were willing for that to happen.

Mr. MITLER. Thank you, Doctor.

Chairman KEFAUVER. Anything else, Dr. Kolb?

Dr. KOLB. I believe I have said that marihuana isn't any more harmful than alcohol, and 1 marihuana cigarette, if you get any effect from it at all, is just about exactly the same effect as 1 drink of whiskey, and it is a tragic thing that in the United States, people have been sent to the penitentiary for 10 years for having in their possession or for selling 2 marihuana cigarettes. It is simply absurd to do.

Mr. MITLER. I have no other questions, Senator.

Chairman KEFAUVER. Doctor, whether one agrees with you or whether they don't, it is very worthwhile to have opinions of experts who have had experience, and to get this problem out for discussion and consideration, for the formation of public opinion.

Dr. KOLB. Thank you.

Chairman KEFAUVER. We appreciate very much your coming here and testifying.

Mr. MITLER. Thank you, Doctor.

Chairman KEFAUVER. Dr. Kenneth Chapman.

Dr. CHAPMAN. Yes, sir.

Chairman KEFAUVER. Former Medical Director, United States Public Health Hospital at Lexington, presently consultant on narcotics addiction, National Mental Health Institute, Department of Health, Education, and Welfare.

Tell us about your experience and background, Dr. Chapman.

STATEMENT OF DR. KENNETH CHAPMAN, CONSULTANT, NARCOTIC DRUG ADDICTION, NATIONAL INSTITUTES OF HEALTH, DEPARTMENT OF HEALTH, EDUCATION, AND WELFARE

Dr. CHAPMAN. My first experience in drug addiction started in 1946 on my assignment to Lexington. I was clinical director there until 1949; came to Washington as assistant in charge of the section that Dr. Himmelsbach is now the director of; and then went back to

Lexington in 1952 to 1954, was medical officer in charge; and since then I have been the consultant that you referred to.

In addition to that, I have been for the past 4 out of 6 months, I have served as a special consultant to the World Health Organization, working out of Geneva, studying the problem of care and treatment of drug addicts in the Near East and in Europe.

Chairman KEFAUVER. What was your educational background?

Dr. CHAPMAN. I graduated from the Yale Medical School in 1938.

Chairman KEFAUVER. Yale Medical School?

Dr. CHAPMAN. Yes.

Chairman KEFAUVER. That is a good university.

Where did you start out?

Dr. CHAPMAN. I am sorry.

I then went into the Public Health Service as an intern, and have been in the Public Health Service as a commissioned officer since 1939.

Mr. MITLER. Doctor, in connection with your work with the World Health Organization, did you make a study of the treatment program in Great Britain, Egypt, and Iran?

Dr. CHAPMAN. Yes, I did.

Mr. MITLER. Could you tell us—we have heard about Great Britain. Could you tell us briefly about the program in those three countries?

Dr. CHAPMAN. Well, in Great Britain, to dignify their program as a treatment program, I think would be an extension of the fact. There is no organized-treatment program of drug addicts in Great Britain. Even to call the system a system, I think would be an extension of the fact.

There is a method, if you would call it that, sort of a loosely defined method. It is constantly in the process of refinement, cooperative arrangements between the medical profession and the Home Office, one branch of which is responsible and would be a parallel to our Narcotics Bureau in this country. They are constantly refining their techniques and methods for handling this particular problem.

There is no compulsory treatment of drug addicts, as such, in Great Britain. They are considered the individual medical problem and province of the physician, unless they come into contact with the law in some way, and it has been described, both by Dr. Lindesmith and Dr. Kolb, the ways in which they can come into conflict with the law.

It has been estimated, as matter of fact, Mr. Green of the Home Office told me, that probably 10 or 15 addicts get in conflict with the law every year and wind up in the penitentiary.

This has usually been in the nature of forging prescriptions or dealing in narcotics, perhaps, or trying to get a couple of doctors to give them extra doses.

The medical profession does not look upon the giving of drugs to drug addicts as support of drug addiction. That is condemned very severely and, as a matter of fact, I have had the extreme pleasure of being a guest of the British Addiction Society, a private organization, when I was there, and the members, all reputable physicians, were quite concerned over what they had said or implied that the British supported addiction, the British physicians were in favor of handing out drugs to addicts, and they were very indignant about this.   And they said, "We don't in any way, shape, or form feel it is good medical practice to provide drugs to drug addicts for the sake of support of drug addiction," and that is spelled out, as Dr. Kolb mentioned, in the Dangerous Drugs Act.

Chairman KEFAUVER. You disagree with Dr. Kolb on that score. You seem to feel that in certain cases there is no alternative.

Dr. CHAPMAN. Pardon me, Senator, I think there is a slight semantic disagreement here.   I think, if I recall correctly, Dr. Kolb said—he read from there that there was no support of addiction as such, but under certain circumstances persons who are addicted to narcotic drugs can receive drugs.

There is a semantic difference of terminology, perhaps.   The British do provide, in a medical sense, narcotics for persons who have been addicted to narcotic drugs, but for medical reasons, and they are defined; namely, for withdrawal, for persons who cannot be taken off drugs because it will be injurious to their health, or because it has been found for medical reasons that to take them off drugs would make it impossible for them to get along in society.

But this is not defined, sir, as supplying addicts with drugs for purposes of addiction.   These are for medical reasons.

Mr. MITLER. Could I interrupt?   I think it is very important.   The difference is, we in the United States do not permit a disbursement of drugs for the last reason that you gave; that is, the last reason you gave.

Dr. CHAPMAN. The last two reasons, I think it would be safe to say.

Mr. MITLER. Excuse me for interrupting you.

Dr. CHAPMAN. Although that is quibbling, because the second point, the matter of they cannot be safely withdrawn, would probably be provided in the United States to an old person who has heart disease, or something like that.   There would be an extension of fact in that area.

Mr. MITLER. Excuse me for interrupting you.

Chairman KEFAUVER. But ordinarily, in the last two cases—that is, where they cannot be withdrawn or where it would be injurious to their health to withdraw them—ordinarily in the United States continued medical sales cannot continue unless there is some other physical matter like heart disease, or something of that sort?

Dr. CHAPMAN. That is correct, sir.

Chairman KEFAUVER. But in those cases, it would ordinarily force the patients into buying wherever they can get the drug.

Dr. CHAPMAN. That is correct, sir.

Chairman KEFAUVER. Buying from peddlers, buying as much as they have money to buy.

Dr. CHAPMAN. Or unscrupulous physicians, which occurs occasionally.

Chairman KEFAUVER. Yes.

Dr. CHAPMAN. Well, in brief, that is the framework in which persons who come to the attention of physicians are handled in Great Britain.

I say I was cautioned repeatedly by people, well experienced in this field, to please not misrepresent or let people in this country misrepresent their method, and dignify it as a system or method of treatment.   It is no more a method of treatment than method of treating pneumonia or anything else.   It is just part of their practice.

As a matter of fact, the average British physician does not see drug addicts. I talked with quite a number, and in all their practice they had never seen a drug addict.

Mr. MITLER. What is the scope of addiction? Is it about the same as Dr. Lindesmith presented?

Dr. CHAPMAN. Well, in a sense, yes. The known drug addicts——

Mr. MITLER. Yes.

Dr. CHAPMAN (continuing). Fall somewhere in the neighborhood of 400 in Great Britain. I don't know the exact figure. As a matter of fact, it varies up and down from time to time, and may or may not relate to the actual number of persons who are being handled by physicians.

A physician may in the course of his practice decide that he is perfectly justified to withdraw this patient over a long period of time. You and I would identify him as a drug addict, or you would say he was certainly addicted. This may not come to the attention of the Home Office unless he cannot get him off drugs or unless he runs into some difficulty, or the patient won't cooperate, or something like that, and they told me themselves, the people in the home office, that they have no idea of how many of these occur. They think there are few.

Mr. MITLER. Does that represent the highlights of the British program, or are there some things you would like to add?

Dr. CHAPMAN. I think there are perhaps 1 or 2 other things that might be clarified in this regard.

When they run into the problem of addiction, they have, as you know, the National Medical Service, and through that technique about 90 percent, I believe, of all prescriptions written in Great Britain come to the attention of a central pharmacist, and they are categorized in terms of the kind of drug that is prescribed.

They have a tickler system, if you will, which makes it possible to identify an excessive use of drugs in any given place or time by any given physician. The pharmacy service is in the National Health Service, and this information is then usually handed to the chief regional medical officer, who advises his regional medical officer—kind of local health officer, if you will—to go out and talk with the physician concerned, and see what's cooking.

More often than not, a simple explanation is that this person has severe arthritis, and he wants to treat him, and everybody is happy, and that is all there is to it. It is noted on the file—the medical file, mind you—that this person is receiving drugs under perfectly legitimate circumstances, and no more issue is made of it.

If, on the other hand, the regional director finds that, unknowingly or unwittingly, perhaps, this physician is confronted with a person who is an addict, he may caution him. These people are on the books from time to time, they have been in and out of jail, or something of that nature, or they may have been using other doctors to get drugs, and they may caution him as to what is happening.

Then again, every effort will be made to smooth the situation over. If they can't, and after considerable effort and trial the physician feels that his hands are tied and he can't move any further with this patient—he can't get him off, he won't cooperate, or something like that—then he is advised that the best next step would be to consult with another physician in this matter, and have an agreement that this is probably the best course of action; namely, that this person should, for medical reasons, be continued on drugs.

Under these circumstances—it is not required, but he usually does for his own protection, advise the Home Office, and gives them the name of the patient that he is treating, and the reasons for which he is treating him, and the dosage of narcotics. This protects everyone.

The pharmacist knows about it, so there can be close checks so if this patient tries to get it from another doctor, they can catch up with him.

These are the essences of the methods entailed.

Chairman KEFAUVER. Doctor, before you leave the subject of the English system, do you want to tell us what you think about it?

Dr. CHAPMAN. Well——

Chairman KEFAUVER. Whether you think it—of course, we operate under a different basis here.

Dr. CHAPMAN. May I, with your permission, read excerpts from a letter; the same sort of question was asked me by the Honorable Senator Meyer from Illinois when they were running a commission on narcotics, and he asked me recently what my recommendations were on that.

I said there are many facets of this method, if one can call it that, which at first glance appear to offer solutions to the current United States problem. For example, the regulations of the Home Office, under the Dangerous Drugs Act, provide—and those I have already told you about, which would seem to provide a means of reducing the amount of legal effort to obtain drugs by confirmed addicts.

However, there is no reason to assume that there is any parallel to be drawn between the problem in the United States and that in Great Britain, nor can we assume that the program which works for a few noncriminals in the United Kingdom could be applied successfully to the preponderantly socially and emotionally maladjusted group which seem to make up the bulk of the United States addicts.

It has been added that Great Britain does not have a problem as we do because of their system. There are no valid reasons, in my opinion, to reach this conclusion. However, there are certain tolerances allowed a physician in Great Britain in the above-outlined management of persons using drugs for medical reasons, which are of value.

In the first place, drug addiction is looked upon as a medical problem. In that light, the maintenance of addiction is not considered good medical practice. Nevertheless, it is possible for a physician for medical reasons, other than for acute chronic or terminal illnesses, to administer drugs to a patient for continuing periods of time, providing he consults and receives the concurrence of the proper medical authority.

I think that, about as succinctly as I can boil it down, is my considered view. I don't think you can translate what the experience is in Great Britain to the United States. I think there are some elements in their methods which warrant consideration if revisions are made.

But I would be the first one to say, "Let's not just pick this up and move it over here."

Chairman KEFAUVER. I think we understand you on that.

Mr. MITLER. Could you tell us briefly, just touch on it, about your visit to Egypt, what is the scope of and how do they approach the problem, and what is the scope of addiction in that country?

Dr. CHAPMAN. Well, the Egyptians have many problems, to say the least, even at' the time I was there, which was right after the Suez crisis.

Chairman KEFAUVER. You say right after the Suez crisis?

Dr. CHAPMAN. Yes.

Chairman KEFAUVER. That has been right recently.

Dr. CHAPMAN. Right after the first kickoff in August.

Chairman KEFAUVER. Oh, yes.

Dr. CHAPMAN. At that time, I would say in talking to the persons concerned with the general health of the nation, and Dr. Shoib, the Director of Health, International Health Relationships, he felt that drug addiction was the least of their health problems in Egypt, and I think that pretty well characterizes it.

Mr. MITLER. Did he say how many addicts there were?

Dr. CHAPMAN. The estimates of the enforcement personnel in Egypt give an estimate of somewhere between 400,000 and 500,000, hasheesh users.

Mr. MITLER. Could you tell us what hasheesh is?

Dr. CHAPMAN. H-a-s-h-i-s-h or h-a-s-h-e-e-s-h is a concentrated variety of a base drug known as cannabis, c-a-n-n-a-b-i-s, which is the element of marihuana.

This is the base ingredient, the base chemical compound which is present in a number of drugs, known in this country as marihuana, known as hasheesh, known as bangh, b-a-n-g-h, known as "ganjee"— I don't know how to spell that. There are a number of drugs which have this base which are used almost in areas entirely by smoking, one or the other methods of smoking, throughout the Near East, South America, Mexico, and in the United States.

I think probably the highest concentration is in the Near East and in southern Asia. This is smoked—since it is a concentrated variety, it is usually mixed with tobacco and smoked either in cigarettes or a water pipe, probably in a water pipe.

Mr. MITLER. What effect does it have; the same effect as heroin?

Dr. CHAPMAN. No. As a matter of fact, it is used by the majority of the people who use it, socially.

You invite a friend in and you offer him your water pipe with a little hasheesh in it to smoke, and it is passed around the room; everybody has a few whiffs, and it acts similarly to a cocktail, if you will.

It is a social custom almost, I am advised—I did not see this—by doctors who have worked out in the smaller communities out around Cairo and down in the delta region.

It is used socially, and it is also abused by numbers of Egyptians in much the same fashion that alcohol is abused in this country.

As they typified it, one of these fellows was an Arabian physician who had been in the United States—he says, "It is like your street-corner gangs almost, these kids, young fellows, hanging around smoking hasheesh. They are giggling, and laugh and carry on; but they don't get into crimes or rarely any fights."

Mr. MITLER. Young people use it?

Dr. CHAPMAN. Young people, old people, all varieties.

I was also advised that the marital counselors have been quite concerned about the smoking of hasheesh on the part of wives complaining that their husbands were inadequate husbands because they smoked hasheesh.

Mr. MITLER. What do they do about the enforcement of the laws?

Dr. CHAPMAN. Well there is a considerable problem because of the many coastal areas and the easy import—they have 250 people, I believe, in their narcotics enforcement group trying to cover all of the borders of Egypt, which are many and extensive, and they are constantly making arrests, trying to cut down on the introduction of the drug into the country.

I dare say there is none grown in Egypt, so far as I could determine. Almost all of it comes in through the borders.

They have so many severe problems of mental health, public health generally, that there has been no attempt at all made to have any treatment centers.

They have taken a few patients who could afford it into their large psychiatric hospital for treatment, but these are relatively few in number.

Mr. MITLER. With respect to Iran, could you just very briefly tell us about that?

Dr. CHAPMAN. Yes.

As was mentioned yesterday, the present Shah became very much interested in the problem of opium smoking. It has been estimated prior to last November a year ago that there were better than a million or a million and a half opium smokers in Iran. This is not unusual for the Near East.

The Minister of Health, who was an American-trained physician, Dr. Saleh, has for all of his life been very much interested in this problem for his people, and as soon as he had a chance, succeeded in getting passed an opium-control bill which prohibits the growth, development, import, or use of opium in Iran.

Concurrent with that, feeling that this was a strong medical problem he set up in the 10 Provinces treatment centers.

Now, according to American standards, I am certain these would not meet our American standards of treatment centers, but according to the general medical treatment in Iran, these are nicely developed and nicely run places.

Opium addicts can come there for withdrawal of their opium habit. They stay around for from 15 to 30 days, and then are sent back to their communities.

There is no way of knowing how successful this program is. It is largely a matter of doing something about this big problem right now, first, and after that "We will count noses and see how many people we have successfully cured."

It is the general feeling and the consensus of those foreigners who have visited there and studied, and have been around the country, that this program apparently is quite successful.

There are quite a few casual users who have gotten to smoking opium for a million reasons, none very serious, and you say, "Don't smoke opium," and they will quit, or you take them off opium and they will quit. It is no real problem.

They are not solving problems with opium.

There are a number of confirmed opium smokers about whom they have the same concern as to ultimately curing as we do confirmed addicts in the United States, but they are small in number, roughly speaking.

Mr. MITLER. Does that give the highlights of the situation in Iran?

Dr. CHAPMAN. I think so; yes.

Mr. MITLER. I wanted to turn to the one hospital in the whole world that is exclusively devoted to the treatment of drug addicts under 21, and that, of course, is the Riverside Hospital in New York.

Dr. CHAPMAN. Yes.

Mr. MITLER. You made a study on behalf of the United States Public Health Service. Maybe I made a mistake in that, but you did make a study for your governmental agency of that hospital?

Dr. CHAPMAN. Yes. Commissioner Basil MacLean, commissioner of hospitals for the city of New York, asked the Public Health Service for a survey in February 1955.

The survey was completed and given back to him about the following year.

Mr. MITLER. Could you tell us, sort highlight it, how that hospital operates and what it is doing for youngsters under 21 who are drug addicts?

Dr. CHAPMAN. Well, I think probably by now you have a fairly good picture of the circumstances in the establishment of the hospital.

There was a large problem in New York City. The authorities were forced to do something about juvenile addicts. There were insufficient facilities, and this hospital, in combination with a public-health law, was established for a kind of involuntary treatment of drug addicts. I use that word advisably. It is bandied about here and there and yon.

It is a public-health type of commitment, within itself having no particular legal teeth, relying on the legal teeth in the violation of going before other groups.

A person under 21, which Inspector Terranova mentioned yesterday, is sent to the hospital on North Brothers Island which, interestingly enough, historically was used in 1919 and 1920 to treat a great number of heroin addicts when they had a considerable upsurge of drug addiction in New York. It has been varyingly used for a number of purposes.

The hospital has facilities for about 120 men and 30 women. It is expandable up and down; it has a considerable staff of psychiatrists, social workers, nurses, attendants, and so forth.

I think the ratio of personnel to patients is something like 2 to 1, more personnel than patients.

Patients are withdrawn according to standard techniques; are given a very careful psychiatric examination, social service evaluation and what-not, a thorough going study of their assets and liabilities of personality being made, and they are placed in a treatment program which may go for a month to as many months as indicated.

The average stay is in the neighborhood of, I think, from around 2 to 3 months; that is the average stay. There are many patients who have been there for as long as 6 months.

The program is so geared, I think profitably, that this overall commitment is delegated to the medical officer in charge of the hospital, Dr. Gamso, and he can exercise it as he sees fit.

In other words, if he feels at any time in the patient's treatment there ought to be a "college try" in the community, so to speak, the patient is given a chance to go out and make an attempt at it.

If he fails or there is evidence of failure, he goes back to the hospital without going through any other procedures.

He stays under the aegis of the hospital until he is discharged or until there is no need of treatment, or until the end of this 3-month period of treatment is up.

For this reason any one casually examining the admissions and discharges from the hospital itself might be disturbed and say, "They all come back." Not by any manner of means. Many of them have repeated admissions for a number of reasons: difficulties at home—not because there is a need for drugs, but there might be a need for the support that is given by the hospital. This happens many times.

The group in the community which looks after the patient when he is outside of the hospital program is located at Metropolitan Hospital, the clinic there operating 5 days a week, and is staffed by social worker, nurse, and with a regular attendance of psychiatrists and other social workers who come in for casework on patients.

Mr. MITLER. That is sort of a followthrough program?

Dr. CHAPMAN. It is a followthrough program.

Mr. MITLER. Definitely.

Dr. CHAPMAN. It is an aftercare program, and it is definitely tried. The staff of the clinic is under the staff of the hospital.

Mr. MITLER. It is the only one in existence, as a matter of fact, in the United States?

Dr. CHAPMAN. That is right.

During the aftercare program, efforts are made to establish contact in the community.

I might say, and this is one of the greatest problems they have, that the problem is getting community agencies to assist them in the followup and aftercare of these patients. It is pretty difficult for one little place up on 86th Street to cover the whole of Manhattan, Brooklyn, and all of that section all by themselves, with that small staff, so they all have to rely on local agencies; and, in truth, the local agencies have not supplied the kind of assistance which should be necessary for a great many of these patients.

Chairman KEFAUVER. What kind of assistance do you mean, job counseling?

Dr. CHAPMAN. Job counseling, social work, family assistance, improving the home situations, the normal things that social agencies usually are expected to deal with.

Chairman KEFAUVER. Why don't the social agencies cooperate? They just do not like to fool with addicts; is that it?

Dr. CHAPMAN. Sir, I do not know. I think that is probably part of it. Certainly the caseload of almost all the social agencies is up to the waiting list standpoint, and this is one more case of the kind that they are not too happy to deal with, and it is easy to push them down to the bottom of the list.

Chairman KEFAUVER. And probably not too experienced to deal with?

Dr. CHAPMAN. That is true, too.

It calls for a great deal of patience and understanding to deal with this kind of an individual who is miscast in many ways for the problems that he has.

In the face of insurmountable, almost insurmountable, difficulties, I think it is surprising the favorable way in which they have been able to keep, maintain contact, and deal successfully, apparently successfully, with a number of patients.

Now, at the present point in time I cannot tell you how many they have dealt with successfully.

They made a study of some 200, and they felt that about 50 percent of those that they were able to contact, and about 19 percent of the 200 at the interval, I think, of a 3-year period, so far as they could determine, I think, were off drugs, so far as they could determine. Sometimes they could not be sure.

So I think——

Chairman KEFAUVER. In fairness, let us get this correctly. They only contacted about 50 percent?

Dr. CHAPMAN. They were only able to find 50 percent.

Chairman KEFAUVER. And of the 50 percent they found about 19 percent of the total were off drugs?

Dr. CHAPMAN. No, sir; 19 percent of the 200.

Chairman KEFAUVER. Of the 200?

Dr. CHAPMAN. Yes.

Chairman KEFAUVER. All right.

Mr. MITLER. Now, that is not a maximum security institution at all, is it?

Dr. CHAPMAN. No, sir, and it was not meant to be.

I think one should, in studying Riverside, look into all of the ramifications of the circumstances of establishing the hospital.

It is stated specifically in the original discussions of proposing the setup, this should not be a matter of a maximum security institution, and should not have a penal atmosphere. It should not be like Lexington.

These points are specifically made. The patients should not feel that they are under the kind of penal coercion for this reason: One has to then expect to have a number of things happen in such a place which would not happen in an institution which was more tightly controlled from a security standpoint.

Mr. MITLER. There were some mistakes at first, and there were a lot of attacks on Riverside.

Dr. CHAPMAN. They were starting from zero.

Mr. MITLER. They started from the beginning, but they are developing.

Dr. CHAPMAN. That is right.

Chairman KEFAUVER. Who pays the cost of this operation?

Dr. CHAPMAN. Almost all of it is borne by the city of New York. At the time of my survey—I can give you a breakdown.

Chairman KEFAUVER. Partly by contribution by the city and partly by charitable contributions?

Dr. CHAPMAN. No, sir; by the State; the State Health Department in its division of chronic diseases, I think it is.

Chairman KEFAUVER. That is all right; by the city and by the State.

Dr. CHAPMAN. Yes.

Chairman KEFAUVER. Let us get on with the rest of your testimony.

Mr. MITLER. All right.

Now, could you just briefly summarize what your recommendations are with respect to developing a good program in the United States for the treatment of drug addiction? That is a big question, but could you hit the highlights of your recommendations?

Chairman KEFAUVER. Before you do that, I would like to get clear——

Dr. CHAPMAN. Yes, sir.

Chairman KEFAUVER. Just what do you do for patients leaving Lexington and Fort Worth? It has been testified here that you give them a railroad ticket back home and $3.

Dr. CHAPMAN. Well, it would vary, depending upon whether or not he was a discharged prisoner. If he is a discharged prisoner, I forgot what the going rate is, I think it is somewhere around $25 he is given, and a suit of clothes and his ticket back home.

Voluntary patients, if they stay for the complete period of treatment of 4½ months, are given a railroad ticket back home, and the funds for subsistence while on the train—I think it is around $3—and if he is in need of suitable clothes to go out and be in society, he is given those clothes, not usually new, usually used clothes. He gets nothing else, and by law he cannot.

Now, the patient who leaves against advice gets nothing, not even a railroad ticket.

Chairman KEFAUVER. He just leaves and he is on his own?

Dr. CHAPMAN. He just leaves; he is on his own.

Chairman KEFAUVER. In addition to that is there any effort to have anybody meet him or try to locate a job for the person or are they in contact with the State or social agency to alert them or get their cooperation?

Dr. CHAPMAN. Only in the case——

Chairman KEFAUVER. With this dischargee?

Dr. CHAPMAN. Only in the case of prison patients, Federal Prison patients, is there any concerted constant program in that regard. This is required.

The average—almost all of the voluntary patients leaving the hospital with the advice of the medical staff, those we don't—I did when I was there, I do not think they do now—concern themselves with what happens to them. But for those who stay for the full period of recommended treatment, efforts are made, and I do not know in what percentage of the cases, a very small percentage of the cases, to provide contacts for them in the community, give them the names of the vocational rehabilitation personnel or some social agency that may give them some advice or assistance of that nature.

Occasionally, and this is almost rare, letters are actually written to the respective agencies advising of the arrival of such an individual.

I do not think it is ever—this would really be rare—happen that an individual is being planned to be met at the train and escorted through the throes of getting adjusted back to his community, except by his family.

Chairman KEFAUVER. Please refer to Mr. Mitler's previous question, and go ahead; that is, what do you recommend for a treatment follow-through program that would be most beneficial to the unfortunate addicts.

Dr. CHAPMAN. In the broad, in the main, I feel that the circumstances, if I may use that, the circumstances of the operation of this program are the first and most important considerations before we get down to the details, because this affects the actual details.

By circumstances, I mean, the legal circumstances of this general program, and I feel for the bulk, for the great bulk, as I said in my letter, of addicts as we know them in the United States today and as we see them and as they pose problems to us and to themselves, there is a need for a kind of involuntary commitment procedure to insure that they receive adequate medical care over a long period of time.

Now, I am not specifying the length of time because in the cases of the kind of civil commitment that I have in mind, time is not specified. It is left to the judgment of the medical personnel operating that program.

Now, I could go on at length giving you ifs, ands, and buts of such a commitment program.

I can give you the highlights of what it should contain. It should contain provisions whereby it would be possible to provide a graded or graduated series of steps in security of the patient in treatment. The maximum of those steps of security would be hospital commitment; the next, perhaps, would be one which was suggested by one of the people here either yesterday or today, the halfway house—I think Dr. Schultz mentioned this place where they could go as an intermediate point where they could work from, so to speak, and they would be there 12 hours a day, 16 hours a day, and the other 8 they would be out working somewhere; or, there might be circumstances in which you might wish to provide this general program of treatment out of an outpatient service clinic or something like that or even a doctor's office.

But there ought to be a provision for a graduation of kinds of treatment determined oceording to the individual needs of the patient.

Now, in the United States I feel under the presentday situation most of the addicts would require at least for some part of their program the maximum kind of security in their treatment such as could be supplied at Lexington or any hospital of a similar nature, or at Riverside, a place where they can be kept free from drugs and can be withdrawn and given adequate medical care and treatment.

Then I feel they should be followed within the framework of this commitment procedure the same as you would follow a mental patient who is discharged from a psychiatric, any psychiatric, hospital, into the community where he is paroled, if you will, by the director of the hospital to the community, to the aegis of an agency or an individual such as a mental health clinic or something of that nature, with the understanding that he be under their specific control, and receive the kind of treatment and guidance that is needed.

He would be sent to vocational rehabilitation; he would be sent to a job program; he would be given family advice and guidance, and so forth, all of the things we now provide in our best organized communities for the care and treatment of our mentally ill discharged patients.

If at any time it became apparent to the local supervisory person that he was in immediate need of further treatment, he could be returned to the next higher step or to the institutions for further treatment.

This might be in the case of anticipated failure, it might be in the actual case of failure in treatment. Hopefully, it would be before failure occurred.

To revert back to Riverside, they are gaining experience and, perhaps, almost predicting "Next week this guy is going to fall off the wagon," and at that point to suddenly say, "This is the end; you need to go back for more closely supervised treatment."

This should be over a period of years, again to be determined by the medical staff involved.

I think in broad and in general that would provide the best answers we know at this time for dealing with this kind of drug addict in the main that we are dealing with in the present day.

Mr. MITLER. You have here your report on Riverside?

Dr. CHAPMAN. Yes. Would you like to have a copy of that for the record?

Mr. MITLER. Yes.

Chairman KEFAUVER. We will just make this an exhibit without being printed in the record.

(The document referred to was received as exhibit 12, and is on file with the subcommittee.)

Mr. MITLER. You have touched the highlights of the program, Dr. Chapman?

Dr. CHAPMAN. Yes; I think in the main I have.

Mr. MITLER. I have no further questions.

Chairman KEFAUVER. Dr. Chapman, the Public Health Service in the various States, of course, contributed to by the Federal Government, could they not be used substantially in connection with this followthrough treatment?

Dr. CHAPMAN. Yes; they could, Senator, if—and the "if" is a mechanism, and the machinery would do it. It may be of interest to you to know that we are in the process of, at the current moment, laying the groundwork for the kind of a followup demonstration community program, demonstration followup community program, which we feel should be developed all around the country, in New York City.

We have a very small staff, and, incidentally, I want to emphasize that point—this is one of the keynotes, just as Dr. Lowry emphasized yesterday, in thinking of any program, and that is getting the personnel to operate it.

We are starting with a very small staff in New York City right after the first of the year in working through the problems connected with the operation of such a followup aftercare program.

They are many. We are very reluctant and very hesitant to plunge into a program just because it is good. We want to work solidly; we want to build solidly, so that we can go back 1 year or 5 years from now, and when you ask, "What are the results?" we can give them to you unequivocally without saying, "We ran through a hundred thousand, and we don't know what happened," which is the kind of thing that happens too many times, and for that reason we want to build it solidly. We want to have a good records system; we want to have good contacts in the community; we want to have adequate built-in controls so that we can run research out of this and find out what we have been doing, and change the methods and techniques of treatment so that we can really make it a good sound demonstration.

This takes time and people to get the right kind of people to operate it. We do not lack in money; we lack in people, and I think that we can enlist and recruit people, and gardually as we build and develop something which we can put before the country and say, "This is the kind of program which should be used," within the modifications, of course, of what the local community needs.

Now, mind you, and this is going to be just about a half of what I would like to see ultimately, because as yet we do not have these laws, the legal circumstances of treatment which would make it possible for a more adequate followup.

We have no commitment procedures that authorize us to involuntarily, as far as the patient is concerned, follow him and see what happens to him, whether he moves from 42d Street to 33d Street. We have no way of doing that.

We have to depend upon his cooperation to do this, and until such a time as we do have techniques of legal controls over these individuals, by whatever method, we are going to be faced with the continuing problem of operating so that we can get their assistance.

I might say that, of course, with the Federal probationers we will have no difficulty during the length of time of their Federal probation. But again, it is a sentence. The average Federal prisoner gets out and has a third of his sentence, which gives 1, 2, 3 years, perhaps; no more.

We work very closely with the probation officers in this regard, but for the voluntary patients it is going to be just that question, Is he going to cooperate with us?

I might say in passing we have been sort of counting noses on Lexington discharges in New York City for the past 3 or 4 years, and have been surprise at the cooperation we have gotten from the patients in letting them be counted.

We have been able to contact, I think, some 90 percent of the patients, at least one time, since their discharge which, much to our surprise, we thought they would disappear.

Mr. MITLER. Just one question: To wrap three questions up in one, I have asked you before about why couldn't they have a facility on the west coast, and why couldn't they segregate 17- and 18-year-olds from the prisoners; why couldn't they segregate the volunteers from the prisoners; that all comes back, then, to the question of staff?

Dr. CHAPMAN. No; not entirely, Mr. Mitler. The west coast—well, even if I had people I would hesitate moving into a program on the west coast until we have gone through the mill, the same kind of problems they went through in Riverside; we are going to have to go through that in a different way with this, even if I had the people, which I haven't.

This other question, the matter of mixing volunteers and juveniles with so-called hardened criminals, you remember Dr. Lowry's figures yesterday——

Mr. MITLER. They were small.

Dr. CHAPMAN. The number of people who make up 25 percent of the admissions are only 3 percent of the people that have ever been in the hospital. So at any one time there are not many of these recidivistic hardened criminals at the hospital. As a matter of fact, 50 percent of the admissions have been—I do not know what it is today—

a year ago 50 percent of the admissions were new admissions that had never been at the hospital before, so we are dealing with a relatively small number of people.

Actually, on the point of fact there is a considerable degree of segregation according to the individual needs of the patients at that hospital.

Generally speaking, those who are maximum security patients are kept in an inner center where you can identify them and keep them very closely.

The more peripheral parts of the hospital are reserved for the minimum security patients, and again we try to group them according to interests and needs and desires.

In other words, in one section you will find a lot of doctors or professionally trained people or people with common interests living together. We try to do that, much the same as you do in any community.

Mr. MITLER. I think that answers the question I had in mind. I have no further questions, Mr. Chairman.

Chairman KEFAUVER. Dr. Chapman, we are very grateful to you, and we are interested in your program. We hope that you will make recommendations to the Congress as to how we can assist you, both in the way of legislation and appropriations for carrying out your program.

Thank you very much.

Dr. CHAPMAN. It so happens that that windfall we got last summer on our Mental Health Act is going to give us a long leg over the fence on that. Thank you, sir.

Mr. MITLER. Thank you, Doctor.

Chairman KEFAUVER. I have a statement prepared which will be treated as though read at the conclusion of the hearings.

(The statement referred to is as follows:)

CLOSING STATEMENT OF HON. ESTES KEFAUVER

This concludes our 2-day hearing. We have had an open and healthy discussion concerning drug addiction, with special emphasis on the problems involving those under 21 years of age. It is useful to learn how this problem is approached in other countries. Of course, methods that may have been successful in European countries, in a different culture, may not be practical in the United States. Nonetheless, certainly there are several things of value we can learn from the experiences of other countries. It is hopeful to note that the sharp increase in drug addiction of those under 21, which came to a climax in 1951 and 1952, has not continued.

However, in the major cities there still exists a serious problem of drug addiction in that age group. It is apparent, however, from these 2 days of testimony, that many of our larger cities lack any affirmative program to effectively treat and cure drug addiction among young people. The subcommittee was glad to head about the development of a hopeful program in New York City in the creation of the Riverside Hospital, which is devoted to the treatment of young addicts under the age of 21. Not only is the program there focused on helping younger people, but an effort is made at this hospital to develop an aftercare-treatment program. Testimony has clearly established that such a followthrough and aftercare clinic is the key to a successful treatment program for drug addiction. We are doing only half the job in our existing treatment facilities when we fail to provide guidance and supervision for the patient in his home community after he has left the hospital.

We find that none of the States have an adequate followup program. The recently enacted D. C. program has only been in operation for 3½ months. It is a healthy start of a good program, but experience with this new law already shows needs for modernization, particularly to provide for medical followup after release.

A followup program for those released form the hospitals at Lexington and Fort Worth is badly needed. Such a program should consist of continued medical and psychiatric care, economic counseling, and general assistance.

It is wasteful, both from a human and economic point of view, to spend substantial sums of money for narcotic hospitals without providing for a follow-through clinic in the larger cities of the United States.

It is good to note that some recent studies established that a great many addicts cannot only be removed from the use of drugs for a long period of time, but in many cases can be permanently cured. Knowing this, communities across the country which at present have made no effort to develop a treatment program should consider the development of facilities to help drug addicts by providing not only for withdrawal of the patient from drugs, but attacking the root of the problem, which clearly is a social-psychological one.

A valuable suggestion has been made in the testimony concerning development of a "halfway house" program, by which patients leaving the treatment centers do not return immediately to their former environment, but spend a period of time living with nonaddicts in a wholesome surrounding while engaging in active employment. Sending the addict from the treatment center right back into his former environment only serves to insure his relapse into the habit within a short period of time.

As a result of these hearings, the subcommittee will explore the available means of developing an effective aftercare-treatment program from the existing treatment centers. Other measures to improve and expand existing treatment centers are also under consideration.

The subcommittee wishes to thank the police departments of New York, Chicago, Los Angeles, San Francisco, Des Moines, Dallas, Fort Worth, and the Metropolitan Police Department of the District of Columbia, and many other departments, for their assistance to the subcommittee in its study of the narcotics problem. We have received help from the authorities at the Riverside Hospital in New York. I also want to thank Dr. John Cronin, Chief, Bureau of Medical Services, United States Public Health Service, and Dr. James Shannon, Director, National Institutes of Health, and members of their staffs, for their valuable assistance.

We would also like to express our appreciation to District Attorney Victor Blanc of Philadelphia, Inspector of Detectives John F. Driscoll of the Philadelphia Police Department, and Lt. Glasgow Driscoll of the narcotics squad for their fine cooperation.

A good portion of the study was made in California and we wish to thank Sheriff Eugene Biscaluiz of Los Angeles County; the director of the department of corrections for the State of California, Richard McGee; Chief William H. Parker; Attorney General E. G. Brown, and the many others who were so helpful to the subcommittee.

Chairman KEFAUVER. We will stand in recess until further call of the subcommittee.

(Whereupon, at 4:15 p. m·, the subcommittee adjourned, subject to call.)

[From the Journal of Psychiatric Social Work, January 1954]

SOME NOTES ON DYNAMICS AND TREATMENT IN NARCOTIC ADDICTION

By Leon Brill, psychiatric social worker engaged in a followup study of narcotic addicts who have had instituitonal care and treatment

What is there about narcotic addiction that has made each community so hesitant about confronting the problems of its addict group and shaping services to meet their special needs?

Does the answer lie in the general public's inability to identify with this group because of judgmental attitudes inherent in the belief that all addicts are criminals? In the average individual's difficulty in comprehending how another person can voluntarily surrender control over his behavior and slavishly submit to a tyrannical and insatiable influence? In sheer lack of understanding as to what is actually involved in addiction, coupled with a good deal of hopelessness as evidenced in the saying "once an addict always an addict"? Or in the preoccupation of informed professional groups with other problems of greater statistical importance? Full answers to these questions would seem to require the sum of all that is known about addiction plus intensive studies of individual and group attitudes in representative communities. The series of case discussions that follow are presented for the informational value they may have for professional groups concerned with the planning of therapeutic or educational programs or actively engaged in such services.

We shall proceed inductively, using the findings from selected cases as a basis for some generalization as to (1) dynamics and recurring motifs in addiction, (2) varying reactions to hospitalization and treatment, and (3) problems confronting dischargees from hospitals and the need for followup services. These cases are representative of more than 200 other individuals seen regularly in a followup service in the past year and a half, for whom our findings would be equally valid. The patients' histories are presented in summary form, with focus first on individual, familial, and community factors.

SOME BASIC PATTERNS AND RECURRING MOTIFS IN ADDICTION

Mr. A., a 29-year-old "restless, shy man, in need of emotional support, emotionally labile and vacillating from depression to euphoria," was committed to an institution with a sentence of a year and a day, and with 2 years' subsequent probation for selling heroin. Mr. A. had always felt himself unloved and rejected by his parents. He considered his father, an alcoholic and occasionally suicidal, a "creep" and deplored his mother's abandonment of the household after Mr. A. became addicted. He had served as a parachutist during the war and considered his Army period the happiest he had experienced, though there, as everywhere, he felt "watched." His work record following his Army discharge was exceedingly spotty; he was unable to remain long on any job since he soon felt criticized and watched. His reaction to pressure was to escape through denial of problems and by flight into new activity. His flights into marriage had been unsuccessful; the first two unions were annulled after brief periods and he was now separated from his third wife. These relationships testified to emotional and psychosexual difficulties. The hospital examinations had revealed a great deal of hostility to women and dependency on them; a strong mistrust of people, who he feared were trying to dominate him; feelings of inferiority and unworthiness of love; narcissism; inadequacy as a man; and a desire to achieve distinction through the use of drugs.

Mr. B., an appealing, intelligent Negro boy in his early twenties, whose parents originally came from the British West Indies and whose home reflected cultural strivings rather higher than the average, had been brought up as the only child in a home where the parents separated when he was only 2. The father assumed no further responsibility for him and was, in fact, not seen again until Mr. B. met him on his way overseas. The child was brought up by his mother and his grandmother, a wealthy and dominating woman, living with each one for several years at a time. During the depression, the mother had rough sledding, subsisting on home relief and working as a domestic. The mother and grandmother fought each other bitterly, using the boy as a weapon in their struggles; though he was dependent on them, he learned to fear dependency since a heavy price had been exacted for it.[1]

Mr. B. suffered from severe feelings of inadequacy, which were evidenced to some extent in the area of education; there was invidious self-comparison with his wealthier cousins in the West Indies who had completed high school or college. He had attended a vocational high school, but left after he was caught up in gang life; he was discovered to be carrying a gun because he felt physically threatened and was then sent to his relatives, whom he envied for their superior status and attainments. On returning to the States, he joined the Army, which set off an unfortunate chain of events. Since he was under age, he was permitted to enlist on condition that he not claim dependency. When his mother violated this stipulation, he was discharged "without honor." Though the Red Cross later rectified this, Mr. B. was extremely upset and felt his involvements had represented a strong factor in his initial addiction.

Earlier danger signals had pointed to internal stress. At puberty, Mr. B. was hospitalized for "pains in the stomach"; observation yielded negative physical findings though pointing to psychological causes. His subsequent vocational history was very poor, revealing only sporadic jobs at unskilled occupations. Later, pressure from his gang started him on the road to addiction. He could

---

[1] The origins of this matriarchal setup in the southern slave system and in current minority problems have been carefully elaborated in such works as St. Clair Drake and Horace R. Cayton, Black Metropolis (New York: Harcourt, Brace, 1945), and Gunnar Myrdal, An American Dilemma (New York: Harper Bros., 1944).

not withstand their hectoring for refusing to use drugs and yielded after being called a square, without fully comprehending the effects of drugs. Once "hooked," he lost his "values as well as my material possessions" and was compelled increasingly to associate with individuals whose goals and values he consciously rejected. His anxiety mounted as he narrowly escaped being shot when detected stealing to support his habit; he saw 1 friend killed and 2 others sentenced to jail before he was himself hospitalized.

Whatever earlier feelings of rejection existed were heavily reinforced upon his discharge from the hospital. Mr. B.'s mother refused to admit him into the house, probably fearing a repetition of his earlier behavior but also because a "boy friend" had displaced him. The grandmother was similarly unbending though finally permitting him to occupy a small room in one of her buildings. The mother had perhaps unconsciously been sexually seductive to her son in the past, since they had shared a bed due to overcrowding. Mr. B. spent his first night home pleading to be allowed to sleep there though meeting with a firm refusal. Small wonder that he took a shot the following morning to regain some of the warmth he had missed in his mother and grandmother. In later contacts, there were increasing evidence of self-destructive impulses which in time culminated in his death under circumstances pointing to suicide.

Mr. C. is a heavy-set, mistrustful, hostile, somewhat snobbish boy who verbalized well and intellectualized a good deal. He grew up in a very comfortable home where he was materially indulged in an atmosphere of lax discipline.

The father, a fairly passive, compliant individual, had always tended to shift responsibility for disciplining the son to the mother, a carefully groomed, intelligent woman, proud of her self-control and independence though evidencing much anxiety and insecurity in relation to the son. She appeared to have unconscious destructive impulses toward him, which emerged more clearly as death wishes at the height of his addiction. She feared her own hostility to him and found it difficult to act forcefully at any time to restrain him, possibly because of her own guilt feelings. The son was aware of these feelings and used them as a weapon against her. He believed that though his parents have been overtly kind in giving him material things, they rejected him on another level and tended to "destroy" him by inculcating severe feelings of inferiority. The mother had often emphasized that her relationship with her husband was "everything," while the children were secondary. In drugs, Mr. C. had therefore discovered a potent aggressive tool with which to hurt himself and his parents in the worst possible ways. At the same time, while professing a desire to be independent of his parents, his addiction tied him in ever closer dependency to them. Overtly, the drugs served to hold his aggressive feelings in check.

Mrs. C., while rejecting her son, yet wished to feel needed by him. It later emerged that she was sexually attracted to her son, describing him as a "beautiful hunk of man." The son, in turn, confessed that he was sexually attracted to his mother and could not remain alone in the home with her. These feelings were carried over into his relationships with girls; in Freudian terms, he had not resolved his incestuous, oedipal feelings toward the mother, possibly also toward his sister.

In discussing the beginnings of his addiction, Mr. C. felt that his family's removal to a better neighborhood when he was younger represented the "worst thing," since he began to associate with a fast crowd and spent freely. Until then, before the parents succeeded in establishing themselves, the family had lived in a poor, working-class district. In high school, Mr. C. was frequently suspended for truancy and mischievousness and finally quit school just 2 months before graduation. He later described himself as "quite mixed up" at this time: he wished to get married, tried to join the Air Force, worked at odd jobs as a drummer. The parents then initiated psychiatric treatment, which he refused to continue. He felt that his problems then were the same as now—drug addiction merely representing an additional symptom or defense. Mrs. C. at one point described him as "afraid to face the world because he doesn't feel accepted."

Mr. D., a 39-year-old Jewish patient, claimed that he had been deserted by his parents shortly after birth, hospitalized, and then sent to a State school where he remained until he was 14. According to an uncle, Mr. D.'s mother had died early and the father, an improvident person, institutionalized the children separately so that they later felt isolated from each other. As an adult, Mr. D. suffered from asthma, to which he attributed his addiction, and from ulcers. All his illness was felt as a punishment. He later lived with his widowed sister-in-law, to whom he related as to a mother person, deploring her lack of narcissistic attention to him.

There were evidences of masochistic satisfaction in his stockpiling of difficulties in interviews, and of an extremely pervasive dependency from infancy, and there was little hope that anything could be changed. There was also evidence of a passibe-aggressive reaction and an attempt to control and manipulate people and his environment through dependency and helplessness. Further, there were persecutory (paranoid) feelings; self-defeating elements; and possibly destructive impulses toward his sister-in-law; an expectation of ridicule and hurt, with resulting depression; and occasional suicidal thoughts.

Mr. E., an effeminate-looking Negro in his early twenties, intelligent and personable, had worked as a male nurse before his hospitalization. The hospital listed one adverse behavior report, since Mr. E. had "performed the female part in the homosexual act." His aunt and uncle were greatly upset when they noticed his plucked eyebrows and set hair following his discharge—"he looked like a woman." Mr. E. managed to find employment in a hotel for transient men, presumably to effect better contacts. There were evidences of emotional disturbance in his mistaking of people's remarks (paranoid trends) to which he reacted by becoming depressed, in his use of drugs to get the "world at my feet" (inferiority feelings), and in his frequently psychopathic behavior.

Mr. F., a 40-year-old Puerto Rican engineer, was shy, subject to mood changes, and unable to verbalize his hostility. His mother described him as "always too quiet," though "a good boy" who had assumed responsibility for her support. A sister and brother had been hospitalized at mental institutions. More than 5 years before, Mr. E. had suffered a "nervous breakdown," been treated by a medical doctor, and had received shock treatments from a psychiatrist. After this treatment, he resorted to drugs but later regretted not having waited to learn whether the treatment had been helpful.

During hospitalization, Mr. F. hinted that his illness was of sexual origin, and later he experienced a period of excitement described by the psychiatrist as "homosexual panic." In discussing his experiences subsequently, Mr. F. expressed delusional and paranoid ideas about the doctors and felt they were in communication with his employer. During his interviews with a hospital social worker, he admitted that he felt unloved and had no one to love. It was the psychiatrist's opinion that Mr. F.'s "schizophrenia had been kept in a state of remission by drugs during the past 5 years." On returning home, he was disoriented, delusional, suffered from persecutory ideas and sudden mood changes. His former doctor suggested that he apply to a local mental hospital for treatment.

There is increasing evidence from these and other studies that the addict group includes diverse individuals from every segment of the population, with varying strengths and weaknesses, goals and strivings, so that it is unreal to speak of an "addict type," although the incidence of addiction seems higher in certain minority groups where broken homes, deteriorated slum environment, and racial discrimination interlock with psychological factors. Common to all patients in this series is some form of emotional disturbance, usually intense, prolonged, and complex. The specific meanings which the use of drugs has for different users are therefore as varied as the disturbing conflicts and emotional needs which serve as motivating forces.

While the casual nexus between emotional difficulties and addiction is not always clear, some basic patterns seem to recur, such as feelings of rejection with disturbances in the maternal relationship; dependency strivings and fear of dependency; low frustration tolerance and escapism; confusion of identity and role; poor orientations to people and situations; conflicts around hostile feelings and psychosexual disturbance; and feelings of inadequacy and insecurity.

1. The significance of rejection and disturbances in the maternal relationships

The findings in our own studies point to severe disturbances in the maternal relationship, ranging from open rejection to unconscious use of the child by the mother to satisfy her own impulsive needs. Ernst Simmel has elucidated the primary role played by maternal rejection in alcoholic and other addiction. For Simmel, the mother becomes the vital factor in addiction, "since she, for whom the addict longs, offers him no security whatever. All addicts hate their mothers: They want to love them, but the mothers do not permit this. * * * The addict [therefore] has an unconscious wish to destroy the mother on whom he depends and the need to hate where he wants to love." [2]

---

[2] Ernst Simmel, Alcoholism and Addiction, in Yearbook of Psychoanalysis (New York: International Universities Press, 1949), V, 250–251.

Since rejection in some form or other has been noted to underlie all emotional illness, further clarification is needed as to why it should lead to addiction in certain cases. One suggested answer implies that addicts lack the capacity or "inner strength" to build the ordinary ego defenses with which to confront their own conflicts and life's discomforts and therefore need to lean on devices like drugs. As we shall see later, these conflicts frequently involve extremely powerful aggressive or incestuous feelings which threaten to overwhelm the individual so that he calls in additional defenses, such as drugs. The original rejection may also frequently be stockpiled since it not only includes the rejection by the mother or mother figure, but also rejection implicit in a broken home, in being a member of a minority group, and in suffering the deprivations of life in a slum environment under marginal economic circumstances. The net result of such compounded deprivation may be an extreme disturbance in the child's self-concepts with ensuing confusion as to his actual identity and role (who am I? Am I male or female? Where do I belong?) and in his ability to engage in meaningful interpersonal relationships. We may then observe a rather hazy and tenuous adaptation to the world of people and things and the development of faulty methods of interpreting and relating the self to reality.

In their recent article on drug addiction and adolescence, Dr. Zimmering and his collaborators at Bellevue Hospital describe patterns of behavior which are in general accord with this view. At one point, however, they state that "there was always a history of a sustained relationship with the mother-figure,"[3] and, "they [addicts] show a particularly strong mother attachment."[4] It is our own belief, from the 200 cases studied, that this attachment, while frequently very strong, represents pathological or unmet needs rather than a truly loving relationship. While addicts are frequently the mother's favorite, they are "favorite" only in the sense of being selected by the parent for this symbiotic relationship. In numerous instances we have noted rather invidious comparison with other siblings as well. As Zimmering et al. point out later, "this [mother attachment] also seems to create a great deal of conflict and anxiety * * * the mother figure is also viewed with fear and frustration."[5] Our series of patients differed in one regard from the Bellevue series: ours included many, whereas the Bellevue group had none, with a history of institutionalization, foster home placements, and shifting mother figures.

2. Difficulties in relating to people

Most addicts have some difficulty in relating to people; many form only very shallow relationships. They do find some support through their gang associations; and even at the height of their addiction they relate themselves to other users. In interviews they are "more than passing" agreeable, frequently making a very good initial impression because of their pleasant demeanor, soft-spoken manner, and freedom from overt hostility. But they seem incapable of maintaining a sustained relationship over a period of time, as numerous therapists and social agencies have discovered to their sorrow.[6]

Fenichel has described addicts as persons ready to give up all "object-libidinal relationships" because they never valued them very highly:

"They are fixated to a passive-narcissistic aim and are interested solely in getting their gratification, never in satisfying their partner, nor for that matter, in the specific personality of their partner. Objects are nothing else for them, but deliverers of supplies. The drug is felt as food and warmth on which the self-esteem eventually exists."[7]

3. Uses of hostility and aggressiveness

The role of hostility and aggressiveness in addiction deserves much more careful study. Earlier writers tended to describe the effect of addiction as

---

[3] Paul Zimmering et al., Drug Addiction in Relation to Problems of Adolescence, American Journal of Psychiatry, CIX (1952), 273.

[4] Ibid.

[5] Ibid., p. 275.

[6] Though numerous writers have emphasized addicts' difficulties in relating to people, not enough attention has been given to their frequent ability to manipulate people by ferreting out their hidden feelings and unconscious motivations as these relate to their own "sensitive areas"—to use Fritz Redl's term. Redl's remarks about the "delinquent egos" of his disturbed children seem to have some relevancy to addicts as well, in their awareness of people's weaknesses and desires and how to use these to serve their own impulsive needs. Fritz Redl and David Wineman, Children Who Hate (Glencoe, Ill.: Free Press, 1951).

[7] Otto Fenichel, The Psychoanalytic Theory of Neuroses (New York: W. W. Norton, 1945), p. 377.

increasing aggressiveness, perpetuating the myth of the "heroin hero" who engaged in violent deeds. It is now recognized that this picture is largely false since drugs act primarily as a sedating influence, inducing apathy, drowsiness, and release from tension. Of importance psychologically is the probability that addicts may consciously or otherwise be using drugs as a means of inhibiting powerful hostile impulses which they cannot manage. This question acquires special importance among minority groups where greater penalties may be imposed following any expression of hostility, as was discussed recently in relation to alcoholism.[8]

4. Low frustration tolerance and dependency strivings

In most of our series, we observed a markedly low tolerance for the ordinary frustrations and pressures of life and strong dependency strivings in the face of feelings of deprivation and inadequacy. These addicts frequently described feelings of emptiness or of some void to be filled and talked much of the welcome surcease from painful anxieties. Addicts may thus use drugs as a means of escaping painful realities, "by reinstating the infantile pleasure principle," in Simmel's words.[9] Fenichel describes addicts generally as "impulsives" who are intolerant of tension and cannot endure pain, frustration, and situations of waiting. All strivings and tensions are gradually replaced by the "pharmaco-toxic longing." Interest in reality gradually disappears, except that having to do with procuring the drug. The tendency toward such a development, rooted in oral dependency on outer supplies, is the essence of drug addiction. "In the end all reality may reside in the hypodermic needle." [10]

Among underprivileged groups especially, drugs may assume an important function when the individual finds himself blocked on a psychological level because of his conflicts and the feeling that traditional goals and strivings are not accessible to him; and on a physical plane, because he is encapsulated in a tight geographical area from which there is no escape except perhaps through fantasy and devices such as drugs. It is in such situations particularly that gang pressures become a factor in addiction. We note in the case of Mr. B., for instance, that when he felt rejected in the home, was struggling with feelings of inferiority, and desperately needed some feeling of belonging—or the support of individuals with needs similar to his own—the opinions of his peers in the gang become an important immediate influence, impelling him to use drugs.

5. Psychosexual conflicts.

The question of psychosexual conflict as a factor in addiction has attracted the attention of various workers and warrants further study. It is generally understood that when an individual becomes addicted, a marked diminution in sexual desire will result, often reaching the point of complete indifference. (Interestingly, there is also a marked loss in desire for food.) Where there is considerable conflict around sexual impulses, drugs may assume great importance as a means of relieving sexual tensions. Fenichel believes:

"Their [addicts'] genital primacy is unstable. In analysis, all kinds of pregenital wishes and conflicts may reveal themselves in a confusing manner. The latter stages of addiction may be compared to the oral orientation of the infant who asks for gratification without any capacity for giving and without any consideration of reality.[11]

"For them, it [drugs] means the fulfillment of a deep and primitive desire more urgently felt by them than are sexual or other instinctual longings by normal persons." [12]

Homosexual activity among addicts seems to be fairly widespread. This fits in with Fenichel's belief that there is a greater prevalence of perverse and infantile strivings in the addict group. The use of drugs, involving as it does auto-erotic activity and a preoccupation with one's own body, may also tie in with Simmel's idea of addiction as a substitute for masturbatory activity. Some writers have pointed to the symbolic meaning of the hypodermic needle and injections as a genital apparatus, while others have gone further in describing them as a symbol of the mother's breast, which provides narcissistic supplies, eases all tensions, and brings solace.

---

[8] Nathan Glazer, Alcoholism Among Minority Groups, Commentary. February 1952.
[9] Simmel, op. cit., p. 239.
[10] Fenichel, op. cit., p. 377.
[11] Ibid.
[12] Ibid., p. 376.

The addict's argot betrays this connection between addiction and sexual activity, as in the addict's poem :

> "We'll live so happily,
> I'll bang her if she'll bang me." [13]

"Bang," here, refers not to sexual activity but to the use of drugs. A "lay" represents a bout in an opium den. Terms ordinarily used in relation to women here refers to drugs, as "a piece," or a "pickup." By "the business," is meant a hypodermic injection, "to shoot" and "to blow" mean to administer drugs. Anal ideas of birth and psychosexual confusion seem to crop up in the idea of a "yen-shee baby," the difficult bowel movement following indulgence in opiates.[14]

PROBLEMS OF OLDER ADDICTS

A number of older addicts are able to maintain a seemingly normal existence, operating their own businesses, working steadily, and participating in family and social relationships. For many older addicts, however, age represents increasing illness and isolation from people, increasing financial pressures, physical and emotional strain, and inability to tolerate the effects of drugs.

Mr. G., a husky-looking, middle-aged Italian, married, had worked continuously as a foreman and supervisor over a 35-year period and had shouldered his responsibilities very adequately. He had begun using drugs before the Harrison acts were passed, in the days when drugs were known as "happy dust" and could be purchased without prescription at the corner drugstore for a quarter. Mr. G later felt nervous and jittery, having charge of so many men, and found that his shots served to relieve this tension and increase his alertness and mastery of the job situation—or so he fervently believed. It was his feeling that drugs represented a beneficial and legitimate way of life and had helped him head off all illness, including the common cold—statements supported by his sister.

Mr. H., a 60-year-old patient of French Creole origin, had returned from a hospital to discover that his last remaining friend had died. Mr. H. had been treated for a tubercular condition at the hospital and now worried not only about that but about his stomach and pancreas trouble as well. He spoke of having had a difficult life, since he was one of many children, orphaned when he was 8, reared in an orphanage, then adopted into a workhouse where he was exploited until he ran away at 12. He later joined the Navy and was addicted by the age of 20. At one point Mr. H. mentioned having shared a common-law relationship over a period of 30 years until his mate died. She also had been an addict. Mr. H. had been arrested many times and admitted having stolen "out of necessity, since how else can one support a $30-a-day habit?"

Following his discharge from the hospital, he experienced a great deal of difficulty when the department of welfare attempted to refer him to the municipal lodging house. Mr. H. refused to be associated with the "winies" and Skid Row characters there and was finally permitted to occupy a furnished room. He reverted to drugs quickly and, when seen, seemed to be falling apart. He was fearful of the effects drugs exerted on him, worried about a nervous breakdown, was concerned about his generally poor health, felt isolated and suspicious, and tended to look to rehospitalization as a kind of sanctuary from the pressures of the world.

Mr. J., an intelligent and well-educated, middle-aged individual who had begun using drugs as a teen-ager, was rehospitalized for the —th time after he had been arrested for selling drugs. His FBI record dated from 1916. A progress report showed 3 Federal penitentiary sentences, 4 penitentiary, 1 workhouse, and 2 jail sentences as well as 1 probation and 5 arrests. He was separated from his wife and children and boycotted by his siblings.

Mr. J. attributed his addiction to his environment and made it clear he had no intention of remaining off drugs. Though he expressed the belief that drugs had been instrumental in lowering his social status, he evidenced few real feelings of guilt. He had been a bookmaker and professional swindler and derived a great deal of satisfaction from the publicity attached to his various sentences—especially to the hearings before the Kefauver committee, in which he figured. Psychiatrically, he gave an impression of "strong psychopathic trends * * * without values or goals that could be constructed as socially constructive."

---

[13] David W. Maurer, The Argot of the Underworld Narcotic Addict: pt. II, American Speech, XIII (1938), 191 ; see also pt. I, American Speech, XI (1936), 116–127.
[14] Ibid., XIII, 192.

FEMALE ADDICTS

The problems presented by female addicts are remarkably similar to the ones observed in our male cases. We note the underlying psychological disturbances, feelings of rejection and isolation, dependency, difficulties in relating to people, low frustration tolerance, escapism and denial of problems, and antisocial behavior. Some differences may reside in the prostitution resorted to by women and in the fact of society's greater tolerance in permitting dependency in women. It is not at all clear why addiction occurs so much less frequently among women than among men. Further study is needed to answer this.

Miss K., a striking-looking woman in her early forties, was the daughter of a wealthy father who could not relate to people and who isolated her from other children. She was otherwise indulged, tutored privately, and later sent to exclusive colleges where she received a liberal education, including training in music which she later applied as a night-club pianist and music teacher. She entered into several common-law relationships; one with an alcoholic had lasted many years, into the present. She nevertheless engaged in prostitution to support her habit and was sentenced several times when apprehended. She was dependent on her mother, with whom she always managed to live, together with her spouse. The mother was surprisingly tolerant of Miss K.'s addiction and prostitution and supported her in times of stress, as did her alcoholic mate.

Miss K. impressed the hospital social worker with traits of immaturity, dependency, and impulsiveness. She characterized herself as an "escapist" and talked about the rejection and lack of affection in her childhood as causes of her addiction. The recognized that drugs constituted an emotional problem, but evidenced no desire or ability to change. Drugs were described in musical terms as a "soft pedal" between herself and life. After 20 years of addiction, Miss K. was increasingly concerned about her addiction only because of the increased costs and the greater impurity of drugs as well as fear of further imprisonment. The hospital diagnosis was "schizoid personality with character disorder."

Mrs. L., an 18-year-old, attractive white "married and separated" woman, has been hospitalized voluntarily for the first time, for a habit less than a year old. The psychiatric history records that the patient lived in a foster home, where she felt happy and close to the foster parents until she was six. At that age, her mother removed her from the home, and she then lived nomadically, at times staying with her mother though more often in other homes and schools. She felt that she had been "boarded out" most of her life and had not really been happy since leaving her first foster home. The record describes Mrs. L.'s relationship with her mother as full of conflict and, frequently, hatred. At 15, the patient married a man 24 years her senior, but separated from him after only 6 weeks.

Regarding her use of drugs, Mrs. L. states that she began "out of curiosity and for kicks." She fell in with a reefer crowd in Miami and graduated to heroin upon returning to New York. She claimed to dislike the effect of drugs, blamed her associates, and laughingly remarked, "I always seem to get in with the wrong crowd." In spite of, or along with, her friction with her mother went a good deal of dependency and expectation of help in crisis. At the height of her addiction she had rejected her mother's help and left the home, returning only when down and out to accept hospitalization. The hospital social worker's impression was of a superficially "sweet," passive, dependent, and immature person, with underlying aggressiveness, who could not relate adequately to people. The hospital diagnosis was "immaturity reaction, passive-aggressive type."

Mrs. M., a 24-year old, married Negro woman, attractive, pleasant, articulate, and somewhat dramatic in discussion, had come to the hospital voluntarily for the first time to cure herself of a 20-month-old habit. Mrs. M. was the daughter of a Pullman porter who left his wife when the patient was only 2. The mother had worked continually since then to support her three children, of whom Mrs. M. was the youngest, resorting to relief when things became especially difficult.

Mrs. M. had reached the third term of high school when she was compelled to leave because she had become pregnant, at the age of 15. Details as to her subsequent history are rather sparse. Though she had no real vocational skills she worked steadily in a factory for about 2½ years. She was married at the age of 21 and separated from her husband after 2 years because he "ran around with other women." It was about this time that Mrs. M. began to use drugs "through associations and curiosity." Interestingly, she pointed out that her friends had used drugs for a long time before she herself succumbed. She had been confident that she was "different" and would not get hooked, but later realized this was an illusion and she was "like everyone else." She admitted to some ambivalence about drugs, stating that they "relieved me of all worries so that nothing mattered at all." She nevertheless resented her dependency on drugs and expressed a desire to change.

Mrs. M. gave numerous indications of confused identifications resulting from the absence of any father figure in her life and the disturbed relationship with her mother, whom she saw largely as a stern and disciplining person. She had never felt close to her mother, nor, for that matter to any other member of the family, fleeing to outsiders for warmth. She described her mother as never having been "direct" (honest? accepting?) with her, but rather "beating around the bush," which augmented her feelings of insecurity. The social worker's impression was of a likable narcissistic person for whom "drugs satisfied very deep emotional needs" and "whose relationship with people was on a superficial, probably manipulative basis so that she had probably never enjoyed a really close relationship with another person."

It is the prevailing belief that hospitalization, away from the old environment with its pressures and temptations, offers the best and perhaps the only effective means of withdrawing addicts from drugs. The question of facilities has presented extraordinary problems; the Public Health Service hospitals at Lexington, Ky., and Fort Worth, Tex., constituted the only resources available for treatment until very recently, when the situation was somewhat ameliorated by the addition of such local resources as the Riverside Hospital in New York and the various clinics under Dr. Leonidas H. Berry in Chicago.

Hospitalization may ordinarily be considered to include three steps: (1) Withdrawal from dependency on drugs, (2) physical-medical rehabilitation, and (3) psychological reorientation and social rehabilitation. Although the process of withdrawal is usually comparatively simple, requiring from a few days to a couple of weeks, this phase formerly received predominant attention, to the detriment of the last step. In the past few years, the Lexington Hospital has taken steps to give due emphasis to the treatment and social rehabilitation aspects as well.

PSICHOLOGICAL ASPECTS OF HOSPITALIZATION

1. What hospitalization means to different addicts

Work with different groups of patients in various types of hospitals has shown that hospitalization represents different things to different individuals. For some, it means an opportunity to satisfy dependency strivings, to be fed and cared for on an infantile level; others will approach it in their customary mood of rebelliousness against all authority, resenting the bars and guards and reacting violently to any attempts at supervision and control. Many patients are hospitalized after having been frightened by the consequences of their use of drugs and the possibility of becoming involved with the police; others come in for more practical reasons: to reduce their habits for various reasons, to escape the pressure inherent in keeping up their mounting need, or merely to tide themselves over a period of financial stress. Many patients come in voluntarily, out of a sincere desire to break the patterns of their vicious dependency whose meaning they may just be starting to understand; others come in reluctantly, impelled by strong family pressure; and still others, as prisoner patients, committed for illegal acts. For many, the initial reaction after withdrawal may be one of intense relief over having been removed from the merry-go-round existence of their addiction.

It is an obvious truism by now that people project into the hospital situation old anxieties, expectations, and remembrances of former hurtful experiences as well as their general ways of relating themselves to other individuals. In Mrs. O for instance we see a rather strong reaction to hospitalization conditioned in part by earlier experiences with doctors and nurses:

Mrs. O., a 33-year-old married woman, suffering from duodenal ulcers, aplastic anemia, and a spastic nerve condition which she attributed to the shock of her mother's death 5 years before, had come to the hospital voluntarily to be treated for a 5-year-old habit. She had originally visited a local doctor for help with her nervousness and sleeplessness and now carried a strong resentment toward him, blaming him for her addiction and accusing him of "exploitation": The doctor had compelled her to clean his office in return for her "shots." Since she had required more than 40 transfusions in the past 2 years, she had developed a fear of nurses as well. She had never associated with other users and had led a generally secluded existence so that the first impact of her hospitalization was shocking indeed.

In discussing the hospital Mrs. O. first stated that doctors had been "very good" to her in withdrawing her; though she added immediately that she had almost suffered a nervous breakdown. She was "abashed" by her experiences with other patients, was concerned about some homosexual activity she observed, and remained extremely fearful of the other patients throughout her hospital stay: "Their lingo stymied her and their bold advances frightened her." She disliked the attitudes of hospital personnel at times. Followng this, she lashed out at her local doctor again, stating that she never wished to see him "or any other doctor, for that matter." If she were ever ill in a hospital, she wouldn't "want a nurse with a hypo to come within 50 feet of me." In discussion, Mrs. O. revealed that her negative attitude toward medical personnel had been further conditioned by her having lost four children through miscarriage "from nervousness.".

It should be helpful now to examine more closely how our 12 patients reacted to hospitalization. Though the recorded information is rather sparse, we do find sufficient clues to their varying behavior, in keeping with the general profiles as outlined:

Mr. A. had been committed for selling and using heroin. The history describes a "marginal hospital adjustment and fair work record." Though three adverse behavior reports are listed, the nature of his infractions is not detailed. In general, Mr. A. resented hospitalization as "a kind of jail" and complained about the food and lack of recreational facilities, though admitting that he had been helped in being withdrawn from drugs. He was able to relate somewhat to the hospital social worker, who described him as stating in interviews "that he had never done anything right, that he is incapable of doing anything well, is probably not very bright, and that he is incapable of being loved while having an insatiable need for affection." No fuller discussion of his problems was possible in view of extreme disturbance and his involvement with self.

Mr. B. entered the hospital relieved to have been let off so easily after seeing 1 friend killed and 2 others jailed. During hospitalization he participated in the juvenile research project and was seen in individual and group therapy for a short time. He insisted that he had "always wanted to get off drugs," was glad he had come to the hospital, and was sure he could now remain off. He discussed plans to complete his education and training which savored of fantasy; and evidenced mixed feelings about enlisting his mother's and grandmother's help in support of his plans. His work adjustment was listed as "fair"; one adverse behavior report is recorded, nature unspecified.

Mr. C. was rebellious and hostile during his first stay at the hospital, but seemed to be responding much more positively the second time. He participated in both individual and group therapy sessions and professed to have a better intellectual understanding of the emotional problems in his addiction; he expressed a desire to stop hurting his mother since "you can be a bastard just so long," and showed some awareness that this treatment was only a "beginning" and should be continued on the outside.

Mr. D. saw in hospitalization an opportunity to satisfy his dependency needs and used his woes as a means of soliciting attention. His stay was beset with disturbances. He became emotionally upset during withdrawal, suspected the doctors and felt they were ridiculing and persecuting him. He feared the hospital bars, wondering "what he had done wrong" to be here. He was unable to shoulder even limited responsibility, claimed too much was expected of him, said he was being rejected, cried, and resorted to threats in order to win the attention he needed, which, when granted, was never commensurate with his expectations.

Mr. E. was happy in this one-sex environment, in which he saw a chance to satisfy his homosexual strivings, and stated this was the first time he had participated in group activities and felt part of the group. He was sent to another part of the hospital when discovered to be engaging in homosexual activity. He enjoyed his work as a male nurse, but evidenced some anxiety regarding his postdischarge adjustment since he was on leave of absence from a city hospital and was apprehensive that he would not be rehired.

Mr. F. felt demeaned by his close association with addict patients and felt he had "gone down" in the hospital. He was apparently unable to tolerate any closer associations and experienced a period of excitement described as "homosexual panic" after several interviews with a female social worker. He had been committed for violation of probation because of his use of drugs and was not fearful of another breakdown if he attempted to avoid using drugs. He was suspicious of the doctors and expressed paranoid and delusional ideas about them.

Mr. G. This was the fifth admission for Mr. G. He had been frightened by his workhouse sentence and was now caught up in mixed feelings, on the one hand determining to break himself of his habit to avoid further involvements with the police, while simultaneously doubting that he could stop now after a lifetime of use. He made a good hospital adjustment, participating in research and expressing resentment toward other patients who deprecated the hospital's work.

Mr. H. was helped with his physical ailments and was happy to be brought back to par. His stomach pains disappeared, and he claimed he was now free of his "main" reason for using drugs. During his last hospitalization he had come to think increasingly of the hospital as a kind of sanctuary from the problems of life and the difficulties occasioned by a habit.

Mr. I. maintained a bland, suave manner and managed to be "in the know" about any matters which might pertain to him. Though cooperative, he managed to keep his real feelings to himself and preserved a "correct attitude" toward the hospital administration. Mr. I. indirectly showed that he had no intention of remaining off drugs and evidenced little anxiety in regard to the postdischarge period, though he was scheduled to be picked up on old charges after leaving the hospital.

Miss K. had managed to pick up a good deal of the psychiatric jargon as a result of her participation in group therapy and had some awareness that drugs constituted an emotional problem, though she showed no ability to use this knowledge to change. She admitted that she had come to the hospital because she was frightened by the "lumps" impure drugs had raised, but planned to avoid such difficulties in the future by obtaining her supplies from a doctor.

Mrs. L. This was the first admission, voluntary, for Mrs. L. The history records a "satisfactory" institutional adjustment, "good" work adjustment, and one adverse behavior report, unspecified. Though she expressed her gratitude for the hospital's having withdrawn her from drugs, Mrs. L nevertheless wrote to her mother, congratulating herself on her success in evading treatment. She assumed an extremely dependent attitude in relation to her mother, expecting her to make full arrangements for employment, etc., in her absence.

Mrs. M was hospitalized voluntarily for the first time. The history lists a "satisfactory" institutional adjustment and one adverse behavior report, unspecified. It was Mrs. M's feeling that hospitalization was not "so bad"; but she admitted she saw the institution "as a kind of jail" and wished to break herself of her habit since she did not want to spend the rest of her life in places "like this." She continued to show some ambivalence about drugs, however, stating that they did relieve her tensions, and she was tempted to continue though resentful of her dependency on them.

2. Treatment opportunities during hospitalization

Patients, for the most part, seem to have little understanding of their emotional conflicts, and are hesitant about confronting them in any case. One of the advantages of hospitalization lies in the unique opportunity it affords for reaching individuals never approached before, away from the pressures of their regular environment. Patients may then gain at least a beginning awareness of their personal difficulties through individual and group therapy, and through various group activities, and their isolation, and learn to identify with others on the basis of common problems and strivings. The means may be provided for building a great tolerance for the ordinary frustrations of living and for channelizing energies along more constructive lines. Since treatment is ordinarily an extended process, it cannot be hoped that very ambitious goals can be realized in the 135 days customarily spent at the hospital. It should be possible for patients to obtain a beginning understanding of their interpersonal difficulties, however, and to pave the way for continued treatment following discharge.

This discussion points up the need for research into possible modifications in existing treatment techniques—possibly along the brief psychotherapy lines suggested by the Chicago Psychoanalytic Institute—so that we may learn how best to approach this group. It is a fact that a large section of the hospital population has steadfastly refused to permit itself to be involved in any of the available treatment resources. A corollary of any effective planning is the conception of the hospital fundamentally as a treatment center, with due provision for the careful screening out of those chronic patients who have no desire to change and wish to use the hospital only as a convenient stopping-off place in times of stress.

3. Social rehabilitation

As in the case of psychological help, hospitalization offers a rare opportunity for advancing the social reorientation of patients. While addicts may have initial difficulties in relating to other individuals, their antisocial attitudes are reinforced by periodic removal from the community by imprisonment and hospitalization, so that they become even less fitted than before to cope with people and the ordinary problems of living. In such settings, patients sometimes identify treating persons with the authoritarian environment, which may block treatment unless the doctors somehow show that they are identified with, and related to, the problems of the patients. Youthful offenders frequently resent the bars and guards of the hospital, the lack of adequate segregation, and their treatment as second-rate citizens by hospital personnel who sometimes fail to distinguish between different categories of patients. Any hopefulness the first-timer may have can be shattered by the fatalism of the hardened addicts; he may, contrariwise, be encouraged to emulate the glamorous adventures of the older patients. Our recent literature has stressed the positive influence all hospital personnel, from doctors to attendants, can exert in countering such attitudes and in creating the permissive environment so necessary for progress. How best to achieve this, in face of the need for effective precautionary measures to prevent smuggling of drugs, remains a ticklish question.

Apart from therapy itself and the opportunities afforded for constructive socialization, hospitalization provides additional possibilities for recreational activities involving teamwork and cooperation, arts and crafts, to stimulate further interests and ego-building achievements, schooling to advance the educational level of patients, and vocational training to develop new skills—a point especially important in the case of younger patients who have spotty work records and little or no training.

In this reorientation process, the hospital cannot isolate itself from the community but must gear its planning toward the eventual return of the patient to his old environment. It is apparent that the best work of the hospital may be negated by failure to anticipate the postdischarge problems of the patient and to offer facilities for continued help with them. Contact with the patient by doctor and social worker might very well start at the very beginning of hospitalization with some interpretation of the purposes of hospitalization and efforts to establish a working relationship as a means of eliciting his confidence and helping him with his problems. By discussion with the patient and, if necessary, by communication with families and agencies in a position to be of assistance, social workers can do a great deal to instill feelings of direction and hopefulness and to ease the difficulties of adjustment during the crucial first weeks following discharge.

A logical sequence of this discussion is the necessity for careful followup activities on the part of an agency related to the hospital—the indispensable "step 4" of any effective hospital program. Such a followup agency familiar with the special problems of addicts and in close communication with the hospital social-service staff would be in a strategic position to pick up on predischarge planning and offer the patient complete support in effecting a satisfactory adjustment in his community. It is disturbing to think how few facilities exist for helping addicts as a group. Most agencies have been reluctant to become involved because they think of addicts as an unrewarding group to treat and because they are fearful of being placed in a position where it may be said they are supporting addiction. Some agencies that tried in all good faith retreated after negative experiences. The work of numerous followup agencies, nevertheless, confirms how basic these services are in helping patients adjust adequately. Albert Deutsch has described the lack of followup resources as a major reason for the high relapse rate of discharged addicts.[15]

POSTDISCHARGE PROBLEMS OF ADDICTS

Every dischargee has some problem confronting him after he leaves the hospital. Even if there were no financial, vocational, medical, marital, or familial problems, there would still be personal difficulties and probems of transition to the old environment after an absence of months. Added to this, each dischargee

---

[15] Albert Deutsch, What Can We Do About the Drug Menace? (Public Affairs Pamphlet No. 186).

must face the question of whether he can avoid a relapse—if he has not already decided to return to drugs.

Mr. A returned to find a bleak home, abandoned by the mother and occupied only by a depressed and unemployed father. A brother was serving time in the workhouse for addiction. Mr. A had been disappointed in his hope of being reconciled with his wife, and was under considerable pressure by his probation officer to find immediate employment. This proved difficult in the face of his feelings of depression and apathy. Mr. A did not see how he could function without using drugs, yet he was fearful of violating probation and again becoming involved with the police. Though he was in need of help, his usual difficulties in relating to people made it hard to accept any approaches on the part of interested agencies.

Mr. B came home to face almost total rejection by his mother and grandmother, who were leery of again becoming entangled in his addiction. Though he had been referred to a social agency by the hospital social service, he was ambivalent about accepting help and approached the social workers with a good deal of suspiciousness. Mr. B found himself unable to remain on the job he had found and could not follow through in his planning with the agency. He thought of desperate maneuvers to remove himself from the community, especially as he found himself taking more and more shots to find release from tension.

Mr. C was soon involved in friction with his parents, and became discouraged when appointments with social agencies, arranged by the hospital social service, were not immediately forthcoming. He became too apathetic to carry out his hospital resolutions and readily fell into his earlier pattern of punishing his parents by relapsing to drugs. The parents despaired and required a good deal of support and interpretation as to how to proceed in relation to their son.

Mr. D. assumed an attitude of complete helplessness and requested help of anyone available. He was under a good deal of pressure during the first 2 weeks; for the department of welfare was slow in granting assistance and his sister-in-law refused to have him in her home, especially since she suspected that he had again begun to use drugs. Mr. D. was deeply hurt by his sister-in-law's rejection of his demands for attention and expressed suicidal thoughts.

Mr. E. was confused as to his employment plans and not at all certain that the city hospital would rehire him after his absence of months. He had naively assumed that his aunt and uncle would support him until he could find employment but was disappointed in this expectation and responded with strong words. Further difficulties ensued when his relatives became aware of his homosexual activities and began to resent his cavalier attitude toward repaying his old debts.

Mr. F. was confused, disoriented, and depressed following his discharge and was unable to return to his old employment because of paranoid ideas to the effect that hospital doctors had been in communication with his boss. Since he was responsible for the support of his mother, he had to borrow money from relatives to maintain the home and to pay for the treatment he resumed. He was suspicious of all offers of help and felt he must stand on his own feet, even though clearly unable to do so. Mr. F.'s mother did not understand his condition and agitated him further by pressing him to return to work.

Mr. G. was depressed by the sudden death of his father and seemed to be having difficulties with his invalided wife. Though his old job was waiting, he feared remaining in the same environment and was anxious to find work in another neighborhood. The remembrance of his earlier imprisonment was still vivid, yet he could not see how he could manage without drugs after a lifetime of use.

Mr. H. found that his last remaining friend had died in his absence. Though without funds, he had a very difficult time being accepted for relief by the department of welfare, which attempted to refer him to the municipal lodging house. Though finally set up in a furnished room, Mr. H. continued to be troubled by his chest condition, stomach, and pancreas pains. After relapsing into his addiction, he feared the effects of drugs, especially as he had to resort to any mixture he could find; and worried about breaking down or ending up on Skid Row. He felt quite lonely and thought of the hospital as a kind of sanctuary.

Mr. I apparently developed a swelling of the limbs on his way home and was hospitalized. Little information is available about him.

Miss K was unemployed and needed funds to maintain her habit. She was early picked up on charges of prostitution and given a suspended sentence and warning. Miss K worried about jail as before and feared the "impure" drugs on the street. She managed by relying on her mother and her separated spouse.

Mrs. L permitted her mother to arrange an extended stay with relatives in

Canada for her. As in the hospital, she saw no need for psychiatric treatment, though this had been suggested. No further thought was devoted to her husband, who had become an incident of the past.

Mrs. M relapsed to drugs after being at home only 1 month. Though she found employment, she was discharged after 1 week and saw no means of supporting a habit she deplored. There was a great deal of friction with her mother, who resented caring for Mrs. M and ordered her out of the home if she could not pay her rent. She was depressed and despairing and looked forward to returning to the hospital as a means of escaping from her predicament.

Along with the numerous immediate problems described here, dischargees are frequently under strong pressure from various sources to prove themselves. In the face of universal suspicion as to their intentions and ability to remain off drugs, their own uncertainty is augmented considerably. Where they are determined to remain "clean," they find themselves in no man's land since they can no longer mingle freely with their user-friends and may be rejected by their original companions. They are thus subjected to a combination of pressures which test their frustration tolerance unbearably in the first weeks following their discharge and foster the temptation to fall back on familiar patterns of resolving tension. As we saw in these cases, they are frequently suspicious of outside agencies and fearful of revealing any information about themselves. Many are closely supervised by probation officers and even more so by their families, who do not understand what was involved in their addiction and hospitalization and are now fearful of a repetition of earlier events, including the pawning of family possessions, stealing, etc.

Most discharges are unfamiliar with the resources of the city in relation to obtaining help with specific problems even if they should desire it. Agencies may cut off their tenuous approaches and reinforce whatever feelings of discouragement and hopelessness they have by adopting a standoffish attitude. The Riverside Hospital in New York and the Chicago clinics mentioned previously seem to represent the first local concerted attempts to meet their problems effectively.

VARIOUS GROUPS HAVE SPECIAL PROBLEMS

1. Adult discharges without family or financial resources

As we saw in the case of Mr. J., the problems of this group may be more acute than those of other dischargees since they are frequently isolated from "normal" individuals and can expect little emotional or financial support. A number of men in the older age level have additional medical problems and increasing difficulty in tolerating the effects of the drugs they use and in keeping up with their sources of supply. Where their main hope for subsistence resides with the department of welfare, they are often subjected to severe pressure until they can complete the application process and weather the delay involved in establishing eligibility and need. Their difficulties have been exacerbated by the department's hesitancy in granting assistance. In view of public pressure in the past, welfare centers appear reluctant to place themselves in a position where it may be said they are supporting the habits of addicts. They may try to take the easiest way out by referring the older, single dischargees to the municipal lodging house or suggesting some work program where the expenditure of department funds can be justified. An interested followup agency could contribute a great deal by helping dischargees establish their eligibility and need without undue delay, by verifying the facts of hospitalization, interpreting their problems, and obviating their being shunted about from office to office until they can find the proper point of application. In general, such an agency could attempt to meet every problem presented by dischargees and to assist them by supportive help and by referral, interpretative, and intensive casework services.

2. Adult dischargees with family and other resources

When adult dischargees return to families and other relatives, some of the problems detailed above are relieved—only to be replaced by others. Dischargees still face the problem of financing themselves, finding employment, etc. Though families try to help, they may themselves be living in marginal circumstances and able to offer only limited assistance. They may not, for example, be able to help dischargees with clothing—an important item since many dischargees pawn their clothing at the height of their addiction before hospitalization. Even where families are in a position to assist, they may hesitate to offer substantial sums of money which may be used to purchase drugs.

Many dischargees are ambivalent about returning to their families and previously hurtful relationships; they may resent the close scrutiny and pressure although they require the warmth and support of the familiar environment. This ambivalence is frequently augmented by the family's mistrust of a dischargee's ability to remain off drugs, so that they question him and even examine his body for telltale needle marks. These suspicions may tend to undermine the dischargee's confidence in his ability to remain off drugs. When the dischargee has resistence to seeking employment because of various blockings, fears, or confusion as to how to proceed, the family's criticism may increase his resentment or depression.

Families may further complicate dischargees' difficulties by superimposing their own ambivalent feelings. Though they fear that the dischargees may relapse or again become involved in illegal activities, they may simultaneously resent the need to support an adult person who should be independent. In their anxiety, families are themselves in need of much interpretative and supportive help. They may not trust their own ability to help dischargees remain off drugs and seek to obtain outside assistance, though occasionally also identifying with dischargees in their fear of outside agencies. Families are frequently avid for information which will help them cope with the problems of the dischargees.

Where dischargees have relapsed, the pressures upon the family may become intolerable. They are then placed in the untenable position of either supporting the expensive habit or seeing the dischargees resort to illegal activities. At such times, families are desperately in need of some counseling service which can help them resolve their conflicting feelings and plan for a resolution of their dilemma.

3. Adolescent dischargees with family resources

It is clear that many of the problems discussed under paragraphs 1 and 2 have reference to this group as well. To these, others may be added: families of adolescents generally feel a great responsibility to scrutinize all the activities of their teen-age youngsters and may adopt an authoritative tone which may increase the rebelliousness of the boys, though at times they are too anxious to act decisively in any direction. Much more turmoil and frustration may be involved when the families are still hopeful about their ability to break the vicious cycle of the habit.

Certain problems, such as the vocational, require special attention in view of the lack of training and employment experience of the youngsters. Of even greater importance are the conflicts around dependency. Adolescents have not yet resolved the question of breaking away from the family and may have extraordinary difficulties in making the transition to adult responsibilities. Their inner tensions may be made more acute by the anxieties inherent in an atom-bomb age and a time of crisis and war. They may then prefer to eschew any long-range planning in favor of a catch-as-catch-can existence.

Some therapists and social agency representatives have tended to deplore the too facile inclination to consider adolescent addicts as a group uniformly accessible to treatment and about whom we can afford to maintain an undiluted optimism. It is their feeling, rather, that adolescent drug users frequently pose treatment problems as stubborn as those of older men—to which may be added unbelievable lapses in judgment and failures in discrimination. Gerard and Kornetsky [16] indicated in a recent study of adolescent opiate addiction that ado-

---

[16] D. L. Gerard and C. Kornetsky, Preliminary Report on Adolescent Opiate Addiction, paper read at the American Orthopsychiatric Association meeting in Cleveland on February 25, 1953.

lescent patients exhibit a level of addiction similar to that of older addicts, in terms of their physical and emotional dependence on drugs, and that the addiction was clearly associated with emotional maladjustment of a severe, deep-seated nature. Their patients fall into the following groups: (1) overtly schizophrenic; (2) incipient or borderline schizophrenic; (3) delinquency-dominated character disorders—(a) pseudo psychopathic delinquents, (b) oral dependent characters; (4) inadequate personalities.

It becomes apparent, then, that further help must be offered the dischargee, thus far compelled to confront alone a complex of problems—psychological, financial, vociational, and medical—during a period of stress when he is uncertain of his ability to avoid a relapse and fearful of any pressures which may undermine his determination to stay "clean." Even should there be no immediate problems, there is a kind of confusion, isolation from people, suspicion of the outside world, and hesitancy as to how to proceed. These points suggest that, ideally, a followup agency closely associated with the hospital program would be the logical starting point for continuing plans made during hospitalization and sustaining the dischargee in the stressful first weeks following his discharge. Such an agency, equipped to offer general and intensive casework services, could contribute much toward preserving the gains made during hospitalization, helping provide the basis for change, and avoiding the relapses so costly to the individual and to society as well.

AN ANALYSIS OF THE NARCOTIC DRUG MENACE FROM A PHYSICIAN'S POINT OF VIEW

By Hubert S. Howe, M. D.

No one in this audience will doubt that, under circumstances as they now exist in the United States, drug addiction and its attendant crime is a serious problem.

As addiction and related crime have both legal and medical aspects, and as I feel that the medical aspects of addiction have not always been fully understood, I am glad of the opportunity to emphasize some of the points which have come up in my study of the subject.

It may be well to say at the outset that when I speak of narcotics, or drugs, or narcotic drugs, tonight, I am referring to opium and its alkaloids, and to certain synthetic narcotics. Therefore morphine, heroin, and demerol are those particularly referred to unless I indicate otherwise. Marihuana and cocaine are not included.

To begin with, it may be appropriate to say that there is no "wonder" drug, and no magic treatment for the cure of drug addiction. Addiction produces habits of both mind and body, as well as habits of association and conduct, which result in a complex of great subtlety.

Addiction to a narcotic drug is medically considered to be an altered condition of the cells, tissues, and organs of the body, brought about by the continuous administration of the drug, with the result that the coordinated body functions require the presence of the drug in the body fluids. Cessation of use of the narcotic causes painful physical and mental disturbances. Nonaddicted persons generally do not fully realize the suffering an addict experiences when the concentration of the drug in his body is diminished below a certain point. To maintain the necessary concentration, administration of the drug must be repeated at intervals of 4 to 5 hours.

The physical pain resulting from absence of the drug can be overcome by proper withdrawal procedures in a relatively short time. Relief from the physical distress, however, has frequently been mistaken for a cure.

In addition to the physical bondage, there remains a mental dependence of a much more stubborn character. Not only does the mental dependence become a conditioned reflex which is not easily broken—even if the individual himself wishes to do so—but the situation is further complicated by the fact that one of the physiological effects of narcotic addiction is to diminish the mental stamina, or will power, of the individual, as well as his ability to withstand pain or discomfort of any kind without returning to his drug.

In addition to these problems, there are matters of environment, evil associates, lack of skill to earn a living by honest means, and a highly developed skill to provide a living by resort to criminal expedients.

To understand the problem of drug addiction, it is necessary to recognize the distinct characteristics of two classes of addicts.

There are, first, persons who have become addicted as a byproduct of treatment for serious medical disease; and, second, victims who have become involved through the agents of organized crime.

It is this second group with whom we are at this time primarily concerned, and to whom we refer when the term "addict" is used. The latter group presents by far the most complex problem which has been the object of a rising tide of public anxiety. As report has followed report, there has been a growing realization of the personal debauchery suffered by the addicted individual, and the danger to the entire community from the crimes which invariably follow in addiction's train. It is generally recognized that an addict is under extreme compulsion to obtain his drug, but few people perhaps understand the economic strain under which he is put by the necessity of his having to patronize the available channels of illicit trade. Evidence from thousands of cases studied underline the now undisputed fact that in order to pay for his narcotic drug, the addict must regularly engage in crime. In fact, the physical, emotional, and economic demands of his habit are so great that he has no real opportunity for honest labor, and so addiction becomes not merely a habit but an all-controlling way of life. Addiction is his habit—but his education is for the practice of crime.

In the early portion of the 19th century, opium was freely prescribed by physicians. There was practically no other satisfactory remedy for pain or for relief from the myriad of symptoms grouped under the designation of "nervousness." During this period narcotic drugs were as freely accessible as aspirin is today. There was little public knowledge concerning their sinister properties, and their use became a common practice. In 1882 there were an estimated 400,000 addicted individuals in this country from a population of 50 million.

Through the education of the public, and greater care being exercised by physicians, the number of persons addicted decreased, so that by 1914, with almost double the population of 1882 (92 million), there were an estimated 150,000 to 200,000 addicts. The Harrison narcotic law was enacted by the Federal Government in 1914. This law effectively stopped the unrestricted sale of opiates by drugstores and made it illegal for physicians to furnish narcotic drugs to addicts.

Unfortunately, however, the Harrison law provided the necessary setting for a flourishing illicit traffic in narcotic drugs. From this point on, the character of the narcotic problem profoundly changed. We exchanged one type of evil for another.

In 1918, a commission appointed by the Secretary of the Treasury estimated that there were 1 million drug-addicted persons in this country. Thus it will be seen that within 4 years' time we had 5 times as many affected individuals as before the passage of the Harrison law. There was, however, a radical change in the method of obtaining opiates by addicts. The closure of the legitimate channels brought into existence an illicit traffic of tremendous proportions. Thus, virulent criminality was added to what was formerly simple immorality.

It is also well established that the type of individual becoming addicted has greatly changed. During the pre-Harrison law period, addiction was usually contracted as a result of what would now be considered improper use of drugs in illness, and because of their unrestricted availability in pharmacies. In that period addicts were mostly older persons. Prices of narcotics were low and most addicts were able to support themselves by legitimate means. Their associates were mostly law-abiding citizens. They and their families suffered a severe inconvenience by their addiction, but in general they were not forced to crminal acts, either by their unrestricted associates or by the expense of their habit. At present, however, the new addict generally starts as an immature youth. Adolescent children, with their natural curiosity and desire to experience new sensations, are the logical prey of the narcotics merchant who offers them free marchandise. Their sales resistance is lowered by an utter lack of knowledge of the devastating slavery which these drugs induce.

The situation of the individual addicted as an adolescent, under present conditions, is far different from the pre-1914 type. The cost of his narcotic need is high—seldom less than $5,000 a year. He has become addicted before he has acquired any skills by which he can earn any such amount of money by honest means. Addiction of the adolescent is particularly unfortunate also because the use of the drug deprives hilm of his normal emotional development. It impairs the normal maturation of his sex life. Moral values are warped before they have been normally formed, and he is rendered relatively incapable of benefiting from any educational training he may receive because of the time and effort ncessary to satisfy his habit, and also as a result of the sedative and emotional effects of the drug.

If the adolescent addict seeks legitimate employment he finds either no opportunities at all, or very unattractive and unremunerative ones. Employers do not want him. He tends to drift away from his unaddicted friends, and at last he is ostracized by them and finds himself mainly in the company of criminals. He can earn the money required by his habit only by becoming a pusher himself, or by resorting to theft or other criminal pursuits. He knows no life but crime, and feels a bond with no one but criminals.

In addition to all these complex forces, he lives in an atmosphere of compound fears. These fears are of three basic types: Fear of not being able to obtain his drug; fear of being apprehended for his criminal activities; and, finally, fear of the persons who supply his drug. This latter fear stems from the fact that by delivering to the addict an overdose, the supplier can cause the addict to kill himself. The user has no way of determining the amount of the dose until after it is too late. This simple fact imposes a stern discipline over the slavery which the drug induces.

Here, then, we find economic and social compulsions leading to crime and the sternest of all human disciplines—the power of the pusher to inflict torture by withholding the supply, or death by delivering too much. Furthermore, this is a day-to-day, hour-by-hour compulsion which is never absent. One can hardly conceive a stronger, more constant, incentive to crime.

In a report to the United States Senate on the "Illicit Narcotic Traffic," published January 23, 1956, it is stated that "The Nation's illicit narcotic traffic grosses more than a half-billion dollars a year." This report also states that "Drug addiction is responsible for approximately 50 percent of all crimes committed in the larger metropolitan areas, and 25 percent of all reported crimes in the Nation."

The Federal Bureau of Investigation Uniform Crime Reports for 1954 state that "Crime, up 26.7 percent since 1950, has increased almost 4 times as fast as the population, and that persons under 18 years of age represented 57.6 percent of all arrested for auto thefts, 49 percent of all arrested for burglary, and 43.6 percent of all those arrested for larceny." What percentage of these crimes against property were committed by individuals addicted to narcotics is unknown, but it may be safely estimated that they comprise a large proportion.

The United States has the highest crime rate of any civilized country in the world, and the largest black market in narcotic drugs. Mr. J. Edgar Hoover states that crime costs each family in the United States an average of $495 per year.

It must be clearly recognized that addicts are of many types. Although the present pattern seems to indicate that most addicts commence the use of narcotics in youth, it would be a serious error to believe that they are all youths at present. Some are newly addicted, while others have been addicted for many years. Their mental makeup varies as much as in any other class of diseased humanity. Some are educated; many are ignorant. Some have valuable skills; others have none. Some are deeply addicted; others are not. Nothing could be clearer than the fact that the same pattern of treatment will not succeed for all. Like other diseased persons, a high quality of individual judgment must be applied in the solution of their physical, emotional, social, and economic needs.

Among those who deal with the problem of addiction there is a growing realization of the fact that there is little justification for the hope of a complete and permanent cure of many addicted individuals. A fact that has never been officially accepted in the United States is that some addicts can be, and remain, useful and law-abiding citizens if they are provided with their minimum requirements.

Cure, therefore, is a very difficult problem, involving much more than simply getting the addict "off the drug" for a few days, a few weeks, or a few months. Institutions sometimes seem to proceed as though this is all there is to it, with the result that they are processing, and often reprocessing, an ever widening stream. Permanent cures are few and far between.

Genuine, permanent cure involves social and economic rehabilitation, rebuilding habits of moral and mental stamina and self-reliance, as well as relief from the physical bondage of the drug. Such a program is unlikely to succeed as a result of filling larger and larger penal institutions with more and more addicts. This is especially true because of the fact that while in institutions, addicts are in contact with many other addicts and criminals, from whom they obtain further education in all the ramifications of addiction, and the techniques and contacts of organized crime. Placing addicts in institutions under compulsion (unless they are imprisoned for life) would be simply to establish under the aegis of the state, great incubators of addiction and crime. Addicts should be privately treated and kept away from other addicts as much as possible.

Rehabilitation, under the present regulations, can only be carried out after the patient has undergone withdrawal treatment. Rehabilitation of addicts skilled only in the devices of crime is not simple; it involves not alone teaching them some peaceful occupation, but remedial, psychiatric, and social guidance over a considerable period of time. In the Report on Drug Addiction recently issued by the New York Academy of Medicine, in regard to rehabilitation in our Federal hospitals, it is stated: "Under the present system, rehabilitation ceases before it is finished. The addict, following his stay at the institution, is given carfare to his home and a warm farewell; then he is dumped as a solitary figure, penniless, very often friendless and without work, in a hostile society. It would test the mettle of a healthy man to undergo this experience; it must be a real trial to the discharged addict.

Under these conditions it is to be expected that a large proportion of these discouraged individuals will quickly return to drug use.

Most addicts cannot be kept away from drugs long enough to effect even the most superficial rehabilitation. It seems reasonable to suggest that rehabilitation could be undertaken before the addict is required to give up his drug. When he has regained his place in society, and had training to enable him to support himself by productive means, he may consent to be relieved of his physical dependence on the drug, with more expectation that the cure will be enduring.

So much has been said about the partnership of addiction and crime that it may be useful to comment on the conduct of addicts while under the influence of their drug. Many uninformed persons believe that addicts, under the influence of opiates, are dangerous. This is a false conclusion, resulting probably from the common familiarity with the effects of alcohol.

There is, however, a fundamental difference between the disease of alcoholism and that of opiate drug addiction. The alcohol habitue is normal only when he has no alcohol, while the narcotic addict is normal only when he takes his drug. Thus the narcotic addict is dangerous, not when he has his drug, but rather when he is without it. This is a very important fact, and one which has escaped many observers. Crime comes, not from the use of the drug, but in order to assure a supply of it.

You may ask, even if narcotic addition is difficult to cure, can't we at least prevent its spreading? From a medical point of view, this would seem entirely possible to do, for there is no uncontrollable desire resulting from the clinical or psychiatric effect of narcotics which drives one addict to infect another. Furthermore drugs are ordinarly taken in solitude and not in groups so that there is little social impulse to the spreading of addiction. While there is no clinical, physiological, psychiatric or social desire to spread addiction, the incentive to do so, in order to obtain funds to supply the addict's own needs, is tremendous. Addicts turn to all types of crime from which they hope to obtain money for their drug, but "pushing" or selling to other addicts is especially common. Thus we have a situation resulting from a high-priced illegal black market in which the financial necessities of the users have made addiction practically a chain reaction.

The growth of crime connected with the illegal narcotic traffic, of course, has not gone unobserved by the agencies of law enforcement. Early in the game, smart Government lawyers noted that it would be a violation of the Constitution to prohibit persons from taking drugs. They, therefore, invented the idea of placing a high tax on the product. The legal infraction in the narcotics business is, therefore, tax evasion, and that presumably is why the Federal Bureau of Narcotics is under the Treasury Department. Be it not thought that the effectiveness of the Bureau of Narcotics has been hampered by constitutional obstacles. On the contrary, their ardor is unexcelled.

In this country, drug addiction has been thought of most ofen as a vice, rather than a disease requiring individual medical and psychiatric care. In fact, this concept has gone so far in enforcement circles as to practically deprive addicts of competent medical advice, even when they want it. Under directives issued by the Commissioner of Probation, with the approval of the Secretary of the Treasury, from 1919 to 1921, physicians are restricted with respect to the prescription of narcotic drugs.

The first directive specifically forbidding prescribing drugs to addicts was issued on July 31, 1919, and states: "An order purporting to be a prescription issued to an addict or habitual user of narcotics, not in the course of professional treatment in an attempt to cure the habit, but for the purpose of providing the user with narcotics sufficient to keep him comfortable by maintaining his customary use, is not a prescription within the meaning and intent of the act; and the persons filling and receiving drugs under such an order, as well as the person issuing it, will be regarded as guilty of violation of the law."

As a verdict of guilty carries a prison sentence, it is easily understood why most physicians refuse to have anything to do with addicts.

Addiction is the only disease, with which I am acquainted, in which physicians are prohibited by law from furnishing the patient sufficient comfort that he may engage in a useful occupation.

Of course the most obvious solution to the whole problem would be to completely and permanently cut off the supply of drugs. This was the philosophy of the Harrison Act passed in 1914. We have been trying this for over 40 years. It has proved more difficult than was originally suspected.

Our Federal Government attempts to curb the spread of addiction through suppression of illicit traffic in narcotic drugs by international and domestic action. The situation has become so acute and so difficult to handle that even the great and efficient law-enforcement agencies of the United States Government have been unable to cope with it. The Commissioner of the Bureau of Narcotics has recently testified before the Senate Judiciary Committee that smuggling is impossible to control. He said: "If you had the Army, the Navy, the Coast Guard, the FBI, the Customs Service and our (narcotics) service, you would not stop heroin coming through the port of New York." This is another of the basic facts of the situation which must be considered and weighed.

The remaining method of prohibition inovlves plans to invoke more severe penalties for possession and selling drugs. As previously stated, the discipline of the vendor is so much more definite and powerful, and the compulsion of being without the drug so much more vivid and painful than the fear of being apprehended that no threat of legal punishment deters the addicts still at large. Those who know the magnitude of the problem believe it would be impractical to keep all addicts in permanent confinement; if not completely impractical, it would certainly be fabulously expensive. The ultimate alternative in terms of severity, is, of course, the death penalty. This has been suggested in some quarters, not so much on the theory it would restrain the addict yet alive, but on the hypothesis that it would thin their numbers. I cannot believe the public would permit such mass bloodshed, nor is it either necessary or desirable as long as any other approach is possible.

Of course drug addiction is not new. It has been going on for centuries in many parts of the world. This automatically raises the question as to whether the situation in other countries has been the same as ours. The fact is, that in many places their experience has been quite different.

In the United Kingdom, the regulation regarding the prescription of narcotic states: "The continued supply of drugs to a patient, either directly or by prescription, solely for the gratification of addiction, is not regarded as a 'medical need'." However, morphine or heroin may properly be administered to addicts in the following circumstances, namely: "(a) Where patients are under treatment by the gradual withdrawal method with a view to cure. (b) Where it has been demonstrated, after prolonged attempt to cure ,that the use of drugs cannot safely be discontinued entirely because of the severity of the withdrawal symptoms produced. (c) Where it has been similarly demonstrated that the patient, while capable of leading a useful and relatively normal life when a certain minimum dose is regularly administered, becomes incapable of this when the drug is entirely discontinued."

In the United Kingdom there are only 317 known addicts, of whom 169 are women and 148 are men, and most of them are over 30 years of age. Morphine is used by 65 percent, heroin by 17 percent, and demerol by 16 percent. The patient's physician is the sole judge as to whether the patient should have continued administration of drugs and the amount prescribed. The physicians may give drugs or the prescriptions for drugs to addicts, and the drugs may be obtained free through the national health scheme. The only circumstances in which the police communicate with physicians treating addicts is where fraud is suspected, or when the pharmacist reports a suspicion of altered prescriptions, or had evidence of the addict receiving drugs from several sources at the same time. With no black market, there is no effort to form new addicts. In 1954, the British Customs made 108 seizures; 68 were of marijuana, 39 of opium, and only 1 of opium alkaloids.

In a report on Drug Addiction in Canada, prepared by a Special Committee on Narcotics Community Chest and Council of Greater Vancouver, we find the following: "North American efforts at control have been spectacularly in ineffective in reducing drug addiction, and drug trafficking, the thieving and moral degredation that supports the illegal drug trade * * * Several other countries also concentrate their punitive activities against illegal traffic, but look upon the addict as a medical problem. Thus, Norway, Sweden, Denmark, Netherlands, Belgium, France, Austria, Switzerland, Italy, Australia, and New Zealand number their addicts in hundreds or less. For example, in 1949, with a population of 1,902,000, New Zealand estimated her addict problem at 45. These countries are virtually free from illegal drug traffic. They have difficulty in understanding our concept of the criminal addict, for their addicts are not driven to crime in order to support their addiction."

Many people recoil with horror at the suggestion of furnishing low-cost drugs to addicts, even under the best system of supervision which our Government can devise. For those of us who want to pass laws prohibiting everything undesirable, and many Americans seem to, it is a thoroughly startling idea. The public has yet to grasp the fact that addicts are dangerous when they are without their drugs, not when they are with them. They do not realize that in Britain this problem has been solved. The question, therefore, clearly is: Why should we have narcotic laws, the practical effect of which is to force people to rob, steal, proselyte and prostitute, in order to support their habit, especially when the need for criminal activity can be prevented for a few cents' worth of drug per addict per day.

One may also consider that, after 40 years of the Harrison Act, the addict still obtains his drug unless he is in the strictest form of incarceration. Why not let him have his minimum requirements under licensed medical supervision, rather than force him to get it by criminal activities, through criminal channels? We have now, in the narcotic black market, a matchless machine for the manufacture of criminals. Isn't it about time we looked over the horizon to see how the problem has been solved elsewhere?

×